Carbon Management in Tourism

Climate change is one of the single most important global environmental issues facing the world today and is emerging as a major topic in tourism studies. Tourism is one of the world's largest industries; it both contributes to, and will be notably affected by, climate change. Given the emerging global legal frameworks to reduce emissions of greenhouse gases, growing costs of carbon and pro-environmentally orientated customers, carbon management in tourism is a necessity. Tourism must take responsive actions to enable travel and tourism to deliver the peak experiences that tourists seek with a lower carbon footprint.

Carbon Management in Tourism is the first book devoted to carbon emission reductions and to showcase a wide range of practical mitigation measures. This book provides a comprehensive overview by combining theory and practice of climate change mitigation in global tourism, addressing various levels of scale, such as global, national, and regional tourism systems, as well as individual tourism businesses. It integrates a thorough scientific discussion of the causes of emissions growth, along with an analysis of the major options to reduce emissions, and state-of-the-art carbon management practices. Detailed case studies provide examples of tourism businesses or destinations that have successfully reduced emissions of greenhouse gases, with consideration of economic and sociocultural issues integrated throughout.

This timely and important volume is essential reading for undergraduate and postgraduate students as well as academic researchers interested in tourism, environmental management, geography and carbon management.

Stefan Gössling is a Professor at the Department of Service Management, Lund University, and the School of Business and Economics, Linnaeus University, Sweden. He is also the research coordinator at the Western Norway Research Institute's Research Centre for Sustainable Tourism.

Routledge International Series in Tourism, Business and Management

Series editors: Tim Coles, University of Exeter, UK and Michael Hall, University of Canterbury, New Zealand.

Taylor & Francis Group
LONDON AND NEW YORK

This innovative book series explores the key contemporary issues in the business and management of tourism. The series is organised around two strands: core themes in the business and management of tourism; and comparative international perspectives. The series is committed to exploring how the tourism sector reflects, informs and drives current thinking and practice in business and management in such areas as HRM, entrepreneurship, service quality management, leadership, CSR, strategy, operations, branding and marketing.

Books in the series will offer upper level undergraduates and masters students, comprehensive, thought-provoking yet accessible books that combine essential theory and international best practice on issues in the business and management of tourism. The series will have interest to those students on tourism programmes, as well as wider audiences in the social sciences (e.g. economics, geography, international studies, regional science, sociology, politics, leisure studies and recreation) and, more especially, business studies, management, marketing and international business.

Published books include:

International Business and Tourism (2008)
Tim Coles and Michael Hall

Carbon Management in Tourism (2010)
Stefan Gössling

Forthcoming titles:

Tourism and Social Marketing
Michael Hall

Carbon Management in Tourism

Mitigating the impacts on climate change

Stefan Gössling

Routledge
Taylor & Francis Group

LONDON AND NEW YORK

First published 2011
by Routledge
2 Park Square, Milton Park, Abingdon, Oxon, OX14 4RN

Simultaneously published in the USA and Canada
by Routledge
270 Madison Avenue, New York, NY 10016

Routledge is an imprint of the Taylor & Francis Group, an informa business

© 2011 Stefan Gössling

The right of Stefan Gössling to be identified as author of this work has
been asserted by him in accordance with the Copyright, Designs and
Patent Act 1988.

Typeset in Times New Roman by Swales & Willis Ltd, Exeter, Devon
Printed and bound in Great Britain by TJ International Ltd,
Padstow, Cornwall

British Library Cataloguing in Publication Data
A catalogue record for this book is available from the British Library

Library of Congress Cataloging in Publication Data
A catalog record has been requested for this book

ISBN: 978–0–415–56632–2 (hbk)
ISBN: 978–0–415–56633–9 (pbk)
ISBN: 978–0–203–86152–3 (ebk)

To Linnea
who turned five at the time of writing this book

Contents

Figures

Tables

Carbon management in focus case studies

Preface

The final chapters of this book were written in the months after the December 2009 UN Conference on Climate Change in Copenhagen (Conference of Parties 15), which ended as a failure, largely due to the refusal of the Chinese government to accept any binding global reduction targets for climate mitigation – even if these targets were set by other countries or regions, such as the European Union (EU), and only comprised these countries' or regions' own emissions. Despite observations of climate-related ongoing changes in the environment, and increasingly urgent warnings by key climate scientists, national interests and a new wave of 'climate scepticism' have dominated rational action to find a solution to what is one of the most important long-term problems of our time: limiting climate change on global average to a maximum warming of 2 °C by 2100 compared to pre-industrial levels.

It is not too difficult to see why there is reluctance to engage in mitigation: in the USA, the country solely responsible for about a quarter of global emissions of greenhouse gases (GHG), ambitions by the Obama administration to initiate significant cuts in emissions have stopped short in Congress, where the country's industrial lobby has exerted considerable pressure to counter what is (correctly) perceived as a threat to the emission-intense US-American lifestyle. The same lobbyists are also involved in various actions to question and discredit climate science – a process supported by a conflict-hungry media – leading parts of the population to believe that there is no scientific consensus on climate change as a phenomenon, and uncertainty regarding its human causes. In China, the country responsible for another quarter of global GHG emissions, the past ten years have seen unprecedented economic growth. The Chinese government, keen on leapfrogging a large and often impoverished population to economic prosperity, has been keen to outline that per capita emissions are still moderate in the country and that, in historical terms, China has been a negligible contributor to the problem. One might add that a considerable share of the country's current emissions is a result of production for industrial countries.

This leaves the world with a challenge: there is consensus that warming beyond 2 °C, often defined as the level that constitutes 'dangerous interference with the climate system', will be largely detrimental to humanity, but there is no willingness to initiate measures that will significantly cut emissions of greenhouse gases. The EU is so far the only region in the world with binding emission reduction targets, even though many states within the USA and Canada envisage making cuts in their own emissions. Moreover, a number of emission-intense countries have announced ambitions to reduce emissions on a voluntary basis. The Stern Review (2006) and other studies have shown that in the long run, mitigation is less costly than non-action, and the refusal of many countries to join a global agreement on binding mitigation goals would strike many as a paradox, particularly as even far-reaching measures to decarbonize the global economy would only cost a fraction of what it has cost to address the global financial crisis. Again, an explanation could be that many actors seem to think that adaptation to climate change is a more viable alternative to deal with the problem, notably postponing action to the future, and possibly leading humanity on a path to geo-engineering, i.e. the manipulation of global biogeochemical systems. This opens up a new dimension of risk, possibly on a scale never experienced before by humanity, as the consequences of changing global systems as well as the limits to adaptation are not well understood (see e.g. Trick *et al.* 2010). A rational conclusion is that mitigation based on reducing energy use and the development of renewable energies needs to be a key priority.

Reducing emissions at the speed required to stay within safe limits of climate change is an enormous task, however, demanding far-reaching changes in the way economic systems operate, the degree of innovation and restructuring needed, as well as the lifestyle choices made. While the global economy might actually profit from massive investment in green technologies, unleashing a new cycle of more sustainable growth, it will be far more difficult to change lifestyles. Tourism and leisure in particular will be central elements in this endeavour, as relaxation, experiences of new cultures and environments, and visiting friends and relations are powerful elements in contemporary lifestyles. Moreover, tourism and travel are associated with strong emotions and belief systems, where cheap motorized private mobility has come to be understood as a basic human right in industrialized countries. At the same time, tourism is one of the main, or *the* main, source of individual emissions for a considerable share of humanity. This makes mitigation in tourism potentially difficult.

The idea for this book was born out of two major observations. First, in encounters with stakeholders of large and small tourism enterprises, there has often been an expression of deep scepticism regarding the seriousness of climate change and its relevance for tourism. Few stakeholders seem to wish to engage with the abstract concept of CO_2, the main GHG responsible for climate change. While this is understandable from an organizational point of view – after all, there are already too many problems to be dealt with on a day-to-day basis – it is surprising that this disinterest also seems to comprise energy-related issues more generally: energy has essentially remained a non-issue in tourism, even though saving energy can entail considerable short-term profits. Hilton Worldwide, for instance, reports that energy management helped to reduce emissions by 15 per cent, corresponding to savings of US$16 million in the period 2005–08. Many case studies in this book have shown similar potential for emission reductions that are entirely economical – in most cases a range of simple measures can cut 10–15 per cent from energy consumption. If savings can be this substantial, why is there not a greater interest in energy management in the global tourism industry?

Several explanations seem possible. Broadly speaking, energy use has remained a non-issue because it has been cheap – and humans only tend to preserve what is scarce and expensive. More specifically, business management programmes have only recently taken an interest in environmental management, and graduates with a basic understanding of these issues have not as yet entered the decision-making ranks of the industry. In tourism businesses where more substantial pro-environmental management has occurred, for instance in the Scandic Hotel chain, this engagement has often been born out of the need for innovation and/or the environmental interest of top executives. For most players in tourism, however, energy and emissions remain issues of little interest and value: high energy use is even, in some businesses, seen as a sign of quality and potency, while climate change remains disregarded as a concept abstract in time and space.

This book argues that this perspective ought to change. Of the arguments presented to support this view, two might be particularly powerful. The first is economic: in mid-2008, oil prices reached a price of US$147 per barrel, leading to considerable changes in the perception of energy as a cost factor, particularly in the aviation sector. Even though energy prices declined again to about US$40 per barrel in autumn 2009, it seems clear that in the medium-term future, fossil fuels will become more costly again. Reducing energy use consequently means saving costs and increasing competitiveness. A second argument is that even though a global agreement on emission reductions has so far failed to materialize, the EU and some other countries have established emission reduction targets of their own. The UK has a legally binding national target for emission reductions. These developments are likely to lead to growing costs for mobility and energy-intense activities – notably even for countries not seeking to reduce emissions: the EU's integration of aviation in its Emission Trading Scheme (EU ETS), for instance, will include international carriers as well. Businesses should thus prepare for tougher climate policy to emerge in the next decade. In summary, carbon management is an issue of economics in the short-term future, and an important adaptation process in the medium-term future. As always, forerunners are likely to have a competitive advantage in dealing with change.

This book is intended as a resource for students, academics and stakeholders in tourism. It provides a comprehensive introduction to a complex and often theoretical and abstract topic: carbon management. To facilitate reading and understanding, 33 'Carbon Management in Focus' case studies illustrate management pathways that have already been proved to work. Tourism is, currently, one of the least eco-efficient sectors in the world. *Carbon Management in Tourism* is intended to address this, with the ultimate goal to make the sector more competitive, innovative and profitable.

Many friends, colleagues and partners in industry have supported this book with their time, energy and advice. On the industry side, I am particularly thankful to Michaela Weitkamp, Aarnout Mijling, Angela Giraldo, Bård Huseby, Bart Otto, Bruno Peters, Dirk Heese, Dr Peter Brandauer, Gerd Deininger, Inger Mattsson, Jens Morawetz, Jörg Adler, Dirk Wewers, Karlyn Langjahr, Bertram Späth, Michael Liebert, Hans-Peter Christoph, Kati Ihamäki, Kristine Simonis, Laurent Le Breton, Lottie Knutson, Valere Tjolle, Manfred Kojan, Marie Malmros, Marion Heider, Mark de Bruin, Matthias Meier, Michael Grehl, Michael Schürch, Oliver Noppen, Pär Larshans, Paul Cooper, Rolf Pfeifer, Pascal Jenny, Edgar Meier, Simone Probost, Arnfinn Oines, Auden Schendler, Stefanie Hidde, Stephanie Schulze, Susi Zentner, Sybille Riedmiller, Thomas van den Groenendaal, Pascal Jenny,

Preben Byberg and Ute Linsbauer for providing me with information that has been essential input for the various case studies.

Among the colleagues that have helped to develop much of the knowledge this book is based on, I am particularly indebted to Wolfgang Strasdas, who has helped to identify the case studies and collected some of the material contained in the presentations, for which I am extremely grateful; Paul Peeters, who has patiently responded to a hundred requests for data, calculations and the latest update on all sorts of transport-related topics; Bernard Lane, who is an enormous resource within all areas of sustainable tourism development and always willing to share his knowledge; as well as the troika Michael Hall, Paul Peeters and Daniel Scott, with whom I have written more articles in recent years than with anyone else. Most of this book is based on this work.

I also owe many other colleagues for their support, suggestions, critical assessments, ideas and friendship, including, in alphabetical order, Carlo Aall, Ralf Buckley, Susanne Becken, Robert Bockermann, Paulina Bohdanowicz, Petra Bollich, Dietrich Brockhagen, John Broderick, Jean-Paul Ceron, Tim Coles, Janet Dickinson, Ghislain Dubois, Alain Dupeyras, Eke Eijgelaar, Frida Ekström, Elin Eriksson, Warwick Frost, Mathias Gößling, Roger Graf, Johan Hultman, Karl Georg Høyer, Marcell Kästner, Jennifer Laing, Lone Lamark, Leslie Lumdson, Michael Lück, Chris Lyle, Dagmar Lund-Durlacher, Jan Henrik Nilsson, Romain Molitor, Shuna Marr, Karmen Mentil, Sabine Minninger, Jörn W. Mundt, Jamie Murphy, Rolph Payet, Helena Rey, Brent Ritchie, Murray Simpson, Paul Upham, David Weaver, Emma Whittlesea and Andreas Zotz. I am also indebted to all those colleagues who make my different working environments liveable places – Agnes Landstad, Agnes Brudvik Engeset, Marte Lange Vik, Eivind Brendehaug, Otto Andersen, Erling Holden, Ståle Brandshaug, Ivar Petter Grøtte, Eli Heiberg, Idun Husabø, Guttorm Flatabø, Christer Eldh, Erika Andersson Cederholm, Richard Ek, Hervé Corvellec, Katarina Zambrell, Per Pettersson-Löfquist, Hans Wessblad, Christer Foghagen, Maxmikael Björling, Anneli Andersson, Hartmut Rein, Holger Lütters and Dörte Beyer. Agnes Landstad and Katarina Zambrell supported me with funds to employ assistants, without which I could not have managed to finish this book in time. Malin Jonell has done a superb job in collecting material for the case studies and copy-editing the material, and has later on been supported by Karin Froms-Andersson. I am also extremely grateful to Emma Travis for her very efficient, personal and professional support at Routledge, and Faye Leerink for efficiently managing the production process. My sincere thanks to all of you.

In concluding this preface, I wish to express my deepest gratitude and love to Linnea and Meike Rinsche, because much of the time invested in this book should have been yours. This book is yours, Linnea, and that of your generation. It is all I can do to address our wastefulness of this planet.

Berlin, Helsingborg, Kalmar & Sogndal, March 2010
Stefan Gössling

1 Travel, tourism and carbon management

Tourism has grown immensely over the past 60 years. From 1950 to 2005, international arrivals have grown by 6.5 per cent per year, i.e. from an estimated 25 million in 2050 to 806 million in 2005 (Figure 1.1; UN World Tourism Organization (UNWTO) 2001, 2010a). In the following three years to 2008, international arrivals increased by more than 100 million to 920 million. By then, however, the global financial crisis set a stop to the strong growth trend, and arrivals declined by 4 per cent in 2009 to 880 million (estimate, UNWTO 2010b). However, UNWTO (2010b) projects that the world economic system will stabilize and that growth will resume at 3–4 per cent in international tourist arrivals in 2010 to reach 1.6 billion in 2020 (UNWTO 2001).

Domestic tourism has grown even faster, and accounts now for almost 10 times more tourist trips than international tourism (UNWTO-UNEP-WMO 2008). The enormous growth in

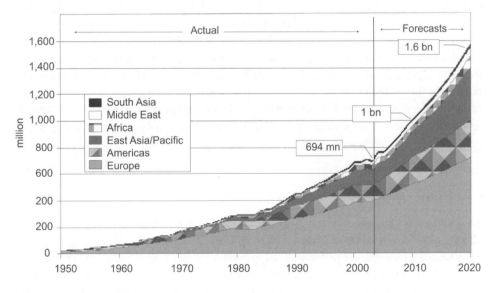

Figure 1.1 *International tourist arrivals 1950–2020*
Source: based on UNWTO 2001, 2010a

global mobility for leisure and business has been going along with high and growing energy use: travel to the destination, staying at the destination, and tourist activities are all energy-intense. As most energy for tourism is derived from fossil fuels, tourism is also a significant contributor to climate change. In the future, with an expected 1.6 billion international tourist arrivals by 2020 (UNWTO 2001), tourism is likely to become an ever more important factor in global warming, particularly in a world seeking to decarbonize. So far, few actors in tourism appear to have been concerned with this. As this book argues, there is thus an urgent need to address energy consumption and associated emissions of GHGs in tourism planning, management, politics and education.

Even though *Carbon Management in Tourism* is the first book to exclusively deal with emissions from tourism, aspects of climate change mitigation in tourism have been considered in a number of scientific books, including C. Michael Hall and James Higham's (2005) edited volume *Tourism, Recreation, and Climate Change*, which covers a wide range of related issues; Stefan Gössling and C. Michael Hall's (2006) *Tourism and Global Environmental Change*, another edited volume with an ecosystem-/theme-specific approach; and Susanne Becken and John E. Hay's (2007) *Tourism and Climate Change*, which provides a general overview of tourism, adaptation and mitigation, and a very readable introduction to many basics of mitigation.

Moreover, there have been two reports summarizing the knowledge in the field and providing specific advice of how to achieve emission reductions. These are 'Tourism and Climate Change: responding to global challenges', published by the UN World Tourism Organization (UNWTO), United Nations Environment Programme (UNEP) and World Meteorological Organization (WMO) in 2008, as well as 'Climate Change Adaptation and Mitigation in the Tourism Sector: Frameworks, Tools and Practice', published by UNEP, Oxford University, UNWTO and WMO, also in 2008. 'Tourism and Climate Change: responding to global challenges' is still the most comprehensive overview of the two-way relationship of tourism as a sector being affected by climate change as well as contributing to climate change. The report is also highly relevant for this book, because it contains the first detailed assessment of emissions from tourism transport, accommodation and activities (for an earlier rough assessment see Gössling (2002)). UNEP-Oxford University-UNWTO-WMO (2008) contains some theory and examples of tourism businesses that have sought to engage in climate change mitigation. This book seeks to go beyond these reports by summarizing the knowledge in the field in a comprehensive state-of-the-art review, and by providing in-depth case studies illustrating carbon management in practice.

HOW TO READ THIS BOOK

To facilitate an understanding of the complex interrelationships between tourism and climate change mitigation, the book's main text is accompanied by 33 case studies from 17 countries of companies and organizations under the heading 'Carbon Management in Focus'. These provide in-depth descriptions of innovative management strategies, where possible in combination with calculations of carbon savings, costs and profits – the latter either financial or including marketing, branding, loyalty, insurance or other benefits. This division was chosen for various reasons. First of all, not all readers will be interested in a full review of the carbon management field in the context of tourism. For these readers – and everyone else – Carbon Management in Focus provides a shortcut to an understanding of how leading innovators have managed to achieve carbon reductions, often providing details that could not have been integrated in the main text without interrupting the flow. Carbon Management in Focus also provides practical advice: in tourism, role models are of great importance, as the sector is not usually innovative and relies on 'tested' ideas (see Hall and Williams 2009). Vice versa, for readers of the main text, which is more theoretical in character, Carbon Management in Focus provides readable illustrations, practical examples and advice, often with comments from the respective companies' and organizations' sustainability managers (who might now be termed 'carbon managers').

With regard to the case studies, examples were identified through journal articles presenting specific businesses, personal contacts, colleagues' recommendations, a request made through the Tourism Research Information Network, and Internet searches. In total, some 50 suitable case studies were identified to cover a variety of carbon management strategies. This number declined to 33, however, as some companies were not willing to reveal details of their management strategies, while others had to be dismissed as not being credible. As indicated in Figure 1.2 there is a heavy focus on Europe, where most of the case studies are located. This should not come as a surprise, however, as Europe has a comparatively long history of modern environmental awareness, environmental policy and legislation, as well as an interest by companies to act pro-environmentally that has evolved subsequently over the past three to four decades. Europe is also the first region in the world that has seriously considered climate change mitigation in its policy, and implemented an Emission Trading Scheme (ETS), which ran through its first trading period in 2005–07, and has now entered its second trading period (2008–12). Awareness of emissions and the

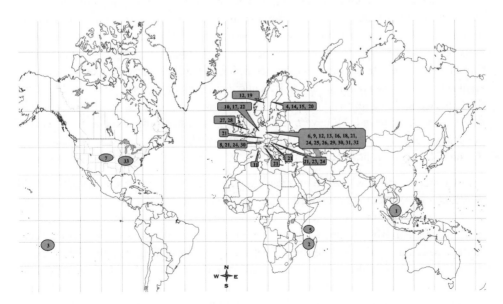

Figure 1.2 *Geographical overview of case study locations*

need to reduce these is consequently high. However, many other case studies have been identified elsewhere in the world, covering all continents and even remote countries such as French Polynesia.

With regard to the strategies chosen to reduce emissions, case studies explore options to eliminate, substitute, reduce and offset emissions, the latter referring to compensational measures for emissions that cannot be avoided (see UNEP-Oxford University-UNWTO-WMO 2008). As elimination, substitution, reduction and offsetting are embedded in the overarching framework of technology, management, education, behaviour, politics and research, these are chosen as the thematic arenas within which mitigation approaches are discussed. Note that case studies represent all transport sub-sectors with the exception of aviation, as no larger airline with a credible strategy to achieve absolute emission reductions could be identified. Case studies also include accommodation establishments, restaurants, attractions, destinations, travel agents and tour operators. Approaches to carbon management do not only include the measures carried out to reduce emissions, but also describe the processes necessary to involve actors and to communicate climate change mitigation goals. Each of the case studies highlights a specific aspect of carbon management that is innovative and original, even though few of the case studies can be seen as fully comprehensive approaches to climate change mitigation.

To illustrate this with an example: Costa Rican NatureAir, though not a case study in this book, is an airline that has chosen to compensate for all of its emissions, clearly an innovative practice, given that few airlines acknowledge their contribution to climate change in the first place. In order to compensate its contribution to global warming, NatureAir pays for rainforest conservation projects, based on the notion that the preservation of tropical forests is only possible when compensation for sustainable use or strict protection is paid. This is a logic many would follow. However, even if it can be shown that a rainforest tract is threatened by conversion and that payments will prevent this – implying proof that deforestation or forest degradation does not simply shift elsewhere – conservation will mean that a carbon pool is maintained, but it does not mean that an additional sink corresponding to emissions from the airline is created. In other words, if compensation works on the basis of forest preservation, atmospheric CO_2 concentrations would still increase. Consequently, as an offset, forest conservation is an ambivalent option, even though it is undoubtedly essential to preserve global forests. For many of the case studies presented in this book, similar concerns could be raised. All have in common, however, that carbon management is economically viable and desirable, with only a few case studies having implemented measures that do not pay off in shorter timeframes.

All case studies are presented in an identical way: the company name and specific field of carbon management are presented in the title. In a short introduction ('The issue'), the need to engage in climate change mitigation is motivated. This is followed by 'The solution', a section briefly introducing a company or organization and its carbon management strategy, including a detailed description of the carbon management approach, difficulties encountered in implementation, costs involved, and goals achieved – where possible measured in terms of economic savings (€) or GHG reductions (t CO_2), recognition through awards, positive customer perspectives, brand-building, or growth in customer numbers.

The importance of the approach chosen for the development of low-carbon tourism systems is discussed in a concluding section ('Impact'). Finally, related websites, useful links and references are provided at the end of the case studies.

Case study material was often collected with considerable effort, including the screening of relevant websites, search for academic papers or reports, and personal contact with the companies and organizations to gain knowledge about implementation processes or access to more sensitive data not posted on websites. The geographical distribution of the case studies warrants more research into areas such as South America, Africa and Asia, where more relevant approaches to carbon management might be found.

2 Climate change mitigation

Reasons for advocacy

There are many reasons for tourism stakeholders to embrace climate change and carbon management as a key challenge. A selection of arguments are discussed in the following in more detail to create a normative basis for this book, including (1) moral dimensions of climate change mitigation, (2) the vulnerability of the global tourism industry to climate change, (3) rising energy costs as an increasingly important factor in operational costs, (4) the low efficiency of current tourism operations, where much energy is wasted, (5) emerging climate policy seeking to make GHG emissions more expensive, (6) growing public awareness of climate change and expectations for businesses to engage in mitigation, and (7) the importance of an understanding of climate change and its consequences for longer-term strategic planning.

MORAL DIMENSIONS

The environmental and economic risks of the magnitude of climate change projected for the twenty-first century are considerable and have featured prominently in recent international policy debates (see Alliance of Small Island States (AOSIS) 2009; G8 2009; Stern 2006). The Stern Review (Stern 2006; see also Stern 2009), a key document focusing on the economics of climate change, has stated that the costs of taking action to reduce GHG emissions now are much smaller than the costs of economic and social disruption from unmitigated climate change in the future. Notably, the costs of unmitigated climate change are not evenly distributed, and the Intergovernmental Panel on Climate Change (IPCC) has concluded with very high confidence (IPCC 2007a) that climate change would impede the ability of many developing nations to make progress on sustainable development by mid-century (see also United Nations Development Programme (UNDP) 2007; Asian Development Bank 2009). In many countries, climate change is projected to lead to increasing conflicts and severe human suffering. Burke *et al.* (2009), for instance, show that warmer years in sub-Saharan Africa have led to significant increases in the likelihood of war because of reduced access to food, and project a greater than 50 per cent increase in armed conflicts in sub-Saharan Africa by 2030.

The Global Humanitarian Forum (GHF) (2009: 1) indicates that climate change already seriously affects the livelihoods of 325 million people, causing 300,000 deaths per year and economic losses of US$125 billion (see also McMichael *et al.* 2003; Patz *et al.* 2005). Four billion people are regarded as vulnerable to climate change, and 500 million people are at extreme risk with an estimated half a million lives expected to be lost because of climate change by 2029. Burke *et al.* (2009) suggest that an additional 390,000 people could die in sub-Saharan Africa because of an increase in warming-related armed conflicts by 2030. In terms of non-human losses, a considerable share of species could become extinct because of climate change (e.g. Pounds and Puschendorf 2004; Thomas *et al.* 2005). The relevance of these findings for tourism is that as a sector contributing to 4.4–9.0 per cent of the current global warming (UNWTO-UNEP-WMO 2008), tourism would proportionally be responsible for at least 13,200 deaths, seriously affect the livelihoods of 14.3 million people, and produce economic losses of US$5.5 billion as a result of its emissions (Gössling *et al.* 2010). This estimate is based on the lower estimate of tourism's 4.4 per cent share in global radiative forcing and based on GHF (2009) death estimates. Recently, tourism's contribution to climate change has, however, been updated to a minimum of 5.22 per cent and an upper range of 12.5 per cent (Scott *et al.* 2010), and tourism-related deaths, species extinction and economic losses might thus be proportionally higher. These findings are also of major significance to the discussion of tourism as a development strategy, as the estimated share of annual economic losses caused by emissions from tourism (US$5.5 billion) is higher than the US$5.42 billion tourism expenditure in the 49 least developed countries (Hall *et al.* 2009).

While this is an uncommon and provocative perspective on tourism, it might indicate the emergence of new, more complex and critical stances on tourism-based socioeconomic development in the wake of the global financial crisis beginning in 2008. For tourism stakeholders, this demands consideration of new dimensions in decision-making, and more engagement based on sound and holistic moral reasoning. On this basis, difficult questions will arise for tourism stakeholders, because each tonne of additional carbon emitted in the atmosphere essentially leaves more people dying or seriously affected, both in terms of health or income. Ultimately, this might lead to a situation where the death of people has to be weighed against economic turnover and jobs, or the relative value of the quality of life associated with travel and vacationing for the more wealthy part of the global population against the maintenance of the integrity of the livelihood systems of the poor majority of humanity. This argument gains particular weight with regard to mobility, where the highly wasteful lifestyles of a very small share of people potentially affect billions of people.

It is beyond the scope of this book to provide a background for such a debate, or to outline its ethical dimensions in greater detail, particularly because this debate is also closely related to differing and varied views on development (e.g. Costanza 1992). It is clear, however, that tourism organizations and stakeholders who have so far focused on the social and economic benefits of tourism can no longer turn a blind eye to environmental change caused by tourism, including energy use and emissions, but also land-use change, unsustainable resource use, or tourism's role as a vector of diseases including human immunodeficiency virus (HIV), severe acute respiratory syndrome (SARS) or, more recently, H1N1 (swine flu) (see Gössling 2002; Hall and Lew 2009). To more comprehensively acknowledge both the beneficial and problematic sides of tourism, however, is likely to lead to ethical dilemmas, and the risk of emotionalized and subjective discussions in the media, on social networking sites, blogs and other public fora. To presuppose these developments and circumvent negative headlines for tourism means that stakeholders need to become sensitized for the moral dimensions of climate change and to proactively embrace the challenges associated with climate ethics.

AFFECTED BY CLIMATE CHANGE

All observed and projected changes in the global climate are of particular relevance to tourism, because tourism businesses, destinations, and tourists are all sensitive to variability and change in climate and weather parameters, which affect the length and quality of tourism seasons and resources, and consequently tourist experiences. In many destinations, tourism is dependent on the qualities of the natural environment, affecting a wide range of the environmental and cultural resources that are attractions, such as snow conditions, wildlife productivity and biodiversity, water levels and quality, beaches, as well as landscapes and species diversity in national parks or World Heritage sites (e.g. Becken and Hay 2007; Bigano *et al.* 2008; Gössling and Hall 2006; Hoegh-Guldberg *et al.* 2007; IPCC 2007b; UNWTO-UNEP-WMO 2008; Hall 2009a, 2009b; Hall and Lew 2009; Scott and Lemieux 2009; Scott *et al.* 2010).

Climate change can also amplify environmental conditions that can deter tourists, including infectious disease, wildfires, insects or water-borne pests (e.g. jellyfish and algal blooms), and extreme weather events such as tropical cyclones or droughts. Even though it is not as yet understood how such changes will ultimately affect travel choices, it seems clear that changes in destination image, perceptions of personal safety, and changes in travel costs because of climate policy will induce shifts in consumer travel demand. Particularly under high-emission scenarios, key elements of the global tourism sector are likely to transform fundamentally (Hall and Higham 2005; Gössling and Hall 2006; Scott 2006; UNWTO-UNEP-WMO 2008; Scott *et al.* 2008; Scott and Lemieux 2009; Hall and Lew 2009).

This is also increasingly realized by industry. For instance, a multi-sector comparison by KPMG (2008) concluded that both tourism and aviation sectors had a comparably low awareness of climate change risks and showed little evidence of strategic planning to cope with the challenges of climate change. Risks might also be greater in specific countries, with for instance a number of Australian key attractions being at risk from climate change, even under moderate warming scenarios (Sustainable Tourism Cooperative Research Centre (STCRC) 2009). In the light of these findings, tourism businesses should therefore have great interest in addressing and mitigating climate change, and take notice of the emerging adaptation literature (e.g. Scott and McBoyle 2007).

RISING ENERGY COSTS

High and rising energy costs should self-evidently lead to interest in more efficient operations, but this does not appear to be the case in tourism more generally. Since the turn of the nineteenth century, world oil prices have only once exceeded those of the energy crisis in 1979 after the Iranian revolution. Even though oil prices declined because of the global financial crisis in 2008 (Figure 2.1) – for the first time since 1981 (International Energy

Figure 2.1 *Crude oil prices 1869–2009*
Source: after WTRG Economics 2010, http://www.wtrg.com/prices.htm

Agency (IEA) 2009) – world oil prices have already begun to climb again in 2009, and there is evidence that they will continue to rise.

The IEA (2009) anticipates that by 2030, energy demand will be 40 per cent higher than in 2009, with fossil fuels continuing to dominate demand. At the same time there is reason to believe that 'peak oil', i.e. the maximum capacity to produce oil, could be passed in the near future. The UK Energy Research Centre (UKERC) (2009), for instance, concludes in a review of studies that a global peak in oil production is likely before 2030, with a significant risk of a peak before 2020. The decline in conventional oil production will lead to the development of costlier options, though IEA (2009) emphasizes the need for invest-ments, and oil prices can consequently be expected to rise, particularly with a view on demand growth. Note that while there are options to develop alternative fuels, considerable uncertainties are associated with these options, for instance with regard to costs, safety, ecosystem conversion, or competition with food production. Rising costs for conventional fuels will therefore become increasingly relevant, particularly for transport, i.e. the sector most dependent on fossil fuels with the least options to substitute energy sources. Within the transport sector, aviation will be most affected due to limited options to use alterna-tive fuels, which have to meet specific demands regarding safety and energy-density (cf. Nygren *et al.* 2009; Upham *et al.* 2009a, b). Likewise, while there are huge unconventional oil resources, including natural gas, heavy oil and tar sands, oil shales and coal, there are long lead times in development, necessitating significant investments. The development of these oil sources is also likely to lead to considerably greater environmental impacts than the development of conventional oil resources (IEA 2001, 2009).

These findings are relevant for the tourism system as a whole because mobility is a precondition for tourism. As the cost of energy is one of the most important determinants in the way people travel, the price of oil will influence travel patterns, with some evidence that low-fare and long-haul flights, in particular, are susceptible to changes in prices (e.g. Mayor and Tol 2008). Moreover, it deserves mention that oil prices are not a simple function of supply and demand, rather, they involve different parameters such as long-term contracts and hedging strategies, social and political stability in oil-producing countries as well as the global security situation more generally. This is well illustrated in the volatility of oil prices in the five-year period 2002–09, when the world market price of aviation fuel oscillated between a low of US$25 in 2002 (Doganis 2006) and US$147 in mid-2008 (Gössling and Upham 2009).

The huge rise in oil prices, which was not expected by most actors in tourism, had a severe impact particularly on aviation. As late as December 2007, the International Air Transport Association (IATA 2007) projected the average 2008-price of a barrel of oil at US$87, up 6 per cent from the average price level in 2007. In early 2008, IATA corrected its projection of fuel prices to an average of US$106 per barrel for 2008, an increase of 22 per cent over its previous estimate. However, in July 2008, oil prices reached US$147 per barrel, and IATA corrected its forecast for average oil prices in 2008 to almost US$142 per barrel, a price 75 per cent higher than a year before (IATA 2008a). In autumn 2008, again seemingly unexpected by the overwhelming majority of actors in tourism, the global financial system collapsed due to speculation of financial institutions with various forms of investment. As a result, the global economy went into recession, and by the end of 2008, oil prices had reached a low of US$40 per barrel.

Fuel price volatility, in late 2008 exceeding 30 per cent of operational costs (IATA 2009a; see Figure 2.2), had a range of negative impacts for airlines. Before the financial crisis, it

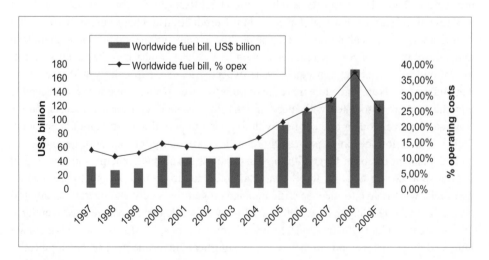

Figure 2.2 *Fuel costs as part of worldwide operating cost*
Source: IATA (2009a)

appeared as if low-fare carriers would be severely affected by high fuel prices, with even profitable airlines reporting falling profits, grounded aircraft and cancelled routes: high fuel prices had clearly affected the perception of travellers that they were flying at quasi-zero costs (see Gössling and Upham 2009). However, because of the financial crisis, fuel costs declined, with evidence suggesting that low-fare carriers were now seen by many travellers as the only airlines still offering flights at reasonable prices, reversing passenger choices to the disadvantage of the flag carriers. These examples show that high and rising oil prices, as well as price volatility can significantly affect tourism and, in particular, airlines. This should be another reason for tourism stakeholders to more proactively reduce energy demand.

WASTING ENERGY

Tourism is a highly energy-intense as well as highly energy-wasting sector. Many studies have shown that it is possible for tourism businesses to reduce emissions considerably, by as much as 10–20 per cent, mostly with low-cost measures with short payback times. Many of the case studies in this book illustrate this. For instance, Hilton Worldwide saved energy and water costs in the order of US$16 million in the period 2005–08, primarily based on behavioural changes of employees with a training in resource-efficiency. Evason Phuket & Six Senses Spa, Thailand, reports payback times of between six months and 10 years for measures saving hundreds of thousands of euros per year. Often, it is also economically feasible to replace conventional, fossil fuel-based energy systems with renewable ones, with payback times of three to seven years (e.g. Bakos and Soursos 2002; Dalton *et al.* 2009).

As payback horizons between five and seven years are usually seen as attractive from an economic point of view (e.g. Gössling and Schumacher 2010), there is a considerable potential to realize savings and to combine emission reductions with economic gains, which can often also be associated with other benefits, such as improved guest and employee loyalty, or positive branding effects. Savings might be possible in all tourism sub-sectors, including aviation, where the recent increase in oil prices as well as discussions of aviation's climate sustainability has led to greater interest in realizing efficiency potentials. For instance, so-called 'green' inflights and winglets are measures with no, or very moderate, costs, yet they lead to considerable reductions in fuel use. Despite this, strategic energy management appears not, as yet, to be a standard in most tourism businesses.

CLIMATE POLICY

Climate change has, since the publication of the IPCC's Fourth Assessment Report (IPCC 2007b), been high on the global political agenda. Even though the UN Framework Convention on Climate Change (UNFCCC) Conference of Parties (COP-15) in Copenhagen did not lead to binding emission reduction targets, consensus was reached that increases in temperature should be stabilized at a maximum of 2 °C by 2100 (UNFCCC (2009); note that the 39 member states of the AOSIS have called in a recent Declaration to the United Nations for a new climate change agreement that would ensure global warming be kept at a maximum of 1.5 °C (AOSIS 2009)), and negotiations for globally binding emission reduction goals are ongoing, with a view on finding consensus in Mexico during COP-16 in December 2010. So far, the EU is the only region in the world with a legally binding target for emission reductions, imposed on the largest polluters. While it is likely that the EU ETS will not seriously affect aviation, the only tourism sub-sector to be directly integrated in the scheme by 2012 (e.g. Mayor and Tol 2009; see also Gössling *et al.* 2008), discussions are ongoing of how to control emissions from consumption not covered by the EU ETS. This is likely to lead to the introduction of significant carbon taxes in the EU in the near future (Euractiv 2009). Moreover, the EU ETS will set a tighter cap on emissions year-on-year, and in the medium-term future, i.e. around 2015–25, it can be assumed that the consumption of energy-intense products and services will become perceivably more expensive. There is also evidence of greater consumer pressure to implement pro-climate policies, as outlined in the following section. Again, tourism businesses and, in particular, destinations need to look into these longer-term issues to identify development pathways that will remain economically viable (e.g. Yeoman *et al.* 2007).

CUSTOMER EXPECTATIONS

Awareness of climate change has substantially increased in recent years, as well as the understanding that action is necessary to reduce its negative impacts. While tourists are not necessarily willing to pay considerably higher prices for holidays that are more climatically friendly or to engage in sustainable holiday practices (e.g. Barr *et al.* 2010; McKercher *et al.* 2010), there is evidence that pro-climate action by tourism businesses is perceived positively by travellers and seen as a significant add-on (e.g. Simpson *et al.* 2008; Carbon Management in Focus case studies). A number of tourism businesses have even built strong brands based on their corporate social responsibility. On the other hand, there is increasing pressure on suppliers to engage in mitigation, and the likely risk of being pointed out as an irresponsible polluter with the emergence of new certification, carbon-labelling and ranking schemes revealing a business's climate performance (e.g. ET Carbon Rankings 2010).

There is thus evidence that environmental image is something to be seriously considered by businesses, because customers favour products and services from responsible and transparent companies (e.g. Mitchell 2001), while exposed greenwashing can negatively affect the image of a company (Gabriel *et al.* 2000). In recent years, customers have become more aware of, in particular, energy and emission-related issues. For instance, in 2009, 99.8 per cent of the Swedish population claimed to know the term 'climate change', and 95 per cent expressed beliefs that Sweden would be affected by climate change (Naturvardsverket 2009).

More generally, Simpson *et al.* (2008) identified three areas in which changes in attitudes will become relevant for tourism and air travel in particular, including the perception of the environmental impact of (air) travel, support for policies to reduce the impact of (air) travel, and willingness to take personal action to reduce the impact of (air) travel, for instance through reduced flying or payments for offsets. The review of studies from various countries revealed that there is evidence for public support of government policies to regulate GHG emissions from aviation in Europe, even though no such support seems to exist in

North America. European surveys also revealed greater concern about the contribution of air travel to climate change and a higher stated willingness to act to reduce or offset emissions from personal travel. For example, support for a carbon tax on air travel was highest among European travellers (80 per cent), followed by North American (75 per cent) and Asian travellers (59 per cent). Support for passenger taxes on air travel was highest when the revenues would go towards improving the environment. There is also some evidence that a small portion of travellers in Europe and Australia are considering flying less for their holidays in order to reduce their personal carbon footprint, but surveys are fragmentary and it is questionable whether intentions will result in action (e.g. McDonald *et al.* 2009; McKercher *et al.* 2010). It is also as yet unclear how the recent public discussion of the work of the IPCC (2007b) has influenced perceptions and willingness to act (cf. RealClimate 2010).

LONG-TERM STRATEGIC PLANNING

The importance of energy, including its availability, production, distribution, or factors influencing its price, appears to not usually be well understood by tourism stakeholders and society more generally. Similar uncertainties seem to exist with regard to energy systems and energy infrastructure (e.g. Kuklinski *et al.* 1982; Bang *et al.* 2000; Gössling *et al.* 2004). Cheap energy is often taken for granted, posing a serious impediment to action. Even less developed is the knowledge and understanding of GHG emissions, a concept abstract in time and space: emissions are not comprehensible by human senses, while their impact will become most relevant in the future and to people other than those being currently responsible for their release. As a concept, GHG emissions, including carbon dioxide (CO_2), methane (CH_4) or nitrogen oxides (NO_x), could thus not be less suitable to engage stakeholders. Yet, addressing climate change is a key issue in achieving sustainable tourism. To improve the understanding of the interrelationships between energy use, GHG emissions and climate change, which appears not to be well developed at the moment (see Becken 2004), is thus paramount for all actors in tourism. Notably, engaging in longer-term strategic planning means not only dealing with problems emerging with the transformation to low-carbon societies, but also capitalizing on the opportunities arising from such processes (Becken and Hay 2007).

3 Climate change

The physical basis

Climate is a statistical longer-term description of average weather patterns, usually measured by variables such as surface temperatures or precipitation over 30-year periods, as defined by the WMO (IPCC 2007b). Climate change refers to significant alterations in climate variables that can, for instance, be identified through statistical tests. These changes can refer to mean values or variability, and have to persist over decades. Notably, there has always been natural climate change and climate variability, and climate change refers in this book to the anthropogenic component, i.e. human activities leading to the conversion of land and changes in GHG concentrations in the atmosphere. This is consistent with the UNFCCC definition (Article 1), according to which climate change is 'a change of climate which is attributed directly or indirectly to human activity that alters the composition of the global atmosphere and which is in addition to natural climate variability observed over comparable time periods'.

GREENHOUSE GASES

The changing composition of the atmosphere causes global warming, the 'greenhouse effect', because human activities lead to emissions of, for example, CO_2, CH_4 and nitrous oxide (N_2O). These are GHGs because they absorb, together with clouds, thermal infrared radiation, emitted by the Earth's surface. GHGs thus trap heat at the Earth's surface and in the troposphere, the lowest atmospheric layer, leading to an increase in the average surface temperature of the Earth of $+14\,°C$ (for more detailed descriptions see IPCC (2007b)). The most important GHGs released by human activities are CO_2, CH_4, N_2O, hydrofluorocarbons, perfluorocarbons, and sulphur hexafluoride (F-gases). These six gases are also the basis for GHG inventories, i.e. statistics on the contribution made by countries, regions, or companies to climate change.

An important characteristic of GHGs is their lifetime in the atmosphere, which can vary from hours to hundreds of years, and their relative potential to absorb outgoing thermal infrared radiation, i.e. to trap heat. CO_2 is a by-product of burning fossil fuels, including oil, coal and gas; as well as the burning of biomass, land-use changes and industrial processes. CO_2 is the most important GHG affecting the Earth's radiative balance (see also Figure 3.1(b)). Because of this, the contributions of other GHGs to radiative forcing (RF)

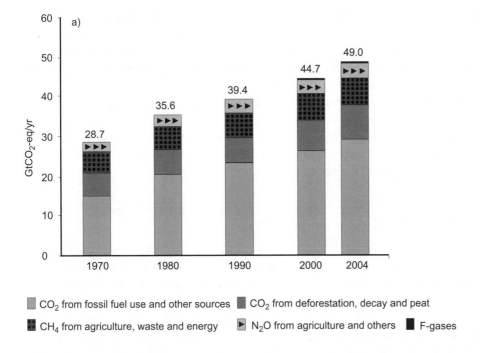

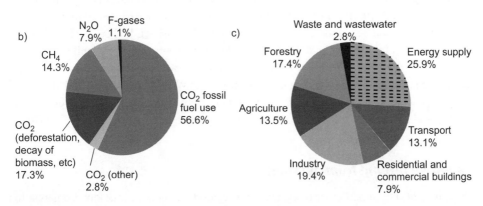

Figure 3.1 Growth in emissions of GHGs, and distribution by sector
Source: IPCC 2007b

are measured against CO_2 in terms of their respective Global Warming Potential (GWP). The GWP compares the radiative properties of the well-mixed GHGs over a chosen time horizon, usually 100 years, relative to the RF of CO_2 (GWP: 1), and expressed as CO_2-equivalents (CO_2-eq) (IPCC 2007b).

As shown in Figure 3.1(a), emissions of GHG have grown from 28.7 $GtCO_2$-equivalent ($GtCO_2$-eq) per year in 1970 to 49.0 $GtCO_2$-eq in 2004, and emissions have further increased since then (Le Quéré *et al.* 2009). The importance of, in particular, CO_2 emissions is that they are long-lived, i.e. they stay in the atmosphere for at least 100 years, and their contribution to global warming is thus cumulative. Figure 3.1(b) shows that CO_2 from the burning of fossil fuels accounted for 56.6 per cent of the contribution to climate change in 2004, with another 17.3 per cent being caused by deforestation and the decay of biomass, and 2.8 per cent by other processes. CO_2 thus accounts for 76.7 per cent (fossil fuel burning and other processes) of the total anthropogenic warming caused by the six major GHGs, followed by CH_4 (14.3 per cent), N_2O (7.9 per cent) and the F-gases (1.1 per cent). Figure 3.1(c) shows emissions by sector, indicating that energy supply (25.9 per cent) is most important, followed by industry (19.4 per cent), forestry (17.4 per cent), agriculture (13.5 per cent), transport (13.1 per cent), residential and commercial buildings (7.9 per cent) and waste and wastewater (2.8 per cent).

Radiative forcing

Of relevance in the context of tourism is that the contribution of various GHGs (as well as clouds) to the warming in a given year is measured as radiative forcing (RF) in watts per square metre (W/m^2; Figure 3.2). The difference to the longer-term assessment provided above is that even the short-lived GHGs become relevant in this comparison (see also Fuglestvedt et al. 2009). Figure 3.2 shows that when measured as RF, accumulated CO_2 is still the most important factor in global warming, accounting for an estimated $1.66 W/m^2$, followed by CH_4, N_2O and halocarbons, which account for 0.48, 0.16 and $0.34 W/m^2$, respectively. A slight increase in RF is caused by stratospheric water vapour from CH_4 ($0.07 W/m^2$), and linear contrails ($0.01 W/m^2$). Depending on its location, ozone causes cooling or warming. In the troposphere, ozone causes warming of $0.35 W/m^2$, while there is slight cooling ($-0.05 W/m^2$) in the stratosphere. Surface albedo changes are caused by land use, leading to cooling at $0.2 W/m^2$, and black carbon on snow, causing slight warming at $0.1 W/m^2$. Aerosols cause considerable cooling in the order of $-0.5 W/m^2$ (direct effect) and $-0.7 W/m^2$ (cloud albedo effect). Taken together, anthropogenic global warming thus contributes $1.6 W/m^2$ to global RF, which can be compared to natural warming of $0.12 W/m^2$ (IPCC 2007b).

Radiative forcing from aviation

These insights are of particular relevance with regard to aviation. Emissions from aviation are released at high altitudes and make a contribution to RF different from surface-bound transport (Lee 2009; Lee et al. 2009). Particularly relevant are nitrogen oxides (NO_x), aerosols and their precursors (soot and sulphate), as well as increased cloudiness in the form of persistent linear contrails and aviation-induced cirrus (AIC). Lee et al. (2009) present an update of values for RF radiation for 2005 (Sausen et al. 2005). They note that there is still limited confidence in quantifying AIC effects, leading to a best estimate value of aviation RF in the order of $0.055 W/m^2$, excluding AIC, and $0.078 W/m^2$ including AIC (with a range of $0.038–0.139 W/m^2$, 90 per cent likelihood range). This represents 4.9 per cent of total anthropogenic forcing in 2005 (2–14 per cent within the 90 per cent likelihood range).

Figure 3.3 illustrates how different emissions from aviation contribute to this total. The most important component of the RF balance is CO_2, for which the Level of Scientific

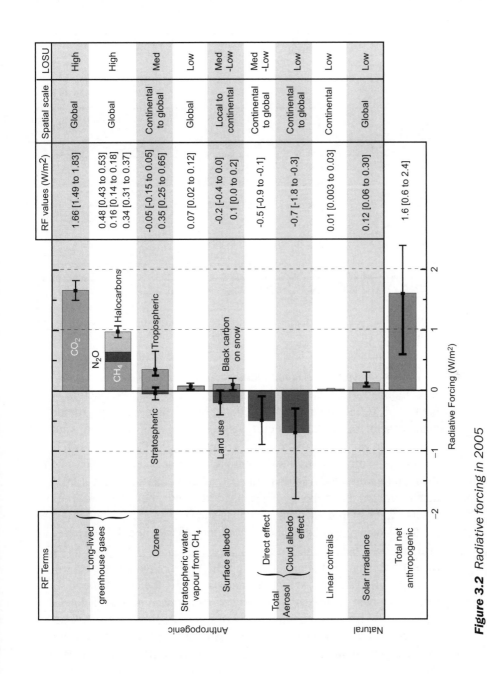

Figure 3.2 *Radiative forcing in 2005*
Source: IPCC 2007b

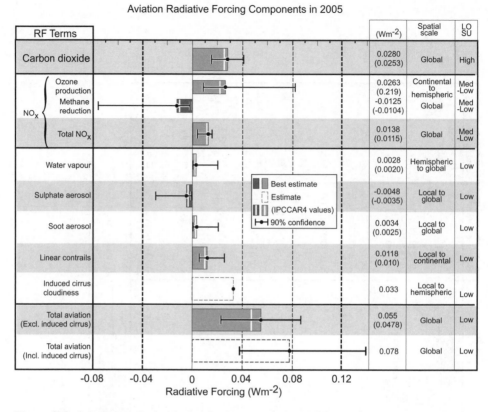

Figure 3.3 *Aviation radiative forcing components in 2005.*
RF components from global aviation as evaluated from pre-industrial
times until 2005. Bars represent updated best estimates or an estimate
in the case of AIC. IPCC AR4 (Fourth Assessment Report) values are indicated by the white lines in the bars as reported by Forster *et al.* (2007).
The AIC estimate includes linear contrails. Numerical values are given on
the right for both IPCC AR4 (in parentheses) and updated values. Error
bars represent the 90 per cent likelihood range for each estimate. The
median value of total RF from aviation is shown with and without AIC. The
median values and uncertainties for the Total NO_x RF and the two total
aviation RFs are calculated using a Monte Carlo simulation. The Total NO_x
RF is the combination of the CH_4 and O_3 RF terms, which are also shown
here. The AR4 value noted for the Total NO_x term is the sum of the AR4
CH_4 and O_3 best estimates. Note that the confidence interval for 'Total
NO_x' is due to the assumption that the RFs from O_3 and CH_4 are 100 per
cent correlated; however, in reality, the correlation is likely to be less than
100 per cent but to an unknown degree. The geographic spatial scale of
the RF from each component and the LOSU are also shown on the right.
Source: Lee *et al.* 2009

Understanding (LOSU, right-hand column in Figure 3.3) is high. CO_2 contributes to positive RF of $0.02\,W/m^2$. NO_x contribute to positive RF of $0.0138\,W/m^2$, the sum of the production of tropospheric ozone, a longer-term reduction in ambient CH_4 (negative RF), and a further longer-term small decrease in O_3 (negative RF). Emissions of water (H_2O) also lead to a small positive forcing ($0.0028\,W/m^2$), while sulphate aerosols cause negative forcing ($-0.0048\,W/m^2$). Soot aerosols cause positive forcing ($0.0034\,W/m^2$) as do persistent linear contrails ($0.0118\,W/m^2$). As outlined, the contribution made by AIC is uncertain (LOSU: very low), but might be in the order of $0.033\,W/m^2$ (best estimate). The positive contribution of aviation to RF is thus considerable, in particular if the positive forcing of AIC is confirmed.

In conclusion, it is important to note that different GHGs contribute differently to climate change, which for GHGs with long lifetimes is measured in CO_2-eq. In the context of tourism, a better measure than the different GHGs' GWP is RF, which more adequately assesses the contribution made by all emissions from the sector to global warming in a given year, i.e. not ignoring the role of short-lived non-CO_2 emissions from aviation.

CONSEQUENCES OF CLIMATE CHANGE

In Earth's geological history, the climate has always changed. The most important difference to climate change related to human activities is the timeframe within which these changes have taken place: humans have emitted GHGs at a significant scale for little more than 160 years, i.e. since the Industrial Revolution, an extremely short period compared to the thousands and tens of thousands of years over which natural climate change has occurred. The primary concern with anthropogenic climate change is consequently that the speed at which atmospheric concentrations of GHGs change is unprecedented in the Earth's geological past (cf. IPCC 2007b).

Since 1990, the year of publication of the IPCC's First Assessment Report (FAR; IPCC 1990), climate change has become an increasingly relevant issue for society and, in particular, politics and business, because of its anticipated consequences for ecosystems as well as human socioeconomic systems. In 2007, the IPCC's AR4 concluded that anthropogenic emissions of GHGs are the major cause for the observed and projected changes in the global climate system, noting that 'warming of the climate system is unequivocal, as it is now evident from observations of increases in global average air and ocean temperatures, widespread melting of snow and ice and rising global average sea level' (IPCC 2007b). Climate change has started to affect many natural systems, including hydrological systems (e.g. increased runoff and earlier spring peak discharge, warming of lakes and rivers affecting thermal structure and water quality); terrestrial ecosystems (e.g. earlier spring events including leaf-unfolding, bird migration and egg-laying, biodiversity decline, and poleward and upward shifts in ranges in plants and animal species); and marine systems (e.g. rising water temperatures, changes in ice cover, salinity, acidification, oxygen levels and circulation, affecting shifts in ranges and changes in algae, plankton and fish abundance) (IPCC 2007b).

Observed and projected climate change will affect ecosystems in ways that increase vulnerabilities with regard to food security, water supply, natural disasters, as well as human

health. Together, these changes are projected to severely affect socioeconomic development and well-being (e.g. Stern 2006, 2009; IPCC 2007b; UNDP 2007; Asian Development Bank 2009). Ultimately, the impact of climate change on socioeconomic development
will be dependent on the speed at which global average temperatures change, as well as
overall temperature increases. The IPCC (2007b) has illustrated this for water resources,
ecosystem health, food security, coastlines, and human health. Beyond temperatures of
$2\,°C$, changes start to become negative for most of these areas, including water stress, loss
of species including coral bleaching and wildfires, shifts in cereal productivity, increasing
damage from floods and storms, and changed distribution of disease vectors.

The IPCC (2007b) also shows that at temperature increases greater than $4\,°C$, significantly
more negative impacts will occur. Similar findings were more recently presented by Smith
et al. (2009a) based on the illustration of 'burning embers', an expert assessment of the
risks posed by increases in temperature to unique and threatened systems, extreme weather
events, distribution of impacts, aggregate impacts, and large-scale discontinuities. They
conclude that even temperature increases lower than $2\,°C$ could pose considerable risks.
Notably, there is now growing concern in parts of the scientific community that there will
be an overshooting of the $2\,°C$ target (e.g. Anderson and Bows 2008; Hansen *et al.* 2006;
Parry *et al.* 2008; Meinshausen *et al.* 2009; Rogelj *et al.* 2009; see also recent conferences such as '$4\,°C$ and beyond', hosted by the Environmental Change Institute, the Tyndall
Centre for Climate Change Research and the Met Office Hadley Centre in Oxford, UK in
September 2009).

AN UPDATE ON IPCC 2007

Since the publication of the AR4, an increasing number of publications have made the
point that the report might have understated both the rate of climate change (e.g. Lean and
Rind 2009; Richardson *et al.* 2009) and the associated potential risks. In December 2009,
an update on AR4 was published by 26 leading climate scientists as an intermediary report
to the IPCC's Fifth Assessment Report (AR5), which is due in 2013. The report, entitled
Copenhagen Diagnosis (2009), provides an analysis of papers related to the work of Working Group I of the IPCC, i.e. the physical science basis of climate change research, which
were published after the IPCC's AR4 publication in 2007. Some of the most pertinent findings are presented in the following.

Atmospheric concentrations of greenhouse gases

With regard to concentrations of GHGs in the atmosphere, emissions continue to increase,
as also outlined by UNFCCC (2009), based on national submissions of GHG inventories.
Compared to 1990, the base year for emission reduction negotiations, global emissions
of CO_2 from fossil fuel burning and cement production have increased by 40 per cent (in
2008; Le Quéré *et al.* 2009). Notably, observed global emissions of CO_2 from fossil fuel
burning and cement production are at the higher end of scenarios as presented by IPCC
(Figure 3.4).

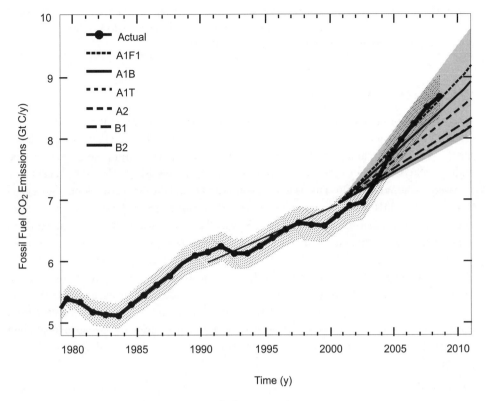

Figure 3.4 *Fossil fuel CO₂ emissions (GtC per year).*

Observed global CO_2 emissions from fossil fuel burning and cement production compared with IPCC emissions scenarios (Le Quéré *et al.* 2009).
Observations are from the US Department of Energy Carbon Dioxide
Information Center (CDIAC) up to 2006. 2007 and 2008 are based on
BP economic data. The emission scenarios are averaged over families of
scenarios presented in Nakicenovic *et al.* (2000). The shaded area covers all scenarios used to project climate change by the IPCC. Emissions in
2009 are projected to be ~3 per cent below 2008 levels, close to the level
of emissions in 2007. This reduction is equivalent to a temporary halt in
global emissions for a period of only 2–4 weeks.

Source: Copenhagen Diagnosis (2009)

In line with continued emissions of CO_2, its atmospheric concentrations have increased,
reaching 385 parts per million (ppm) in 2008, i.e. a level 105 ppm above pre-industrial
levels and at least 40 per cent higher than at any time in the last 800,000 years (Copenhagen Diagnosis 2009). CO_2 levels increased at a rate of 1.9 ppm per year between 2000 and
2008, corresponding to 3.4 per cent per year, up from 1 per cent per year in the 1990s (Le
Quéré *et al.* 2009). According to the Copenhagen Diagnosis (2009), there are three major
reasons for the acceleration in the growth of emissions of CO_2, including industrial growth
in developing countries, and particularly China, the increased international trade of goods,
primarily involving China (see also Peters and Hertwich 2008; Andersen *et al.* 2010), and a

slowdown in previous improvements in CO_2 efficiency (Raupach *et al.* 2007). At the same time, there are concerns that the capacity of terrestrial and marine sinks to take up CO_2 is approaching saturation (Copenhagen Diagnosis 2009).

Warming trends

As concentrations of GHG continue to increase, global temperature trends continue to accelerate, with atmospheric warming now reaching a trend of +0.187 ± 0.052 °C per decade for the 25-year period ending in 2008, up from +0.177 ± 0.052 °C from the 25-year period ending 2006 (Copenhagen Diagnosis 2009: 14). These trends are confirmed by recent data released by the WMO (2009) the Hadley Centre (2009) and the Goddard Institute for Space Studies (GISS 2010), which all conclude that the last decade was the warmest since temperature measurements began. The year 2009 was the second warmest year in the northern hemisphere since temperature measurements began in 1880, and the warmest since 1880 in the southern hemisphere (GISS 2010). The Copenhagen Diagnosis notes that (2009: 9): 'Even over the past ten years, despite a decrease in solar forcing, the trend continues to be one of warming. Natural, short-term fluctuations are occurring as usual, but there have been no significant changes in the underlying warming trend'. Notably, every year from 2001–08 has been among the warmest since temperature measurements began, even though solar irradiance has been comparably weak over the past few years (see also Easterling and Wehner 2009).

The importance of these findings is even more evident when illustrated over a longer period of time. For instance, Mann *et al.* (2008) present northern hemisphere temperature reconstructions. The temperature curve shows considerable variation over the past 1,800 years, but it is clear that there has been an observed rapid temperature increase in the past decades.

Sea-level rise, extreme events and ocean heat balance

Along with temperature increases, changes in other parameters have been observed to accelerate, including sea-level rise at 3.4 mm per year since 1993 (satellite measurements). The Copenhagen Diagnosis (2009) suggests that this acceleration is consistent with ice-sheet mass loss, and concludes that sea-level rise will be higher than projected in the IPCC AR4, i.e. possibly more than 1 m by 2100 in an emission scenario without mitigation. Several metres of sea-level rise would occur over the next centuries. With regard to weather extremes, hot and cold periods are expected to amplify further, with increases in precipitation extremes and drought. The intensity of tropical cyclones has also increased in the past three decades, along with tropical ocean temperatures, even though future changes in cyclone activity cannot yet be modelled. Increases in the frequency of severe thunderstorms in some regions, including the tropics and south-eastern USA, are however expected because of climate change (Trapp *et al.* 2007, 2009; Aumann *et al.* 2008; Marsh *et al.* 2009). Observed changes in extreme events also include recent increases in both the frequency and intensity of wildfires, for instance in Spain, Greece, southern California, and south-east Australia, which are expected to continue (Westerling *et al.* 2006; Pitman *et al.* 2007).

With regard to oceans, estimates of ocean heat uptake have been found to be higher than previously calculated, and global ocean surface temperatures reached the highest levels ever recorded in summer 2009. This has been going along with processes of ocean acidification and de-oxygenation, which could prove to be highly problematic for marine ecosystems (Orr *et al.* 2005; McNeil and Matear 2007; Fabry *et al.* 2008; Oschlies *et al.* 2008; Stramma *et al.* 2008; Rosa and Seibel 2008; Brewer 2009; Lam *et al.* 2009; Hofmann and Schellnhuber 2009; Riebesell *et al.* 2009).

Tipping points

The Copenhagen Diagnosis (2009) also identifies tipping points, i.e. a situation where current trends in emission pathways are likely to lead to considerable increases in global average temperatures and other climate-related impacts, which in turn would increase the risk of reaching tipping points, where abrupt and rapid changes in the climate system will occur. There are five tipping points that could undergo a transition this century:

1 *Arctic ice-mass loss*. In the Arctic, an acceleration of the melting of glaciers and ice sheets has been observed, indicating 'beyond doubt' (Copenhagen Diagnosis 2009: 9) that Greenland is losing ice mass at an accelerating rate. Notably, the summertime melting of the Arctic in 2007 (Mote 2007), has been far greater than projected in the IPCC AR4 climate models, with sea-ice melt during 2007–09 being 40 per cent greater than average projections (Copenhagen Diagnosis 2009). This might mean that the Greenland ice sheet is nearing a tipping point where it is 'committed to shrink' (Copenhagen Diagnosis 2009: 43, based on Lenton *et al.* 2008 and Kriegler *et al.* 2009).

2 *Antarctic ice-mass loss*. There is greater uncertainty regarding the West Antarctic ice sheet (Lenton *et al.* 2008; Kriegler *et al.* 2009), but there is the potential for rapid change in ice-mass loss. There are also indications of changes in the East Antarctic ice sheet.

3 *The Amazon rainforests*. The region experienced widespread drought in 2005 which turned the region from a sink to a source of carbon in the order of 0.6 to 0.8 GtC per year (Phillips *et al.* 2009). If droughts increased or became more severe, the system could reach a tipping point resulting in a potential dieback of up to 80 per cent of the rainforest (Cox *et al.* 2004, 2008).

4 *The Sahel and West African monsoon*. One of the few positive tipping points could be a weakening of the Atlantic thermohaline circulation, which could disturb the West African Monsoon, leading it to move northwards into the Sahel. As moist air would be drawn from the Atlantic to the west, this could lead to a greening of the Sahel (Cook and Vizy 2006; Chang *et al.* 2008; Patricola and Cook 2008).

5 *Indian summer monsoon*. There are indications that the Indian summer monsoon is already affected (Ramanathan *et al.* 2005; Meehl *et al.* 2008). This is likely to be primarily a result of emissions of soot from small burning fires, absorbing sunlight. This causes heating of the atmosphere, leading to a decline in the land–ocean temperature gradient critical for triggering monsoon onset (Ramanathan *et al.* 2005).

The Copenhagen Diagnosis indicates other tipping elements and mechanisms, such as carbon loss from permafrost. These could amplify global warming. The authors caution, however, that amplifying feedbacks from individual tipping elements are fairly weak at the global scale:

> However, other (non-tipping element) amplifying feedbacks, including a potential future switch in the average response of the land biosphere from a CO_2 sink to a CO_2 source, could significantly amplify CO_2 rise and global temperature on the century timescale (Friedlingstein *et al.* 2006). The Earth's climate system is already in a state of strong amplifying feedback from relatively fast physical climate responses (Bony *et al.* 2006) (e.g. water vapor feedback).
>
> (Copenhagen Diagnosis 2009: 44)

FUTURE CLIMATE CHANGE

Projections of the responses of the climate system to changing concentrations of GHGs in the atmosphere are based on simulation runs of climate models. As such simulations need to consider future emission pathways, which are uncertain, various assumptions are usually made regarding future socioeconomic and technological development. Through such modelling based on a range of assumptions, scenarios can be developed covering different development pathways. Figure 3.5 shows a range of scenarios from the SRES-family (A1F1, A2, B1), which represent different socioeconomic development and emission scenarios. The figure shows that even in the mitigation B1 scenario – characterized by global population growth to 9 billion in 2050 and its subsequent gradual decline, considerable achievements in eco-efficiency, the introduction of green technologies, and wider global approaches to sustainable development – there is a risk that an increase in global average surface temperature of 2 °C will be exceeded.

In the scenarios, global mean air surface temperatures are projected to increase by +2 °C to +7 °C above pre-industrial levels by 2100. Indeed, various authors have warned that if current emission trends continue, or even if emission reduction commitments currently made by nations are successfully achieved, temperatures will exceed 2 °C average global warming by 2100 (Hansen *et al.* 2006; Anderson and Bows 2008; Parry *et al.* 2008; Meinshausen *et al.* 2009; Rogelj *et al.* 2009). The Copenhagen Diagnosis consequently concludes that there is a very high probability (>90 per cent) that warming will exceed 2 °C by 2100, unless global emissions peak soon and start to decline rapidly by 2020, and that warming rates will accelerate if positive carbon feedbacks significantly diminish the efficiency of land and oceans to absorb CO_2:

> At the high end of emissions, with business-as-usual for several decades to come, global mean warming is estimated to reach 4–7 °C by 2100, locking in climate change at a scale that would profoundly and adversely affect all of human civilization and all of the world's major ecosystems. At the lower end of emissions, something that would require urgent, deep and long-lasting cuts in fossil fuel use, and active preservation of the world's forests, global mean warming is projected to reach 2–3 °C by century's end. While clearly a better outcome than the high emissions route, global mean warming of even just 1.5–2.0 °C still carries a significant risk of adverse impacts on ecosystems and human society.
>
> (Copenhagen Diagnosis 2009: 51)

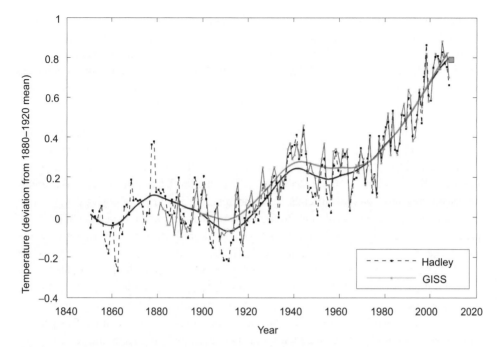

Figure 3.5 Reconstructed temperatures and projected temperature increases. Reconstructed global average temperature relative to 1800–1900 and projected global average temperature out to 2100 (the latter from IPCC AR4). The envelopes B1, A2, A1F1 refer to the IPCC AR4 projections using those scenarios. The reconstruction record is taken from Mann *et al.* (2008).

Source: Copenhagen Diagnosis 2009

Importantly, even when emissions of GHGs have peaked and decline or even stop completely, atmospheric temperatures cannot be expected to peak and decline for centuries because of the long lifetime of CO_2 and other GHGs in the atmosphere (Matthews and Caldeira 2008; Allen *et al.* 2009; Solomon *et al.* 2009; Eby *et al.* 2009). In conclusion, humanity needs to urgently engage in mitigation, while simultaneously preparing for adaptation.

CLIMATE CHANGE SCEPTICISM

Little room is given in this book to climate sceptics and climate change scepticism, because there cannot be any serious doubts about the findings of the IPCC (2007b), despite recent claims of mistakes and inconsistencies. Climate change is complex, as will be understood by any reader of the three volumes of the AR4, i.e. the consensus of the science on climate change compiled by IPCC Working Groups I (The Physical Science Basis), II (Impacts, Adaptation and Vulnerability) and III (Mitigation of Climate Change). As underlined in all IPCC reports, key uncertainties in climate science persist, a problem dealt with by climate scientists by assigning probabilities and describing the level of scientific knowledge as low-moderate-fair (see also Copenhagen Diagnosis 2009 for a summary on research needs and uncertainties). Notably, key findings in the IPCC reports have been consistent over time, and subsequently moved from lower to higher levels of scientific certainty. Conclusions have consequently essentially remained the same since the publication of the First Assessment Report in 1990.

As long as there have been IPCC reports, there has been scepticism about climate change. In part this might be explained by failures in the transfer of knowledge from scientists to the media, and from the media to the public, as well as the problems incurred in maintaining journalistic norms, i.e. the distribution of information leading to 'enhanced accountability on the part of elected officials', and adherence to principles of objectivity, fairness, accuracy and balance (Boykoff and Boykoff 2004). In analyses of media content in the US prestige-press between 1988–2002, Boykoff and Boykoff found that in the majority of articles (53 per cent) 'balanced' accounting of climate change prevailed, i.e. giving equal attention to the views that there are human causes for climate change and that climate change is a natural phenomenon. While adhering to the journalistic principle of balance, Boykoff and Boykoff conclude that these articles lead to informational bias, given the agreement in the scientific community of the human causes of global warming. Thirty-five per cent of articles covered climate change with a greater focus on human activities as contributing to climate change, thus, according to the authors, in some sense representing scientific discourse, while the remainder of articles either emphasized that it was dubious whether humans contributed to climate change (6 per cent), or that global warming clearly had anthropogenic causes (6 per cent). There was thus clear evidence of a significant difference between the scientific community consensus on climate change and the US prestige-press discourse of the issue.

Overall, Boykoff and Boykoff (2004, 2007; see also Boykoff 2007 for an analysis of TV reports) conclude that reporting in the media is problematic, as it fails to correctly transfer information from science to the public, and that the employment of professional journalistic norms such as balanced reporting can even adversely affect interactions between science, policy and public. Boykoff and Boykoff (2004, 2007) do not address the problem of organizations seeking to distribute false information on climate change, however, which might be significant, as a recent report by Greenpeace (2010) on the funding of climate sceptics by the US oil industry highlights. Nevertheless, media misrepresentations of scientific findings have also been caused by non-government organizations (NGOs) (Ladle *et al.* 2005), and have, as a whole, had the consequence of eroding public trust for science.

More recently, in late 2008, a science 'scandal' as well as purported errors in the IPCC AR4 made global headlines, fostering the notion that climate science was unreliable and that at least some scientists 'believing' in climate change had sought to deliberately reject scientific papers from 'sceptical' scientists in the review process leading to publication in peer-reviewed journals. It is beyond the scope of this book to discuss the conflict in more detail, however, and readers are referred to two websites dedicated to explaining misunderstandings, www.skepticalscience.com and www.RealClimate.org. A number of misconceptions on climate change are also addressed in the Copenhagen Diagnosis (2009).

In summary, it is clear that climate change and climate change mitigation are perceived as a threat by many, as serious climate policy will demand a restructuring of the global oil industry and other energy-intense industries, as well as changes in the energy-intense lifestyles of the wealthy. Should there be, on the other hand, reasonable doubt on climate change, it would be justified to maintain business-as-usual, a preferred option for individuals whose business models or lifestyles will be affected by climate politics (Stoll-Kleemann *et al.* 2001). However, scientific evidence of global warming is, as outlined, 'unequivocal' (IPCC 2007b), while there appear to be few studies of the 'climate sceptics' and their arguments, which notably can range from reasons such as ensuring adherence to the principles of good sciences, to legitimate questions regarding uncertainties in climate science, to the discrediting of climate science for reasons of personal profit (see also Markussen and Svendsen 2005; Greenpeace 2010).

4 Climate change mitigation

From the above discussions it is clear that mitigating climate change is a key challenge for humanity. The IPCC (2007b) has put emphasis on the fact that global emissions should decline in the near future to avoid 'dangerous interference with the climate system', as outlined in the United Nations Framework Convention on Climate Change. To achieve this, a global average maximum level of warming has been identified at 2 °C by 2100 compared to 1990, beyond which largely negative impacts for ecosystems and socioeconomic systems are likely to occur (Hansen et al. 2006; Anderson and Bows 2008; Parry et al. 2008; Meinshausen et al. 2009).

EMISSION TRENDS AND MITIGATION NEEDS

Current emission trends, if continued, would 'very likely' (>90 per cent probability) lead to accelerated increases in globally averaged surface temperatures, reaching between 1.8 °C and 4.0 °C by 2100 (IPCC 2007b), i.e. exceeding 'safe' levels of climate change. A more recent assessment of the German Advisory Council on Global Change (WBGU 2009) concludes that if cumulative CO_2 emissions in the period 2010–50 were limited to 750 Gt, there is a 67 per cent probability of limiting global warming to within 2 °C. Based on this approach, there is thus an overall 'cap' on the emissions that can be emitted up to 2050, which in turn allows for calculation of the level of emissions that can be emitted every year. Depending on when emissions peak, this will demand a flatter (peak earlier in time) or steeper (peak later) decline in emissions over time (Figure 4.1).

From these scenarios it becomes obvious that even if emissions peaked in the immediate future in 2011, which is highly unlikely, there would have to be a subsequent decline in global emissions at a rate of 3.7 per cent per annum relative to 2008 and maintained up to 2050, which appears hardly realistic to achieve, given observed and projected growth in energy use (cf. IEA 2009). Scenarios peaking in 2015 and 2020 demand subsequent emission reductions of 5.3 per cent per year and 9.0 per cent per year, respectively, which are even less realistic goals. Emission reductions thus need to take place immediately, and at a considerable rate, if there is to be a real chance of avoiding warming beyond 2 °C by 2100. Notably, at current emission rates, the global GHG budget for 2010–50 would be used up within just 20 years (Meinshausen et al. 2009). Delays in peaking thus have

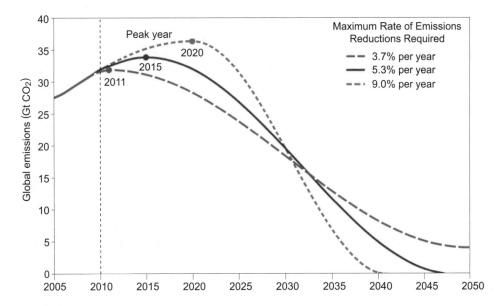

Figure 4.1 *Emission reduction pathways in relation to emission peaks.*
Examples of global emission pathways where cumulative CO_2 emissions
equal 750 Gt during the time period 2010–50. At this level, there is a 67
per cent probability of limiting global warming to a maximum of 2 °C. The
graph shows that the later the peak in emissions is reached, the steeper
their subsequent reduction has to be. The figure shows variants of a glo-
bal emissions scenario with different peak years: 2011, 2015 and 2020.
In order to achieve compliance with these curves, maximum annual
reduction rates of 3.7 per cent, 5.3 per cent or 9.0 per cent would be
required (relative to 2008).
Source: based on UNWTO 2001, 2010a

significant consequences for the scale of climate politics in the post-Kyoto period (see
also England *et al.* 2009). In terms of absolute emissions, even if emissions peaked as
soon as 2011, sustainable emissions would be down to 4 Gt CO_2 in the year 2050, or less
than half a tonne CO_2 per year per person at a projected world population of 9 billion
(Copenhagen Diagnosis 2009), i.e. less than one eighth of current globally averaged per
capita emissions.

The situation is further complicated by the fact that emission reductions are comparably
cheap at the moment, but expected to rise in the future (Figure 4.2). In other words, while
reducing emissions by some 10–15 per cent through behavioural change and low-cost technical measures would be cost-neutral or even lead to savings for both producers and consumers, further reductions in emissions will become rapidly more expensive. The IPCC
(2007b) estimates, for instance, that individual stakeholders, such as companies, could save
at least 5 Gt of CO_2-eq without costs (Figure 4.2; scenario for 2030, considering growth
in emissions; see (c)). At investments of up to US$100 per tonne of CO_2-eq, this amount

would increase to at least $15\,GtCO_2$-eq and up to $>30\,GtCO_2$-eq (Figure 4.2(a)). However, the amount of emissions abated at US$100 is only marginally greater than the amount abated at US$50, indicating that mitigation costs rise exponentially beyond a given point. Top-down approaches, according to the IPCC, would lead to lower emission reduction levels (Figure 4.2(b)), indicating that voluntary action would be more efficient from an overall systemic point of view. Self-regulation is, however, not a realistic option due to obstacles such as the lack of interest in energy-related issues, perceived difficulties in retrofitting and restructuring, or an understanding of high costs incurred in saving energy (e.g. Oberthür 2003; Haites 2009; Smith and Rodger 2009; T&E 2009a, b).

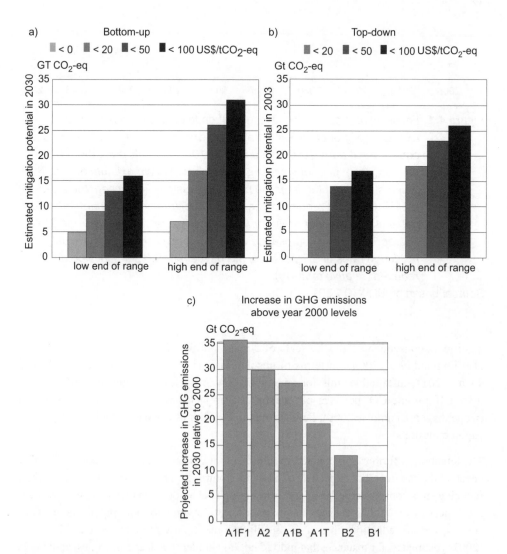

Figure 4.2 *Emission reductions achieved at various cost levels and in bottom-up versus top-down approaches*
Source: IPCC 2007b

THE EMERGENCE OF GLOBAL CLIMATE POLICY

As a response to a growing understanding of the consequences of climate change for eco-systems and socioeconomic development, a range of conferences have been held since 1992, when the United Nations Conference on Environment and Development (UNCED) took place in Rio de Janeiro. One of the outcomes of the UNCED was the United Nations Framework Convention on Climate Change (UNFCCC), a treaty with the objective to sta-bilize GHG concentrations in the atmosphere to prevent 'dangerous interference with the climate system'. The UNFCCC was opened for signature in 1992 and entered into force on 21 March 1994. As of December 2009 it was ratified by 192 countries, which have met annually since 1995 in COP to establish a framework for intergovernmental initiatives to deal with the challenges posed by climate change:

> The ultimate objective of this Convention and any related legal instruments that the Conference of the Parties may adopt is to achieve, in accordance with the relevant provisions of the Convention, stabilization of greenhouse gas concentrations in the atmosphere at a level that would prevent dangerous anthropogenic interference with the climate system. Such a level should be achieved within a time-frame sufficient to allow ecosystems to adapt naturally to climate change, to ensure that food production is not threatened and to enable economic development to proceed in a sus-tainable manner.
>
> (UNFCCC 2010b)

Table 4.1 provides an overview of emissions from 192 countries. The table shows that there are huge differences in overall emissions, measured in million t CO_2-eq, emissions per capita of the population, and total emissions including land use, land-use change and forestry (LULUCF) and land-use change and forestry (LUCF). The table also indicates that emissions might have substantially increased or decreased since the base year 1990. Moreover, for many countries, emission inventories are more than 15 years old.

Table 4.1 Greenhouse gas emissions by country

Country	Latest year available	Total GHG emissions (Mt CO_2-eq)	% change since 1990	Total GHG emissions per capita (t CO_2-eq)	Total GHG emissions with LULUCF/LUCF
Albania	1994	5.53	−22.5	1.74	7.06
Algeria	1994	91.76	—	3.31	100.34
Antigua and Barbuda	1990	0.39	—	6.30	0.29
Argentina	2000	282.00	22.0	7.63	238.70
Armenia	1990	25.31	—	7.14	24.70
Australia	2006	536.07	28.8	25.99	549.85
Austria	2006	91.09	15.1	11.01	72.94
Azerbaijan	1994	43.17	−29.0	5.62	42.09
Bahamas	1994	2.20	14.9	7.97	2.20
Bahrain	1994	19.60	—	34.90	19.60

Table 4.1 Continued

Bangladesh	1994	45.93	—	0.37	53.76
Barbados	1997	4.06	24.8	15.90	4.05
Belarus	2006	81.00	−36.4	8.29	55.00
Belgium	2006	136.97	−5.2	13.08	135.91
Belize	1994	6.34	—	29.63	2.31
Benin	1995	39.35	—	6.88	−8.18
Bhutan	1994	1.29	—	2.51	−2.26
Bolivia	2000	21.46	40.1	2.58	49.94
Botswana	1994	9.29	—	6.15	−29.44
Brazil	1994	658.65	11.1	4.14	1 476.73
Bulgaria	2006	71.34	−38.9	9.28	53.12
Burkina Faso	1994	5.97	—	0.61	4.58
Burundi	1998	2.00	—	0.32	−1.00
Cambodia	1994	12.76	—	1.15	−5.15
Cameroon	1994	165.73	—	12.11	187.91
Canada	2006	720.63	21.7	22.09	751.97
Cape Verde	1995	0.29	—	0.73	0.22
Central African Republic	1994	37.74	—	11.61	−101.58
Chad	1993	8.02	—	1.20	−38.18
Chile	1994	54.89	—	3.87	45.69
China	1994	4 057.62	—	3.39	3 650.14
Colombia	1994	137.49	22.9	3.84	152.08
Comoros	1994	0.52	—	1.08	−0.38
Congo	1994	1.38	—	0.51	−68.49
Cook Islands	1994	0.08	—	4.33	−0.07
Costa Rica	1996	10.79	76.9	3.03	10.07
Cote d'Ivoire	1994	24.73	—	1.71	4.88
Croatia	2006	30.83	−5.2	6.95	23.34
Cuba	1996	40.19	−36.8	3.67	18.54
Czech Republic	2006	148.20	−23.7	14.49	144.83
Dem. Rep. of the Congo	1994	44.64	—	1.03	−176.84
Denmark	2006	71.91	2.2	13.24	70.11
Djibouti	1994	0.51	—	0.84	−0.09
Dominica	1994	0.15	−98.8	2.18	−0.22
Dominican Republic	1994	20.44	61.7	2.56	13.94
Ecuador	1990	30.77	—	2.99	77.72
Egypt	1990	116.74	—	2.02	106.84
El Salvador	1994	11.72	—	2.07	15.66
Eritrea	2000	0.76	—	0.21	0.76

Estonia	2006	18.88	-54.6	14.04	15.40
Ethiopia	1995	47.74	11.0	0.84	37.87
Fiji	1994	1.39	–	1.83	-6.31
Finland	2006	80.29	13.2	15.26	46.85
France	2006	546.53	-3.5	8.90	476.63
Gabon	1994	6.52	–	6.19	-494.35
Gambia	1993	4.26	–	4.24	-45.73
Georgia	1997	12.89	-71.6	2.62	14.04
Germany	2006	1 004.79	-18.2	12.20	968.39
Ghana	1996	13.14	17.8	0.74	-5.88
Greece	2006	133.11	27.3	12.01	127.91
Grenada	1994	1.61	–	16.21	1.51
Guatemala	1990	14.74	–	1.65	-24.80
Guinea	1994	5.06	–	0.70	-12.54
Guinea-Bissau	1994	1.69	–	1.49	–
Guyana	1998	3.07	40.8	4.05	-27.80
Haiti	1994	5.13	–	0.67	6.06
Honduras	1995	10.83	–	1.94	15.46
Hungary	2006	78.62	-20.0	7.82	72.72
Iceland	2006	4.23	24.2	14.05	5.36
India	1994	1 214.25	–	1.30	1 228.54
Indonesia	1994	334.19	25.2	1.77	498.31
Iran (Islamic Republic of)	1994	385.43	–	6.30	417.01
Ireland	2006	69.76	25.6	16.33	69.27
Israel	2005	73.41	–	10.97	73.02
Italy	2006	567.92	9.9	9.63	455.71
Jamaica	1994	116.31	–	47.58	116.15
Japan	2006	1 340.08	5.3	10.51	1 248.58
Jordan	1994	21.94	–	5.33	18.37
Kazakhstan	2004	210.21	-34.7	13.93	202.77
Kenya	1994	21.47	–	0.80	-6.53
Kiribati	1994	0.03	–	0.39	0.03
Korea, Dem. People's Rep.	1990	201.93	–	10.02	187.30
Korea, Republic of	2001	542.89	87.6	11.62	508.25
Kyrgyzstan	2000	15.05	-58.3	3.04	14.08
Lao, People's Dem. Rep.	1990	6.87	–	1.63	-97.44
Latvia	2006	11.62	-56.1	5.10	-6.19
Lebanon	1994	15.70	–	4.63	15.91
Lesotho	1994	1.82	–	1.07	3.08
Liechtenstein	2006	0.27	19.0	7.79	0.27
Lithuania	2006	23.22	-53.0	6.85	15.27

Table 4.1 *Continued*

Luxembourg	2006	13.32	1.0	28.37	13.03
Madagascar	1994	21.93	–	1.72	–217.04
Malawi	1994	7.07	–12.1	0.71	24.59
Malaysia	1994	136.68	–	6.81	75.60
Maldives	1994	0.15	–	0.62	0.15
Mali	1995	8.67	–	0.91	–1.08
Malta	2000	2.85	28.4	7.33	2.61
Mauritania	1995	4.33	–	1.91	3.58
Mauritius	1995	2.06	–	1.83	1.84
Mexico	2002	548.50	29.2	5.38	638.35
Micronesia, Federated States of	1994	0.25	–	2.36	0.25
Monaco	2006	0.09	–13.0	2.88	0.09
Mongolia	1998	15.90	–17.7	6.82	15.60
Morocco	1994	44.37	–	1.67	39.88
Mozambique	1994	8.19	20.8	0.53	15.97
Namibia	1994	5.60	–	3.54	–0.11
Nauru	1994	0.04	–	4.06	0.03
Nepal	1994	31.19	–	1.48	39.31
Netherlands	2006	207.48	–2.0	12.66	210.05
New Zealand	2006	77.87	25.7	18.75	55.12
Nicaragua	1994	7.65	–	1.68	–5.40
Niger	1990	4.86	–	0.61	10.96
Nigeria	1994	242.63	–	2.25	347.64
Niue	1994	4.42	–	2 052.95	4.51
Norway	2006	53.51	7.7	11.44	25.68
Pakistan	1994	160.60	–	1.26	167.12
Palau	2000	0.09	–	4.67	0.09
Panama	1994	10.69	–	4.08	34.40
Papua New Guinea	1994	5.01	–	1.09	4.60
Paraguay	1994	140.46	149.9	29.94	159.96
Peru	1994	57.58	–	2.45	98.80
Philippines	1994	100.87	–	1.47	100.74
Poland	2006	400.46	–11.7	10.49	359.95
Portugal	2006	82.74	40.0	7.81	78.58
Republic of Moldova	1998	10.51	–68.4	2.49	9.07
Romania	2006	156.68	–36.7	7.27	119.19
Russian Federation	2006	2 190.24	–34.2	15.37	2 478.03
Rwanda	2002	2.38	–	0.28	–4.63

Saint Kitts and Nevis	1994	0.16	—	3.77	0.07
Saint Lucia	1994	0.89	—	6.12	0.54
Samoa	1994	0.56	—	3.36	0.48
Sao Tome and Principe	1998	0.12	—	0.89	-1.42
Saudi Arabia	1990	165.27	—	10.16	150.03
Senegal	1995	9.57	—	1.11	3.57
Seychelles	1995	0.26	—	3.43	-0.58
Singapore	1994	26.86	—	7.96	26.86
Slovakia	2006	48.90	-33.6	9.07	45.87
Slovenia	2006	20.59	10.8	10.27	15.86
Solomon Islands	1994	0.29	—	0.82	0.29
South Africa	1994	379.84	9.4	9.38	361.22
Spain	2006	433.34	50.6	9.94	400.34
Sri Lanka	1995	29.13	—	1.60	408.21
St. Vincent and the Grenadines	1997	0.41	4.6	3.80	0.28
Sudan	1995	54.24	—	1.76	71.97
Suriname	2003	3.34	—	6.85	4.87
Swaziland	1994	2.64	—	2.78	-0.62
Sweden	2006	65.75	-8.7	7.21	27.74
Switzerland	2006	53.21	0.7	7.11	50.98
Tajikistan	1998	4.29	-81.9	0.71	2.80
Thailand	1994	223.98	—	3.76	285.84
The Former Yugoslav Rep. of Macedonia	1998	15.07	-2.4	7.56	12.79
Togo	1998	6.28	—	1.28	34.41
Tonga	1994	0.23	—	2.37	-0.08
Trinidad and Tobago	1990	16.01	—	13.14	14.51
Tunisia	1994	25.14	—	2.85	23.37
Turkey	2006	331.76	95.1	4.60	255.66
Turkmenistan	1994	52.31	—	12.77	51.93
Tuvalu	1994	0.01	—	1.09	0.01
Uganda	1994	41.55	—	2.05	49.80
Ukraine	2006	443.18	-51.9	9.51	410.56
United Arab Emirates	1994	130.44	—	56.71	126.21
United Kingdom	2006	655.79	-15.1	10.83	653.83

Table 4.1 Continued

United Rep. of Tanzania	1994	39.24	0.6	1.35	952.80
United States	2006	7 017.32	14.4	22.96	6 170.53
Uruguay	2000	29.73	7.5	8.95	17.19
Uzbekistan	1994	153.89	-5.7	6.85	153.49
Vanuatu	1994	0.30	–	1.79	0.30
Venezuela	1999	192.19	–	8.03	177.90
Viet Nam	1994	84.45	–	1.18	103.84
Yemen	1995	17.87	–	1.15	8.20
Zambia	1994	32.77	–	3.70	36.23
Zimbabwe	1994	27.59	–	2.40	-34.65

Source: UNSTATS 2009

With regard to emission reductions, the UNFCCC does not set mandatory limits on GHG emissions and is not legally binding. Rather, under the UNFCCC, governments gather and share information on GHG emissions, national policies and best practices; launch national strategies for addressing GHG emissions and adapting to expected impacts, including the provision of financial and technological support to developing countries; and cooperate in preparing for adaptation to the impacts of climate change (UNFCCC 2010c).

As outlined, global targets for emission reductions are guided by recommendations made by the IPCC. The burden sharing, i.e. the contribution made by different countries to global emission reductions are negotiated within the UNFCCC, and more specifically the COP, under the guiding principle of 'common but differentiated responsibilities' (CBDR), where developing countries can increase emissions to facilitate economic development, while developed countries reduce emissions more substantially in order to approach more equitable per capita GHG emissions globally. The UNFCCC is charged with establishing and monitoring national GHG inventories, which for most countries are compared to 1990 base year levels for emission reductions as identified in the Kyoto Protocol, the legal framework for emission reductions. Base year emissions are defined as aggregate anthropogenic CO_2-eq emissions of GHG listed in Annex A (see Table 4.2) in a historical base year (UNFCCC 1998). For most Annex I countries, the base year is 1990, but countries included in Annex I undergoing the transition to a market economy can choose a base year other than 1990. An important addition is that if land use, land-use change and forestry constituted a net source of GHG emissions in the base year, emissions from deforestation will be included in the base year inventory.

The Kyoto Protocol to the UNFCCC was adopted in 1997 in Kyoto, Japan, at the Third Session of the Conference of the Parties (COP-3) to the UNFCCC. The Kyoto Protocol entered into force on 16 February 2005, when Russia signed the Protocol and the conditional criterion of a minimum share of 55 per cent of global emissions of CO_2 being emitted by signatory countries was met. The Kyoto Protocol ascribes different responsibilities to countries to reduce GHG emissions, depending on their economic development and emission levels, and contains legally binding commitments for Annex B countries (see Table 4.2). Annex B

Table 4.2 Countries as grouped under the Kyoto Protocol

Annex B countries

The countries included in Annex B to the Kyoto Protocol that have agreed to a target for their greenhouse-gas emissions, including all the Annex I countries (as amended in 1998) except for Turkey and Belarus.

Annex I countries

Including all the OECD countries in the year 1990 and countries with economies in transition. Under Articles 4.2 (a) and 4.2 (b) of the Convention, Annex I countries committed themselves specifically to the aim of returning individually or jointly to their 1990 levels of greenhouse gas emissions by the year 2000. By default, the other countries are referred to as Non-Annex I countries.

Including: Australia, Austria, Belarus, Belgium, Bulgaria, Canada, Czech Republic, Denmark, Estonia, European Community, Finland, France, Germany, Greece, Hungary, Iceland, Ireland, Italy, Japan, Latvia, Liechtenstein, Lithuania, Luxembourg, Monaco, Netherlands, New Zealand, Norway, Poland, Portugal, Romania, Russian Federation, Slovakia, Slovenia, Spain, Sweden, Switzerland, Turkey, Ukraine, United Kingdom.

Annex II countries

Including all OECD countries in the year 1990. Under Article 4.2 (g) of the Convention, these countries are expected to provide financial resources to assist developing countries to comply with their obligations, such as preparing national reports. Annex II countries are also expected to promote the transfer of environmentally sound technologies to developing countries.

Including: Australia, Austria, Belgium, Canada, Denmark, Finland, France, Germany, Greece, Iceland, Ireland, Italy, Japan, Luxembourg, Netherlands, New Zealand, Norway, Portugal, Spain, Sweden, Switzerland, United Kingdom.

Source: IPCC 2007b, UNFCCC 1998, 2010c

countries include most countries in the Organization for Economic Cooperation and Development (OECD) as well as countries with economies in transition. Countries included in Annex B of the Protocol have agreed to reduce their anthropogenic GHG emissions including CO_2, CH_4, N_2O, and the F-gases hydrofluorocarbons, perfluorocarbons, and sulphur hexafluoride by at least 5 per cent below 1990 levels in the commitment period 2008 to 2012.

GLOBAL MITIGATION TARGETS

Table 4.3 shows emission reduction commitments for Annex I Parties included in Annex B to the Kyoto Protocol for the period 2008–12. Based on the principle of CBDR, emission reduction commitments are not equal, with some countries being allowed to increase emissions in this period, and others having to decrease, on average to 92 per cent of 1990 emissions, representing an emission reduction by 8 per cent. For the purpose of monitoring, Annex I countries have to submit updated inventories once a year.

Table 4.3 *Base year emissions and reduction commitments in the period 2008–2012*

Party	Base year level of total national emissions (t CO_2-eq)	Emission reduction commitment (percentage of base year)
Australia	547,699,841	108.0
Austria	79,049,657	87.0
Belarus*		92.0[a]
Belgium	145,728,763	92.5
Bulgaria*	132,618,658	92.0
Canada	593,998,462	94.0
Croatia*		95.0
Czech Republic*	194,248,218	92.0
Denmark	69,978,070	79.0
Estonia*	42,622,312	92.0
European Community	4,265,517,719	92.0
Finland	71,003,509	100.0
France	563,925,328	100.0
Germany	1,232,429,543	79.0
Greece	106,987,169	125.0
Hungary*	115,397,149	94.0
Iceland	3,367,972	110.0
Ireland	55,607,836	113.0
Italy	516,850,887	93.5
Japan	1,261,331,418	94.0
Latvia*	25,909,159	92.0
Liechtenstein	229,483	92.0
Lithuania*	49,414,386	92.0
Luxembourg	13,167,499	72.0
Monaco	107,658	92.0
Netherlands	213,034,498	94.0
New Zealand	61,912,947	100.0
Norway	49,619,168	101.0
Poland*	563,442,774	94.0
Portugal	60,147,642	127.0
Romania*	278,225,022	92.0
Russian Federation*	3,323,419,064	100.0
Slovakia*	72,050,764	92.0
Slovenia*	20,354,042	92.0
Spain	289,773,205	115.0
Sweden	72,151,646	104.0
Switzerland	52,790,957	92.0
Ukraine*	920,836,933	100.0
UK and Northern Ireland	779,904,144	87.5

Notes: (1) The base year data are as determined during the initial review process. (2) Targets under the "burden-sharing" agreement of the European Community are shown in italics: the EC agreed to reduce emissions to 92% of those of 1990 as an entity, but with different responsibilities for countries within the EC. *A Party undergoing the process of transition to a market economy (an EIT Party). ªThe amendment to the Kyoto Protocol with an emission reduction target for Belarus adopted by decision 10/CMP.2 has not entered into force yet. (3) Annex I Parties with the base year other than 1990 are Bulgaria (1988), Hungary (average of 1985-1987), Poland (1988), Romania (1989), Slovenia (1986).
Source: UNFCCC 2010d

Voluntary post-Kyoto emission pledges were submitted to the UNFCCC in January 2010, i.e. after consensus was reached at the COP-15 in Copenhagen to stabilize global warming at 2 °C by 2100, though without agreement on binding mitigation targets. By 31 January, the UNFCCC had received national pledges to cut and limit GHG by 2020 from 55 countries accounting for 78 per cent of global emissions from energy use (UNFCCC 2010d). As shown in Table 4.4, most pledges are conditional, however, indicating that progress on binding emission targets could prove to be slow.

Table 4.4 *Quantified economy-wide emission targets for 2020, Annex I Parties*

	Emissions reduction in 2020	Base year
Australia	–5% up to –15% or –25% Australia will reduce its greenhouse gas emissions by 25% on 2000 levels by 2020 if the world agrees to an ambitious global deal capable of stabilizing levels of greenhouse gases in the atmosphere at 450 ppm CO_2-eq or lower. Australia will unconditionally reduce our emissions by 5% below 2000 levels by 2020, and by up to 15% by 2020 if there is a global agreement which falls short of securing atmospheric stabilization at 450 ppm CO_2-eq and under which major developing economies commit to substantially restrain emissions and advanced economies take on commitments comparable to Australia's.	2000
Belarus	–5–10% reduction, which is premised on the presence of and access of Belarus to the Kyoto flexible mechanisms, intensification of technology transfer, capacity building and experience enhancement for Belarus taking into consideration the special conditions of the Parties included in Annex I undergoing the process of transition to a market economy, clarity in the use of new LULUCF rules and modalities.	1990
Canada	17%, to be aligned with the final economy-wide emissions target of the United States in enacted legislation.	2005
Croatia	–5%	

Table 4.4 *Continued*

	Temporary target for Croatia. Upon the accession of Croatia to the European Union, the Croatian target shall be replaced by arrangement in line with and part of the European Union mitigation effort.	1990
EU	20%/30%	
	As part of a global and comprehensive agreement for the period beyond 2012, the EU reiterates its conditional offer to move to a 30% reduction by 2020 compared to 1990 levels, provided that other developed countries commit themselves to comparable emission reductions and that developing countries contribute adequately according to their responsibilities and respective capabilities.	1990
Japan	25% reduction, which is premised on the establishment of a fair and effective international framework in which all major economies participate and on agreement by those economies on ambitious targets.	1990
Kazakhstan	15%	1992
Liechtenstein	Liechtenstein commits itself to reduce greenhouse gas (GHG) emissions 20% below 1990 levels by 2020. If other developed countries agree to comparable reductions and emerging economies contribute according to their respective capabilities and responsibilities within a framework of a binding agreement, Liechtenstein is prepared to raise its target up to 30%.	1990
New Zealand	New Zealand is prepared to take on a responsibility target for greenhouse gas emissions reductions of between 10 per cent and 20 per cent below 1990 levels by 2020, if there is a comprehensive global agreement. This means:	

- the global agreement sets the world on a pathway to limit temperature rise to not more than 2° C;
- developed countries make comparable efforts to those of New Zealand;
- advanced and major emitting developing countries take action fully commensurate with their respective capabilities;
- there is an effective set of rules for land use, land-use change and forestry (LULUCF); and
- there is full recourse to a broad and efficient international carbon market.   1990

Norway	30–40% As part of a global and comprehensive agreement for the period beyond 2012 where major emitting Parties agree on emissions reductions in line with the 2 degrees Celsius target, Norway will move to a level of 40% reduction for 2020.	1990
Russian Federation	15–25%*	1990
USA	In the range of 17%, in conformity with anticipated U.S. energy and climate legislation, recognizing that the final target will be reported to the Secretariat in light of enacted legislation.[1] [1]The pathway set forth in pending legislation would entail a 30% reduction in 2025 and a 42% reduction in 2030, in line with the goal to reduce emissions 83% by 2050.	2005

* Addition in Russian, no translation provided, thus deleted
Source: UNFCCC 2010e

Figure 4.3 further illustrates the issue of emissions in absolute and per capita terms, distinguishing Annex I and non-Annex I countries. Annex I countries account for about 20 per cent of the world population, but account for 45.7 per cent of global GHG emissions. The USA and Canada have particularly high per capita emissions, exceeding $25\,t\ CO_2$-eq per year, followed by Japan, Australia and New Zealand (JANZ), with per capita emissions of $15\,t\ CO_2$-eq per year. In the EU, emissions are in the order of $11\,t\ CO_2$-eq per year. Annex I countries had, on average, emissions of $16.1\,t\ CO_2$-eq per capita per year, compared to average non-Annex I emissions of $4.2\,t\ CO_2$-eq per capita per year. Emissions are as yet lowest in South Asia at about $3\,t\ CO_2$-eq per capita per year.

While this figure illustrates the need for CBDR regarding emission reductions, i.e. demanding more ambitious climate policy in high-polluting countries, there is another, emerging issue regarding sustainable per capita emissions. Current systems to measure, compare, and reduce emissions based on the principle of CBDR have emerged out of international policy frameworks focusing on nation states. Consequently, national emission inventories represent averaged per capita emissions of a country's residents, plus in some cases incoming tourism, with the Kyoto Protocol identifying emission reduction responsibilities with a view on averaged per capita emissions. However, as outlined by Chakravarti *et al.* (2009), emissions are not evenly distributed within countries, as there are high- and low-emitting individuals in both countries that are high or low per capita average emitters. Gössling *et al.* (2009a) suggest that the greatest differences in per capita emissions, if measured in percentiles, might eventually be found within countries, not between countries. Currently, average per capita per year CO_2 emissions are in the order of roughly $4\,t\ CO_2$, while Chakravarti *et al.* (2009) show that a considerable share of individuals in some countries might cause emissions exceeding $30\,t\ CO_2$ per year. Given these insights, new models might have to be found in the future to negotiate burden sharing, i.e. not only *between* countries, but also *within* countries.

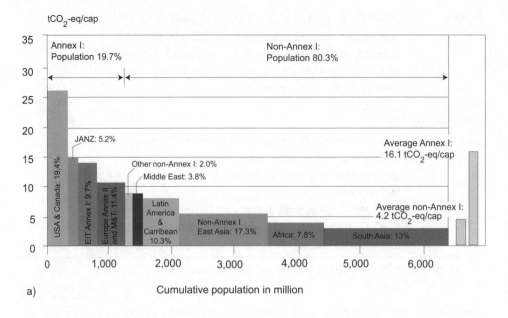

a)

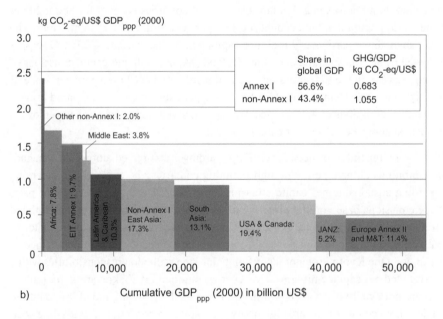

b)

Figure 4.3 *GHG emissions in comparison to population*
Source: IPCC 2007b

HOW REALISTIC ARE POST-KYOTO EMISSION REDUCTION COMMITMENTS?

As outlined, consensus was reached during COP-15 in Copenhagen that global warming should not exceed 2°C by 2100. To stay within this goal, it would be necessary for global emissions to decline by 50 to 85 per cent of 2000 emissions by 2050 (IPCC 2007b). Such emission cuts have been endorsed by most countries, as well as international business organizations such as the World Economic Forum (WEF) (2009) and the Copenhagen Climate Council (2009). The leaders of the G8 also endorsed the emission reduction target of 50 per cent by 2050, even though they could not agree on a baseline of 1990 or 2005 (G8 2009).

Overall, there is thus agreement on considerable emission reductions. However, an analysis of non-binding reduction targets by individual countries, recently presented at the Potsdam Climate Conference 2010 in Germany, suggests that if countries actually achieved their voluntary targets as currently proposed, temperatures would still be likely to increase by 3.5 °C by 2100 (Hans-Joachim Schellnhuber, director Potsdam Institute for Climate Impact Research, 2010), i.e. overshooting the target by 75 per cent. Moreover, emission reduction targets as currently announced are non-binding, while commitments as submitted to the UNFCCC (2010e) are, in many cases, conditional. Many Annex B countries have not even achieved stable emissions compared to the base year 1990, as agreed upon in the Kyoto Protocol. As shown in Figure 4.4, many of the countries that have made pledges to reduce emissions are, in fact, struggling with emission growth, including, for instance Norway, New Zealand, Japan, and several countries in the EU 27. It is thus unclear whether these countries will achieve absolute reductions in emissions in the near future or not.

Figure 4.4 shows that there are huge differences in emission growth/decline between Annex B countries. About half have not achieved any reductions in emissions, and some have experienced further growth of up to 119 per cent (Turkey) over 1990 emissions. Countries that have reduced emissions mostly include Eastern European countries, with for instance Latvia, Ukraine, Lithuania, Estonia and Romania cutting their emissions by about half (UNFCCC 2010f). More generally, UNFCCC (2010f) reports a slight fall in some GHGs and an increase in others. Between 1990 and 2007, and excluding LULUCF, global emissions of CO_2 decreased by 0.5 per cent, CH_4 by 17.3 per cent and N_2O by 24.7 per cent. Conversely, emissions from F-gases increased by 14.8 per cent. As it is unclear how emission reductions have been achieved in those countries with binding commitments, with at least some evidence pointing at the role of movements of production to Asia and in particular China, as well as the non-inclusion of international aviation and shipping in national GHG inventories (Andersen *et al.* 2010; Davis and Caldeira 2010), it seems clear that emissions cuts have been modest, if positive at all. This raises the question of the future capability of Annex I countries to further reduce emissions without a binding target.

REGULATORY MECHANISMS TO ACHIEVE EMISSION REDUCTIONS

There is consensus among business leaders and politicians that emission reductions should be achieved at the lowest possible cost. The Kyoto Protocol thus foresees a 'cap-and-trade' system, which imposes limits, 'caps', for national emissions of Annex I countries. Within countries, emission cuts are usually achieved by transferring emission reduction targets to industry, i.e. following a production-based approach that foresees emission reductions by the major polluters (see Aall 2010). The EU was the first region to develop a cap-and-trade system that is currently running in its second trading period from 2008–12, the EU ETS. The EU ETS is the largest carbon market both by volume and value (Capoor and Ambrosi 2009). Notably, within the EU, emission reductions targets are unevenly distributed within

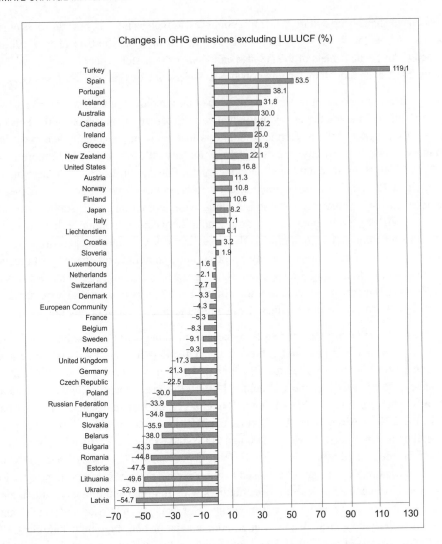

Figure 4.4 *Changes in GHG emissions 1990–2007 excluding LULUCF*
Source: UNFCCC 2010f

countries, with high polluters (measured in per capita emissions) usually making a greater contribution in percentage reduction terms to achieving the EU's goals. Within the EU 27, emission reductions focus on about 12,000 industrial units, which together are responsible for about 45 per cent of CO_2 emissions (Broderick 2009). As this does not consider 55 per cent of emissions embedded in consumption of goods produced in smaller industrial units, EU leaders have begun to discuss an introduction of CO_2 taxes on consumption (Euractiv 2009). For the moment, however, all efforts to reduce emissions focus on production in large industrial units, which poses difficult new questions regarding the allocation of emissions embedded in imports/exports (Helm *et al.* 2007; Aall 2010; Andersen *et al.* 2010; Davis and Caldeira 2010).

Non-Kyoto carbon markets

In North America, the Chicago Climate Exchange (CCX) is an ETS with legally binding reduction targets, which companies can voluntarily join. Participation in the CCX is still very limited. In the absence of any climate policy leadership prior to the Obama administration, regional regulatory frameworks in the USA have, however, evolved in many states and provinces. A total of five Canadian provinces and eight US states have set GHG reduction targets of 10–30 per cent for 2020 (below a 1990 baseline) and six states and two provinces have also set 2050 reduction targets between 75–80 per cent (below a 1990 baseline). This has also led to the establishment of carbon markets on a regional basis (Table 4.5).

Table 4.5 *Non-Kyoto carbon markets*

Exchange/Scheme	Website
Chicago Climate Exchange, USA	http://www.chicagoclimatex.com/
The Chicago Climate Exchange (CCX) is North America's only cap and trade system for all six Kyoto GHG, which is voluntary for businesses to join, but binding.	
New South Wales Greenhouse Gas Abatement, Scheme Australia	www.greenhousegas.nsw.gov.au
The objectives of the Greenhouse Gas Reduction Scheme (GGAS) are to reduce GHG emissions associated with the production and use of electricity and to develop and encourage activities to offset the production of GHG emissions. There is a GHG benchmark per capita. The initial level was set at 8.65 t CO_2-eq per capita in 2003. The benchmark progressively drops to 7.27 t CO_2-eq in 2007 which represents a reduction of five per cent below the Kyoto Protocol baseline year of 1989–90. The per capita amount continues at this level until 2021.	
The Regional Greenhouse Gas Initiative (RGGI), USA	www.rggi.org
The first mandatory, market-based effort in the United States to reduce greenhouse gas emissions. Connecticut, Delaware, Maine, Maryland, Massachusetts, New Hampshire, New Jersey, New York, Rhode Island, and Vermont haved capped and will reduce CO_2 emissions from the power sector with 10% by 2018.	
Western Climate Initiative (WCI), USA and Canada	www.westernclimateinitiative.org

Table 4.5 Continued

The WCI is a collaboration of independent jurisdictions who
commit to work together to identify, evaluate, and
implement policies to tackle climate change at a regional
level. Other US states, Canadian provinces, Mexican states
and tribes that are interested in collaborating to combat
climate change at a regional level are encouraged to
participate in the WCI as either members or observers.
Arizona, British Columbia, California, Manitoba, Montana,
New Mexico, Ontario, Oregon, Quebeck, Utah, Washington.

Any 'cap-and-trade' system is based on a limit of emissions set by a government and provides options to trade emissions in a regulatory carbon market (e.g. Broderick 2009). Companies or corporations are issued emission permits, Assigned Allocation Units (AAUs),
which represent the right to emit a specific amount of emissions in a given year or period
of time. The amount of AAUs given to a company is based on emission levels in previous
years, and the percentage share of reduction the company/corporation should achieve within
a given timeframe. The amount of AAUs distributed among companies cannot exceed the
cap, limiting emissions to a set level. Companies forced to reduce emissions can choose to
engage in measures to reduce emissions. If this is achieved within the company, reductions
exceeding the target can be sold as emission permits to other companies. Conversely, companies growing in emissions or not managing to keep emissions below assigned levels have
to buy credits corresponding to their excess emissions. They can do this through carbon
markets, where companies can buy AAUs, or credits achieved through Joint Implementation (yielding Emission Reduction Units, ERU) and the Clean Development Mechanism
(yielding Certified Emission Reduction Units, CER).

Joint Implementation and Clean Development Mechanism

Joint Implementation (JI) is a market-based implementation mechanism defined in Article
6 of the Kyoto Protocol, allowing Annex I countries or companies from these countries to
implement projects jointly that limit or reduce emissions or enhance sinks, and to share the
resulting ERUs (cf. IPCC 2007b). The Clean Development Mechanism (CDM) is intended
to meet two objectives: to assist parties not included in Annex I in achieving sustainable
development and in contributing to the ultimate objective of the convention of cost-efficient emission reductions; as well as to assist parties included in Annex I in achieving compliance with their quantified emission limitation and reduction commitments. The CDM
is the most important framework for the supply of carbon credits from emission reduction
projects, which are approved, validated and exchanged by the UNFCCC secretariat. CDM
projects can be implemented in all non-Annex I countries, and are certified by operational
entities (OE) designated by UN COP (IPCC 2007b). Both JI and CDM thus generate credits, typically from electricity generation from biomass, renewable energy projects, or capture of CH_4, which can be bought directly from a broker or a JI/CDM developer, or through

an exchange by companies exceeding their AAUs. Each AAU, ERU or CER corresponds to 1 tonne of CO_2, the standard exchange unit.

In theory, 'cap-and-trade' systems ensure that emissions will be reduced at the lowest cost to society, with the buyer paying a fee for polluting, and the seller being rewarded for reducing emissions by a greater amount than legally demanded. In reality, there are several shortcomings to this system. First of all, there is no global cap on emissions, and trading with CERs is open between Annex I and non-Annex I countries. This allows cheap imports from countries with no caps on emissions. Hypothetically, a CDM developer can thus clean up emissions stemming from a highly polluting business in a given non-Annex I country, while another highly polluting business is built simultaneously in another part of that country. Also for this reason, there are limits on the total quantity of credits that can be imported through the CDM, which are specified in National Allocation Plans (NAPs). Furthermore, there are problems related to 'additionality', as projects that lead to cost savings greater than the cost of the project cannot be approved as CDM projects – which has not always been the case in the past (cf. Michaelowa and Michaelowa 2007; Holm Olsen 2007). In response to criticisms forwarded to the CDM, the World Wide Fund for Nature (WWF) and other NGOs have developed the 'Gold Standard' (GS), which sets out more stringent project criteria (Gold Standard 2006). In particular, the GS is based on stricter screens for additionality and sustainability at project inception, for example permitting renewable energy projects but excluding forestry, and requiring Environmental Impact Assessments and local stakeholder consultation. Mandatory, independent monitoring of sustainable development benefits during project operation further improves outcomes. Validation and verification has to be carried out by independent UNFCCC-accredited bodies (www.cdmgoldstandard. org). For critical perspectives on 'cap-and-trade' systems, carbon markets and offsetting see, for example, Böhm and Dabhi (2009) and David Suzuki Foundation (2008).

The regulatory carbon markets have grown considerably in recent years and were worth more than US\$126 billion (about €80 billion) in 2008 (Capoor and Ambrosi 2009). The price of emission allowances or credits has however varied considerably, and declined considerably after the failure of the COP-15 meeting in Copenhagen to achieve consensus on binding emission targets. Table 4.6 shows quantities of Kyoto Protocol units (AAUs, ERUs, and CERs) for Annex B Parties at 31 December 2008 (Mt CO_2-eq). Notably, only New Zealand has produced ERUs, indicating that the generation of CERs is far less costly. For more detailed information on regulatory carbon markets, as well as CDM project development and CER certification, see Broderick (2009).

Regulatory markets are currently less relevant for tourism, as the trading schemes are production-oriented and tourism businesses are not usually large enough to be considered in cap-and-trade systems. Tourism is thus only indirectly affected by carbon trading, for instance when purchases of energy from larger power-generating utilities are made. Aviation is an exception, as the sector will be included in the EU ETS from 2012 onwards. There are, as yet, no plans to include cruise ships in any ETS, but the sector has, as aviation, received recent attention, because cruise tourism is growing fast (Mintel 2008), while there is no legislation to address the sectors' emissions.

Table 4.6 *Total quantities[a] of Kyoto Protocol units for Annex B Parties as at 31 December 2008, MtCO$_2$-eq*

Annex B Party	AAUs	ERUs	CERs
Australia	—	—	—
Austria	334.83	NO	3.23
Belgium	659.59	NO	1.18
Bulgaria	610.05	NO	NO
Canada	—	—	—
Czech Republic	864.59	NO	4.33
Denmark	294.22	NO	3.47
Estonia	197.21	NO	NO
European Community	19 668.74	NO	139.45
Finland	352.77	NO	1.84
France	2 821.36	NO	12.18
Germany	4 875.56	NO	40.14
Greece	668.65	NO	0.05
Hungary	534.46	NO	0.61
Iceland	—	—	—
Ireland	314.97	NO	3.67
Italy	2 432.77	NO	9.30
Japan	5 944.87	NO	42.27
Latvia	119.36	NO	0.11
Liechtenstein	1.06	NO	NO
Lithuania	224.95	NO	0.23
Luxemburg	47.15	NO	0.17
Monaco	—	—	—
Netherlands	1 005.36	NO	16.51
New Zealand	309.44	0.12	0.01
Norway	250.58	NO	0.05
Poland	2 648.93	NO	2.08
Portugal	377.52	NO	1.25
Romania	1 275.16	NO	0.02
Russian Federation	16 617.10	NO	NO

AAUs = assigned amount units, CERs = certified emission reductions, ERUs = Emission Reduction Units
[a]'Total quantities' refers to the sum of the Kyoto Protocol units in each account type for 33 Annex B Parties.
Source: UNFCCC 2010a

CLIMATE POLICY FOR AVIATION AND SHIPPING

For aviation and the emerging, though in relative terms less significant sector, of cruise ships, emissions need to be addressed by legislation to regulate international bunker fuels and associated emissions, as these sectors are not covered by the Kyoto Protocol. Responsibility for emission reductions is currently with the international aviation and shipping organizations International Civil Aviation Organization (ICAO) and International Maritime Organization (IMO) (see Haites 2009).

Aviation

Civil aviation has grown constantly and rapidly since the 1960s. The sector is now respon-sible for emissions of about 700 Mt of CO_2 in 2004, i.e. 2.6 per cent of total anthropogenic CO_2 emissions in that year, and 1.3 per cent to 14.0 per cent of RF (90 per cent likelihood range) (Lee *et al.* 2009).

Article 2 of the Kyoto Protocol states that limiting and reducing GHG emissions from international aviation in Annex I nations is the responsibility of the ICAO, while emissions from domestic flights are included in national GHG inventories of Annex B countries and part of national emission reduction targets. As outlined by Haites (2009), the UNFCCC has focused on different approaches to allocate emissions from international aviation to Parties in the 1990s, but agreement has been impossible. The basis for discussions was that emissions attributed to Annex I Parties would be regulated, but not those of non-Annex I Parties, consistent with the CBDR principle. Haites (2009) reports that out of eight options originally identified for allocation of emissions from international aviation and shipping, only five were selected in 1996 as the basis for further work (cf. Bode *et al.* 2002; Oberthür 2003):

1 No allocation.
2 Allocation to Parties according to the country where the bunker fuel is sold.
3 Allocation to Parties according to the nationality of the transporting company, the country where the aircraft or vessel is registered, or the country of the operator.
4 Allocation to Parties according to the country of departure or destination of an aircraft or vessel or shared between the countries of departure and arrival.
5 Allocation to Parties according to the country of departure or destination of passenger or cargo or shared between the countries of departure and arrival.

However, no progress on a method for allocating emissions was made on this basis. Haites (2009: 417) suggests that this is because allocation on the basis of Annex I/non-Annex I Parties would have induced behaviour reducing the effectiveness of the regulations, either because purchases of fuel would cause shifts to non-Annex I Parties (option 2) or because air traffic on identical routes between Annex I and non-Annex I countries would develop in favour of the latter, as these are not affected by regulation (option 3). While these argu-ments may be partially valid – aviation is in reality forced to bunker fuels in the destination it is serving – a globally consistent approach may according to UNWTO still fail to emerge, because:

* ICAO's geographic and policy ambit reflects its membership of 190 States, well beyond the 39 ratifying Annex I countries;
* there are significant barriers to applying a Kyoto Annex I/non-Annex I industrialized/ other country type concept in relation to equality of treatment and certain other provi-sions in aviation's Chicago Convention;

- international aviation is unable to benefit from application of the Kyoto provisions regarding JI, the CDM and emissions trading.

(Lyle 2010)

The ICAO annual assembly in 2004 dismissed the idea of establishing a global ETS for aviation itself or establishing a separate organization to do so, but endorsed the inclusion of aviation in existing national/regional ETS as a more cost-effective approach than fuel taxes or charges on aviation activity. However, in October 2007, the annual assembly of ICAO decided against requiring airlines to limit GHG emissions through participation in the EU ETS, effectively rejecting their earlier decision. Instead, ICAO created a panel to develop a comprehensive climate change plan for the international aviation industry. The 42 countries in the European group of ICAO strongly disagreed with the decision by making a 'reservation' against the resolution, indicating that these member states could choose to ignore the resolution on legal grounds in that it compromises the EU's capacity to achieve its international GHG emission obligations under the Kyoto Protocol (Environment News Service 2007). Instead, ICAO suggested self-regulation, even though the problems incurred in this are well documented (see Oberthür 2003; Haites 2009; Smith and Rodger 2009; T&E 2009a, b). Limited progress on the issue also led the Australian and UK governments to call for the UNFCCC to take charge of emissions from both aviation and shipping in a sectoral approach (T&E 2009b).

In this context, it deserves mention that international aviation is exempt from taxes on fuel or Value Added Tax:

> ICAO has since 1951 issued guidance material promoting exemption of aviation fuel from taxation on a reciprocal basis and this concept has been included in the vast majority of the air services agreements, which regulate international air transport (no less than 98 per cent of the more than 2,200 bilateral agreements filed with ICAO). Thus, except within regions such as Europe where there is a multinational body (the EU) with the authority to supplant air services agreements between individual states, agreement on taxation of aviation fuel for international operations has proved intractable to date.
>
> (UNWTO 2009: 7)

As of March 2010, ICAO had not presented a binding emission reduction goal. The latest document published by the organization on climate change and aviation (GIACC (Group on International Aviation and Climate Change), June 2009), presented no consensus on several key issues, and vague statements on how to achieve emission reductions:

> 1. GIACC recognizes the critical importance of addressing climate change, and thus recognizes the need to strive to find ways and means to limit or reduce the impact of greenhouse gas emissions from international civil aviation on the global climate.
>
> . . .
>
> 5. While there was no consensus, some GIACC Members are of the view that the Programme of Action does not address the commitments under Article 2.2 of the Kyoto Protocol. (*Note by author: Article 2.2 of the Kyoto Protocol requires industrialized countries to pursue the limitation or reduction of GHG emissions from international civil aviation through ICAO*).
>
> 6. Notwithstanding the substantial fuel efficiency improvements achieved by the aviation sector

and the impact of the current economic downturn, GIACC recognises that the projected growth of international air traffic will outweigh the gains made by currently projected fuel efficiency improvements resulting in an average year over year increase in total fuel burned.

7. GIACC recommends a strategy for efforts to achieve global aspirational goals.

8. The short term goal to 2012 agreed by the GIACC is for improvements in the in-service fleet average fuel efficiency of international aviation operations at the rate of 2% per year, calculated on the basis of volume of fuel used per Revenue Tonne Kilometre performed.

9. Agreement was reached in GIACC on goals in the form of fuel efficiency for the medium and longer terms. Specifically, the Group recommends an annual improvement of 2% over the medium term until 2020. For the long term, the GIACC recommends an aspirational global fuel efficiency improvement rate of 2% per annum from 2021 to 2050.

10. These goals are established on the basis of forecasts and GIACC recommends that they be reviewed on a periodic basis in light of scientific and technological advances. To achieve these goals will require a significant investment in technological development.

11. In addition to fuel efficiency goals, the group considered goals that could indicate stronger ambition. For the medium term, the discussions focused on a goal of carbon-neutral growth by 2020. For the long term, the GIACC discussed carbon emissions reductions. No consensus was reached in either case, and GIACC recommends further work on both medium and long term goals.

12. While there was no consensus, some GIACC Members are of the view that it would be necessary and feasible to achieve carbon-neutral growth in the medium term, relative to a baseline of 2005, and to achieve substantial CO_2 emissions reduction for the long term for global international aviation.

13. Under the recommended strategy, goals would not attribute specific obligations to individual States. The different circumstances, respective capabilities and contribution of developing and developed States to the concentration of aviation GHG emissions in the atmosphere will determine how each State may contribute to achieving the global aspirational goals.

14. GIACC recommends that the Council should adopt the basket of measures developed by GIACC, from which States may choose (http://www.icao.int/), covering aircraft-related technology development, improved air traffic management and infrastructure use, more efficient operations, economic/market-based measures, and regulatory measures. The basket includes measures to facilitate access to assistance, particularly for developing countries.

15. GIACC has provided an initial table showing the basket of measures, which can be further developed through ICAO. GIACC also recommends that ICAO should continue to develop, and update as necessary, guidance to States on the adoption of those measures, including measures to assist developing countries, as well as access to financial resources, technology transfer and capacity building.

16. GIACC acknowledges that there remains disagreement on the application of market-based measures across national borders. GIACC recommends that the ICAO Council establish a process to develop a framework for market-based measures in international aviation, taking into account the conclusions of the High-Level Meeting and the outcome of the UNFCCC COP-15 with a view to complete this process expeditiously.

17. GIACC recommends that Council should encourage States, to develop action plans, which articulate the proposed approach in that State, and file those plans with ICAO.

18. GIACC recommends that Council direct the Secretariat to develop and implement a mechanism under Article 67 of the Convention to collect annually from States data on traffic and fuel consumption.

19. GIACC also recommends that Council seek to develop approaches for providing technical and financial assistance in the reporting process to developing countries.

20. GIACC also recommends that the Council seek to develop a CO_2 Standard for new aircraft types.

21. The cumulative progress achieved by States on a global level should be reported by ICAO on a triennial basis to the Assembly.

(ICAO 2009)

One of the modest achievements since publication of GIACC (2009) is ICAO's Committee on Aviation Environmental Protection's (CAEP) discussion of a timetable for the development of a CO_2 Standard for commercial aircraft to be imposed on manufacturers, which is to be identified by 2013 (Chris Lyle, Air Transport Economics, personal communication February 2010). It is unclear, however, which metric would be used for such a standard and whether such a standard would actually achieve emission reductions and at which scale. It can also be assumed that aircraft manufacturers do their best to reduce fuel use anyway, as this is one of the most important cost factors (cf. IATA 2009a).

In view of limited progress on reducing emissions from aviation by ICAO, the European Commission (EC) has for several years had plans to include emissions from all aircraft departing EU airports (i.e. intra-EU as well as all other flights) in the EU ETS. In November 2007, the EU parliament voted to include national and international aviation in the EU into the EU ETS (European Parliament and Council 2007). After modifications of its original plans, the EU now plans to include shipping and aviation in a forthcoming open ETS (European Parliament and Council 2009). The current proposal is that:

- Aviation will be included in the EU ETS from 2012.
- Emissions from aviation will be capped at 97 per cent of their average 2004–06 level in 2012. This will decrease to 95 per cent from 2013, although this percentage may be reviewed as part of the general review of the Emissions Trading Directive;
- Airlines will receive 85 per cent of their emission allowances for free in 2012. This percentage may be reduced from 2013 as part of the general review of the Emissions Trading Directive;
- An exemption has been introduced for commercial air operators with very low traffic levels on routes to, from or within the EU or with low annual emissions (less than 10,000 tonnes CO_2 a year). This means many operators from developing countries with only limited air traffic links with the EU will be exempt. This will not have a significant effect on the emissions covered by the EU ETS;
- A special reserve of free allowances has been added for new entrants or very fast-growing airlines. The reserve does not increase the overall cap on allowances and therefore does not affect the environmental impact of the system. Airlines that are growing will be able to benefit from the reserve up to a limit of one million allowances.
- A new mechanism has been introduced to ensure consistent and robust enforcement throughout the EU. As a last resort, Member States could ask for an operator to be

banned from operating in the EU if it persistently fails to comply with the system and other enforcement measures have proven ineffective.

(Europa 2008)

Notably, EU policy will include all flights originating from or ending in the EU 27, irrespective of the country of origin of airlines/aircraft. Airlines are required to auction 15 per cent of all emission permits, while the rest will be distributed based on the principle of grandfathering, i.e. based on historical emission reductions. Given the observed strong growth in aviation emissions, the gap between the caps set for 2012 and to be set for 2020 and a business-as-usual growth scenario are likely to be substantial. Aviation in the EU has grown substantially since 1990, the original base year for the Kyoto Protocol, with EU GHG emissions from international aviation growing by 87 per cent in the period 1990–2004, and further projected growth by 84 per cent to 100 per cent expected for the period 2005–20 (Commission of the European Communities 2006; Boon *et al.* 2007). This 'business-as-usual' trajectory can be compared against the proposed emission caps (Figure 4.5), where solid grey columns show allowable emissions in 2005 (average period 2004–06), 2012 and 2020, while the light grey column shows anticipated emission growth by 2020, indicating the gap between caps and the development of emissions.

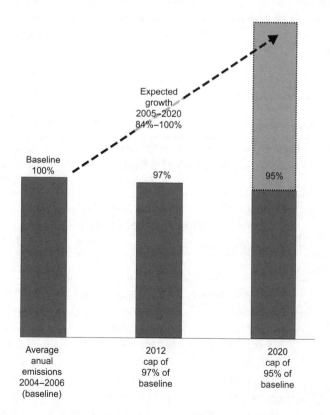

Figure 4.5 *EU aviation business as usual emissions growth scenario and ETS proposed emission caps for 2012 and 2020*
Source: Commission of the European Communities (2006); Boon *et al.* (2007)

As outlined by Simpson *et al.* (2008), two recent legislative decisions could have important implications for GHG emissions in the aviation industry in the USA. In 2007, the US Senate Committee on Environment and Public Works approved the 'Lieberman-Warner Climate Security Bill' and forwarded it to the full Senate for consideration. This proposed legislation includes a cap and trade GHG emissions trading scheme. If enacted, the Lieberman-Warner Bill would create a regulatory system similar to the ETS for the American aviation industry. The US commercial aviation industry (Air Transport Association, Air Line Pilots Association, Cargo Airline Association, and the Regional Airline Association) expressed strong opposition to the proposed legislation (Air Transport Association 2007), and it is currently unclear if and when such an ETS will be implemented.

In Canada, provincial governments in British Columbia and Quebec have proposed implementation of a carbon tax (Simpson *et al.* 2008). In early 2008, the National Round Table on the Environment and Economy provided a detailed report to the federal government, recommending the establishment of a carbon tax, a cap-and-trade system, or a combination of the two, as soon as possible. This advisory body is made up of business, government and non-government members that represent the interests of a wide range of stakeholders that would be potentially affected by a carbon tax, and was specifically requested by the Government of Canada to provide advice on a GHG reduction strategy for the federal government. Thus, its recommendations are expected to carry considerable weight with governments in Canada. The proposed carbon tax was to include all sectors of the Canadian economy, including domestic aviation.

Table 4.7 shows the positions of ICAO, IATA and the Aviation Global Deal group (AGD group) on emission reductions in aviation. Both ICAO and IATA envisage absolute

Table 4.7 Emission reduction targets and suggested action in aviation

Organization	International Civil Aviation Organisation (ICAO)	International Air Transport Association (IATA)	Aviation Global Deal Group (AGD group)
Emission reduction goal	–50% until 2050, stabilization by 2030 (base year 2005)	–50% until 2050, stabilization by 2020 (base year 2005)	–50% to –80% by 2050, up to –20% by 2020
GHG considered	CO_2	CO_2	CO_2
Suggested measures	• Energy efficiency measures • Air traffic management Biofuels • Open and unlimited emission trading with other sectors	• Energy efficiency measures • Air traffic management Biofuels • Open and unlimited emission trading with other sectors	• Energy efficiency measures • Air traffic management Biofuels • Open and unlimited emission trading with other sectors

Source: ICAO 2009, IATA 2009a, AGD group 2009

emission reductions in aviation by 50 per cent over 2005 by 2050. While ICAO foresees stabilization of emissions by 2030, IATA anticipates stabilization already by 2020. Notably, 'stabilization' in both cases refers to no further growth in net emissions. Hence, there will not be stabilization but, rather, compensation for growth by emission reductions in other sectors, i.e. primarily the purchase of carbon credits. The Aviation Global Deal group (AGD group) (including Air France-KLM, BAA, British Airways, Cathay Pacific Airways, Finnair, Qatar Airways, Virgin Atlantic and The Climate Group) is more ambitious, foreseeing emission reductions by 50 per cent to 80 per cent by 2050, and up to a 20 per cent emission reduction by 2020.

Notably, all organizations refer to CO_2, and it is somewhat unclear how non-CO_2 emissions will be addressed. A policy document by UNWTO (2009a) comments that:

> Current scientific evidence suggests that aviation's non-CO_2 effects in relation to basic CO_2 effects are well above the average multiplier or ratio for all man-made emissions. There are also differences in the relative impact of individual non-CO_2 GHGs between aviation and man-made emissions at large (and, in the case of aviation, there are GHGs not covered by the Kyoto Protocol which ultimately may prove more significant than some included in the Protocol, for example contrail-induced cirrus). The non-CO_2 impact for aviation might be addressed by integration into CO_2-based policy frameworks through conversion to CO_2 equivalents or by the use of a multiplier to gross up the CO_2 impact to cover both CO_2 and non-CO_2 effects. However, at present there remain difficulties in assessing accurately the non-CO_2 climate impacts from aviation at high altitude. Thus aviation may warrant transitional arrangements from initial inclusion of CO_2 only to coverage of climate impacts of all aviation emissions once there is a clear scientific basis for this.

With regard to mitigation measures, fleet renewal, air traffic management (ATM), biofuels, and, most importantly, open and unlimited emission trading with other sectors, are presented as strategies to deal with emission growth (ICAO 2009; IATA 2009a; AGD group 2009). Notably, unlimited and open trading means that the share of RF from aviation is likely to grow rapidly, because other sectors would decline in absolute emissions (cf. Bows *et al.* 2009a), while aviation will be inclined to purchase emissions permits from other sectors in an open trading scheme. This is because improving fuel efficiency in aviation is comparably costly, or, vice versa, emission permits will be comparably cheap (UNWTO-UNEP-WMO 2008: 12). For example, at permit prices of €25 per tonne CO_2, the cost of flying would increase by about €3.0 per 1,000 passenger kilometres (pkm) (at an emission factor of 0.129 kg CO_2/pkm), notably in a situation where all emissions have to be accounted for through permits by the airline (cf. Scott *et al.* 2010).

An open trading scheme will thus mean that aviation can continue to grow in its emissions, as anticipated by the AGD group (Aviation Global Deal group 2009), which foresees that the sector's emissions will more than double by 2035. This scenario might incur risks. First of all, as outlined by Lee and Sausen (2000), if non-CO_2 effects of aviation are not considered in emission trading, the sector might actually increase overall global warming because of buying permits for CO_2, but emitting GHG with a greater RF than that of CO_2 alone. Moreover, Scott *et al.* (2010) outline that in an open trading scheme, emissions from aviation would continue to increase rapidly for some years. When cheap credits purchased by the aviation industry become exhausted over time, multiple sectors would begin to compete for increasingly expensive emission credits, which could lead to a sudden dramatic change in cost structures within the aviation sector and other economic sectors; putting large investments in air transport and destinations at risk. In order to avoid such potentially rapid growth in prices for permits and the detrimental impact on international tourism, Scott *et al.* (2010) conclude that it seems advisable to establish a closed ETS for aviation, or to include aviation in an open trading scheme with a gradually tightening cap on the number of permits that can be bought from other sectors. In this context, it deserves mentioning that there is also a case for the taxation of aviation, as this sector remains the only untaxed tourism transport sector (domestic flights can be an exception) (cf. Piket 2009), also resulting in competitive distortions between aviation and the more environmentally friendly transport modes.

International shipping

Considerably less information is available on the role of emissions from shipping, which only recently received attention as an emissions-intense sector. Emissions from shipping are estimated to have been in the order of 1,046 Mt CO_2 in 2007, which corresponds to 3.3 per cent of global CO_2 emissions in that year. International shipping is estimated to have emitted 870 million tonnes, or about 2.7 per cent of global emissions of CO_2 in 2007 (IMO 2009a). As shown in Table 4.8, emissions other than CO_2 are less relevant. The IMO (2009a, b), anticipates that, in the absence of mitigation policies, emissions from shipping will grow by 1.9–2.7 per cent per year until 2050, leading to overall growth by 150–250 per cent in the period 2007–50 (Figure 4.6).

As reported by Eijgelaar *et al.* (2010), tourism is an important component in this growth: worldwide cruise demand has grown steadily at an average annual rate of 7.4 per cent since 1990 (CLIA 2009), and emission growth from this sector has consequently been faster than from shipping more generally. In relative terms, cruise ships and ferries are less relevant, however. Eijgelaar *et al.* (2010) calculate CO_2 emissions (in metric tonnes) based on data provided by IMO and data from individual cruise companies. For the year 2007, IMO estimates the global fuel use of all passenger ferries and cruise ships at 31.3 Mt, corresponding to 96 Mt CO_2 (Buhaug *et al.* 2009). WEF (2009) provides a sub-sector estimate for ocean-going cruises, which are said to have accounted for 34 Mt CO_2 in 2005, i.e. roughly one third of the total for ferries and cruise ships, but does not provide information on sources and methodology used for calculating these. Based on the IMO estimate, cruise ships and ferries account for 9.2 per cent of emissions from shipping. The sector is thus less important

Table 4.8 Summary of GHG emissions from shipping during 2007

	International shipping	Total Shipping	
	million tonnes	million tonnes	CO_2 equivalent
CO_2	870	1046	1046
CH_4	Not determined	0.24	6
N_2O	0.02	0.03	9
HFC	Not determined	0.0004	≤ 6

Source: IMO 2009b

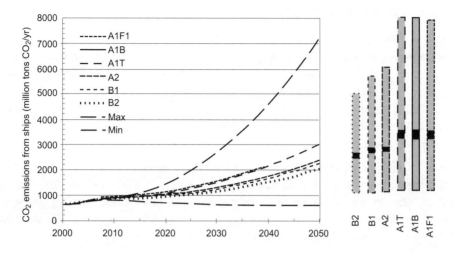

Figure 4.6 *International shipping CO$_2$ emission scenarios.*
Trajectories of the emissions from international shipping. Columns on the right-hand side indicate the range of results for the scenarios within individual families of scenario.

Source: IMO 2009b

in relative terms, even though it should be noted that as cruise ships have carried only 16 million passengers in 2007 (Mintel 2008), the sector constitutes the most energy-intense form of tourism on a per tourist basis.

A notable paradox with emissions from shipping is that the sector has so far contributed to global cooling, despite its significance in CO$_2$ emissions, because simultaneous emissions of sulphur dioxide (SO$_2$) lead to a net negative RF effect from shipping (Eyring *et al.* 2009; Winebrake *et al.* 2009). New regulations regarding SO$_2$ and NO$_x$ will reduce emissions of these gases, but contribute to greater warming, at least in the short-term future. In the long run, because of the short residence times of SO$_2$, effects of CO$_2$ will dominate (Fuglestvedt *et al.* 2009). Reductions in SO$_2$ and NO$_x$ through regulation also show that regulatory frameworks can be established, with current caps on fuel sulphur (S) content foreseeing a reduction from currently 4.5 per cent S content to 3.5 per cent S content by 2012, and progressive reduction to 0.5 per cent S content by 2020 (IMO MEPC 2009). However, as is the case with aviation, efforts to reduce CO$_2$ emissions from international shipping have been unsuccessful (Haites 2009). IMO called for a study of CO$_2$ emissions from shipping and feasible reduction strategies as early as September 1997 (Oberthür 2003). However, as of January 2010, neither binding targets nor measures have been adopted by IMO.

Overall, the above sections have shown that considerable problems have to be solved in reducing emissions from aviation and shipping, while there is a notable absence of a global strategy for emission reductions, and not even a framework for including emissions from aviation and shipping into carbon trading schemes. As of January 2010, the EU is the only region in the world that plans to extend its ETS to cover international shipping from 2013 onwards (CE Delft 2009).

VOLUNTARY CARBON MARKETS

Voluntary offsetting schemes have grown rapidly in the past 12 years due to the interest of companies, organizations, event managers and individuals to offset their emissions even in the absence of legal demands. The World Bank estimates that at least 54 Mt CO_2-eq were traded in 2008 in voluntary markets, up from 43 Mt CO_2-eq in 2007 (Capoor and Ambrosi 2009), indicating considerable interest in voluntary offsetting. Voluntary carbon markets also include the CCX, a cap-and-trade system with credit-generating projects, voluntary membership and legally binding commitments (see Table 4.5).

The first voluntary offsetting agencies were founded in the early 1990s, but there has been rapid expansion in the sector in the past 10 years (Figure 4.7). Gössling *et al.* (2007) identified 40 voluntary carbon offsetting agencies offering carbon credits, including or specifically for aviation, and the website Carbon Catalog (www.carboncatalog.org/providers) lists 108 agencies offering all sorts of offsets (16 January 2010).

Unlike emissions trading, which is regulated by a strict formal and legal framework, carbon offsets by individuals or companies that are arranged by commercial or not-for-profit carbon-offset providers lack formal standards and certifications. A number of concerns have been raised about the unregulated voluntary carbon-offset market, including calculation methods, the principle of 'additionality', the possibility of double-counting and multiple sales of the same carbon credits, the lack of standards for verification, the time scales and location of projects, and the ethics of some projects (Tufts Climate Initiative 2006; Gössling *et al.* 2007). Furthermore, DEFRA (2008) lists the risk of carbon leakage, i.e. the risk of an increase in emissions on one site due to reductions elsewhere; permanence, i.e. the need to ensure that emissions will not be released later in time; certification through independent accounting bodies; and transparency on the methodologies and procedures used (Table 4.9).

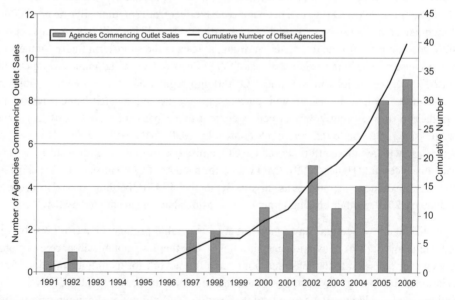

Figure 4.7 *Number of organizations commencing voluntary carbon offset sales, 1991–2006*
Source: Gössling *et al.* 2007

Table 4.9 *Principles of credibility and efficiency*

1. In order to produce a saving in carbon that would not have happened otherwise, projects must be able to prove that their savings are **additional** to business as usual. The project could not take place without the carbon finance from selling credits. The project is not required by legislation or to demonstrate compliance against legally binding targets.

2. As well as demonstrating that a project is additional, consumers will also want a guarantee that the project they have helped to fund has not caused an increase in carbon emissions elsewhere. **Leakage** is when the carbon saving made at a project/location/time increases emissions elsewhere. To provide the consumer with this assurance an assessment must be made of any effects from the project whether up stream or down stream. This must be taken into account in determining the total emissions that can be sold from that project.

3. The consumer needs to be confident that the carbon saving they are purchasing is **permanent**. If there is potential for the project to be impermanent, for example forestry projects are at risk of disease or fire, then this must be accounted for. The consumer needs a guarantee that they are purchasing a permanent emissions reduction. To achieve this projects must be periodically independently reviewed and, if necessary, credits must be replaced when they expire or cease to be valid.

4. A consumer needs to be confident that a project meets this criteria and the project can best prove this by seeking **independent verification**. The verifier must be an accredited and recognised independent third party.

5. As with the CDM, information should be **transparent**. Consumers and other interested stakeholders should be able to view and scrutinise information on the projects supported. Project documentation should be publicly available on a website to set out the underlying projects (when they were considered approved and implemented), the quantification methodology applied and independent validation and verification procedures and reports for project and credits.

6. Consumers need to be confident that the offset they purchase meets the above criteria and has indeed happened. Therefore, the **time** credits are issued is important, ie they must be issued *ex post* to the emissions reduction taking place.

7. When a consumer purchases an offset they need to have confidence that the credits they are purchasing to offset their emissions cannot be used by anyone else either to offset their emissions or demonstrate compliance against a target. It is vital that a system is in place to register and track credits to avoid **double counting** or double selling. This registry must be used to permanently cancel credits. Consumers must also be confident that there is no potential for a project to be double counted against another policy or mandatory targets.

Source: DEFRA 2008

Finally, the Gold Standard (2006) recommends with regard to additionality that it should be demonstrated that:

- The project would not have occurred without the project being a voluntary offset project; due to financial, political or other barriers;
- The project goes beyond a 'business-as-usual' scenario, i.e. reductions that may have been achieved in the usual energy efficiency or technological renewal cycles;
- Greenhouse gas emissions are lower with the project than they would have been without the project (i.e. the baseline situation);
- Overseas Development Aid is not involved.

Several difficulties characterize voluntary carbon markets. These pertain to the credibility of emission credits sold, i.e. data collection, calculation, and offset certification, as well as the question of how to include non-CO_2 emissions from aviation. Notably, this will also become a problem for the upcoming EU ETS for aviation, but already needs to be dealt with in the voluntary carbon markets.

With regard to offset types, agencies in the voluntary carbon market offer Emission Unit Allowances or European Union Allowances (EUAs), CERs, ERUs, Verified Emission Reductions (VERs), as well as Gold Standard versions of VERs and CERs. This is highly confusing for consumers, as there are huge differences between these credits, and the problem entailed in this is that VERs are currently the most common type of offset sold in the voluntary market, even though VERs have the lowest level of credibility in terms of meeting acclaimed emission reductions, and with regard to additionality (see below; cf. Gold Standard 2006). One conclusion could thus be that the most reliable high-quality reduction

Table 4.10 *Types of credits in the voluntary markets*

EAUs: High level of credibility, but interfere with regulatory markets. *Purchase for voluntary purposes not recommended.*
CERs: Are imported from countries without caps on emissions, local sustainable development benefits are questionable. High level of credibility. Can include forestry projects. *Purchase not recommended.*
ERUs: As nationally registered offsets, they help countries to reduce their emissions, which may affect a country's ambitions to further reduce emissions. *Purchase recommended if it can be ensured that imported ERUs are cancelled in UN registry, to avoid interference with regulatory markets.*
VERs: Offer low level of credibility, often unclear whether emission reductions have been achieved. *Purchase not recommended.*
GS CERs: High level of credibility, local sustainable development benefits. *Purchase recommended if cancelled in UN registry.*
GS VERs: Offer lower level of credibility, combine sustainable development benefits with emission reductions. *Purchase recommended if there are no GS CERs or ERUs available.*

Source: Gössling 2008

units with greatest transparency and sustainable development benefits are GS CERs, if offsetting agencies ensure that reduction units are cancelled in the UN-registry to avoid interference with regulatory markets.

Overall, it remains unclear whether voluntary carbon offsets can play a significant role in addressing emission growth from aviation. Smith and Rodger (2009), for instance, report that offsetting aviation-related emissions through national measures to reduce emissions is not feasible in New Zealand. While voluntary offsetting of 'unavoidable' flights must be seen as better than not engaging at all, they are also temporary solutions, to 'buy time':

> (Voluntary) offsets are environmentally risky options that do nothing to directly reduce aviation emissions. If not presented as a temporary or complementary strategy, offsets carry the political risk of encouraging people to believe that they need not change their behaviour, thus creating irreversibility in current consumption and production patterns. ... one of the main disadvantages of a voluntary approach is that it gives limited incentive to airlines to increase their fuel efficiency ... Voluntary carbon offsetting schemes remain an ambiguous solution to aviation's environmental impacts, and therefore an ambiguous tool for sustainable tourism management.
>
> (Gössling et al. 2007: 241)

5　Tourism and climate change

Climate change has become a key issue on the international political tourism agenda only recently. While global warming received some political attention with the foundation of the IPCC in 1989 and subsequent publication of the IPCC's First, Second and Third Assessment Reports (FAR, SAR and TAR; IPCC 1990, 1995, 2001), it was not before the publication of the Fourth Assessment Report (AR4, IPCC 2007b) that climate change became a politically broadly acknowledged issue. An understanding of the importance of climate change for tourism also emerged comparably late (Figure 5.1).

The first scientific papers linking climate change and tourism were published well before the FAR and covered the issue of impacts of climate change on tourism. McBoyle *et al.* (1986, 1987) and Wall *et al.* (1986) were the first to discuss the effects global warming would have for tourism. Tourism was, however, not mentioned in the FAR (Wall 1998), and became only integrated on a more regular basis in the TAR and AR4 (Amelung *et al.* 2008, Hall 2008). With regard to tourism's contribution to climate change, it took another decade before an explicit linkage between the sector and its contribution to GHG emissions was made (Bach and Gössling 1996). Even though the role of aviation in climate change had received attention since the 1970s (Fabian 1974, 1978), tourism continued to be seen as a 'white', non-polluting industry until recently.

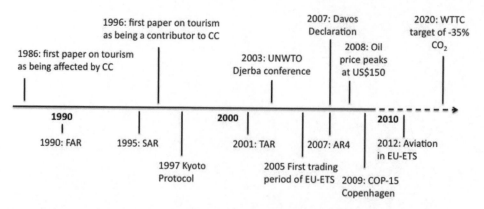

Figure 5.1 *The emergence of climate change as an issue for tourism*

In the global political arena, the interrelationships of tourism and climate change gained importance when UNWTO convened the First International Conference on Climate Change and Tourism in Djerba, Tunisia, in 2003. The conference's focus was on adaptation to climate change (Ceron and Dubois 2003), even though the UNWTO (2003) conference proceedings acknowledge tourism as both 'affecting and being affected by climate change', i.e. as a contributor to GHG emissions. A first global assessment of emissions from tourism was published shortly before the conference (Gössling 2002), together with the first national assessment of GHG emissions from tourism (Becken 2002).

The first UNWTO tourism and climate conference led to the Djerba Declaration (UNWTO 2003), which 'recognized the complex inter-linkages between the tourism sector and climate change and established a framework for future research and policy making on adaptation and mitigation' (Cabrini 2009: 162). In October 2007, this was followed by the Second International Conference on Climate Change and Tourism in Davos, Switzerland, convened by UNWTO, UNEP and the WMO, and with the support of the WEF and the Swiss Government. The conference led to the formulation of the more specific Davos Declaration (UNWTO 2007: 2), acknowledging that:

- climate is a key resource for tourism and the sector is highly sensitive to the impacts of climate change and global warming, many elements of which are already being felt. It is estimated to contribute some 5% of global CO_2 emissions.
  …
- given tourism's importance in the global challenges of climate change and poverty reduction, there is a need to urgently adopt a range of policies which encourages truly sustainable tourism that reflects a 'quadruple bottom line' of environmental, social, economic and climate responsiveness.

UNWTO also called for the tourism industry to contribute to reductions in emissions (UNWTO 2007: 2):

The tourism sector must rapidly respond to climate change, within the evolving UN framework and progressively reduce its Greenhouse Gas (GHG) contribution if it is to grow in a sustainable manner. This will require action to:

- mitigate its GHG emissions, derived especially from transport and accommodation activities;
- adapt tourism businesses and destinations to changing climate conditions;
- apply existing and new technology to improve energy efficiency;
- secure financial resources to help poor regions and countries.

The Davos Declaration calls for a range of actors to take action. This includes a call for governments and international organizations to (UNWTO 2007: 2–4):

- Collaborate in international strategies, policies and action plans to reduce GHG emissions in the transport (in cooperation with the ICAO and other aviation organizations), accommodation and related tourism activities.

For tourism industry and destinations to:

- Take leadership in implementing concrete measures (such as incentives) in order to mitigate climate change throughout the tourism value chain and to reduce risk to travellers, operators and infrastructure due to dynamic climate variability and shift. Establish targets and indicators to monitor progress.

- Promote and undertake investments in energy-efficiency tourism programmes and use of renewable energy resources, with the aim of reducing the carbon footprint of the entire tourism sector.
- Seek to achieve increasingly carbon free environments by diminishing pollution through design, operations and market responsive mechanisms.

For consumers to:

- In their choices for travel and destination, tourists should be encouraged to consider the climate, economic, societal and environmental impacts of their options before making a decision and, where possible to reduce their carbon footprint, or offset emissions that cannot be reduced directly.
- In their choices of activities at the destination, tourists should also be encouraged to opt for environmentally friendly activities that reduce their carbon footprint as well as contribute to the preservation of the natural environment and cultural heritage.

For research and communications networks to:

- Encourage targeted, multi-disciplinary research on impacts of climate change in order to address regional gaps in current knowledge, develop tools for risk assessment and cost-benefit analyses with which to gauge the feasibility of various responses.
- Include environmental and climate specific subjects in the study curricula of tourism training programmes and extend these to broader educational systems.
- Promote responsible travel that supports 'quadruple bottom line' sustainable tourism, incorporating climate, environmental, social and economic considerations.
- Raise awareness on tourism's economic role as a tool for development, and present information on causes and effects of climate change based on sound science, in a fair, balanced and user-friendly manner.

The Davos Declaration, which also introduced a quadruple bottom line to sustainability, has subsequently developed into more accentuated goals with regard to mitigation. The emerging consensus is that tourism needs to take responsibility for emission reductions in line with other sectors (UNWTO 2009b), and the World Travel and Tourism Council (WTTC 2009) specified 'aspirational' goals for sector-wide absolute emission reductions in the order of 25–30 per cent by 2020 and 50 per cent by 2035 (both from 2005 levels). The need to act on the challenge of climate change is also emphasized by various other organizations, including the WEF (2009), Copenhagen Climate Council (2009) and G8 (2009), and outlined in UNWTO's (2009b: 14) 'Roadmap for Recovery':

> The tourism community should continue to champion carbon-neutrality and confront commitments agreed by parties to the UNFCCC to respond to climate change. This should include incentives for adaptation, substantial financial support and low cost technology transfer to the poorest economies. All strategies and the associated financing should help drive sectoral low carbon transport and accommodation, as well as the use of green technology.

While such calls indicate that the problem is recognized on supra-national and national levels, and by political and economic actors, these documents might as yet have very limited consequences for the continuation of daily business in tourism, also because relative efficiency gains are outweighed by growth in tourist numbers and the associated development of infrastructure and capacity (Gössling *et al.* 2009b).

CURRENT EMISSIONS FROM TOURISM

The tourism sector uses energy for the transport of visitors to and from, as well as within destinations, in accommodation establishments and for a range of tourist activities, such as visitation of sites and attractions, participation in meetings and conferences, visits to bars, discotheques, cafés, or events such as festivals and concerts. Tourism includes, by UNWTO definition, 'the activities of persons travelling to and staying in places outside their usual environment for not more than one consecutive year for leisure, business and other purposes not related to the exercise of an activity remunerated from within the place visited'. This is of importance, as tourism-related emissions thus comprise different travel motives (leisure–business), geographical patterns (international–domestic) and temporal ranges (overnight–same-day trips), as well as activities (conferences, festivals, shopping, nature walks).

As most of the energy used in tourism is derived from fossil fuels, tourism is associated with considerable emissions of GHGs. In 2007, UNWTO, UNEP and WMO commissioned a report on the interlinkages between climate change and tourism, also including a calculation of the contribution made by tourism to global emissions of CO_2 (see UNWTO-UNEP-WMO 2008). The report estimated these emissions to be in the order of 5 per cent of global CO_2 emissions in 2005, noting that the sector's contribution to RF is probably higher, in the order of 4.4–9.0 per cent – the range is attributed to uncertainties. As indicated in table 5.1, most tourism emissions are a result of transport, with aviation accounting for 40 per cent of tourism's contribution to CO_2, followed by cars (32 per cent) and accommodation (21 per cent). Note that 'tourism' is estimated to be responsible for 80.5 per cent of all emissions from aviation, i.e. excluding transports and military flights. Cruise ships are included in other transport, and with an estimated 19.17 Mt CO_2, responsible for around 1.5 per cent of global tourism emissions. Note, however, that emissions from ferries and cruise ships have more recently been estimated to account for 96 Mt CO_2, i.e. a considerably higher value (cf. Chapter 4).

All calculations presented above are based on energy throughput. As the construction of hotels, airports and aircraft, cars and roads, boats and marinas all consume considerable amounts of energy, a lifecycle perspective accounting for the energy embodied in the tourism system would lead to higher estimates. Furthermore, tourism also leads to indirect emissions not considered in the UNWTO-UNEP-WMO (2008) assessment, including the energy use in associated sectors, such as tour operators and their offices, travel to work by those employed in tourism – which can involve significant numbers of staff driving or flying, often over considerable distances – as well as significant amounts of freight, as involved in the transport of food and other goods for tourism, which are relevant particularly in small island destinations (e.g. Gössling and Schumacher 2009). The UNWTO-UNEP-WMO (2008) emission assessment must thus be seen as conservative (Table 5.1).

The GHG inventory for global tourism presented by UNWTO-UNEP-WMO (2008) largely matches an analysis by the WEF (2009), which is based on a somewhat different methodology including a different set of sub-sectors, i.e. including cruise ship travel, but excluding

Table 5.1 Distribution of emissions from tourism by sub-sector

Sub-Sectors	2005	
	CO_2 (Mt)	%
Air transport	515	40
Car transport	420	32
Other transport	45	3
Accommodation	275	21
Activities	48	4
TOTAL	1,304	100
Total World (IPCC 2007b)	26,400	
Tourism contribution		5

Source: UNWTO-UNEP-WMO, 2008

activities. WEF presented a 13 per cent higher estimate of global travel and tourism (T&T) CO_2 emissions in 2005 (1,476 Mt) than UNWTO-UNEP-WMO (2008). Notably, WEF (2009: 13) distinguishes direct and indirect emissions from tourism, with direct emissions being defined as 'carbon emissions from sources that are directly engaged in the economic activity of the T&T sector'. While these are included in the WEF estimate, indirect emissions are excluded, i.e. emissions caused 'as a consequence of the activity of the companies in the T&T value chain, but occur from sources not directly engaged in the economic activity within the T&T sector. For example, emissions from electricity usage in airline or travel agent offices, and emissions from transportation of hotel consumables, such as food or toiletries' (WEF 2009: 13).

The exclusion of indirect emissions, as well as a lifecycle perspective by WEF could be seen as a serious omission, however, because emissions from tourism are often directly or indirectly compared with the sector's economic performance, with the result that tourism appears to be a comparably eco-efficient sector (cf. WEF 2009). As economic accounts are based on satellite accounting, i.e. including indirect and even induced economic effects, while a considerable share of emissions from tourism is excluded from analysis, it is nevertheless incorrect to compare emissions and turnover (see also Becken and Hay 2007 for a discussion of methodologies for GHG accounting). Note as well that UNWTO-UNEP-WMO (2008) findings cannot be compared to WEF (2009) due to the lack of transparency regarding the sources and assumptions made by WEF (2009).

Yet another update on emissions from tourism has recently been published by Scott *et al.* (2010), based on RF, i.e. measuring the overall contribution of all GHG emissions by the sector to global warming in 2005. The calculation provided in table 5.2 shows that tourism's contribution to global climate change might have been between 5.2–12.5 per cent in 2005. These figures are an update on UNWTO-UNEP-WMO (2008) and higher because of a recent update on the contribution of aviation to RF by Lee *et al.* (2009), who for the first time consider AIC. As shown in table 5.2, including emissions from aviation based on the calculation of RF has a considerable impact on the contribution of tourism to global warming.

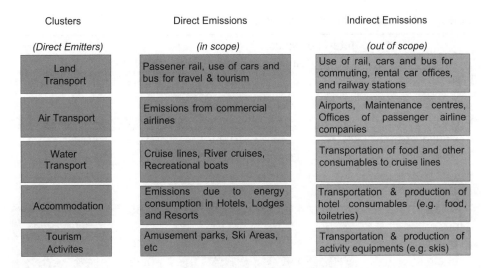

Clusters	Direct Emissions	Indirect Emissions
(Direct Emitters)	*(in scope)*	*(out of scope)*
Land Transport	Passener rail, use of cars and bus for travel & tourism	Use of rail, cars and bus for commuting, rental car offices, and railway stations
Air Transport	Emissions from commercial airlines	Airports, Maintenance centres, Offices of passenger airline companies
Water Transport	Cruise lines, River cruises, Recreational boats	Transportation of food and other consumables to cruise lines
Accommodation	Emissions due to energy consumption in Hotels, Lodges and Resorts	Transportation & production of hotel consumables (e.g. food, toiletries)
Tourism Activites	Amusement parks, Ski Areas, etc	Transportation & production of activity equipments (e.g. skis)

Figure 5.2 Direct and indirect sources of CO_2 from tourism and travel
Source: WEF 2009

Table 5.2 Contribution of tourism to radiative forcing, 2005

	Mt CO_2	RF (excluding AIC), W/m²	RF (with average AIC), W/m²	RF (with maximum AIC), W/m²
Air transport	515	0.0452	0.1080	0.1829
Car transport	420	0.0204	0.0204	0.0204
Other transport	45	0.0022	0.0022	0.0022
Accommodation	275	0.0133	0.0133	0.0133
Activities	48	0.0023	0.0023	0.0023
Total tourism	1,304*	0.0835	0.1462	0.2211
Total world	26,400	1.6	1.678	1.771
Share (%)	4.94	5.22	8.72	12.49

Source: Scott *et al.* 2010
* rounded

A DETAILED ANALYSIS OF EMISSIONS FROM TOURISM

All tourism, including overnight, same-day, international, and domestic travel is estimated to have accounted for 9.75 billion trips in 2005, out of this 5 billion are same-day trips (4 billion domestic and 1 billion international) and 4.75 billion are trips involving overnight stays (4 billion domestic and 750 million international). As an international trip can include arrivals in more than one country, the number of international tourist arrivals is higher at 480 million. Consequently, international trips represent 16 per cent of all tourist trips, and are outweighed by domestic trips constituting 84 per cent of all trips. Table 5.3 also presents arrivals and trips by transport mode, shows that air transport is the least relevant means of transport, accounting for 17 per cent of tourist trips (with overnight stays), and 1 per cent of same-day trips.

Table 5.3 Approximate tourism volumes, 2005[a]

(billions)	Total	of which: Domestic	International	Of which: Intraregional	Interregional
Total trips	9.75	8.00	1.75		
Same-day	5.0	4.00	1.00	1.00	0.00
over land/water	5.0	4.00	0.99	0.99	
by air	0.05	0.04	0.01	0.01	
by air (%)	1	1	1	1	
Tourist					
Arrivals	4.80	4.00	0.80	0.65	0.15
Trips [b]	4.75	4.00	0.75	0.61	0.13
Over land/water	3.93	3.52	0.41	0.40	0.01
by air	0.82	0.48	0.34	0.22	0.12
by air (%)	17	12	46	35	92

(a) Dark grey: estimated volumes based on UNWTO country data or other sources; light grey fields: approximate volumes (as only little data are available);
(b) Trip volumes are derived from available arrivals data as one trip can produce more than one arrival.
Source: UNWTO-UNEP-WMO 2008

Transports

Emissions from tourism-related transports are calculated by multiplying transport distances with averaged emission factors, i.e. the averaged amount of CO_2 emitted for transporting one person over one kilometre (pkm). For any global estimate, such a top-down approach is fairly exact, even though downscaling to single flights or emissions by, for instance, a tour operator would require data on transport modes, their energy use, load factors, and, for aviation and the calculation of RF contributions, also including knowledge on flight routes and altitudes. As shown in table 5.4 for transport in the EU, averaged emission factors for different transport modes can vary considerably.

Coach and rail transport are the most efficient, causing emissions of 0.022 kg CO_2/pkm and 0.027 kg CO_2/pkm, respectively. This difference is mainly caused by occupancy rates: if compared on a per seat kilometre (skm) basis, i.e. considering the number of people that could theoretically be transported at full occupancy, rail is more efficient at 0.016 kg/skm, compared to coach at 0.020 kg/skm. Even lower emissions can result from rail travel when electricity is sourced from renewable energies (see Carbon Management in Focus 8, SBB, Switzerland). Emissions from cars amount on average to 0.133 kg CO_2/pkm, while flights of 1,000 km or more cause 0.130 kg CO_2/pkm, and short flights of less than 500 km produce 0.206 kg CO_2/pkm. The high value for short-haul flights is due to the high amount of energy used for take-off and climbing. Most emission-intense are cruise ships, even though no comprehensive database is available for this. Carnival Corporation & plc (2008) reports, for instance, direct air emissions of 0.330 kg CO_2 per Available Lower Berth km (ALB km)

Table 5.4 *Emission factors for tourism transport modes in the EU context*

Mode	CO_2 factor (kg/pkm)	Occupancy rate/load factor %
Air <500 km	0.206	
500–1,000 km	0.154	
1,000–1,500 km	0.130	
1,500–2,000 km	0.121	
>2,000 km	0.111	
Air world average	0.129	75
Rail	0.027	60
Car	0.133	50
Coach	0.022	90

Source: Peeters *et al.* 2007

for its fleet, a measure considering passenger capacity. As cruise ships will not be 100 per cent occupied, emissions on a pkm basis will be higher.

Table 5.5 summarizes CO_2 emissions from international and domestic tourism transport. Note that more detailed emission factors are often available from national authorities (e.g. UK Department of Energy and Climate Change 2009). The most important land transport mode for tourism in industrialized countries is the car (Peeters *et al.* 2007a). Other transport modes, such as rail and coach, and water transport are less important in terms of global passenger volumes, and even less so with respect to CO_2 emissions. Of all emissions by surface traffic, the roughly 5 billion same-day trips, i.e. 51 per cent of all trips, cause emissions of 133 Mt CO_2, i.e. 10.2 per cent of surface traffic emissions. Another important relationship is that the 750 million international tourist trips cause emissions of 371 Mt CO_2 (494 kg per trip), while 4 billion domestic tourist trips cause 478 Mt CO_2 (119 kg per trip). More detailed data on trips, distances travelled, emissions, and distributions between domestic and international tourism can be derived from Table 5.5, as well as Figures 5.3, 5.4 and 5.5.

As shown in Figure 4.3, the vast majority of tourism journeys, measured as trips, are made by car and other transport modes, i.e. bus, train and water-borne transport modes. Air travel is, compared to other transport modes, far less relevant, accounting for 8.9 per cent of all trips.

A considerably different picture arises if one considers the distances covered by different transport modes. This is because air travellers usually cover comparably large distances, and this category is consequently the most relevant in terms of passenger kilometres.

Finally, yet another picture emerges when emissions from the various transport modes are compared. Here, the contribution made by aviation to global warming increases even further, as it is a comparably energy-intense form of transport. In particular, the role of other transport declines to a very low level, as emissions per pkm are only a fraction of those caused by air travel.

Table 5.5 *Interrelationships between transport and emissions, 2005*

	Total	Same-day visitors (domestic & int.)	Tourists Domestic	Tourists International total	Intraregional	Interregional
All tourism						
Total number of trips (million)	**9,750**	5,000	4,000	750	615	135
Passenger kilometres (billion)	**9,147**	1,237	4,832	3,077	1,313	1,763
Average return distance (km)	**938**	247	1,208	4,102	2,135	13,063
Total CO_2 emissions (Mt)	**981**	133	478	371	153	218
CO_2 kg per km	**0.107**	0.107	0.099	0.121	0.116	0.124
CO_2 emissions (kg/trip)	**101**	27	119	494	248	1616
Air						
Total number of trips (million)	**870**	50	480	340	215	125
Passenger kilometres (billion)	**3,984**	60	1,340	2,585	833	1751
Average return distance (km)	**4,580**	1,200	2,791	7,602	3,875	14,012
Total CO_2 emissions (Mt)	**515**	11	185	321	104	217
CO_2 kg per km	**0.129**	0.177	0.138	0.124	0.125	0.124
CO_2 emissions (kg/trip)	**592**	212	385	945	484	1737
Surface						
Total number of trips (million)	**8,880**	4,950	3,520	410	400	10
Passenger kilometres (billion)	**5,162**	1,177	3,493	492	480	12
Average return distance (km)	**581**	238	992	1,200	1,200	1,200

Total CO_2 emissions (Mt)	**464**	122	293	49	49	1
CO_2 kg per km	**0.090**	0.104	0.084	0.101	0.101	0.079
CO_2 emissions (kg/trip)	**52**	25	83	121	121	95
of which:						
Car						
Total number of trips (million)	**5,956**	3,641	2,028	287	282	5
Passenger kilometres (billion)	**3,354**	892	2,117	344	338	6
Average return distance (km)	**563**	245	1,044	1,200	1,200	1,200
Total CO_2 emissions (Mt)	**419**	115	258	46	45.0	0.8
CO_2 kg per km	**0.125**	0.129	0.122	0.133	0.133	0.133
CO_2 emissions (kg/trip)	**70**	32	127	160	160	160
Other (train, coach, ship, etc.)						
Total number of trips (million)	**2,924**	1,309	1,492	123	118	5
Passenger kilometres (billion)	**1,809**	285	1,376	148	142	6
Average return distance (km)	**619**	218	922	1,200	1,200	1,200
Total CO_2 emissions (Mt)	**45**	7	34	4	4	0.2
CO_2 kg per km	**0.025**	0.025	0.025	0.025	0.025	0.025
CO_2 emissions (kg/trip)	**15**	5	23	30	30	30

Source: UNWTO-UNEP-WMO 2008, based on data provided by UNWTO, ICAO and IATA

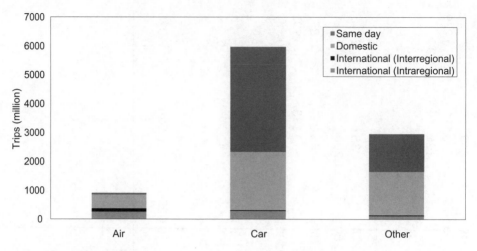

Figure 5.3 *World tourism transport volume by mode, 2005*
Source: UNWTO-UNEP-WMO 2008

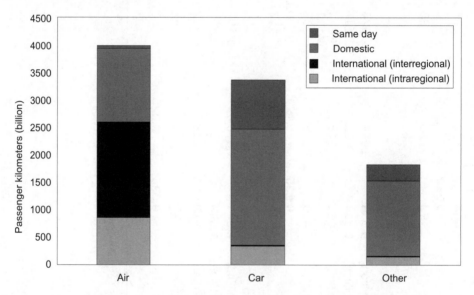

Figure 5.4 *World tourism passenger kilometre volume by mode, 2005*
Source: UNWTO-UNEP-WMO 2008

Accommodation

Energy use in accommodation includes heating/cooling, lighting, cooking (in restaurants), cleaning, and, in tropical or arid regions, the desalination of seawater. UNWTO distinguishes a wide range of accommodation establishments, such as hotels, youth hostels or second homes, but there is no comprehensive data on the number of beds and energy use in each respective category. A general rule is that the more luxurious the accommodation, the more energy will be used, a fact explicable by greater room space heating/air conditioning (A/C) requirements in higher standard accommodation, as well as a greater range of

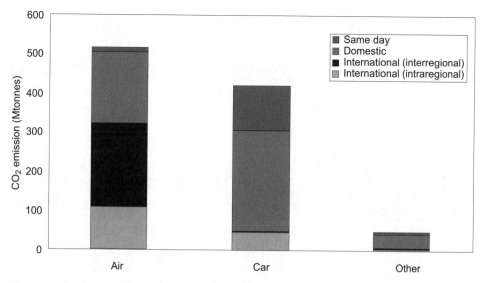

Figure 5.5 CO_2 *emissions by tourism transport, 2005*
Source: UNWTO-UNEP-WMO 2008

electrical appliances in the room (see also Table 5.6). A standard five star room, for instance, might now include two telephones (including one in the bathroom), kettle, iron, hair dryer, safe, TV, electric scales, and speakers (also in the bathroom), with upcoming appliances including heated bathroom mirrors as well as heated toilet seats.

In a review of energy use in hotels, Bohdanowicz and Martinac (2007) found energy-use values of between 51–256 MJ/guest night, while Becken and Hay (2007) found a range of 25–284 MJ/guest night. In terms of emissions, there are ranges between <1 kg (renewable energy use) to 125 kg CO_2 (self-supporting power generation) per guest night identified in the literature (UNWTO-UNEP-WMO 2008). However, few studies exist that have more comprehensively assessed emissions. Bohdanowicz and Martinac (2007) studied energy use in the Scandic and Hilton chains, finding average energy use values of 322 MJ/guest night in Hilton hotels, and 172 MJ/guest night in Scandic Hotels. The study does not provide any information on emissions, however. As about half of the energy use in both chains is electricity, this could correspond to emissions of 4.6 kg CO_2/guest night for Scandic Hotels, based on the Nordic electricity mix with emissions of about 0.096 kg CO_2 per kWh (Andersson and Lukaszevicz 2006), and about 44 kg CO_2 per guest night in Hilton hotels, based on a value of 0.5 kg CO_2/kWh in the UK or Germany. All other studies appear to have country- or accommodation-specific approaches to energy use. For instance, Becken *et al.* studied various forms of accommodation in New Zealand, finding energy-consumption values ranging from 32–110 MJ, and emissions ranging from 1.4 kg CO_2/guest night to 7.9 kg CO_2/guest night (Becken and Hay 2001, 2007). Beccali *et al.* (2009) find energy-use values between 32–112 MJ/guest night in hotels in Sicily/Italy. Most other studies are indicative of energy use in single hotels, and in the absence of systematic reviews of energy use in accommodation establishments, global assessments of energy use and emissions remain difficult. Table 5.6 summarizes the results from existing studies on energy use and emissions in accommodation.

Table 5.6 Energy use in accommodation

Accommodation type, country	Energy use per guest night (MJ)	Emissions per guest night (kg CO_2)	Including	Source
1/2* hotels, Zanzibar/Tanzania	205	14.5	Diesel generator	Gössling 2000
4* hotels, Zanzibar/Tanzania	1,050	73	Diesel generator	Gössling 2000
3* hotel, Zanzibar/Tanzania	3.5	<0.1	Electricity (solar)	Carbon Management in Focus 5
5* hotel, Seychelles	1,787	125	Diesel generator	Gössling 2007, unpublished data
Average Sicilian hotel	65 (+50 thermal)	9.2	Electricity only	Beccali et al. 2009
1/2* hotel, Sicily	32 (+50 thermal)	4.7	Electricity only	Beccali et al. 2009
3* hotel, Sicily	50 (+50 thermal)	7	Electricity only	Beccali et al. 2009
4/5* hotel, Sicily	112 (+50 thermal)	15.8	Electricity only	Beccali et al. 2009
5* hotel, Oman	3,717	260	Direct/indirect emissions	Case study x, 2010
Hotels, Australia	110–265 (mean: 191)	n.a.	Electricity and gas consumption	Warnken et al. (2005)
Eco-resorts, Australia	68–256 (mean: 165)	n.a.	Electricity and gas consumption	Warnken et al. (2005)
Caravan parks	22–43 (mean: 32)	n.a.	Electricity and gas consumption	Warnken et al. (2005)
4* hotel, Germany	119	0.1	Electricity and wood pellets	Carbon Management in Focus 6
2* hotel, Vietnam	94–976 (mean: 364)	n.a.	Electricity only	Trung and Kumar (2005)

Accommodation			Fuel types	Source
3* hotel, Vietnam	148–1,536 (mean: 515)	n.a.	Electricity only	Trung and Kumar (2005)
4* hotel, Vietnam	288–853 (mean: 508)	n.a.	Electricity only	Trung and Kumar (2005)
Hotel, Majorca	51	n.a.	Electricity, gas, oil	Simmons and Lewis (2001)
Hotel, Cyprus	87	n.a.	Electricity, gas, oil	Simmons and Lewis
Holiday village, Germany	91	n.a.	Electricity	Lüthje and Lindstadt (1994)
Hotel, New Zealand	155	7.9	Electricity, fossil fuels and wood	Becken et al. (2001), Becken and Hay (2007)
B&B, New Zealand	110	4.1	Electricity, fossil fuels and wood	Becken et al. (2001), Becken and Hay (2007)
Motel, New Zealand	32	1.4	Electricity, fossil fuels and wood	Becken et al. (2001), Becken and Hay (2007)
Camping, New Zealand	25	1.4	Electricity, fossil fuels and wood	Becken et al. (2001), Becken and Hay (2007)
Hostel, New Zealand	39	1.6	Electricity, fossil fuels and wood	Becken et al. (2001), Becken and Hay (2007)
Summer houses, Sweden	246 (assumed 60 days stay/year)	0.7 (assumed 60 days stay/year)	Electricity	SCB (2002)

Conversion factors: 1 kWh = 3.6 MJ; 1 MJ = 0.28 kWh; 1 diesel = 2.7 kg CO_2; 1 l diesel = 38.6 MJ

Table 5.6 shows considerable differences in energy use and emissions per guest night, even though not all values are comparable, as in some cases only electricity use is considered. Notably, energy use and emissions are not proportional, as on the consumption side, values are influenced by occupancy rates, while on the production side, energy generation can be more or less efficient, and be based on energy sources with higher (e.g. coal) or lower carbon contents (e.g. gas), or renewable sources leading to very low emissions (wind, sun, biomass, hydro). For example, Deng and Burnett (2000) found that electricity accounted for 73 per cent of the overall energy use in hotels in Hong Kong. Similar values were found in New Zealand, where the main energy source for accommodation establishments is electricity (75 per cent of total energy use), while coal is 12 per cent, LPG 9 per cent, petroleum fuel 3 per cent, and natural gas and wood 1 per cent (Becken *et al.* 2001). A survey conducted by Simmons and Lewis (2001) revealed an energy mix of electricity (57 per cent), gas (8 per cent), oil (<1 per cent), gas oil (<1 per cent), and electricity from renewables (34 per cent) for one hotel in Majorca, and an energy mix of electricity (70 per cent), gas (<1 per cent), and oil (29 per cent) for one hotel in Cyprus. Zmeureanu *et al.* (1994) reported a mix of electricity (29 per cent), gas (26 per cent), and steam (45 per cent) for hotels in Ottawa, Canada, and Trung and Kumar (2005) found that electricity accounted for 76–91 per cent of energy demand, the remainder covered by LPG (6–21 per cent) and diesel and other fuels (3–4 per cent).

With regard to the purposes of energy use, a study for Hong Kong found that 32 per cent of total energy was consumed for A/C, 12 per cent for lighting, 5 per cent for lifts and escalators, 23 per cent for other systems/appliances, and 28 per cent for cooking and water heating (the latter based on gas and diesel) (Deng and Burnett 2000). Vietnamese hotels were found to use 46–53 per cent of energy for A/C and ventilation, 13–26 per cent for lighting, and 17–27 per cent for water heating, the remainder (4–13 per cent) being used for lifts, pumps, refrigerators and others (Trung and Kumar 2005). Yet another study of hotels in Sicily suggests that in upscale hotels (four and five stars), electricity consumption on an end-use basis is primarily for heating, ventilating and air conditioning (HVAC) (35 per cent), lighting (35 per cent), cooking and food refrigeration (15 per cent), hotel services (10 per cent) and losses (5 per cent). Thermal energy is primarily used for hot water (40 per cent), cooking (25 per cent) and air heating (35 per cent) (Beccali *et al.* 2009). The Carbon Trust (2010) suggests that most energy use in hotels in the UK is associated with heating, followed by hot water provision, catering, lighting and other factors, including A/C (Figure 5.6). In pubs, heating and lighting take up about equal shares of energy consumption, followed by cellar services, hot water, catering and other.

Given considerable differences in fuel use and emissions, there is uncertainty regarding total emissions from global accommodation. Table 5.7 presents an estimate of global average values for direct energy use and emissions by accommodation category (Gössling 2002), which need to be seen as conservative in the light of the findings presented in table 5.8.

Overall emissions from tourism can be calculated by multiplying the number of tourists by length of stay and an emission factor (CO_2 per guest night). The total number of international guest nights was estimated to be in the order of 6.1 billion in 2005. For domestic tourism, the total number of guest nights was estimated at 13.7 billion. For calculations of total

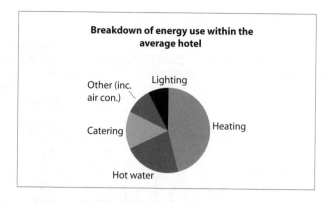

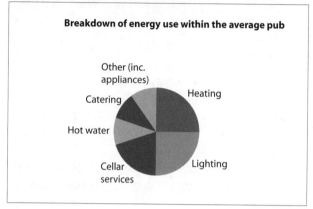

Figure 5.6 *Energy use in hotels and pubs in the UK*
Source: Carbon Trust 2010

Table 5.7 *Estimated global average energy use by type of accommodation*

Type of Accommodation	Energy use per guest night (MJ)	Emissions per guest night (kg CO_2)
Hotels	130	20.6
Campsites	50	7.9
Pensions	25	4.0
Self-catering	120	19.0
Holiday villages	90	14.3
Vacation homes	100	15.9
Estimated Average	98	15.6

Source: Gössling 2002

emissions from accommodation, UNWTO-UNEP-WMO (2008), used an average of 19 kg CO_2 per guest night in international tourism, and 11.5 kg CO_2 in domestic tourism, to correct for lower emission levels in accommodation used by domestic tourists in developing

Table 5.8 *Number of trips, guest nights and CO_2 emissions from tourism accommodation, 2005*

Overview of estimated number of trips, guest nights and CO_2 emissions from tourism accommodation, 2005

			total	of which:	
				domestic	international
total trips			9.7	8.0	1.7
	same-day		5.0	4.0	1.0
	over land, water		5.0	4.0	0.99
	by air		0.05	0.04	0.01
	by air (%)		1	1	1
	tourist				
	arrivals		4.8	4.0	0.80
tourist trips		bn			
(overnight)	– arrivals per trip			1.0	1.07
	total		**4.747**	4.000	0.747
	in hotel and		1.713	1.340	0.373
	similar (H & S)				
	other CE & private		3.034	2.660	0.373
	tourists in		36.089	33.492	50.000
	H & S (%)				
	over land, water		3.931	3.524	0.407
	by air		0.816	0.476	0.340
	by air (%)		17.187	11.896	45.524
guest-nights		bn			
	total		**19.846**	13.706	6.140
	in hotel		5.945	3.772	2.173
	other CE & private		13.901	9.934	3.967
room-nights		bn			
in H & S	**total**		**3.931**	2.494	1.437
	avrg person per room		1.512	1.512	1.512
average		nights			
nights	**total**		**4.181**	3.427	8.220
	in hotel		3.470	2.816	5.818
	other CE & private		4.582	3.734	10.623
CO_2					
emissions	total CO_2		274	158	117
	emissions (Mt)				

average CO_2 per night (kg)	13.8	11.5	19.0
average CO_2 emissions (t/trip)	0.058	0.039	0.156

Source: UNWTO-UNEP-WMO 2008, based on data provided by UNWTO, ICAO and IATA

H & S: hotel and similar establishments
CE: collective establishments, except for hotel and similar, this includes campsites, rented apartments, bungalows, etc.

countries. Total emissions associated with accommodation were thus estimated at 274 Mt CO_2 (in 2005; direct energy use, see Table 5.8). This estimate might, however, considerably underestimate emissions from accommodation.

Other tourism activities

Tourists visit attractions and participate in a wide range of activities at the destination. Emissions caused by these activities vary widely between various categories of attractions, such as museums or theme parks, outdoor-oriented activities and events (e.g. sport events or concerts), or shopping. Data on energy use and emissions caused by tourist activities is, however, scarce and available studies are seldom comparable. Moreover, calculations often focus on energy use but do not detail emissions. Becken and Hay (2007) for instance, provide a summary of energy use associated with activities in Switzerland and Finland, showing that on a per visit basis, energy consumption can

Table 5.9 *Energy use for activities*

Activity	MJ per tourist
Heli-skiing	1,300
Scenic flights	340
Diving	800
Scenic boat cruises	165
Sailing (motor)	140
Guided walks	110
Adventure activities	57
Rafting	36
Experience centers	29
Zoos	16
Museums	10
Visitor centers	7

Including fossil fuels and renewable energy, and considering local transports.
Source: Becken and Simmons (2002)

range between 1.8 MJ and 119 MJ. It is not clear what is included in these figures, however, which partially consider 'embodied energy use'. Of the more detailed studies, Becken and Simmons (2002) show for activities in New Zealand that emissions can range from 7–1,300 MJ per tourist/visit. Again, results in this study are not linked to emissions (see Table 5.9).

A number of studies also investigate specific tourist activities. For instance, Byrnes and Warnken (2006) have shown that boats cause considerable emissions. Per trip, Australian tour boat operators cause on average 61 kg CO_2-eq if the boat uses a diesel engine or 27 kg CO_2-eq if the boat uses a petrol engine (it is not clear, however, how CO_2-eq were calculated). In extreme cases, high-powered vessels can use 300 litres of fuel per hour for two 485 kW engines, even though only 11 passengers can be carried. Dawson *et al.* (2009) have also shown how energy intense activities such as polar bear viewing in Churchill, Canada can be, with about 8,000 tourists per year causing emissions of 20,892 t CO_2, including transportation, accommodation and activities. Activities are only responsible for a minor share of per tourist emissions of >2.6 t CO_2, however, with tundra vehicle trips, helicopter scenic flights, dog sledding and local transport accounting for 73 kg CO_2/tourist. In yet another example, Aspen Skiing Company reports that emissions for running ski lifts, snow making, etc. account for 21.4 kg CO_2 per skier day (see Carbon Management in Focus 7).

Tourism activities

As there is no systematic international dataset on energy consumption and emissions from tourism activities, UNWTO-UNEP-WMO (2008) assume an average of 250 MJ of energy for 'Other activities' for an average international tourist trip, corresponding to 40 kg CO_2, 50 MJ (8 kg CO_2) for shorter and less activity-oriented business trips, and 100 MJ (16 kg CO_2) for Visiting Friends and Relatives (VFR) trips. The weighted global average for activities of international tourists is 170 MJ or 27.2 kg CO_2 per trip. For domestic tourists, UNWTO-UNEP-WMO (2008) assume 11 kg CO_2 per domestic trip in high-income economies and 2.7 kg CO_2 per trip in developing countries. Extrapolated to 4.75 billion tourist trips in 2005, emissions from tourist activities are estimated to be in the order of 48 Mt CO_2. Note that this estimate has comparably high error margins.

Food

GHG emissions associated with food consumption have not been considered in assessments of emissions from tourism such as provided by UNWTO-UNEP-WMO (2008) or WEF (2009), possibly because these are seen not to be specific for tourism, i.e. to be part of 'everyday consumption' (for studies including food, see Gössling *et al.* 2002; WWF-UK 2002; Peeters and Schouten 2006). It might be argued, however, that food-consumption patterns in tourism are different from everyday food consumption, because there are considerable differences in the quality and quantity of the food and beverages consumed, and because food might be imported over considerable distances, particularly in the case of small, isolated islands. The following sections provide a review of the GHG intensity of food, also with a view on an emissions sub-sector that could make a considerable contribution to reducing GHG (Gössling *et al.* 2010).

Food production and consumption are key issues for climate change mitigation, because agriculture accounted for between 10 per cent and 12 per cent of total anthropogenic GHG emissions in 2005 (Smith *et al.* 2009b), to which packaging, retailing, transport and preparation have to be added, as well as the clearing or conversion of ecosystems for food production. Most problematic are the food sector's emissions of methane (CH_4) and nitrous oxide (N_2O), which are potent GHGs (Smith *et al.* 2009b). If emissions from fisheries are added, food production and consumption account for a considerable share of overall emissions. While there appears to be no global assessment available, in the case of Norway, for instance, a calculation of GHG emissions on an end-use-consumption basis revealed that food consumption accounts for more than 20 per cent of the country's total GHG emissions (Hille *et al.* 2008).

Tourism is of relevance in food consumption because it is estimated that some 75 billion meals per year, or just over 200 million meals per day are consumed in tourism-related contexts (Gössling *et al.* 2010). While this would still correspond to a small share of the meals eaten by 6.8 billion people on a daily basis, their consumption in tourism would nevertheless be relevant, because of the considerable impact tourism businesses can have on tourist consumption. For example, the decision by Scandic Hotels to provide organic and fair-traded coffee in their hotels in Sweden has repercussions for the sustainability of millions of cups of coffee served every year (Scandic 2009). Other arguments pertain to the influence of foodservice providers in tourism on the globalization of the food industry. If large hotel chains buy food at a grand scale with a view to reducing costs, for instance, this will increase the pressure on the global food sector to provide cheap foodstuffs. This, in turn, encourages the industrialization of food production, which Vos (2000) argues has led to many of its current problems, and would more recently even include outbreaks of swine fever and bovine spongiform encephalopathy.

Any analysis of the CO_2 emissions associated with particular foodstuffs must specify the production-consumption chain involved and establish suitable system boundaries, also considering a wide range of other factors that are ultimately beyond the scope of most analyses (see also British Standards Institute 2008). For instance, in the case of strawberries, seasonality, use of greenhouses, location and production techniques all influence GHG emissions. Analyses become even more difficult in the case of mixed products, such as for instance strawberry ice cream.

In a comprehensive analysis of European studies assessing the GHG-content of various foodstuffs on a farming lifecycle basis, i.e. production to farm gate, Hille *et al.* (2009) found considerable differences in GHG intensities. For instance, among various vegetables, values ranged from 0.046 kg CO_2/kg to more than 28 kg CO_2/kg of vegetables. The main factor for this was whether these were produced in heated greenhouses or in the field.

Cereals, such as wheat, rye, oats and barley were found to entail comparably low GHG emissions in their production, ranging between 0.180–0.720 kg CO_2-eq per kg of cereal, or 0.045–0.225 kg CO_2-eq per 1,000 kcal. Rice, on the other hand, appeared to be 5–20 times more emissions-intense, with one study suggesting emissions of 4.55 kg CO_2-eq per kg rice, or 1.25 kg CO_2-eq per 1,000 kcal (Kok *et al.* 2001). Consequently, it would seem that the use of potatoes and cereals is, in Europe, climatically far more sustainable than using rice, at least in those countries that are producing potatoes and cereals, and where no significant transport emissions share needs to be added on top of this.

Regarding the most important food category in terms of GHG content – meat – beef production per 1,000 kcal was found to lead to emissions of about 10 kg CO_2-eq, lamb to about 8 kg CO_2-eq, chicken and turkey to 7 kg CO_2-eq, and pork to 2 kg CO_2-eq. Overall, the studies indicated that pork is climatically more favourable than chicken, which again is more favourable than lamb and beef. Beef is found to be around five times more GHG emissions-intense than pork. With regard to seafood, small carbon footprints were identified, even though this depends on fisheries, as lifecycle analysis suggests that 75–90 per cent of energy-use is related to harvesting (Tyedmers 2001). For instance, per tonne of deep sea fish, including important commercial species such as cod, fuel use for ships can vary between 230 and 2,724 litres, while for pelagic species including herring and mackerel, values are lower at 19 to 159 litres per tonne. High fuel use is also entailed in shrimp fisheries, with fuel use per tonne of catch varying between 331 and 2,342 litres. These values affect emissions per calorie of food, which vary between 0.085 kg CO_2-eq/1,000 kcal for mackerel and 109 kg CO_2-eq/1,000 kcal for lobster. However, note that these values are for production only, and transport might heavily influence the carbon balance (for a discussion of the comparability of the above values, see Hille *et al.* 2009).

Food imports are a particular problem on small tropical islands, where foodservice providers are typically serving high-quality, high-protein foods to upscale tourists. Such tourists often, at least in the perception of hotel managers, expect the foodstuffs they know from home (Pattullo 2005). In such locations, a large share of the food is often imported by air, including food items such as soft drinks, dairy products and even vegetables (Gössling & Schumacher 2009). While this represents an extreme situation, even in regions such as Europe, the USA or Australia the transportation of foodstuffs can imply considerable GHG emissions (see Table 5.10).

While there is as yet a lack of studies on the interrelationships of food consumption and GHG emissions in tourism, the above review indicates that food is a relevant sub-sector. The review also reveals, however, that tourism businesses can make a considerable contribution to reducing GHG emissions arising from food consumption, while simultaneously educating travellers. The sub-sector thus deserves special attention in carbon management.

Table 5.10 *Emissions involved in transporting various foodstuffs to Germany*

Food transported (1 kg)	Distance			CO_2	
	Great circle (km)	Corrected (km) [1]	Distance source	kg CO_2/ tkm [2]	kg CO_2/ kg food
1. Grapes by aircraft from South Africa	8,690	9,125	http://www.webflyer.com/travel/mileage_calculator/	0.725	6.62
2. Nile perch by aircraft from Tanzania	6,980	7,329	http://www.webflyer.com/travel/mileage_calculator/	0.725	5.31
3. Strawberries by aircraft from Egypt	2,910	3,056	http://www.webflyer.com/travel/mileage_calculator/	0.725	2.22
4. Melons by ship from Brazil		9,723	http://www.portworld.com/map/	0.015	0.15
5. Tomatoes by truck from Spain		2,333	http://maps.google.com/	0.160	0.37
6. Tomatoes by train from Spain		2,441	http://maps.google.com/ (shortest rail route)	0.015	0.04

Source: Gössling *et al.* 2010

Notes: 1) Aircraft cannot usually fly directly between two points; a detour factor has been used to correct for this; 2) Emission factors based on Gilbert and Perl (2008); Léonardi and Baumgartner (2004), Zarhariadis and Kouvaritakis (2003).

6 | Trends in emissions from tourism

Both domestic and international tourist numbers have grown continuously and at a rapid pace for more than six decades, as mirrored in growth in international tourist arrivals from 25 million in 1950 to 924 million in 2008. Emissions from tourism have grown concomitantly, but more important than understanding current emissions from tourism, as presented in previous chapters, is gaining an understanding of the future growth in emissions. The following sections highlight global, national, individual, and 'per trip' emission trends.

GLOBAL TOURISM EMISSION TRENDS

Based on a business-as-usual scenario for 2035, which considers changes in travel frequency, length of stay, travel distance, and technological efficiency gains, UNWTO-UNEP-WMO (2008) calculate that emissions from tourism could grow considerably in the coming 25 years. Table 6.1 and 6.2 detail assumptions on which the scenario is based, are that travel distances (in pkm) will grow by 2.0–11.1 per cent per year in international/domestic travel, depending on transport mode, while growth in the number of guest nights is expected at 4.0–5.3 per cent per year and growth in trip numbers at 4.5–6.3 per cent per year (table 6.1). Specific efficiency gains, on the other hand, are assumed to be in the order of 32 per cent in the period 2005–35 for aviation, and 1–2 per cent per year for surface-bound transport. There will be growth in specific emissions for accommodation and activities (1–2 per cent per year), as these become more energy-intense over time.

In this scenario, the number of tourist trips is projected to grow by 179 per cent in the period 2005–35, while guest nights would grow by 156 per cent. Distances travelled (in pkm) are

Table 6.1 Scenario assumptions, travel framework conditions

	Air Transport (pkm; %/year)	Car Transport (pkm; %/year)	Other Transport (pkm; %/year)	Number of guest nights (%/year)	Number of trips (%/year)
International	5.3	2.3	2.0	4.0	4.5
Domestic	11.1	7.5	3.7	5.3	6.3

Table 6.2 Model assumptions: efficiency

	Air travel (overall reduction 2005–3035 in %)	Specific energy use car transport (%/year)	Other transport (%/year)	Accommodation (%/year)	Activities (%/year)
International	32	−1	−1	0	+1
Domestic (developed world)	32	−1	−1	0	+1
Domestic (developing world)	32	−2	−1	+2	+2

expected to increase by 223 per cent, while CO_2 emissions from transport are anticipated to grow by 161 per cent due to efficiency gains. Within the accommodation sector, emissions are forecast to increase by 170 per cent while for tourism activities, growth is expected to be 305 per cent. In terms of the contribution made by various sub-sectors, aviation will become the most important (table 6.3).

The business-as-usual scenario shows that CO_2 emissions will grow by more than 130 per cent, if growth in tourism is compared on the basis of overnight stays, i.e. excluding day visits (UNWTO-UNEP-WMO 2008: 143). This means that emissions will be reaching 3,059 Mt by 2035 (excluding day trips), up from 1,304 Mt in 2005 (including day trips) (table 6.3). These estimates can be compared with a projection for emission growth by the WEF (2009), which suggests emissions of 3,164 Mt CO_2 by 2035. Both UNWTO-UNEP-

Table 6.3 Emissions in 2005 and 2035, business-as-usual

Sub-Sectors	2005		2035*	
	CO_2 (Mt)	%	CO_2 (Mt)	%
Air transport	515	40	1631	53
Car transport	420	32	456	15
Other transport	45	3	37	1
Accommodation	274	21	739	24
Activities	48	4	195	6
TOTAL	1,302	100	3,059	100
Total World (IPCC 2007b)	26,400			
Tourism contribution	5%			

Source: UNWTO-UNEP-WMO 2008, Scott et al. 2010
Note:
* the 2035 estimate does not include same-day trips as the 2005 estimate does, and 2005/2035 emissions are thus not directly comparable

WMO (2008) and WEF (2009) present business-as-usual scenarios, i.e. including a forecast of technological efficiency, but not considering policy intervention or behavioural change. Even though the scenarios do not address the economic crisis beginning in mid-2008, evidence from past crises, such as 11 September 2001, SARS in 2003, or the 1997–98 Asian financial crisis, shows that tourism and air travel usually recover quickly: 'Despite some dramatic external factors which have temporarily slowed or reversed the growth rate of aviation, the industry has proven to be remarkably resilient to these events with consistent recovery to long-term growth rates' (Lee *et al.* 2009: 57).

As a result, if aviation and tourism remain on a business-as-usual pathway, they will become key sources of GHG emissions. Figure 6.1 shows this for aviation in the EU, comparing the region's emission reduction targets with the projected growth of emissions from aviation, and Figure 6.2 illustrates a world economy embarked on an absolute emission reductions pathway, with an unrestricted business-as-usual pathway for the tourism sector. Lines A and B in Figure 6.1 represent emission pathways for the global economy under a −3 per cent/year (A) and −6 per cent/year (B) scenario, with emissions peaking in 2015 (A) and 2025 (B), respectively. Both scenarios are based on the goal of avoiding a +2 °C warming threshold by 2100 (for details see Scott *et al.* 2010). As indicated, a business-as-usual scenario in tourism, even considering current trends in energy efficiency gains, will lead to

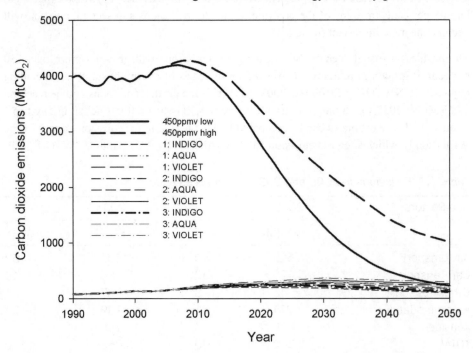

Figure 6.1 *EU emission reduction targets and aviation emissions. CO$_2$ emission budgets for 450 ppmv compared with aviation emissions scenarios based on the UNFCCC data to account for 50 per cent of international flights and all domestic and intra-EU flights. For further details on the scenarios see authors.*

Source: Bows et al. 2009a

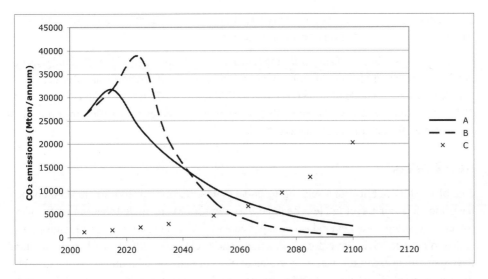

Figure 6.2 *Global CO$_2$ emission pathways versus unrestricted tourism emissions growth*
Source: Scott *et al.* 2010

rapid growth in emissions from the sector (line C). By 2050 to 2060, a business-as-usual scenario would result in tourism sector emissions exceeding the emissions budget for the entire global economy (intersection of line C with line A or B).

These results emphasize the importance of emission reductions in the tourism sector on a global scale, as continued growth in GHG emissions from tourism will be in stark conflict with emission reduction needs as outlined by the IPCC and others, as well as existing climate policy objectives of the international community. Should there be ambitions to reduce emissions from tourism as in other economic sectors, fundamental changes in tourism mobility will be needed (e.g. Dubois *et al.* 2010).

NATIONAL TOURISM EMISSION TRENDS

Despite findings as presented above, many tourism business organizations have – directly or indirectly – argued that tourism is a less relevant emission sector, as it accounts for only 5 per cent of global emissions of CO$_2$ (e.g. WEF 2009; UNWTO 2009). As outlined, this perspective might be correct if the present tourism system is considered on the basis of CO$_2$, but the picture changes when RF is chosen for calculations, increasing tourism's share of global warming from 5.2 per cent to 12.5 per cent, or when future growth in the system is taken into account. The view also ignores that tourism is an activity of the wealthy, with for instance only an estimated 2–3 per cent of the world population participating in international air travel on an annual basis (Peeters *et al.* 2007a). Consequently, residents of industrialized nations show significantly higher levels of tourism mobility if measured on a per trip or travel distance basis (Schafer and Victor 2000; Gössling 2002; Hall 2005), and emissions from tourism in these countries are considerably higher on a per capita basis.

Emissions might also be higher in relative terms, i.e. when the share of emissions from tourism is compared to that of other economic sectors.

There are now studies assessing emissions associated with tourism in New Zealand (Becken 2002; Patterson and McDonald 2004; Becken and Patterson 2006; Smith and Rodger 2009), Sweden (Gössling and Hall 2008), Norway (Hille *et al.* 2007) and Australia (Dwyer *et al.* 2010). Note that these are not comparable, as each of the studies has a different approach to calculations (for details see respective studies).

New Zealand

One of the first publications seeking to understand emissions from tourism on a country basis looked at air travel in New Zealand. Becken (2002) concluded that international air travellers visiting New Zealand added 6 per cent (1.9 Mt) to the country's CO_2 emissions if added to national GHG inventories. Patterson and McDonald (2004) sought to understand the energy intensity of tourism in New Zealand in comparison with other sectors. Combining Tourism Satellite Account (TSA) estimates with environment accounts including direct and indirect emissions from tourism activities in New Zealand in 1997–98, they concluded that tourism was the fifth largest emissions sector when focusing on internal energy use, and the second highest emitter out of 25 sectors when including emissions from overseas travel by inbound tourists. Smith and Rodger (2009) calculated most recently that CO_2 emissions attributable to air travel to and from New Zealand from the 2.4 million international tourist arrivals in 2005 is 7.9 Mt CO_2-eq, if calculated using an 'uplift factor' of 1.9. As New Zealand as a country accounts for emissions of 77.2 Gt CO_2-eq, they conclude that this corresponds to about 10 per cent of national emissions. Air travel attributable to New Zealand residents amounted to 3.9 Mt CO_2-eq, again based on an uplift factor of 1.9.

Norway

Another approach was developed by Hille *et al.* (2007), focusing on emissions related to tourism and leisure activities by Norwegians, i.e. excluding those from visitors in Norway. They included work-related emissions (e.g. conference visits), education such as evening courses or hobbies, free daily time spent, for instance, with shopping, as well as organizational work (for instance in religious contexts), and holidays. GHG inventories focus on CO_2, but include direct and indirect energy use on a lifecycle basis (for a discussion of methods see Aall 2010). Hille *et al.* (2007) conclude that tourism and leisure of Norwegians contribute 4.4 Mt CO_2 to the country's emissions of 33.3 Mt CO_2, i.e. 13.3 per cent.

Sweden

In the case of Sweden, Gössling and Hall (2008) calculated 'Kyoto-relevant emissions', on the basis of a bunker-fuel approach, i.e. including all bunker fuels tanked within the country, but excluding travel by Swedes in countries outside Sweden. Even though it remains unclear whether emissions from bunker fuels will be allocated on this basis, results show that tourism accounts for 11 per cent of national CO_2 emissions in 2001, a figure that is expected to increase to 16 per cent by 2020 in a business-as-usual scenario considering technological efficiency gains.

Australia

In the most recent analysis of the carbon intensity of a national tourism system, Dwyer *et al.* (2010) focus on a TSA approach to calculate emissions on a CO_2-eq basis for the year 2003–04. Dwyer *et al.* (2010) perceive the TSA approach to be more suitable because earlier studies have focused on direct emissions from tourism, not considering indirect impacts associated with supplying inputs to tourism, such as those stemming from travel agencies and tour operator services, taxi, air, rail and water transport, motor vehicle hiring, as well as cafés, restaurants and food outlets, clubs, pubs, bars, food and beverage manufacturing, retail, casinos, libraries and other entertainment services. In estimating emissions from these sectors based on a production approach and an expenditure approach (for details see authors), it is concluded that depending on the approach chosen, tourism is the fifth- to seventh-ranked Australian industry in terms of emissions, accounting for 21.6 to 29.5 Mt CO_2-eq, or 3.9–5.3 per cent of total industry emissions. Note that the lower estimate is not including international aviation (i.e. corresponding to a 'Kyoto-approach', cf. Gössling and Hall 2008), while the higher value includes international aviation of inbound tourists, though only on the basis of CO_2 (i.e. not considering the RF contribution of aviation to global warming). It also needs to be noted that emission factors chosen for aviation appear comparably low and it is unclear whether these consider load factors. Overall, these findings would suggest that on a TSA (carbon *intensity*) basis, and including international aviation, emissions from tourism in Australia are in line with the global UNWTO-UNEP-WMO (2008) estimate, while the carbon *footprint* of Australian tourism is higher, i.e. in the order of 54.4 Mt CO_2-eq in 2003–04 (production approach).

On a methodological note, it is important to understand that studies focusing on energy audits of tourism systems on a national basis use varying system boundaries and allocation principles, and there is no single understanding of what would constitute direct, indirect or lifecycle-related emissions (cf. Gössling 2009a). In the future, a definition of a unifying standard for energy and emission audits is thus warranted.

INDIVIDUAL TOURISM EMISSION TRENDS

The importance of the contribution made by tourism to climate change possibly becomes most obvious when examined on a per capita basis. This is because climate change is ultimately a result of the consumption activities of about 6.8 billion people (July 2009 estimate; CIA World Factbook 2010). In 2004, emissions of GHG in CO_2-eq were about 49 Gt, and of this there was about 27.7 Gt CO_2 (IPCC 2007b). Calculated at 6.5 billion people, average per capita emissions are thus in the order of 7.5 t CO_2-eq or 4.2 t CO_2 per year. However, there are vast differences in per capita emissions between countries and within countries, most of which might be a result of mobility patterns. As Gössling *et al.* (2009: 147) suggest, 'individual emissions associated with food consumption may vary by a factor 2–5, by a factor 5–10 for housing, but possibly by a factor of 100–1,000 for mobility'.

Highly mobile travellers (both for business and leisure) might exceed annual emissions of 50 t CO_2 from air travel alone (Gössling *et al.* 2009; Gössling and Nilsson 2010), corresponding to almost 12 times the global per capita annual average of 4.2 t CO_2 of total emissions, or about 1,250 times the global average emissions from air travel (300 pkm corresponding to about 40 kg CO_2 per capita per year) (IATA 2008a). For the most frequent travellers, there are even reports of flying distances of up to 425,000 pkm per year (Gössling *et al.* 2009a), corresponding to 4,116 times the global average flight distance (IATA 2008b), as well as reported participation in up to 300 return flights per year (Gössling *et al.* 2008).

Even with regard to car and bus travel, there has been considerable growth in distances, with a total of 25 trillion pkm travelled in 2007 (Gilbert and Perl 2008). There are, however, huge differences in individual mobility, particularly with regard to car use: between 1970 and 1990, the average per capita distance travelled by private car increased by 90 per cent in Western Europe to 8,710 pkm (OECD 1996), and similar growth is now observed in China. Gilbert and Perl (2008: 74–75) report that there were less than one million cars on the road in 1985, but numbers had grown to 17 million in 2004 (i.e. by 18 per cent per year). Car owner-ship is still low at 13 per 1,000 inhabitants in 2004, compared to 470 in Western Europe and 760 in the US, and further growth can thus be expected. Likewise, India has still low owner-ship rates of private cars at 7 cars per 1,000 inhabitants in 2000–01, but the average growth rate between the 1980s and 1990s was 9 per cent per year (Gilbert and Perl 2008).

Mobility intensity, transport modes chosen and travel purpose vary between industrialized countries: in Norway, average per capita mobility in 1992 was about 33 pkm per day, half of this for leisure (Høyer 2000). In Australia, average mobility was about 44 km per day per resident (Lenzen 1999), while in Sweden, daily travel was 45 pkm in 2000, about 45 per cent of this for leisure (car: 33 pkm, other: 12 pkm, not further distinguished; SCB/SIKA 2001). In Germany, per capita mobility was 33 pkm in 1995 (car: 24 pkm, air travel: 4 pkm, train: 2 pkm, other: 3 pkm), about half of this for leisure-related purposes (BMV 1996, excluding distances travelled abroad). An analysis by Schafer (2000) indicates daily per capita travel distances (including distances travelled abroad) of 29 pkm in Great Britain (1995/97, leisure-related: 41 per cent), 41 pkm in the Netherlands (1995, leisure-related: 36 per cent), 33 pkm in Switzerland (1994, leisure-related: 50 per cent), and 62 pkm in the USA (1995, leisure-related: 31 per cent).

Available data for the mid-1990s thus seems to indicate that daily mobility in industrialized countries is in the order of 40 pkm per day, about half of this for leisure-related purposes. Out of the roughly 20 pkm travelled for leisure, car travel might account for 70–75 per cent, air travel for 15–20 per cent, and other means of transport for 5–10 per cent. Notably, individual mobility can grow further even in already highly mobile societies, as indicated by car travel in the USA, where average distances travelled by car were in the order of 18,650 pkm in 1990, compared to 8,710 pkm in Western Europe (OECD 1996), a develop-ment that has been going along with simultaneous decline in walking, use of bicycle and bus (see Table 6.4 for data for the UK). Fuel use distribution for car travel is even greater between countries, with for instance annual per capita gasoline consumption being 1,300 litres in the USA, 360 litres in Germany and the UK, 300 litres in Italy, and 240 litres in France (Sterner 2007). In between individuals, it is however known that people with higher incomes travel considerably more than those with lower incomes (SCB/SIKA 2001), point-ing at the importance of individual travel patterns in overall emissions. However, no articles were identified discussing differences in private car mobility on an individual basis.

High mobility in terms of overall distances travelled is, however, primarily associated with the use of aircraft. The role of highly mobile individuals is that a comparably small share of air travellers seems to account for a comparably high share of emissions. This relationship is illustrated in Figure 6.3 for example, of the air travellers from Swedish airport Landvetter, Gothenburg, the 3.8 per cent partaking in more than 50 flights per year were responsible for 28 per cent of all flights in 2007 (Gössling *et al.* 2009c).

Table 6.4 *Average annual distance travelled in the UK per person by all modes (in miles)*

Mode	1975/1976	1989/1991	1999/2001	% Change 1975/1976– 1999/2001
Walking	255	237	189	-26
Bicycle	51	41	39	-24
Private hire bus	150	123	95	-43
Car	3199	4806	5354	67
Motorcycle/moped	47	37	29	-38
Van/lorry	183	301	211	15
Minibuses, caravans, etc.	16	34	24	50
London bus	57	36	46	-19
Other local bus	372	238	199	-47
Non-local bus	54	124	97	75
London underground	36	49	57	58
Surface rail	289	366	368	27
Taxi/minicap	13	42	61	369
Air, ferries, light rail	18	40	48	167
Total of all modes (miles)	4,740	6,475	6,815	44
% mileage by car, van/lorry	71	79	82	
Average trip length (miles)	5.1	5.9	6.7	

Source: Knowles (2006)

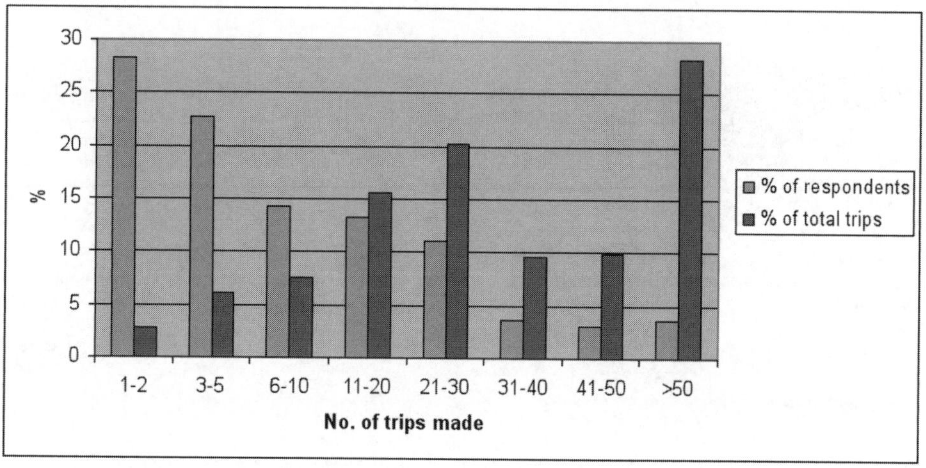

Figure 6.3 *Relationship between air traveller and trip number shares*
Source: Gössling *et al.* 2009

Another example of the importance of highly mobile lifestyles, resulting travel distances and emissions is presented in Figure 6.4, based on the travel diary of a tourism academic keeping track of all flights made since 1983. Flights are registered with Flight Memory, an Internet-based database for people seeking to keep track of their aeromobility. The summary of flights reveals that the academic has spent 1,750 hours in the air in the period 1983–2009, corresponding to 2.5 months of non-stop flying. The 486 flights made in this period covered more than one 1.3 million kilometres, or the equivalent of 32 trips around the Earth. The development of the academic's lifetime aeromobility is shown in Figure 6.5, indicates that there has been constant growth in distances travelled and the number of flights made between 2002 and 2008, when more than 150,000 km were covered by air.

In terms of emissions, the 1.3 million kilometres flown in the period 1983–2009 could have resulted in about 162 t of CO_2, at a conservative emission factor of 0.125 kg CO_2 per pkm, given that aircraft were less efficient in the 1980s and 1990s. The importance of these findings is best illustrated in an extrapolation to a hypothetical mobility of the world population. Taking as a starting point a highly mobile lifestyle involving flight distances of 50,000 pkm per year, i.e. the average annual flight distance of the academic in the period 1983–2009, and multiplying this with an emissions factor of 0.125 kg CO_2 per pkm would result in emissions of 6.25 t CO_2 per year. Extrapolated to the world population of 6.8 billion in 2009, this would result in 42.5 Gt CO_2, i.e. exceeding current emissions of about 27.7 Gt CO_2 (2004) by more than 50 per cent (cf. IPCC 2007b). Such a hypothetical scenario, though far from representing the observed maximum mobility of individuals, illustrates the importance of individual travel patterns in global emission pathways as well as their evolution over time. Growth in tourism and associated emissions should thus be seen in the context of participation (who is responsible for trips), the distances travelled (how far do people travel) as well as travel frequency (how many trips are made per individual) to understand how the system is currently evolving.

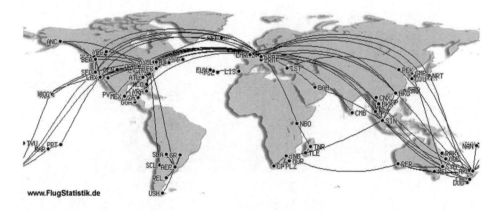

Figure 6.4 *Long-distance flights made by tourism academic 1983–2009*
Source: Flight memory 2010

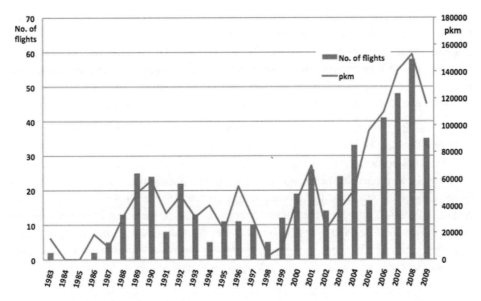

Figure 6.5 *Development of travel distances and flight numbers, tourism academic*
Source: Author's data

PER TRIP PERSPECTIVES

The problem incurred in emissions generated from tourism can also be illustrated from a 'per trip' perspective, as there are huge differences between various forms of holidays, with, for instance, a fly-cruise from Europe to Antarctica (Lamers and Amelung 2007) entailing emissions of about 6 t CO_2, i.e. 1,000 times more than a domestic cycling holiday. For comparison, a 14-day holiday from Europe to Thailand might cause emissions of 2.4 t CO_2, and even holidays often perceived as eco-friendly, such as dive holidays, cause

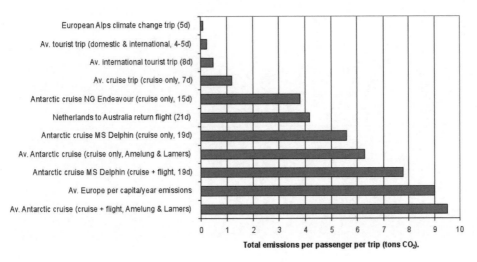

Figure 6.6 *CO_2 emissions of various journeys, 2005*
Source: Eijgelaar *et al.* 2010

emissions in the range of 1.2–6.8 t CO_2 (UNWTO-UNEP-WMO 2008). These figures show that emissions caused by a single holiday can vastly exceed or account for a significant share of annual per capita emissions of the average world (4.2 t CO_2) or the average EU resident (9 t CO_2). In comparison, many holidays cause comparably low emissions, only marginally increasing overall per capita emissions. Consequently, emissions largely depend on the choice of transport mode and the distance travelled (cf. Figure 6.6).

In summarizing these findings, it can be shown that, globally, emissions from tourism can be considered small. They become more relevant when looking at RF in a given year, with tourism emissions accounting for an estimated 5.2–12.5 per cent of global RF in 2005 (Scott *et al.* 2010). However, as climate change mitigation is addressed in national politics, it might be more pertinent for nations to discuss emissions from tourism on a national basis. As outlined, results will be influenced by the system boundaries chosen for calculation, but estimates presented for New Zealand, Sweden, Norway and Australia indicate that in industrialized countries, emissions from tourism can be considerably larger than the global average, both on averaged per capita terms, as well as if calculated as a share of national emissions.

7 Understanding emission growth in tourism

Consumerism has generally increased in past decades, with the Worldwatch Institute (2010) reporting that purchases of consumer goods included 68 million vehicles, 85 million refrigerators, 297 million computers and 1.2 billion mobile phones in 2008. It goes on to report that between 1950 and 2005, metals production grew six-fold, oil consumption eight-fold and natural gas consumption 14-fold. Sixty billion tonnes of resources are now extracted annually, with an average European using 43 kg of resources per day and an American 88 kg. Services, such as tourism, are by no means less energy and resource intense, and the steep rise in production/consumption-related growth in global GHG emissions (Le Quéré et al. 2009) is also a result of tourism. Given the share of tourism in global GHG emissions and the observed and projected growth in this sector, it is essential to understand the mechanisms driving tourist activity.

EMISSION GROWTH IN TOURISM: A SYSTEMIC PERSPECTIVE

Systemically, trends leading to emission growth can be summarized as (1) an increasing number of people (2) travelling over growing distances with (3) increasingly energy-intense modes of transport.

With regard to (1), growth in tourist numbers is reflected in statistics. International tourism arrivals have tripled in the last 30 years from approximately 300 million in 1980 to 922 million in 2008 (UNWTO 2009c). The number of international tourist trips is expected to continue to grow exponentially over the coming decades, and estimated to reach 1.6 billion by 2020 (UNWTO 2001). Domestic tourist numbers are developing at even higher rates, and especially in large markets such as China and India. In China, domestic tourist numbers increased on average by 7.8 per cent per year between 1994 and 2007 and 12.9 per cent per year between 2002 and 2007 (National Bureau of Statistics of China 2009). In India domestic tourism saw 7.1 per cent growth in 2005 and 19.0 per cent in 2006 (Indian Tour Operators Promotion Council 2009).

Second, individual travellers participate in more frequent and more distant holidays (UNWTO 2008), staying over shorter periods of time. These trends will continue: according to WTO's Tourism 2020 Vision (UNWTO 2001), the share of long-haul tourism is

Table 7.1 Energy use associated with different comfort classes

Energy use for air travel over 5000 pkm	Emissions (t CO_2)	Factor*
Commercial aircraft (economy)	0.555	4.1
Commercial aircraft (first class)	1.110	8.2
Private jet	2.125	15.7
A380	253.761	1,880

* Emissions compared to travelling this distance by train

projected to increase from 18 per cent in 1995 to 24 per cent in 2020, which, given the overall growth in tourism, implies that the number of long-haul trips will more than triple between 1995 and 2020. Furthermore, average trip distance is also increasing. In the EU, the number of trips is projected to grow by 57 per cent between 2000 and 2020, while the distances travelled are expected to grow by 122 per cent (Peeters *et al.* 2007a), also because of trends towards more frequent holidays over shorter periods of time (Hall 2005; Dubois and Ceron 2006).

Finally, with regard to (3), travellers increasingly use high-energy transportation and stay in more luxurious hotels (UNWTO-UNEP-WMO 2008). For instance, new upscale hotels might have larger rooms, while existing hotels might upgrade rooms to contain more and more energy-intense appliances. Recently, airlines have, for instance, announced the provision of greater leg-space (e.g. Royal Dutch Airlines 2010), extended features such as wide seats (Traveldaily 2010), or extra baggage allowances of 10 kg for EuroBonus Silver and 20 kg for EuroBonus Gold members by Scandinavian Airlines (SAS 2010). This contributes to higher energy use on a per trip basis. More generally one might also speculate that there is a 'comfort career' of air travellers, going along with higher energy intensities (as indicated in Table 7.1). The hypothesis is that the more frequently people fly, the greater will be their interest in comfort. When this becomes affordable (also through bonus points; cf. Gössling and Nilsson 2010), they will proceed from economy class to first class. Ultimately, travellers would then seek to fly in private jets (a trend visible in e.g. the USA, cf. Cohen 2009), which then would become more luxurious and larger over time, with the most extreme case including a privately owned A380 (USA Today 2007).

With more trips and accommodation capacity worldwide, and the growing energy intensity of trips, future emissions from the tourism sector are expected to increase despite efficiency gains (UNWTO-UNEP-WMO 2008; Gössling *et al.* 2010).

SOCIOECONOMIC DRIVERS OF GROWTH

On the most fundamental level, the two most important explanatory variables for trends in emission growth are (1) changes in income levels and (2) the decline in real costs of mobility. With regard to income levels, there is a strong relationship between income, travel time and travel distance, in the sense that people in a wide range of countries and cultures spend similar shares of their time and income on mobility, a relationship termed Travel Time

Budgets (TTB) and Travel Money Budgets (TMB), originally proposed by Zahavi (1981) and developed by Schafer (1998) and Schafer and Victor (2000) (see also Hertwich and Peters 2009). Travel time remains fairly constant with income growth at around 1.1 hours per person per day on global average, but as higher incomes allow access to faster transportation, the distances travelled grow. This relationship suggests that with any rise in global income levels, overall mobility will grow as well.

While there is evidence that considerable growth in travel time is possible for individuals (cf. Gössling *et al.* 2009a), and that daily travel times vary with residential location, personal characteristics, and household characteristics, Gilbert and Perl (2008) argue that the notion of TTBs may nevertheless apply for aggregate populations. TTBs can thus be used to develop scenarios for mobility growth based on expectation of global income growth (Schafer and Victor 2000). Notably, mobility might also become more energy intense with income growth, as reflected in declining numbers of business travellers during the financial crisis in 2008, and growth in this segment in 2009 (e.g. American Express Business Travel 2009), as well as the more general fact that trains and buses are often used beyond capacity in developing countries, while private mobility is now a norm for a considerable share of citizens in industrialized countries.

As a factor leading to further growth in mobility, and in support of the TTB concept, there has been a decline in real travel costs, in particular through market liberalization and the rise of low-cost airlines, leading to price competition, declining real prices for air travel, and new marketing approaches including 'all-you-can-fly' passes (e.g. Goetz and Vowles 2009 for the USA; Gregory 2009), and concomitant massive growth in mobility in already highly mobile societies (e.g. Palmer and Boissy 2009). For instance, Goetz and Vowles (2009) present data showing constant growth in passenger numbers in the USA (with the exception of the 2001–02 post-11 September period) – despite the fact that almost one third of global passenger transport by air (in trip numbers) already takes place in the USA (IATA 2008b). With the rise of low-cost carriers even in other continents, such as in China (Liang and James 2009) and growing incomes, further strong growth in global air travel and individual mobility is thus likely.

Declining real costs could recently have been reinforced through the global financial crisis in 2008. While the global aviation industry recorded a loss of US$11 billion in 2009, which is projected to decline to US$2.8 billion in 2010 (IATA 2010a), low-fare airlines reported growth in passenger numbers – for instance, Irish airline Ryanair reported a year-on-year growth (Q3 2008 compared to Q3 2007) in passenger numbers of 13 per cent (Ryanair 2009) and now carries 65 million passengers annually (in 2009) (Ryanair 2010). More generally, financial losses in global aviation have been a rule rather than an exception in the past 15 years (cf. Doganis 2006; Gössling and Upham 2009), with accumulated losses of over US$30 billion in the period 2000–05 alone (Goetz and Vowles 2009). Notably, even Ryanair reported losses of €103 million in Q3, 2008, due to rising fuel costs. Another way of looking at aviation is as a system that is heavily subsidized, as airlines could not survive as companies accumulating losses year after year. Subsidies also include the non-taxation of international aviation, leading to competitive advantages for air travel over 'slower' surface-bound transport modes, as well as frequent-flyer programmes, which reward highly mobile travellers with further mobility and other benefits, while seeking to foster high mobility more generally: Air Berlin, for instance, offers 'bargain tickets', 'companion tickets', 'business class upgrades' and 'transferability of miles' to its customers (Air Berlin 2010, see also Thurlow and Jaworski 2006; Gössling and Nilsson 2010). On the production side, because of over-capacity in aviation, airlines appear to be increasingly stuck in the logic of declining profit margins that for years have been compensated for by growth in passenger volumes (Gössling *et al.* 2010). Ryanair (2009), for instance, titeled a February 2009 news headline 'Ryanair beats recession as traffic grows by 13 per cent' (in Quarter 3 of 2008 over the previous year), acknowledging in the same news release that in the same period (Q3) it had made losses of €102 million.

SOCIOCULTURAL AND PSYCHOLOGICAL DRIVERS OF MOBILITY

While the previous sections explained trends, they did not address motivations for increasingly mobile lifestyles, which are usually discussed in the scientific literature in association with changing economic, cultural, social, and political relations (Williams and Montanari 1995; Green *et al.* 1999; Swarbrooke and Horner 2001; Hall and Müller 2004; Connell and Williams 2005; Coles *et al.* 2005; Connell 2006; Lassen 2006; Shaw and Thomas 2006; Dicken 2007; Larsen *et al.* 2007; Ramírez de Arellano 2007; Frändberg 2008a, b). For instance, globalization of business has led to an increase in global mobility, and employees of large companies might also use aircraft as a transport choice (Lassen 2006), even though this might not always be the most cost-efficient or fastest option. Culturally, there might be fundamental changes in the way children grow up in contemporary industrialized countries, with socializing processes fostering and establishing highly mobile lifestyles (Frändberg 2008a, b), and where children are already targeted by frequent-flyer programmes (Gössling and Nilsson 2010). Yet other motives can be found in increasingly global social networks and associated mobilities of labour markets, higher education, family life, migration and diasporic trips (e.g. Larsen *et al.* 2007: 258).

On yet another analytical level, one might discuss cultural and psychological mechanisms fostering mobility, where physical travel has the cultural function of forming and maintaining social capital (for a short review of relevant concepts and a case study see Randles and Mander 2009), ultimately to a point where social structures 'necessitate' (aero)mobility (Thurlow and Jaworski 2006). Culturally and psychologically, mobility interlinks identity and social status, where 'long-haul travel is imagined as providing for the accumulation of experience, which is used to re-narrate and represent self-identity' (Desforges 2000: 942). This might lead to the consumption of distance as a demand imposed on individuals in contemporary society, to which the individual's standing is linked. Highly mobile lifestyles are at the same time supported by mechanisms such as loyalty or frequent-flyer programmes, which reward highly mobile travellers with additional, free mobility or energy-intense upgrades (Gössling and Nilsson 2010). Social status however also appears to be linked to the frequency of travel, the distances covered within given timeframes as well as the energy-intensity of travel. Cohen (2009), for instance, describes trends in the USA towards partial or full ownership of private aircraft, a desire that is also linked to social status as evident from an article in Forbes.com:

What does a billionaire do when having a private jet becomes so affordable that mere million-aires can swing the cost? He trades up – to a Boeing 747–8, say, or to an Airbus 380 – costing $280 million and $300 million respectively. Back in 1996, when Boeing introduced the first 'personal use' version of one of its commercial airlines, the $30 million Boeing Business Jet (a reconfigured 737) was treated as the last word in spaciousness and luxury. Now, compared with competing luxe lifts, a 737 looks like mashed potatoes.

(Sherman, 3 August 2007: no page)

Another example of cultural and psychological change affecting mobility patterns might be new structures in industrialized countries, where social interaction declines, and where there are trends of technological 'individualizing' through the Internet (e.g. Putnam 1995 for the USA). At the same time, human–animal relationships may gain importance, and animals could in many contexts become agents in human health and well-being (Fine 2006), to ultimately become the non-human partners of human beings. This is also reflected in statistics. For instance, the Humane Society (2009) claims that there are approximately 77.5 million dogs and 93.6 million cats owned in the US, with 39 per cent of households owning at least one dog and 33 per cent owning at least one cat. For wealthy people with animal 'partners', it might be increasingly important to move them 'decently' when travelling, and the emergence of airlines such as Pet Airways catering exclusively to animals appears to bear witness to such developments (Figure 7.1).

While the above examples might only be relevant for a minority of humanity, there are also examples of more general relevance for understanding the psychological dimensions of mobility consumption and growth, including the importance of perceptions of getting

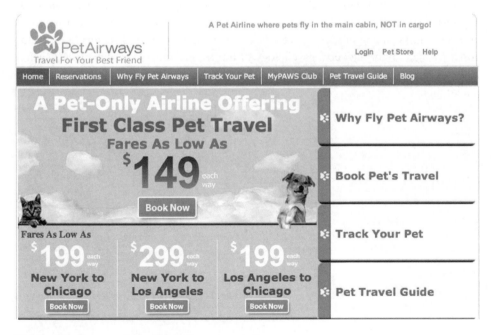

Figure 7.1 *Screen shot of Pet Airways website*
Source: www.petairways.com

a good bargain as a travel motive. For instance, in the case of low-fare airlines, Nilsson (2009) reports that some 60 per cent of low-cost air travel in Europe might be 'induced', in the sense that people choose to fly because the trip is seen as a snatch, not because there has been a specific desire to experience a given destination. From a psychological viewpoint, one can thus analyse low-fare mobility consumption with regard to the role of 'bargains', i.e. people engaging in travel because there is a feeling that they are getting something free of charge or at a comparably lower cost. As Western societies are built on competitive principles (Latouche 1993), a bargain might be perceived as 'winning', for instance over other people paying more for their holiday-trips.

Identity and status as drivers of mobility consumption might also become relevant in other contexts. For instance Randles and Bows (2009) describe the role of flag-carriers in the 1960s as nation-state icons and symbols of national pride:

> We find it also across all the different 'classes of agent' which comprise the aviation sector – aircraft and components manufacturers, airline and airport operators, and air traffic controllers – such that it significantly contributes to a collective aviation psyche. For manufacturers, we see it in state-of-the-art aerospace engineering. For airlines: in the plane-tail livery of 'national flagships'; for airports: in airy chandelier bedecked terminals; for pilots and crew: in passengers moving aside as smartly uniformed teams hurry by: hats and stripes, high heeled shoes, identical overnight trolleys: peacocks of national brands. What we might call the 'clip-clop factor'. In sum it is captured in a word: status.
>
> (Randles and Bows 2009: 1)

Factors such as national pride and the continued role of aircraft and airlines as symbolic icons for nations can thus be added to dimensions of identity and social status in creating systems that are important for societies beyond their contribution to transportation. A better understanding of these processes, or what could be seen as sociocultural factors fostering mobility or the very 'psychology of travel', including even dimensions such as envy, escape, or addiction, may thus be seen as an urgent research field deserving further exploration.

8 Mitigation

Systemic considerations for restructuring

Any systematic approach to mitigation should begin with a review of emission intensities, i.e., a systematic assessment of where emissions occur. This is because dozens of smaller changes in the tourism system to reduce emissions will not yield anywhere near as much as one change in the major sources of GHG. As outlined above, aviation is the key sector in emissions, both in terms of current emissions and future growth, and on scales reaching from global, to national, to individual and per trip dimensions. Consequently, any strategy seeking to reduce emissions from tourism should set out with a review of the aviation system and its foundations. The second sector of importance is car travel, accounting for almost the same level of CO_2 as aviation, though involving far greater trip numbers. Car use is important to address, however, because growth in emissions from this sector is likely with a rapidly increasing number of people becoming motorized, as well as this sector's potential to implement technological change leading to considerably reduced specific emissions. With regard to the third most important sub-sector, accommodation accounts for another fifth of emissions and is another sector that is important to address because of the great potential to reduce emissions from buildings. On this basis, an analysis of UNWTO-UNEP-WMO (2008), based on scenario modelling, has sought to discuss how emissions from global tourism could be reduced.

SCENARIOS FOR MITIGATION: UNWTO-UNEP-WMO

UNWTO-UNEP-WMO (2008) provide mitigation scenarios showing how emissions from tourism could be reduced by 2035. Notably, assumptions made for these scenarios move beyond 'business-as-usual', with for instance 'technology change' assuming far-reaching climate policy environments, including regulation as well as carbon taxes and carbon trading. The scenarios provide a good starting point for an understanding of where mitigation strategies should focus, as well as the challenges associated with achieving absolute emission reductions.

More specifically, two sets of mitigation scenarios were developed by UNWTO-UNEP-WMO (2008), one based on the assumption of technological improvements (higher energy efficiency) and one on changes in tourist consumption patterns, including transport modal shifts, the choice of destinations and increases in average length of stay. To cover a wide range of potential development pathways, a total of seven 'technology scenarios' were combined with 10 'consumption scenarios', resulting in 70 combinations.

'Technical-efficiency' elements:

- Reduction in aviation energy consumption per pkm of 50 per cent by 2035 versus 32 per cent in the 'business-as-usual' scenario;
- additional 2 per cent per year reduction in car transport emissions per pkm over the 'business-as-usual' scenario;
- additional 2 per cent per year reduction in other transport emissions per pkm over the 'business-as-usual' scenario;
- additional 2 per cent per year reduction in accommodation emissions per guest night over the 'business-as-usual' scenario;
- additional 2 per cent per year reduction in activities emissions per trip over the 'business-as-usual' scenario.

'Consumption change' elements:

- No further growth in aviation number of trips and pkm;
- growth in rail/coach of 2.4 per cent to 5 per cent per year to keep growth in the number of trips constant with the 'business-as-usual' scenario;
- 0.5 per cent per year increase in average length of stay instead of a 0.5 per cent reduction per year in the 'business-as-usual' scenario.

In 26 of these scenarios emissions grow by >100 per cent. Only four scenarios result in growth lower than 20 per cent by 2035 over 2005, and only one single scenario actually yields absolute emission reductions (for details see UNWTO-UNEP-WMO 2008). This is a scenario combining high energy-efficiency gains with considerable modal shifts, changes in the choice of destinations, and increases in average length of stay. The results indicate that only strong pressure on the sub-sectors to become more energy-efficient, combined with behavioural change in tourism consumption will lead to absolute reductions in emissions (Figure 8.1 see Peeters and Dubois 2010a).

With regard to results, the 'technical-efficiency' scenario would yield CO_2 reductions of 36 per cent compared to the 'business-as-usual' scenario. This, however, means that although growth in emissions will be slower than in the business-as-usual scenario, no absolute emission reductions, as envisaged by e.g. WTTC (2009), will be achieved, rather than lower growth in emissions than in the business as usual scenario (Figure 8.1). Likewise, in the consumption change scenarios, including modal shift and an increased length of stay, emissions of CO_2 are at best 43 per cent lower than in the business-as-usual scenario, but no absolute reductions are achieved. Only when the two scenarios are combined, can CO_2 emissions decline by up to 68 per cent by 2035, compared to business-as-usual. This corresponds to a decline by 16 per cent below the 2005 baseline, i.e. far less than the WTTC (2009) aspirational target of 50 per cent, and also less than required by international climate policy to stay within the 2°C warming goal in an equal burden sharing between all economic sectors. Nevertheless, several important insights emerge from this analysis:

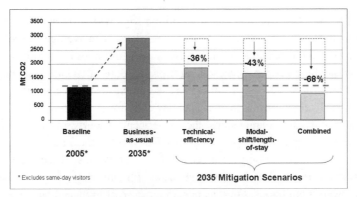

Figure 8.1 *Scenarios of CO$_2$ mitigation potential from global tourism in 2035*
Source: UNWTO-UNEP-WMO 2008

- Increasing length of stay is an economically efficient way to save a significant amount of emissions.
- Aviation efficiency and growth reduction have the most important impacts on emission reductions (–14 per cent if aviation fuel efficiency is increased to the theoretical limits and up to –43 per cent if the global number of air pkm is kept constant at 2005 levels).
- Efficiency measures in accommodations and activities can reduce CO$_2$ emission growth by 14 per cent.
- Only the combination of reduction strategies leads to absolute reductions in CO$_2$ emissions. In all other mitigation scenarios, other economic sectors (e.g. agriculture, manufacturing) would have to take a larger share of the mitigation burden. This underlines the importance of behavioural change and contradicts industry beliefs that technology alone will solve the problem.

The mitigation scenarios indicate that absolute reductions in emissions are possible, even though they are not realistic given the enormous pressure that would have to be put on the sector, ultimately through regulation. Moreover, even in the most ambitious scenario, tourism as a sector would achieve lower emission reductions than other sectors, which would consequently mean that greater reduction burdens would fall to these sectors. As outlined by Scott *et al.* (2010), industry perspectives are not in line with these insights. While UNWTO (2009d) and WTTC (2009) have acknowledged the contribution made by tourism to climate change, these organizations' 'aspirational' goals of emission reductions by 50 per cent by 2050 over 2005 are hardly realistic (see also Chapter 9; Åkerman 2005; Chapman 2007; Dubois *et al.* 2010; Peeters and Dubois 2010a).

SYSTEMIC CHANGE TO ACHIEVE SIGNIFICANT EMISSION REDUCTIONS

Based on these results, it is possible to discuss structural changes that have to be achieved in order to reduce emissions from tourism. Data presented by UNWTO-UNEP-WMO (2008) suggests several relationships of relevance in this context. For instance, on global average and including domestic and international travel, a tourist trip lasts 4.15 days and causes emissions of 0.25t CO_2. This includes 4.75 billion trips with at least one overnight stay. For international trips, average length of stay is 8.3 days, with average emissions of 0.66t CO_2. These results indicate that long trips cause greater emissions in both absolute and relative (on a per day basis) terms, because long trips are more often based on energy-intense transport (by air). Moreover, as outlined, there is a trend for the average length of stay to decline, which is likely to further increase per day emissions in the future. Because of these distance–energy-intensity relationships, the 17 per cent of tourism trips that are made by aircraft cause 40 per cent of the CO_2 emissions. Conversely, the 34 per cent of trips made by coach and rail account for only 5 per cent of all CO_2 emissions. These relationships have been confirmed in regional and national studies, with similar relationships between trip distance and overall emissions. For instance, in the case of France, 2 per cent of the longest flights account for 43 per cent of aviation CO_2 emissions (Dubois and Ceron 2009). In the Netherlands, 4.5 per cent of long-haul trips cause 26.5 per cent of all holiday-making emissions (de Bruijn *et al.* 2008). In the former EU 25, the 6 per cent of outbound trips >4,000 km caused 47 per cent of all emissions (see also Table 8.1).

Figure 8.2 illustrates the trip-length–emissions relationship for all tourism trips with all transport modes made within the EU (plus Switzerland and Norway). Short-haul trips (<750 km one way) currently account for the vast majority of trips (81 per cent), causing 40 per cent of transport-related emissions. Long-haul trips (>2,000 km) and medium haul trips (750–2,000 km) account for 19 per cent of all trips, but cause 60 per cent of emissions. This relationship will become even more skewed by 2020, as the share of long-haul trips is expected to grow from 6 per cent to 12 per cent and the share of medium-haul trips from 13 per cent to 17 per cent.

Overall, a number of conclusions can be drawn from these relationships. First, the main parameters determining emissions are travel distance and transport mode. This is of importance, as tourism actors usually measure their performance based on emissions per pkm or skm, outlining, for instance, the good performance of their carriers on certain relations. However, relatively low 'per pkm' emissions become irrelevant when long travel distances are involved. It thus seems clear that average travel distances have to be reduced in order to reconcile growth in trip numbers with climate policy. An example might illustrate this: for every average air-based trip substituted by an average car trip, CO_2 emissions will decline by 78 per cent. If a long-haul flight of 10,000 km (one way) is substituted with a 'long drive'

Table 8.1 *Distribution of trips, pkm and GHG emissions for distances classes, EU25 outbound tourism*

Return distance (km)	No. of trips (%)	Mobility pkm (%)	GHG emissions (%)
0–1,000	71	31	18
1,000–2,000	16	19	19
2,000–4,000	7	13	16
>4,000	6	37	47

Emissions are calculated on the basis of CO_2-eq, for details see authors
Source: Peeters *et al.* (2004)

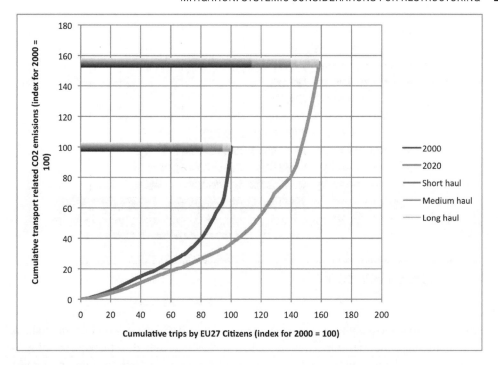

Figure 8.2 *Relationship between trips and transport related emissions of CO$_2$*
Source: Based on Peeters *et al.* 2007

holiday over 1,000 km (one way), transport-related emissions decline by more than 90 per cent (Scott *et al.* 2010).

On longer distances, it is thus essential to reduce trip numbers, or to at least stabilize their overall number. On shorter distances, there is a need to shift mobility from air travel to surface travel, and in particular train and bus travel. Likewise, there would be a need to break the trend towards more energy-intense mobility, i.e. with regard to first- and business-class travel, as well as private mobility based on private or shared aircraft. Examples of the emissions implied in various journeys on a per day basis are given in Figure 8.3, outlining that trains and coaches have on average emissions a factor of 5–6 lower than aircraft (see also Table 8.3). In terms of 'binding' as many vacation days as possible with low 'per day emissions', it is important that average length of stay increases, because in relation to emissions associated with accommodation and destination activities, transport is disproportionally more energy-intense. Calculated on a 'per day' basis, extending average length of stay will thus reduce overall emissions. Notably, the opposite has been observed in recent years, including, for instance, the development of travel patterns such as 'breakneck breaks', i.e. short-stay long-haul trips (cf. Gössling and Nilsson 2010).

These structural changes need to be combined with a perspective on spending and profits to avoid disruptions in the tourism system. Restructuring the tourism system towards low-carbon consumption is, from a business perspective, essentially a process that demands the

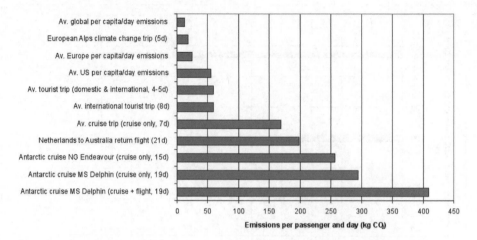

Figure 8.3 *Average emissions for various journeys per passenger and day*
Source: Eijgelaar *et al.* 2010

combination of two parameters, i.e. the lowering of the GHG intensity of tourism products and increasing – not declining – profit margins. This is captured in the concept of eco-efficiency, i.e. the amount of energy or emissions caused to generate one unit of a given currency. Several publications have shown that there are vast differences in eco-efficiency, with for instance one study showing that the eco-efficiency of different tourist types in France varies by at least a factor of 400 (Gössling *et al.* 2005). There are now also studies comparing the eco-efficiency of tourism with other economic sectors (e.g. Patterson and McDonald 2004; Jones and Munday 2007), and, more recently, 'emissions in t CO_2 per US$1 million in revenue' has been used by some companies as a key performance indicator. Carbon Management in Focus 1 shows, for instance, that hotels may emit between 24–490 t CO_2-eq to generate US$1 million in revenue.

So far there are no consistent methodologies allowing accurate comparison of emissions (including direct and indirect, as well as lifecycle emissions, possibly on the basis of RF rather than CO_2) with turnover or profits (including multiplier effects) (see Dwyer *et al.* (2010) for a study working on a TSA basis). On an incoming tourism basis (by national-ity), the usefulness of an eco-efficiency approach is illustrated in Figure 8.4 for Amster-dam, where tourist nationalities where found to have substantially varying eco-efficiencies (Gössling *et al.* 2005). Results allow identification of the tourist nationality with the highest spending patterns in relation to emissions, and, vice versa, those with the highest emissions and the lowest spending pattern. The eco-efficiency approach can also be applied to vari-ous tourist types (e.g. day visitors, nationals, overseas tourists), tourism sub-sectors (hotels, restaurants, or retail), or on a product value chain basis (cf. Jones and Munday 2007). It thus opens up new opportunities to strategically work with emission reductions, because energy use does not seem directly related to the profitability of tourism products, and there is thus room for optimization, i.e. to maintain or increase the profitability of tourism businesses while reducing the environmental impact (Gössling *et al.* 2005).

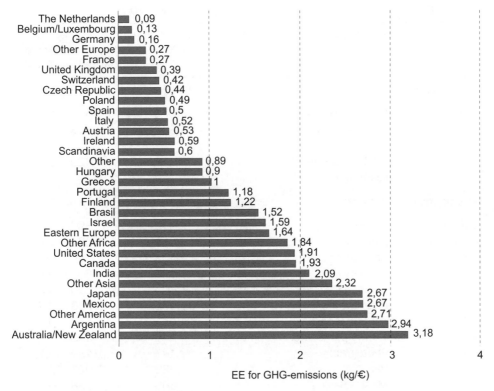

Figure 8.4 *Eco-efficiency by source market for Amsterdam, 2002*
Source: Gössling *et al.* 2005

Eco-efficiencies can also be calculated on a tourism/leisure consumption basis, and be used to identify more climatically and economically beneficial consumption. Hille *et al.* (2007) illustrate this for consumption in Norway, based on expenditure per unit of energy use (in megajoule, MJ). As shown in Table 8.2, there are vast differences in energy use – a parameter closely correlated to emissions on a country comparison basis – per unit of expenditure. Theatres or restaurants, for instance, entail energy use of just 0.2 MJ per NOK, while gyms or all forms of holidays can be more than 12 times as energy intense (see also Figure 8.5).

Results such as these can be used to maintain revenue flows while simultaneously allowing for emission reductions, on the basis of 'high-carbon' and 'low-carbon' spending. This, however, is closely correlated to the issue of profits, as there is evidence that profit margins in tourism have constantly declined in some sub-sectors such as aviation, entailing a need for volume growth to maintain profits. This is, for instance, the current logic of low-cost airlines, which maintain the image of virtually 'free' travel through price structures where the actual cost of jet fuel is often higher than the ticket price charged (Gilbert and Perl 2008). This model has worked for low-cost carriers attracting ever growing passenger numbers, but it has made it impossible for other airlines to remain profitable, with the consequence that fleet renewal appears to have become impossible. Higher profit margins could thus be seen as a precondition for low-carbon restructuring. Taken together, these considerations

Table 8.2 Leisure consumption by people living in Norway in 2001

Categories of leisure consumption		Time spent, mill. hours	Money spent, mill. NOK	Energy use	
				Total (TJ)	Per NOK (MJ)
Holiday journeys		804	18,951	48,039	2,5
Outdoor recreation	Second homes	1,322	14,919	17,555	1,2
	Motorised outdoor recreation	38	3,839	4,813	1,3
	Traditional outdoor recreation	336	17,271	16,029	0,9
Visiting relatives/friends		1,602	24,161	35,718	1,5
Culture/ entertainment	Aqua parks	4	330	397	1,2
	Libraries	16	1,151	684	0,6
	Cinemas	33	1,169	689	0,6
	Concerts	29	1,500	651	0,4
	Museums	16	1,865	1 500	0,8
	Restaurants/cafés	300	30,536	6,783	0,2
	Theatre/opera	6	1,051	175	0,2
	Theme parks, etc.	10	776	293	0,4
Hobbies	Photography	—	2,147	1,439	0,7
	Pets	110	1,929	1,007	0,5
	Music/playing instruments	51	565	328	0,6
Traditional home entertainment	Reading	429	9,701	7 152	0,7
	Traditional games	2,279	3,084	1,726	0,6
Modern home entertainment	Computers/ Internet	580	7 813	11,605	1,5
	TV and radio	3,195	7 683	7,945	1,0
	Audio-visual equipment	562	4,446	5,883	1,3
Sports and working out	Sports – participant	147	5,468	7,401	1,4
	Sports – observer	33	913	700	0,8
	Gyms	46	1,000	1,993	2,0
Organisational work	Religious organizations	61	4,366	3,205	0,7
	Others	111	590	789	1,3
Homes and gardens	Gardening	226	4,170	5,370	1,3
	Redecoration	76	14,169	11,760	0,8
Hobbies-related evening courses		21	593	696	1,2
Conference tourism		144	5,715	7,439	1,3
TOTAL/average		**12,511**	**177,702**	**209,764**	**1,1**

Source: Hille *et al.* 2007

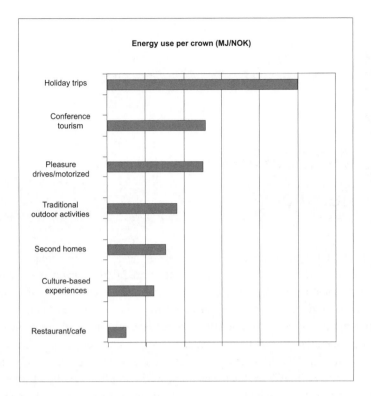

Figure 8.5 *Energy use per Norwegian crown*
Source: based on Hille *et al.* 2007

would lead to suggestions for five key systemic changes to achieve emission reductions in tourism:

1 Flows: from distant to closer markets/destinations.
2 Travel: from high-energy to low-energy transport.
3 Length of stay: from shorter to longer holidays.
4 Spending: from 'high-carbon' to 'low-carbon' spending.
5 Profits: from low profits to high profits.

Mitigation can be based on the principles of eliminating, reducing, substituting, and off-setting (Becken and Hay 2007; UNEP-Oxford University-UNWTO-WMO 2008), i.e. the avoidance of energy use, the achievement of greater energy efficiencies, the use of sustainable energy sources such as renewable energy, and the compensation of unavoidable emissions through offsetting schemes. In considering these principles, the following chapters discuss low-carbon tourism operations with a focus on technology, management, education, behavioural change, politics and research. Each of the chapters focuses on emission-intense or systemically important sub-sectors of tourism, i.e. in particular aviation, cars, accommodation, destinations and food.

9 Mitigation

Technology

Technical breakthroughs are regularly presented as the solution to climate change mitigation, even though speculation on their potential can regularly surpass the real potential of these technologies. Likewise, uncritical reporting on new technologies often fails to adequately address engineering obstacles that have not yet been overcome, or the costs entailed in establishing the infrastructure necessary to replace current technology. In some cases, the information on the emission reduction potential of technology might also be downright wrong, as exemplified by the statement by the Air Transport Association of America (ATA 2009) that 'Since 1978, ATA airlines have improved fuel efficiency by 110 percent, which has resulted in significant reductions of carbon dioxide (CO_2)'. Obviously, it is impossible to improve fuel efficiency by 110 per cent, which essentially would mean that the aircraft generates 10 per cent more energy than it uses to fly. Other reports have suggested aircraft could be powered with solar power, i.e. by equipping wings with solar cells, which is physically impossible given the vast amounts of energy needed to lift aircraft with any significant payload and moving it at commercial speeds (cf. Gössling and Upham 2009). Technology discourses are of considerable importance, however, as they shape public opinion and contribute to the idea that technology can solve all problems while, more realistically, it will be part of, but not the only solution (see also Chapter 8).

AVIATION

In terms of emissions, aviation is the most important sub-sector of the tourism system both in terms of its current and future contribution to emissions. Part of the aviation sector, including IATA, ICAO and most of the major airlines, have outlined a range of technology-based strategies to achieve emission reductions, including new airframes and engines (to be realized through fleet renewal), improved ATM (discussed in Chapter 10, Management), biofuels, and economic measures. These are seen to eventually lead to absolute reductions in GHG emissions about 30 years from now. To this end, IATA suggests that absolute emissions will only increase slightly over the next 20 years because of energy efficiency gains through fleet renewal and ATM system improvements, followed by absolute emission reductions in the medium-term future (by 2035–40), and reaching a stated −50 per cent target in 2050 with respect to current aviation emissions. Importantly, the purchase of emissions credits from other economic sectors is not identified as a component of this strategy (Scott *et al.* 2010). As IATA (2009a) simultaneously suggests that efficiency gains will be in the order of 1.5 per cent per year up to 2020, while growth in passenger numbers is anticipated to be in the order of at least 4.0 per cent per year (Boeing (2008); Airbus (2009) anticipates 4.7 per cent over the period 2009–28), this would suggest that fuel use and emissions will grow by at least 2.5 per cent per year (cf. Lee 2009; see also Owen (2010) for a calculation of recent fuel efficiency gains). Up to 2020, there would thus be considerable growth in emissions from aviation, which is confirmed in other studies, with projected growth rates ranging between 0.8 per cent and 6.2 per cent per year (various periods within 1995–2025; for a review see Mayor and Tol 2010a).

A more realistic scenario on emission growth than provided by ICAO and IATA is presented by the AGD group, including Air France-KLM, BA, Cathay Pacific, Finnair, LOT Polish Airlines, Qatar Airlines, Virgin Atlantic, Virgin Blue, BAA and the Climate Group (AGD group 2009). The AGD group foresees that emissions from global aviation will continue to grow, despite technical and management efficiency gains. In the AGD scenario, emissions from aviation would more than triple by 2050 in a business-as-usual scenario. Technology change, ATM, and sustainable fuels (i.e. 'biofuels') will help to avoid about one third of this growth, and emissions from aviation would consequently grow by just over 100 per cent by 2035 and remain near that level through 2050 in this alternative emission scenario developed within the aviation industry. As outlined by Scott *et al.* (2010), this stands in considerable contrast to the IATA scenario of a 50 per cent emission reduction by 2050 with respect to current emissions.

Efficiency gains

Airlines and their organizations often outline that considerable efficiency gains have been achieved over the past 50 years and that further gains are possible, an argument lately also based on the high price of fuel (cf. Gössling and Upham 2009). Fuel efficiency of aircraft has indeed improved considerably since the 1950s at a rate of about 1.5 per cent per year but, as shown by Peeters and Middel (2007), the speed at which these gains have been achieved has declined (see also Bows *et al.* 2009b). Between 2000 and 2050, the regression line in Peeters and Middel (2007) suggests further gains in the order of 40 per cent, representing a declining trend with annual efficiency gains lower than those expected by IATA. Notably, the new Boeing B787 fits the regression line in Figure 9.1, but the A380 is some 10 per cent above, i.e. not reaching fuel efficiencies as expected in this model. As the development of new aircraft now takes one to two decades, it is questionable whether coming aircraft types will be able to make the hoped for efficiency leaps as indicated in Figure 9.1. Notably, even if such leaps were achieved, it would still take 25 years to replace an existing fleet of aircraft, due to the long lifetime of the carriers.

In this context it should be noted that there are considerable differences in fuel efficiency between airlines. Figure 9.2 illustrates this for airlines serving Sweden, based on a study (Peeters *et al.* 2009) calculating fleet-weighted and seat density corrected energy use per skm in MJ, i.e. not considering actual load factors. Taking these into consideration would lead to even greater differences, as low-cost carriers tend to have newer fleets and

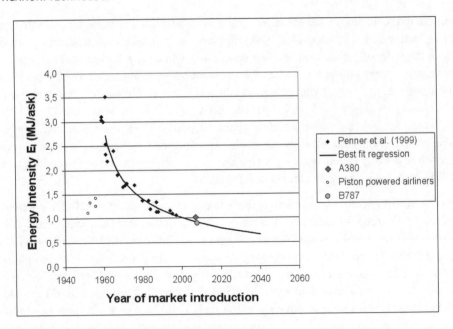

Figure 9.1 *Historic and expected future trends in fuel efficiency for aircraft*
Source: Peeters and Middel (2007)

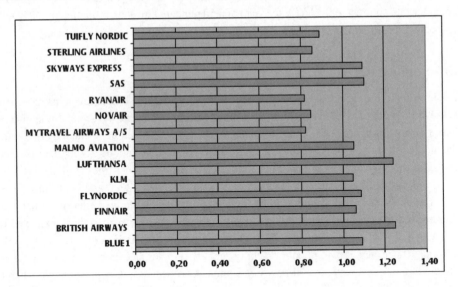

Figure 9.2 *Fleet weighted and seat density corrected average energy consumption per skm (MJ) in 2007*
Source: Peeters et al. 2009

higher load factors. In 2007, Ryanair, MyTravel Airways and Novair had the most efficient fleets, while Lufthansa and British Airways had the least efficient fleets. Flying the same distance with Lufthansa rather than MyTravel would thus have resulted in up to 50 per cent higher emissions, notably not considering load factors.

In conclusion, it appears that considerable improvements in fuel efficiency are indeed possible for most airlines with current technology. Furthermore, new engine and airframe technologies, including gas turbine engines, higher lift-to-drag ratios by increased wing-span, use of wing-tip devices, increased laminar flow on the wings and advanced airframe skin designs such as the 'flying wing', structure weight reductions, and new aircraft configurations could be realized in the future (UNWTO-UNEP-WMO 2008). However, it is questionable whether these will lead to specific fuel-use efficiency gains exceeding 1.5 per cent per year for the world's fleet of aircraft, notably over periods exceeding one or two decades. New technologies also often come as a trade-off – open rotors, for instance, are considerably more efficient but will lead to increasing noise levels (for discussion see Gamah and Self 2010), a major issue, for instance, in Europe. Other technologies might entail very high costs. For instance, restructuring the aviation system on the basis of hydrogen fuels would demand a completely new fuel supply infrastructure. In the light of recent global losses in aviation, it is questionable whether such changes will be financially viable. Realistically, the contribution to mitigation to be made by new technology is thus, over the next 20 years, a relative one, i.e. reducing growth rates in fuel consumption, but not leading to a decline in absolute emissions.

Biofuels

Biofuels are a second option that has received much attention in recent years to reduce emissions from aviation, and they are mentioned by virtually all airlines as a key strategy for mitigation (e.g. AGD group 2009). Clearly, the production of biofuels in commercial-scale volumes after 2030 seems to be the only option to achieve absolute emission reductions in the sector as they do not demand the development of new aircraft and fuel infrastructure, but can be used in existing commercial aircraft (Upham *et al.* 2009a, b; Vera-Morales and Schäfer 2009). However, fundamental questions remain regarding:

1 the type of biofuel to be used (e.g. cellulosic biomass, oil-rich seeds, microalgae);
2 the availability of marginal lands for biofuel production not competing with food production;
3 the biofuel's substitutability for fossil fuels (Jet A), both in terms of energy content (volume) and properties at flight altitude (safety);
4 their energy-input to energy-output ratio;
5 their lifecycle emissions compared to Jet A;
6 their costs.

Several biofuels have been tested in commercial aircraft so far. Virgin Atlantic used a 20 per cent biofuel to 80 per cent kerosene blend in 2008 to fly a Boeing 747 from London to Amsterdam (Virgin Atlantic 2008). In another test, Air New Zealand flew one engine of a Boeing 747–400 with a biofuel blend derived from Jatropha (Air New Zealand 2008). Continental Airlines used a 50 per cent kerosene, 50 per cent biofuel blend (from algae, 2.5 per cent, and Jatropha, 47.5 per cent) to fly a 737–800 in 2009 (Continental Airlines 2009; Vera-Morales and Schäfer 2010). Even though the details of these experimental flights have not been published by the airlines, it might be concluded that biofuels are potentially feasible, at least as a blend with kerosene, as for instance foreseen by AGD group (2009).

Nevertheless, a number of problems remain to be solved. Vera-Morales and Schäfer (2010) outline, for instance, that natural gas-based synthetic oil products would not lead to significant emission reductions, while synthetic oils from cellulosic biomass could reduce lifecycle emissions by up to 85 per cent, but are not feasible at significant scale due to vast land requirements. Microalgae-based fuels demand less, but still considerable, land areas, but need to be supplied with concentrated CO_2, thus potentially increasing lifecycle GHG emissions over those of petroleum-derived jet fuel.

Other problems are incurred in lower volumetric energy-density (MJ/litre) of current biofuels than Jet A fuel (Hileman et al. 2009). Vera-Morales and Schäfer (2010: 6) state for instance, that storing fuel energy of 34.7 MJ requires one litre of fossil fuel-based jet fuel, but 1.5 litres of ethanol, 2.2 litres of methanol, and significantly larger volumes of hydrogen. The implication is that aircraft using biofuels would have a reduced range and for some long-haul routes even blends of biofuels might consequently be impractical. Furthermore, it is unclear which biofuels might be the most feasible. Jatropha was considered as the most promising biofuel as recently as 2007, but it appears to already have been abandoned as a suitable energy crop, while new concerns have arisen about its water requirements (Gerbens Leenes et al. 2009). This is going along with failed investments and socioeconomic expectations – for instance, Lahiri (2009) reports how Jatropha was seen as a major opportunity in India, with millions of US dollars invested by the government to develop plantations. Lahiri (2009) suggests, however, that few saplings have survived, and that it is questionable whether there will ever be any biofuel production.

Other biofuels are currently being developed, with algae being the new focus of investors. Yet again, it appears that expectations on algae exceed their potential, with many technical and biological problems remaining unsolved (Mascarelli 2009). For instance, Vera-Morales and Schäfer (2010) report that growing 1 kg of algae requires 2.2 kg of CO_2 (as fertilizer), of which only a small fraction can be absorbed from the atmosphere. Consequently, CO_2 would ideally have to be provided from fossil fuel burning, leading to a recycling of emissions otherwise released to the atmosphere, but incurring a dependency on fossil fuel combustion. For further discussion regarding the capacity of biofuels to replace conventional jet fuel and wider sustainability issues see also Nygren et al. (2009), Upham et al. (2009a, b) and Thornley et al. (2009).

In 2005, global consumption of jet fuel was 232 Mt (Lee et al. 2009). Replacing conventional fuels with advanced biofuels would, irrespective of the source of the biofuel, lead to considerable area requirements. For instance, Scott et al. (2010) calculated that in order to use Jatropha, an area of more than 1 million km^2 would be required, i.e. roughly the size of Germany, France, the Netherlands and Belgium combined. Based on projected growth in air travel, this area would then grow by a factor of two over the next 15 years. Finding such an immense area for energy crop cultivation, even on the marginal lands on which some Jatropha species can be grown, is likely to be difficult politically. Microalgae use smaller, but still considerable areas. For instance, Vera-Morales and Schäfer (2010) conclude that a land area the size of 11 per cent of peninsular Spain or the state of Colorado would be needed to match current fuel demand in aviation, notably in a maximum productivity scenario for biomass. Other problems pertain to the costs of production as well as the RF caused by non-CO_2 GHG emissions and appear as yet not to have been discussed in the literature. Overall, many studies now seem to indicate that technology alone will not solve emission growth in aviation (Åkerman 2005; Chapman 2007; UNWTO-UNEP-WMO 2008; Bows *et al.* 2009; Dubois *et al.* 2010; Peeters and Dubois 2010a).

CARS

The car is the most widely used mode of surface-bound transport for tourism (UNWTO-UNEP-WMO 2008). Most cars used by tourists are privately owned, but rental cars can be of considerable importance at destinations. Virtually all cars have in common that they are powered by combustion engines running on fossil fuels. These engines, as well as the car design, have become more efficient over time, but most gains have been lost to more powerful engines and higher comfort standards, including A/C or heated seats. Only recently there might be a significant trend towards declining specific emissions per km, at least in Europe, and possibly because of increasing fuel prices, greater environmental consciousness, the financial crisis as well as other mechanisms penalizing or rewarding car choice.

Efficiency gains

As shown by the Council of the European Union (2010), average emissions from new passenger cars in the EU have declined from 0.1722 kg CO_2 per km in 2000 to 0.1535 kg CO_2 per km in 2008, with petrol vehicles becoming 11 per cent more efficient and diesel vehicles 6 per cent in this period. In 2007–08, emissions dropped by 3.3 per cent, the largest drop in specific emissions since monitoring began (Council of the European Union 2010). Paradoxically, however, more fuel-efficient cars can increase mobility in line with the Jevons Principle (cf. OECD 1996), i.e. because of greater efficiency and thus lower costs for travel, travel distances and energy use increase. This is confirmed by Gilbert and Perl (2008), who show that owners of new cars are destined to travel significantly more than owners of older cars, based on six surveys from 1969 to 2001 in the US.

The Council of the European Union (2010) also remarks that the economic crisis has not led to substantial downsizing of the car fleet and that average engine power stayed the same. There has been growing interest in alternative fuel vehicles, however, which almost doubled in number from 2007 to 2008. Yet, they account for only 1.3 per cent of new passenger car registrations (Council of the European Union 2010). Another aspect of importance in this context is the difference in car cultures between countries. These are reflected in national emission averages from newly registered cars, with for instance recent EU statistics showing that cars in Portugal have, on average, emissions of 0.138 kg CO_2/km, while the rates are 0.165 kg CO_2/km in Germany and 0.181 kg CO_2/km in Latvia (Council of the European Union 2010), i.e. representing a difference of up to 30 per cent in new car registrations within countries in the EU. This indicates that in terms of technological innovation, the most substantial reductions in fuel use could be achieved by the use of more efficient small cars, i.e. a combination of lower weights, less power and reduced speeds. This, however, would have to be accompanied by rising fuel prices in order to maintain stable fuel price budgets to prevent people from travelling more, i.e. technology innovation has to go along with policy intervention. Notably, Gilbert and Perl (2008) show that the most important principle to reduce mobility is the prevention of car ownership, an argument supporting Equal Advantage for Non-Ownership (EANO) principles (see Chapter 10, Management).

Alternative energy technology

Future alternative car engine technologies might include electricity-powered vehicles, hybrid cars, and cars using biofuels or hydrogen. Electric cars are more energy efficient than cars with internal combustion engines, and cause no tailpipe emissions. Their overall performance is, however, dependent on how power is generated, with only renewable energies guaranteeing that car use is low-carbon and risk-free, i.e. not leading to emission growth or carrying the possibility of nuclear accidents. Electric cars cannot as yet replace fuel-based cars, however, because battery capacity is limited and loading times are considerable. An exception to these limitations in the use of electric vehicles more generally might be small tourist destinations, where for instance Werfenweng (see Carbon Management in Focus 23) has shown that it is feasible and, in fact, a considerable attraction for visitors to use electric vehicles for tourist movements within the destination – notably with the side effect that visitors arrive predominantly by train.

Hybrid vehicles use both electricity and fuel, i.e. recharging their batteries when running the combustion engine. Hybrid cars can use up to 50 per cent less fuel than cars with combustion engines, but the lifecycle emissions of batteries seem as yet not fully understood. Biofuels for cars have existed for a long time, and in particular E85, ethanol blended with petrol has been used in Brazil for a long time. However, considerable problems are connected with the use of ethanol and other biofuels, for instance regarding land use competing with food production. The Earth Policy Institute (2010) concludes that the USA's focus on biofuel production from grain has had major implications for global food prices, as more and more grain is retained in the USA for domestic consumption as biofuel: 'The 107 million tons of grain that went to U.S. ethanol distilleries in 2009 was enough to feed 330 million people for one year at average world consumption levels. More than a quarter of the total U.S. grain crop was turned into ethanol to fuel cars last year' (Earth Policy Institute 2010: no page). A new report by the Environmental and Health Administration of Sweden (EHAS 2010) also concludes that sustainable production of biofuels for cars is a key issue, but outlines that biofuels could lead to reductions of GHG emissions by somewhere between 4–79 per cent, i.e. their potential is highly dependent on the type of biofuel used and associated lifecycle emissions (for the USA see also DOE/NETL 2009). Another technology to be developed for cars are fuel cells using hydrogen. Difficulties remain, however, with regard to the production of hydrogen, which requires electricity, as well as this fuel's storage and distribution. Overall, there is considerable potential to reduce specific emissions from cars, even though the development of travel distances will, as outlined above, remain a key question in this context: if people continue to travel more, this might outweigh efficiency gains.

CRUISE SHIPS

IMO (2009b: 3) states that there is 'significant' potential for reduction of GHGs through technical and operational measures, with a specific emission reduction potential in the order of 25–75 per cent (Table 9.1), depending on the ship type and operating pattern. IMO (2009b) details four strategies to reduce emissions from shipping: (1) improved energy efficiencies, (2) the use of renewable energy sources (sun and wind), (3) the use of fuels with lower lifecycle emissions, including biofuels and natural gas, and (4) the use of 'emission-reduction technologies' including chemical conversion and capture and storage. As most of these options to reduce emissions refer to technology but sometimes refer to operational and thus management issues, both technology and management changes are discussed in this section.

With regard to improving energy efficiencies, IMO (2009b) distinguishes ship design and operational measures. To this end, an 'Energy Efficiency Design Index' (EEDI) for new ships, as well as an 'Energy Efficiency Operational Indicator' (EEOI) for all ships, as well as guidance principles on best practice for the entire shipping industry are currently being developed. The EEDI determines energy use of new ships, considering intended cargo and speed, and can be used to model different ship choices with the ultimate goal of reducing fuel use requirements. This can include designs of improved hull shape, air lubrication systems to reduce hull resistance in the water, improved engines, propellers and the use of diesel-electric systems as well as wind-assisted propulsion power, solar energy systems to provide lighting, or waste heat recovery systems and shaft generators to improve efficiency. In contrast, the EEOI works as a benchmarking system by measuring how efficiently a ship operates in terms of fuel use per unit of cargo moved over a given distance. IMO (2009b: 4) suggests that the index be used by ports to differentiate their fees, and by 'charterers or cargo owners in connection with energy efficiency branding or in negotiating sub-contracts'.

The use of renewable energy and biofuels is a second pillar of IMO's strategy to reduce emissions, including the use of liquefied natural gas (LNG), fuel cells, fuels with low

Table 9.1 Assessment of potential reduction of CO_2 emissions from shipping by using known technology and practice

	Saving (%) of CO_2/tonne-mile	Combined	Combined
DESIGN (new ships)			
Concept, speed & capability	2–50[+]		
Hull and superstructure	2–20		
Power and propulsion systems	5–15	10–50%[+]	
Low-carbon fuels	5–15*		
Renewable energy	1–10		25–75[+]
Exhaust gas CO_2 reduction	0		
OPERATION (all ships)			
Fleet management, logistics & incentives	5–50[+]	10–50%[+]	
Voyage optimization	1–10		
Energy management	1–10		

Source: IMO (2009b)
+ Reductions at this level would require reductions of speed.
*CO_2 equivalent based on the use of LNG.

lifecycle CO_2 emissions, biofuels, as well as sails and kites. Solar power and wind energy are seen as potentially useful to help meet ancillary requirements such as lighting on board ships, but are not seen as promising as primary propulsion options. IMO (2009b: 6) outlines that:

> Current solar-cell technology is sufficient to meet only a fraction of the auxiliary power requirements of a tanker, even if the entire deck area were to be covered with photovoltaic cells. Wind-assisted power, on the other hand, has a promising potential for fuel-saving in the medium and long term but, as present-day trial experiences of these technologies on board large vessels is limited, it is difficult to assess their full potential and further trials and development should be encouraged. … it seems inevitable, however, that fossil fuels will probably continue to be the predominant source of power for the majority of the shipping industry for the foreseeable future.

Options for reducing emissions of CO_2 through capture are not seen as promising, but there is some potential to reduce other gases, including NO_x, SO_x, CH_4, non-methane volatile organic compounds (NMVOC) and particulate matter (PM). IMO (2009b: 6) acknowledges that projections on efficiency gains are difficult, but suggests that by 2020, a combination of 'regulatory, design and operational measures' might lead to relative fuel savings of around 17–32 per cent per tonne per mile of cargo transported. In other words, absolute emissions from shipping would continue to increase, as efficiency gains are outpaced by growth: 'it would be almost impossible to guarantee any absolute reduction by shipping as a whole, due to the projected growth in demand for shipping worldwide arising from the growing world population and global economy' (IMO 2009b: 7). This certainly is true for cruise ships as well, given above-average growth rates in this shipping sub-sector.

OTHER TRANSPORT

Electric trains, trams, metros and trolley buses that are directly connected to the grid are very energy-efficient transport modes causing low levels of emissions, particularly when purchases of renewable electricity are made. Swedish Railways (Svenska Järnvägen, SJ), for instance, like Swiss Railways, exclusively sources electricity coming from renewable power. According to the company, emissions from one person travelling by train over a distance of 1,000 km based on a lifecycle analysis will amount to as little as 0.0021 kg CO_2, which can be compared to emissions of 0.133 kg CO_2 from cars or short distance emissions of 0.154 kg CO_2 from aircraft (per pkm) (SJ 2010, see also Table 9.2). This indicates that train systems could be operated virtually carbon-free.

There are, however, considerable differences between train systems as shown in Figure 9.3 for intercity trains, mostly due to differences in capacity. Notably, Shinkansen trains achieve the lowest values even though they run at the highest speeds (270–300 km/hour, compared to around 200 km/hour for trains in Europe). Values of 0.03–0.06 kWh/skm correspond to emissions of 0.015–0.030 kg CO_2/skm at an assumed energy-mix emission of 0.5 kg CO_2 per kWh, and are even lower when renewable energy is used.

The actual operational energy consumption for trains depends primarily on speed, landscape relief, and the number of accelerations (Jørgensen and Sørenson 1997). With faster trains covering greater distances, energy use for train systems is likely to increase, but a

Table 9.2 *Environmental impact of travelling 1,000 km by train in Sweden, compared to other transport modes*

Distance	Transport mode	Type	Load factor
1,000 km	Train	X 2000	50%
1,000 km	Bus	Diesel	50%
1,000 km	Car	Fuel, 2005–2009 (Mk 2005)	2 passengers
1,000 km	Aircraft	B737–600	65%

Transport mode	CO_2 (kg)	HC (g)	NOX (g)	Particles (g)
Train	0.0021	0.0057	0.0087	0.0007
Bus	34.8000	15.0000	250.0000	60.0000
Car	95.5000	85.0000	20.0000	20.0000
Aircraft	155.3800	60.0000	460.0000	–

Source: Swedish Railways 2010, translated

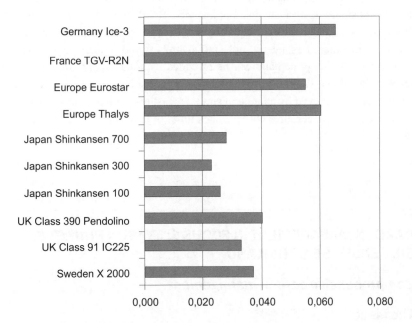

Figure 9.3 *Energy intensity of intercity trains (kWh per skm)*
Source: Kemp 2009

number of technological developments might outweigh growth in demand, including the use of hybrid locomotives, regenerative braking and kinetic energy storage systems (UIC 2007). In order to meet increasing demand in a low-carbon world, railways could also use carriers with greater capacity. For instance, UIC (2007) reports that the French double-decker TGV uses almost the same amount of energy as its conventional trains, but can carry 40 per cent more passengers.

Urban public transport systems include light-rail transit and metro or suburban rail, and increasingly large-capacity buses. Bus Rapid Transit (BRT) systems have been developed in Curitiba, Brazil and are now in place in many South American cities (e.g. Machado-Filho 2009). BRT offers the opportunity to provide high-quality, state-of-the-art mass transit at a fraction of the cost of other options. BRT utilizes buses on segregated busways and can incorporate services such as pre-board fare collection, user-friendly transit stations, simplified transfers and routings, and highly developed customer services. Other destinations in Asia, Australia, Europe and North America also use BRT.

ACCOMMODATION

The accommodation sector represents, globally, approximately 21 per cent of emissions from tourism. Initiatives in this sector are important, as many hotels have considerable options to reduce energy use, which are usually economical. More generally, buildings have been identified as having the greatest potential to reduce emissions (IPCC 2007b), and substantial efficiency gains have been made in recent years in hotels (Bohdanowicz and Martinac 2007; Butler 2008; Bohdanowicz 2009; Ryghaug & Sørensen 2009). Reducing energy can lead to considerable cost savings. For instance, Bohdanowicz (2009, personal communication) estimates that 10–15 per cent of energy consumption can be reduced by simple, behaviour-related measures, i.e. through staff awareness and educational campaigns, while 15–20 per cent of energy demand can be provided by solar thermal in most tropical and sub-tropical locations. The Carbon Trust (2007) suggests that 20 per cent energy efficiency reductions can be achieved by a range of simple measures, with another 12 per cent of savings possible based on measures with payback times of less than two years (see also Carbon Management in Focus 1).

CARBON MANAGEMENT IN FOCUS 1: EVASON PHUKET & SIX SENSES SPA, THAILAND

Comprehensive carbon management

The issue

Accommodation establishments, and in particular resort hotels in the tropics have energy requirements which are considerably different from accommodation in other latitudes. A/C is a primary factor in energy use, demanding large amounts of electricity, which are often produced in less efficient generators (e.g. Gössling and Schumacher 2010; see also Carbon Management in Focus 2, 3, 5, 6). Emissions in tropical resorts can exceed 100 kg CO_2 per capita per day (e.g. Gössling and Schumacher 2010; Chapter 5 this book), and there is thus considerable potential for energy savings.

The solution

Six Senses is a resort and spa management and development company, established in 1995, operating under the brand names Soneva, Six Senses Hideaway,
Six Senses Latitude, Evason, as well as Six Senses Spas and Six Senses Destination Spas. In 2009, Six Senses operated 26 resorts (open or under development) and 41 spas with a total of 1,200 rooms and 3,700 employees under
the Six Senses brand name (Six Senses 2009a). Six Senses has the ambition
to have a net zero carbon footprint in 2010, and to turn into a net sink of emissions by 2020.

In order to achieve this goal, Six Senses has developed an online carbon calculator, which can be adapted to each resort or spa by changing the settings for
emission factors and country-specific details. The calculator was developed by
Carbon Foresight, a company based in Canada specializing in carbon audits
(see Related websites), and considers the GHGs covered in the World Resources
Institute/World Business Council for Sustainable Development Protocol (WRI/
WBSCD 2004). This includes the long-lived GHGs CO_2, CH_4, N_2O, and the use
of a Radiative Forcing Index of 1.9 for emissions from aviation, following the
recommendation by the Department of Energy and Climate Change (2009). Further details on the carbon assessment methodology are provided in Six Senses
(2009b).

Currently, nine resorts have completed a carbon footprint inventory report, i.e.
all that have been operational for at least a year, with data being fed into the carbon calculator on an annual basis. Other resorts are currently recording figures
on energy consumption as well as guest flights, transport of products, water
consumption, waste and food.

Six Senses' carbon footprint inventories cover:

Scope 1: Direct carbon emissions from sources that are owned by the
resort/spa.
Scope 2: Indirect carbon emissions from the generation of purchased
electricity.
Scope 3: Indirect carbon emissions that occur as a consequence of the activities of the resort/spa, but from sources not owned or controlled by the
resort/spa.

The inventory thus covers energy used in buildings (electricity, heating/cooling),
waste, ground travel, air travel, shipping, paper and food, and goes beyond the
framework for emission inventories as recommended by Gössling (2009) for
carbon-neutral destinations, in that even emissions associated with food production are considered. The inventory does however focus on energy throughput, i.e. it does not consider emissions on a lifecycle basis.

Results from the inventories show that the vast majority of emissions are associated with production and consumption outside the hotel, and in particular air travel, which accounted for a minimum of 76.4 per cent of emissions in the nine resorts assessed (Six Senses 2009b). In the case of Evason Phuket resort, 93.8 per cent of all emissions are associated with air travel, with a total of 67,112 t CO_2-eq being emitted by the hotel with its 260 rooms in 2009. Of the remainder, electricity generation is particularly emission intense, accounting for about 4.5 per cent of emissions (Table 9.3).

As shown in table 9.4, Six Senses has compiled an emissions benchmark of the nine resorts audited so far. The benchmark compares overall emissions in tonnes CO_2-eq by scope (1–3), by revenue and by guest night. Results are also compared with assessments by chains Marriott International, Scandic Hotels, and Whitbread. Results show that on a guest night basis, there are considerable differences in emissions, varying between 0.46 t CO_2-eq (Evason & Six Senses Hua Hin) to 1.66 t CO_2-eq (Six Senses Yao Noi). Calculated on a revenue basis, there are also considerable differences, with a factor of 5, in emissions caused to generate US\$1 million (about €700,000) in revenue: for Evason Ana Mandara Nha Trang resort this is 93 t CO_2-eq/US\$1 million and for Six Senses Zighy Bay 490 t CO_2-eq/US\$1 million.

Based on the carbon footprint inventory, Six Senses have implemented various measures at Evason Phuket resort to reduce energy consumption:

- An energy monitoring system has been installed.
- More efficient A/C with mini chiller systems has been installed.
- Water is heated through a solar thermal plant.
- Gas is used as a back-up heat source for solar thermal.
- Water is pumped to a high point, allowing use of gravity for distribution, reducing energy use for pumps.
- Medium voltage (6.6 kV) underground electrical cables have been installed to reduce power loss due to length of running power cables.
- Energy-efficient light bulbs are used.
- A water pond is used to create insulation and cooling for conference room.
- A waterfall serves as insulation and cooling for Kid's Club.
- Natural ventilation is used in lobby and restaurants instead of A/C.
- The main kitchen has been renovated to maximize natural ventilation and light; refrigerators built into wall to dispose of heat outside.
- The power diesel generator has been set on low revolutions per minute.
- A biomass absorption chiller turning garden waste to air-conditioning for the general store has been installed.

The return on investment of these measures has been calculated at ranging between six months to ten years:

Table 9.3 Emissions from various sources, Evason Phuket

Source	Quantity	Unit	CO_2e (kg/yr)	Percentage
Air Travel: Long Haul International (>5,000km)	281,372,662	km	59,369,631.7	88.46%
Air Travel: Medium Haul International (1,000–5,000km)	11,895,131	km	2,224,389.5	3.31%
Air Travel: Short Haul International (<1,000km)	4,028,238	km	1,333,346.8	1.99%
Energy: Diesel	66,633	L	178,576.4	0.27%
Energy: Electricity (Thailand)	5,157,270	kWh	3,006,688.4	4.48%
Energy: Gasoline/Petrol	52,560	L	121,676.4	0.18%
Energy: Liquified Petroleum Gas (LPG)	135,742	kg	207,685.3	0.31%
Food: Non-vegetarian meals	118,265	each	206,963.8	0.31%
Food: Vegetarian meals	39,422	each	49,277.5	0.07%
Freight: Air – Long Haul (>5,000km)	239,680	tonnes*total avg km	143,808.0	0.21%
Freight: Air – Medium Haul (1,000–5,000km)	3,462	tonnes*total avg km	4,569.8	0.01%
Freight: Air – Short Haul (<1,000km)	3,090	tonnes*total avg km	5,716.5	0.01%
Freight: Truck – Long Haul	175,960	tonnes*total avg km	21,643.1	0.03%
Ground Travel: Car – Large Diesel (approx >2L)	131,055	km	34,598.5	0.05%
Ground Travel: Car – Large Petrol/Gas (approx >2L)	9,335	km	2,763.3	0.00%
Ground Travel: Car – Medium Petrol/Gas (approx 1.4–2L)	186,528	km	40,290.0	0.06%
Ground Travel: Motorbike – Small (Moped/Scooter – approx 120 c.c.)	1,173,984	km	85,700.8	0.13%
Ground Travel: Van (diesel, up to 3.5 tonnes)	115,717	km	31,451.9	0.05%
Paper: Office paper (0% recycled content)	920	kg	2,616.5	0.00%
Paper: Office Paper (100% recycled content)	8,223	kg	14,719.2	0.02%
Paper: Toilet paper/ tissue paper/serviettes	22,012	kg	22,012.0	0.03%
Waste: Landfill – Mixed Solid Waste	179,150	kg	21,498.0	0.03%
Waste: Recycled Food Scraps (Organic)	80,935	kg	-9,712.2	-0.01%
Waste: Recycled Garden Waste	149,284	kg	1,492.8	0.00%
Waste: Recycled Glass	8,240	kg	-741.6	0.00%

Table 9.3 *Continued*

Waste: Recycled Metal	979	kg	-1,409.8	0.00%
Waste: Recycled Paper	6,311	kg	-6,689.7	-0.01%
Waste: Recycled Plastic	1,474	kg	-619.1	0.00%
Water: Collected Rainwater	129,638	m³	0.0	0.00%
Water: On-site desalination	2,213	m³	0.0	0.00%
			67,111,943.9	100%

Source: Six Senses 2009b

Table 9.4 Benchmark of key emission indicators, Six Senses Thailand

Site	CO_2e scope 1-3	CO_2e scope 1-2	Hosts	CO_2e per host, scope 1-2	Revenue (million USD)	CO_2e per \$1 million, scope 1-2	Guest nights	CO_2e per guest night, Scope 1-2	CO_2e per guest night, Scope 1-3
Six Senses*	**326,304**	**28,955**	**3,079**	**9.4**	**103.9**	**279**	**432,293**	**0.07**	**0.75**
Soneva Fushi	24,721	4,134	370	11.2	23.3	177	37,458	0.11	0.66
Soneva Gili	20,229	3,236	243	13.3	16.9	191	24,632	0.13	0.82
Six Senses Samui	18,444	2,133	307	6.9	8.5	252	26,913	0.08	0.69
Six Senses Yao Noi	28,846	1,907	246	7.8	5.9	325	17,427	0.11	1.66
Six Senses Ninh Van Bay	33,686	2,054	360	5.7	7.5	274	22,884	0.09	1.47
Six Senses Zighy Bay	42,730	7,104	287	24.8	14.5	490	31,474	0.23	1.36
Evason & Six Senses Hua Hin	52,234	4,201	476	8.8	9.3	454	113,636	0.04	0.46
Evason Ana Mandara Nha Trang	38,302	669	281	2.4	7.2	93	48,504	0.01	0.79
Evason Phuket	67,112	3,517	509	6.9	10.8	326	109,365	0.03	0.61
Resort & Hotel Groups with published Carbon Footprint – only scope 1-2									
Marriott International		2,982,878	151,000	20	13,000	229	–	–	–
Scandic Hotels		23,500	6,600	4	966	24	–	–	–
Whitbread		190,057	33,000	6	4,137	158	–	–	–

Source: Six Senses 2009b

* Figures only include the Six Senses Resorts listed in this table

- The energy monitoring system cost US$4,500 (€3,100), enabling the resort to achieve 10 per cent energy savings as well as to identify areas for further savings.
- Investment for the mini chiller system was US$130,000 (€90,000), which saves US$45,000 (€31,300) annually, and thus pays off in 2.8 years.
- The Quantum heat recovery system cost US$9,000 (€6,300), saving US$7,500 (€5,200) annually, corresponding to 1.2 years payback time.
- The laundry hot water system cost US$27,000 (€18,800), saving US$17,000 (€11,800) annually (1.6 year payback time).
- Efficient lighting cost US$8,500 (€5,900), resulting in US$16,000 (€11,100) savings per year, i.e. taking six months to pay back (not considering the longer life-span of the lights).
- Investment in a water reservoir was US$36,000 (€25,000), leading to annual savings of US$330,000 (€230,000) (less than a month payback time).
- Biomass absorption chiller cost US$120,000 (€83,500) resulting in US$43,000 (€29,900) saving annually, i.e. 2.8 years payback.
- Medium voltage (6.6 kV) underground electric copper cables cost US$300,000 (€209,000). Payback is roughly 10 years from lower energy loss, but other benefits include less radiation, less power fluctuation, reduced fire risk and a prettier resort compared to old hanging low voltage electrical cables.

Impact

Six senses has engaged in an energy and GHG emissions assessment going beyond measurements in most other accommodation establishments, as the company assumes responsibility even for the emissions caused by travel to the destination, and includes non-CO_2 GHGs in its assessment. System boundaries chosen even include food, even though emissions are not calculated on a lifecycle basis. By creating its own carbon calculator, the company can assess various key performance indicators, including emissions per guest night or per US$1 million turnover (€700,000). Benchmarking, even in comparison to other chains, helps to reduce emissions, for which various economical measures have been identified.

Source

Arnfinn Oines, Social & Environmental Conscience, Six Senses Resorts & Spas, Thailand

Website

Six Senses Resorts & Spas, www.sixsenses.com

Related websites

Carbon Foresight, www.carbonforesight.com
Thailand Green Leaf Foundation, www.hotelthailand.com/greenleaf

References

Department of Energy & Climate Change (2009). UK Government Quality Assurance Scheme for Carbon Offsetting. Approval requirements and procedures for offset providers. Available from: http://offsetting.defra.gov.uk/cms/assets/Uploads/New-Folder-2/NewFolder/090514-Scheme-Requirements-version-1.2-final.pdf. Accessed 8 February 2010.

Gössling, S. (2009). Carbon neutral destinations: a conceptual analysis. *Journal of Sustainable Tourism* 17(1): 17–37.

Gössling, S. and Schumacher, K. (2010). Implementing carbon neutral destination policies: issues from the Seychelles. *Journal of Sustainable Tourism* 18(2), in press.

Six Senses (2009a). About Us. Available from: http://www.sixsenses.com/corporate/document/company_profile.pdf. Accessed 4 February 2010.

Six Senses (2009b). Carbon Inventory Report. Evason Phuket 2008–2009. Six Senses Resorts & Spas, Bangkok, Thailand.

World Resources Institute/World Business Council for Sustainable Development (WRI/WBCSD) (2004). Greenhouse Gas Protocol: A Corporate Accounting and Reporting Standard, Revised Edition. Available from: http://pdf.wri.org/ghg_protocol_2004.pdf. Accessed 8 February 2010.

Information on energy use within a given accommodation establishment is scattered, but there are some general insights regarding energy sub-sectors in hotels, with about 45 per cent of energy use in hotels in the UK being associated with heating, followed by hot water provision, catering, lighting and other factors, including A/C (The Carbon Trust 2010). In tropical climates, a study by Trung and Kumar (2005) suggests that 46–53 per cent of electricity consumption is for A/C and ventilation, while lighting and water heating account for 12–27 per cent each. Other electricity use (lifts, pumps, refrigerators) is less relevant at 4–17 per cent. Yet another study of hotels in Sicily suggests that in upscale hotels (four and five stars), electricity consumption on an end-use basis is primarily for HVAC (35 per cent), lighting (35 per cent), cooking and food refrigeration (15 per cent), hotel services (10 per cent) and losses (5 per cent). Thermal energy is primarily used for hot water (40 per cent), cooking (25 per cent) and air heating (35 per cent) (Beccali *et al.* 2009; see also Chapter 5). Studies would thus indicate that a management focus on heating and A/C is paramount.

Accommodation establishments can save considerable amounts of money through various measures, including approaches to heating and A/C, as well as new management approaches with regard to food and beverages such as bottled water. According to the Carbon Trust (2010: no page) in the UK, 'the hospitality sector is responsible for over 3.5 million tonnes of carbon emissions per year. It is estimated that energy savings of up to 20%, equivalent to more than £200 million, are possible across the sector'. Likewise, in the USA, Energy Star (2010: 1) reports that: 'On average, America's 47,000 hotels spend $2,196 per available room each year on energy. This represents about 6 percent of all operating costs.' While hotels thus have much to earn from carbon management, they might also be the sector with the highest support by governments, organizations and customers to restructure and retrofit towards low-carbon operations. For instance, the EU co-financed the Hotel Energy Solutions scheme (www.hotelenergysolutions.net), coordinated with the UNWTO, UNEP, International Hotel & Restaurant Association, European Renewable Energy Council and the French Environment and Energy Management Agency. The scheme helps small- and medium-sized hotels in the EU to increase energy efficiency and use renewable technologies. Notably, there is now also a rapidly growing number of companies specializing in technology-based energy management solutions (see Related websites in Carbon Management in Focus case studies).

The most important measure in existing accommodation establishments is eventually to reduce energy use. Where most energy is used for heating or cooling, adjusting room temperatures is a key measure. This can be facilitated through technology, including digital measurement and control units, which for instance heat/cool rooms only shortly before they are used, or shut down A/C when balcony doors are opened. Building design, including positioning, material and insulation can provide an important precondition for maintaining temperatures in the desired range and considerably reduce overall energy use (e.g. Chan and Lam 2003). Likewise, it is crucial to have A/C units and heating in the right locations to avoid inefficient use, and to regularly service units (cleaning filters and coils for A/C) (Becken and Hay 2007; UNWTO-UNEP-WMO 2008). Carbon Management in Focus case studies also show that wherever A/C is used, there are innovative solutions to reduce electricity use – by 40 per cent (Coral Lodge, Carbon Management in Focus 2) to 98 per cent (Hotel Victoria, Carbon Management in Focus 6). Hilton hotels in Prague, Malta and Tel Aviv have also experimented with using river and seawater for cooling (Paulina Bohdanowicz, Hilton Europe Sustainability Manager, personal communication 2009; see also Carbon Management in Focus 3). Other technical measures can include energy efficient lighting, electricity saving devices such as master switches and key cards, intelligent space temperature controls, heat recovery systems, for instance in kitchen ventilation, and building management systems more generally (see also Carbon Management in Focus 6).

CARBON MANAGEMENT IN FOCUS 2: CORAL LODGE 15.41, MOZAMBIQUE

Reducing energy for air conditioning

The issue

A/C is one the main energy consuming factors in hotels in tropical environments. Reducing A/C energy use is thus an important factor in reducing operational costs, while at the same time contributing to climate change mitigation. Large hotels located close to the sea might be able to use cold deep-sea water for cooling (see Carbon Management in Focus 3) or cold water from wells (see Carbon Management in Focus 6), but such solutions are not feasible for smaller hotels.

The solution

Coral Lodge 15.41 (15.41 refers to the latitude at which the hotel is located) is a small, exclusive lodge opened in February 2010. It offers 10 villas, each of them 100 m² in size. The villas are located in the northern part of Mozambique, close to the Western Indian Ocean. As the size of the villas would have made it difficult and expensive to cool them with a conventional A/C system, Evening Breeze was chosen, a micro-A/C system set up directly over the bed. As the system only cools part of the room, i.e. the immediate bed environment, energy use is considerably lower than that of standard A/C systems. The system is also different in that rooms do not have to be sealed for A/C to work – open windows have no considerable impact on energy use and allow for the exchange of fresh air. During the day, rooms are not cooled, thus further reducing energy use.

Evening Breeze was developed by two Dutchmen, Thomas van den Groendendaal and Yoeri Nagtegaal, in cooperation with Delft University of Technology, with the goal of finding an alternative for standard A/C to reduce energy use. Evening Breeze is connected to an outdoor unit to transport heat outside. The system's cooling capacity is 5,000 BTU. The system is still quite energy-intense, but since only a small area is cooled, the system uses, according to Evening Breeze (2009), 60 per cent less energy compared with a system cooling the full room, i.e. 400 W rather than the 1,200 W of standard cooling systems. Per day, this amounts to savings of about 8 kWh, assuming that the system runs 10 hours per day, or, at an assumed rate of €0.25 per kWh, savings of €2 per day. In terms of investment costs, in- and outside unit, airduct, mosquito net, aluminium rails and textile ventilation sock cost about €1,800 per bed (not including the cost of transport), according to Bart Otto, the Managing Director of Coral Lodge 15.41. At an average occupancy rate of 50 per cent, the investment cost in the system will thus pay off within 5–6 years.

Importantly, the system allows the user to adjust to four cooling stages, 'Breeze', which is just passive cooling by air circulation comparable to a ceiling fan; 'Fresh', which is active cooling up to 3 °C below ambient room temperature; 'Cool', up to 5 °C below ambient room temperature; and 'Cold', up to 7 °C below ambient room temperature. Air is drawn from under the bed into the cooling system, which also reduces humidity before transporting the air back to the bed ceiling, from where it spreads through a textile ventilation system over the bed. Part of the cool air is then re-used in the system, creating an efficient cooling cycle. This results in a noise- and draft-free sleeping environment, according to Thomas van den Groenendaal, Founder and Director of Evening Breeze.

Impact

A/C is the major factor of energy use in many hotels, and alternative cooling systems have thus a considerable impact on overall energy use and costs. Evening Breeze is a cost-efficient solution leading to considerably lower energy use, and could thus make a considerable contribution to climate change mitigation.

Source

Bart Otto, Managing director, Coral Lodge 15.41, Mozambique
Thomas van den Groenendaal, Founder and Director, Evening Breeze, The Netherlands

Website

Evening Breeze, www.evening-breeze.com
Coral Lodge 15.41, www.corallodge1541.com

References

Evening Breeze (2009). Evening Breeze Catalogue 2010. Available from: http://www.evening-breeze.com/presentations/EB_CANOPI_Brochure_ENG.pdf Accessed 7 January 2010.

CARBON MANAGEMENT IN FOCUS 3: PACIFIC BEACHCOMBER S.C., FRENCH POLYNESIA

Sea Water Air Conditioning to minimize energy use

The issue

Hotels, particularly in sub-tropical and tropical climates, use considerable amounts of energy for A/C (Yik et al. 2001). Where A/C is regularly used, it is usually the most important factor in overall energy consumption. Note that this situation is different in temperate climates, where A/C can be one of the most important factors in electricity consumption, but space heating and domestic hot water are usually more important in terms of overall energy use (see Chapter 5 and Carbon Management in Focus 2, 6), accounting for about half of energy requirements (e.g. Bohdanowicz and Martinac 2007). Electricity for A/C is also costly, and can account for a considerable share of the operational costs of a hotel room, particularly in tropical islands (e.g. Gössling and Schumacher 2010).

The solution

Pacific Beachcomber S.C. is a hotel group based in Tahiti, owning six hotels in French Polynesia. Four of the hotels are managed through the InterContinental Hotel Group, and two through Hotel Management & Services, a management company also owned by Pacific Beachcomber. The InterContinental Resort Thalasso & Spa of Bora Bora, French Polynesia, is a hotel with 83 overwater bungalows. It was opened in 2006, and claims to be the first accommodation establishment in the world to use deep-sea water for cooling, a process called Sea Water Air Conditioning (SWAC). When the hotel was planned, several reasons made SWAC an interesting alternative to A/C. First of all, as outlined by Laurent Le Breton, Assistant Manager of the Pacific Beachcomber S.C., A/C is responsible for up to 55 per cent of electricity consumption in hotels in French Polynesia, where electricity is expensive and expected to become even more expensive in the future. As the government of French Polynesia has a goal to produce 50 per cent of energy renewably by 2020, there was also an incentive in terms of government subsidies covering 60 per cent of the investment costs.

The reason why A/C is costly is because cold production with electricity is inefficient (Figure 9.4): 78 per cent of the primary energy is wasted, and only 22 per cent is converted into cold. This is because electricity is produced in generators in many hotels in the tropics, with conversion losses of 60 per cent. Of the

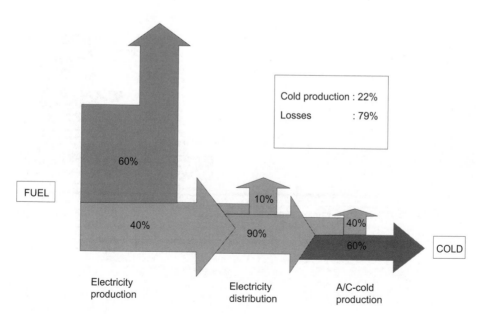

Figure 9.4 *Energy loss for cold production*
Source: Le Breton *et al.* (2008)

electricity produced, another 10 per cent is lost through distribution, and of the remainder, another 40 per cent in air conditioners.

SWAC can be an alternative to conventional air conditioning. Cool deep-sea water, the prerequisite for using SWAC, is readily available at depths of around 1,000 m. At this depth, water temperatures reach 5 °C in the area and is stable all year long, i.e. close to the coldest deep-sea water temperature of 4 °C, the point at which water reaches its greatest density. The SWAC system uses deep-sea water to cool fresh (warm) water through a heat exchanger in a circulating system. The fresh water cools air in hotel rooms, public spaces, and offices and is then recirculated through the heat exchanger. The InterContinental Resort Thalasso & Spa pumps up cold seawater through a 2,300 m-long pipe with a diameter of 400 mm and returns warm water through a return pipeline with a diameter of 630 mm. The temperature of the deep-sea water is 5.0–5.5 °C when pumped up from 900 m depths, and 12 °C when it leaves the system and is discharged into the sea. The pipe has a water intake of 270 m³ per hour and produces 1,500 kW of cold (for a schematic overview of the SWAC system see Figure 9.5).

Figure 9.6 shows how the pipeline is constructed (Le Breton et al. 2008). The first part of it can be buried. When reaching the slope, the pipeline has to be anchored to protect it against storms or other disturbances. Once the pipeline has reached deeper water (45 m), concrete rings are attached as ballast anchors to hold it down. An important technical detail is that the InterContinental Resort Thalasso

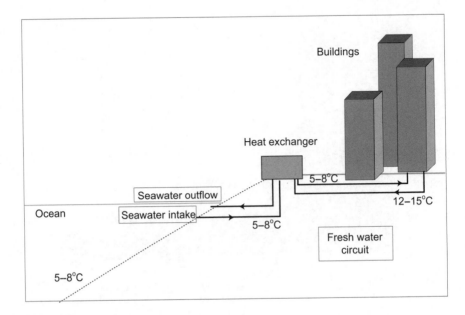

Figure 9.5 *Schematic overview of SWAC system*
Source: Le Breton *et al.* (2008)

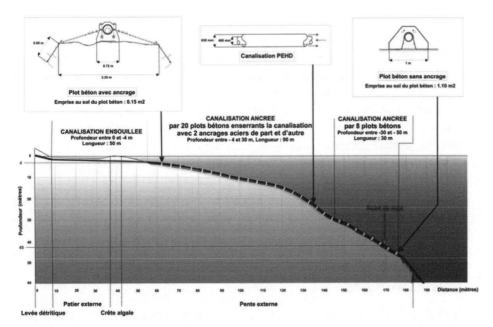

Figure 9.6 Technical details of SWAC system
Source: Le Breton et al. (2008)

& Spa used a coaxial pipeline (shown on top in the middle of Figure 9.6). As the pipeline's diameter is small (40 cm), heat loss is high. To reduce heat loss, the 40 cm pipeline for water intake is placed in a 63 cm pipeline containing the 'used' cold water pumped back from the heat exchange unit at a temperature of around 14 °C. Though no longer suitable for cold production, this water is still considerably colder than the surface seawater at 28 °C, and functions as a heat insulator. Heat loss of cold water is limited to 1 °C in this system.

In terms of difficulties entailed with implementation, the planning and construction process for the SWAC system reportedly took 18 months, as a wide range of aspects had to be considered, including geophysics and hydrodynamics, environmental aspects (ecosystem disturbances, impacts on species, protected areas), as well as pipeline sizing, construction and anchorage, and thermal sizing (heat losses, circulation speed). Investment costs for the system were in the order of €6.6 million, but it is estimated that the return on investments is €1 million per year in avoided generator diesel and related costs, also cutting emissions by 2,500 t CO_2 per year. Electricity consumption of SWAC is estimated to be 90 per cent lower than with conventional A/C.

Impact

SWAC can be considered as a reliable, economic low-carbon technology, which can be operated at low costs for periods of 50 years or more. Implementation of such a project is however complex: 'Building anything in a remote island of the Pacific Ocean is a challenge in itself. The lack of materials and equipment adapted to each of the phases of construction makes things difficult' (Le Breton *et al.* 2008: 7). SWAC can, however, be used for all sizes of projects wherever cold water is available and A/C is needed, from whole cities to small hotels (see also Carbon Management in Focus 6). It is financially viable and increasingly so with rising energy prices.

Source

Laurent Le Breton, Assistant Managing Director, Pacific Beachcomber S.C.

Website

Pacific Beachcomber S.C., www.pacificbeachcomber.com

Related websites

Makai Ocean engineering, www.makai.com/p-swac.htm (instals SWAC systems)
Ocean and Deep Water Engineering, www.odewa.com (instals SWAC systems)

References

Bohdanowicz, P. and Martinac, I. (2007). Determinants of benchmarking of resource consumption in hotels – case study of Hilton International and Scandic in Europe. *Energy and Buildings* 39(1): 82–95.

Gössling, S. and Schumacher, K. (2010). Implementing carbon neutral destination policies: issues from the Seychelles. *Journal of Sustainable Tourism* 18(2), in press.

Le Breton, L., Lombard, P. and Colinet, M. (2008). Sea Water Air Conditioning in French Polynesia. Paper presented at the 2nd International Conference on Ocean Energy (IOCE, 2008), Brest, France, 15–17 October 2008.

Yik, F.W.H., Burnett, J. and Prescott, I. (2001). Predicting air-conditioning energy consumption of a group of buildings using different heat rejection methods. *Energy and Buildings* 33(2): 151–166.

Other technology-based measures include the adjustment of boilers to maintain water temperatures for guest showers at just under 60 °C, while limiting overall water use by installing low-flow showerheads. Further measures, such as heat exchangers to recover heat from wastewater pipes, are technically feasible (UNWTO-UNEP-WMO 2008). Energy use for hotel pools can be reduced by installing solar water heaters and heat pumps, while reducing heat loss by using pool covers. Often, such measures have very short payback times. New light technology, including energy-efficient light bulbs with long lifetimes, as well as LED-based lighting can also considerably reduce energy use, as can room card systems shutting down energy use in rooms when guests are leaving. More recent innovative approaches include water-bottling systems to reduce transports, as shown by Scandic Hotels, which can be economically profitable and have considerable environmental benefits. Food management more generally also offers wide-ranging opportunities to reduce emissions.

CARBON MANAGEMENT IN FOCUS 4: SCANDIC HOTELS, SWEDEN

Phasing out bottled water

The issue

All food transports entail considerable emissions. Bottled water in particular has received attention as a carbon-intense product, as manufacturing of plastic or glass bottles, water treatment, bottling and labelling, chilling for sale and use, collection and recycling, and in particular transport of the heavy end-product all entail considerable emissions (Gleick and Cooley 2009). As water is readily available in drinking quality in many industrialized countries, bottled water has also been called an 'unnecessary luxury' (Konsumentföreningen Stockholm 2007).

In their comprehensive analysis of bottled water, Gleick and Cooley (2009) compare energy inputs of various stages of production in the US. Notably, these are based on an energy input analysis (i.e. not a lifecycle analysis) and do not include disposal and/or collection, processing and recycling. Manufacturing PET (polyethylene terephthalate) plastic bottles requires the largest share of energy in the production process. These results are confirmed by a Swedish study (Angervall *et al.* 2004), which also concludes that returnable glass bottles are environmentally favourable over recyclable plastic bottles. However, the overall outcome depends on transport distance and mode (see also Colman and Päster 2007 for wine). The US, for instance, imports water from as far as France or the South Pacific, which can entail energy use exceeding that used in the manufacturing of plastic bottles by up to 45 per cent (Table 9.5). In total, bottled water requires energy inputs between 5.6–10.2 MJ per litre (Gleick and Cooley 2009).

Extrapolated, the consumption of 33 billion litres of bottled water in the US in 2007 could have required an energy input equivalent to 32 to 54 million barrels of oil, or emissions of 12.6–21.4 Mt of CO_2. Calculated per litre of water, this

Table 9.5 Total energy requirements for producing bottled water (MJ per litre)

	Energy intensity ($MJ_{(th)} l^{-1}$)
Manufacture plastic bottle	4.0
Treatment at bottling plant	0.0001–0.02
Fill, label, and seal bottle	0.01
Transportation: range from three scenarios	1.4–5.8
Cooling	0.2–0.4
Total	5.6–10.2

Source: Gleick and Cooley (2009)

corresponds to 0.380–0.650 kg CO_2. Consumers in the US drank an average of about 110 litres of bottled water per person in 2007 (Gleick and Cooley 2009). Associated emissions would thus have been in the order of 42–72 kg CO_2 per capita per year. This does not seem much, but corresponds to about 1.5 per cent of sustainable annual emissions (calculated at 50 kg CO_2 out of 3,500 kg CO_2).

A similar study for Sweden (Konsumentföreningen Stockholm 2007) found that consumption of bottled water (both glass and PET) caused emissions of 34,000 t CO_2 in 2006, up from 9,500 t CO_2 in 1992. Calculated per litre (total: 247 million litres in 2006) on a lifecycle basis, this corresponds to about 0.130 kg CO_2 per litre. This is an average value including imported waters; Swedish bottled water causes emissions roughly one third of this. The comparison shows that emissions associated with bottled water are considerably lower in Sweden than in the US; nevertheless, there has been remarkable growth in bottled water consumption in recent years, and both the US and Sweden are still far from per capita consumption as observed in for instance Italy (184 litres per capita in 2004; Worldwater 2009). Notably, 16.5 per cent of all bottled water (200 billion litres) is currently consumed in the US (Gleick and Cooley 2009). Results should also be seen in context: bottled water is just one form of beverage with a high carbon footprint. For instance, apart from 33 billion litres of bottled water, US citizens also consume 57 billion litres of carbonated soft drinks and 24 billion litres of beer (Gleick and Cooley 2009). It can be assumed that similar figures can be found in many other industrialized countries.

The solution

Scandic is a European hotel chain with 141 hotels in 10 countries, including Sweden, Denmark, Finland, Norway, Estonia, Lithuania, Germany, the Netherlands, Belgium and Poland. The hotels total 25,333 rooms, and the chain recorded 7.8 million bed nights in 2008. Scandic made a decision to reduce emissions of CO_2 by 50 per cent by 2011 (compared to 1996, when emissions were calculated for the first time), and to no longer emit emissions from fossil fuels by 2025. Even though this goal only includes emissions associated with Scandic's core business, strategies were discussed to even improve the emissions balance of e.g. food and beverage purchases. In 2008, the decision was made to phase out bottled water: according to Konsumentföreningen Stockholm (2007), each 33 cl bottle of water in Sweden results in emissions of 0.044 kg CO_2, and the 3.6 million bottles sold in Scandic Hotels annually thus caused emissions of 160 t CO_2 per year.

As a replacement for bottled water, guests are now provided with filtered and carbonized (if requested) tap water. Where the water quality cannot be taken for granted, water analyses are carried out to ensure high quality. The water is provided in bottles designed specifically for Scandic by Jonas Torstensson and Swedish Olympic swimmer Therese Alshammar. Bottles are produced in Spain from recycled glass. A 40 cl bottle is sold to guests at 25 Swedish crowns (about €2.5) and an 80 cl bottle at 49 Swedish crowns (€4.9). According to Inger Mattsson, Scandic's manager for sustainable business, the new bottled water is well received by guests, and no complaints have been received. Scandic still offers bottled water for guests who want to take a plastic bottle with them outside the hotel, but within the hotel, all sales of bottled water have ceased.

The decision to replace bottled water with tap water was made in spring 2008, notably without any studies on customer perceptions of the new product. Scandic's food and beverage group, together with the former manager for sustainable business operations, suggested replacing bottled water to reduce emissions. The board accepted the suggestion, and by December 2008 bottled water had been phased out in 150 hotel restaurants.

Water analyses, where needed, were carried out by Cafebar. Cafebar also installed water pumps, water filters and carbonizing systems, which are produced by Escowa (see Related websites). Scandic's bottled water system also has a payback time that is 'interesting from a business point of view' (Inger Mattsson). Inger Mattsson emphasizes, however, that the system was not introduced to generate profits, but to strengthen Scandic's profile as the leading sustainability innovator. Scandic also collects 1 Swedish crown (€0.1) from each sold bottle for a new sustainability fund. Not-for-profit organizations and individuals will be able to apply for grants – in 2010, the first 1 million Swedish crowns (€100,000) will be given to projects seeking to develop sustainability issues.

Impact

Scandic's focus on their own bottled water system is not only feasible from a customer perception point of view, it also leads to considerable reductions in emissions and generates profit, as payback times are short. This is thus another business case combining an environmental strategy with new income opportunities, while positively enhancing the brand name.

Source

Inger Mattsson, Manager Sustainable Business, Scandic Hotels

Website

Scandic Hotels, www.scandichotels.com

Related websites

Cafebar, www.cafebar.co.uk/
Escowa, www.escowa.se/

References

Angervall, T., Flysjö, A. and Mattsson, B. (2004). Jämförelse av dricksvatten – översiktlig livscykelanalys (Comparison of drinking water – an understandable lifecycle analysis). Gothenburg: The Swedish Institute for Food and Biotechnology. Available from: http://www.konsumentforeningenstockholm.se/upload/Konsumentfrågor/SIK_vattenrap-port_maj_2004.pdf. Accessed 7 October 2009.

Colman, T. and Päster, P. (2007). Red, white and green – the cost of carbon in the global wine trade. American Association of Wine Economists. Available from: http://www.wine-economics.org/workingpapers/AAWE_WP09.pdf. Accessed 7 October 2009.

Gleick, P.H. and Cooley, H.S. (2009). Energy implications of bottled water. *Environmental Research Letters* 4: doi: 10.1088/1748–9326/4/1/014009.

Konsumentföreningen Stockholm (2007). Totala koldioxidutsläpp fran konsumtionen av buteljerat vatten i Sverige (*Total emissions from the consumption of bottled water in Sweden*). Available from: http://www.konsumentforeningenstockholm.se/upload/Konsumentfrågor/RAPPORT_CO$_2$_av_buteljerat_vatten_2007.pdf. Accessed 7 October 2009.

Worldwater (2009). Per capita bottled water consumption, by country, 1999–2004. Available at: http://www.worldwater.org/data20062007/Table13.pdf. Accessed 7 October 2009.

Investments in energy efficiency might be complemented with a focus on renewable energy, which can either be purchased from power providers, often at no or only small price differences (e.g. Gössling *et al.* 2005), or investments in renewable energy technology more generally. When renewable energy is purchased directly from power providers, it is essential to ensure that additional renewable energy capacity corresponding to the amount of energy purchased is actually installed by the power provider. To illustrate this: when a company decides to buy 1 million kWh of renewable power, the power provider should invest in additional capacity to generate this amount. A critical approach to 'green' power purchases is necessary, because some power providers have started to sell the renewable electricity that is in their portfolio at a premium to environmentally aware customers – with the only consequence that other customers purchase higher shares of coal, nuclear or other power, and consequently with no effect on sustainability.

Another option for accommodation establishments to reduce their emissions is to generate their own renewable energy. An increasing number of studies have recently concluded that renewable energy systems for small- to medium-sized accommodation establishments are feasible. For instance, Bakos and Soursos (2002) have shown that photovoltaic cell (PV) installations for small-scale tourist operations in Greece are economically viable with up to 10 years payback time, and considerably lower payback times if government subsidies are provided, as in this case study (see Bakos and Soursos (2002), who also provide a detailed cost analysis). Likewise, Dalton *et al.* (2009) conclude in their analysis of three case studies with stand-alone renewable energy systems in Australia that PV-based and wind energy conversion systems are all economically viable, but wind energy conversion systems had shorter payback times (3–4 years), and were thus economically preferable to PV systems with payback times of 6–7 years. Two other studies arrive at similar conclusions for larger scale wind-hydro energy systems on a medium-sized Aegean island, Greece (Kaldellis *et al.* 2001) and in Australia (Dalton *et al.* 2008a), with the latter study also finding that larger scale wind energy systems (>1000 kW) are more economical than multiple small-scale systems at 0.1–100 kW. In a review of grid-connected renewable energy systems, Dalton *et al.* (2009) report payback times ranging from 5–8 years for PV systems and 4–30 years for wind energy conversion systems. Overall, these studies indicate that renewable energy systems can be economical, and that it can be worthwhile for accommodation establishments to carry out feasibility studies to assess their potential, particularly in warm and sunny climates or in areas with moderate to high average wind speeds.

CARBON MANAGEMENT IN FOCUS 5: CHUMBE ISLAND, ZANZIBAR, TANZANIA

Low-energy solar-powered small-scale accommodation

The issue

Accommodation establishments need energy for various purposes, such as A/C, heating or refrigeration, lighting and electrical appliances. In tropical islands or peripheral areas in the tropics, the standard solution is to use diesel-driven generators, which function independently of the – often unreliable – public grid and can be adjusted to the hotel's electricity demand. However, depending on the size of the generator, energy use is substantial. Even the smallest units (10–50 kW) will use around 4–10 litres of fuel per hour (cf. Caterpillar 2009), and usually have to run 24 hours a day. In larger hotels, energy use of several thousand litres of diesel per day is not uncommon (e.g. Gössling and Schumacher 2010, see also Carbon Management in Focus 1). However, fossil fuel-based electricity generation is not only leading to considerable emissions of GHGs, which in upscale hotels can exceed 100 kg CO_2 per guest night, it also entails high fuel and maintenance costs and results in dependency on a constant supply of fossil energy.

The solution

A solution to the problem is to become independent of fossil fuels, and to generate electricity from renewable energy sources. However, such an approach requires the minimization of energy demands and the use of different energy sources, such as solar and biogas to back up the system during the night or in rainy periods. Furthermore, given the huge energy requirements in upscale hotels, such solutions are only feasible in small hotels not offering the wide range of electrical appliances including A/C, hair dryers, mini-bars, safes, or TV-sets. The question thus arises as to whether small hotels can appeal to upscale tourists without offering such items and features (for examples see Carbon Management in Focus 12), and whether such renewable energy solutions are feasible from an investment point of view. One successful example of an upscale tropical island without a diesel-driven generator is Chumbe Island.

Chumbe Island is a privately established and managed nature reserve, with the goal of protecting a fringing coral reef and virgin forest that are particularly rich in biodiversity. The islet accommodates a maximum of 14 visitors in seven eco-bungalows. Neither the bungalows nor the island's visitor centre use fossil energy and their entire design is resource autarkic. This has been achieved by reducing energy demand to a minimum, while producing and storing solar energy to cover unavoidable energy requirements. The major energy consuming factor, A/C, has been avoided by positioning the bungalows and visitor centre in predominant wind directions and designing them as open structures cooled by draught. To adjust air flow and thus temperatures, louvres can be opened or closed in the bungalows. With regard to electrical appliances, the only energy-consuming devices in the bungalows and the visitor centre are lights, which are powered by PV panels on the rooftops that provide 12 V energy sufficient for lighting. In total, 48 solar panels producing about 8 kWh per day cover the island's electricity consumption, corresponding to energy use of about 1 kWh per guest night (at an occupancy rate of around 40–50 per cent). This includes the restaurant kitchen with solar freezer, and laptops, cameras and mobile phones that can be charged in the visitor centre, as well as the energy consumption of day visitors not staying overnight. Energy production also covers lights for seven bungalows, the manager's house, a small mosque, two staff quarters, and the main centre with restaurant, kitchen, office and lounge.

Another environmental challenge is water collection, filtration, heating, and the treatment of wastewater and sewage, all of which would demand energy use in the case of conventional hotels. As there is no ground water source – the island is too small to have an underground freshwater lens – all roofs of the bungalows, visitor centre and staff quarters are used to collect freshwater from rainwater during the rainy seasons. The rainwater passes through a sand-gravel filtration system and is stored in cisterns under each bungalow and the visitor centre. The water is then hand-pumped through a solar-powered heating system into hot and cold water containers in raised towers for the shower in the bathroom. Used water is again put through a filter system, and ends up in sealed plant beds to prevent polluted water from seeping into the intertidal areas and coral reef. Plant beds contain species that are demanding in water and nutrients, and therefore absorb remaining nitrates and phosphates. To establish this vegetative filtration or artificial wetland system for the restaurant kitchen, which produces wastewater with much higher nutrient loads than showers, numerous experiments and technical adjustments were required over the years, and several engineers specializing in environmental wastewater systems had to visit (see Chumbe's greywater report; Chumbe 2009). To avoid sewage from toilets (blackwater), composting toilets were installed, where compost rather than flush water is used. Composting toilets decompose human waste and turn it into fertilizer by aerobic composting in a specially designed compost chamber. They need no flush water and thus reduce fresh water consumption as well.

To implement these systems, many obstacles had to be overcome. With regard to energy use, an important precondition for low-energy systems concerns the visitor type. Chumbe Island is explicitly marketed as an up-market eco-destination with all-inclusive prices of US$250 (€174) per person per night. Guests seem to accept the simplicity of the accommodation, and most seem to perceive it even as part of the unique island experience. The solar system was relatively expensive to purchase and maintain, according to Sibylle Riedmiller, the Project Director, entailing costs of US$50,000 (€34,800) since 1994. It is, however, estimated that fuel costs for running a generator would have amounted to US$120,000 (€84,000) per year. Another problem regards the maintenance of the PV system as well as the availability of spare parts. The system has been going through many repairs, and experts had to be brought to the island in 2004 and 2005 to provide assistance. In particular, batteries had to be replaced fairly often, with disposal of used batteries being another environmental problem. The future development of power storage technology is thus a key issue with regard to the overall sustainability of the system. Finally, there are some problems relating to usage, with for instance some kitchen equipment being more high-powered than light bulbs, adding considerably to energy demand, but only during short periods. This can negatively affect batteries and needs to be considered in the technical design.

Impact

Chumbe Island shows that energy use in small islands can be reduced to very low levels, i.e. about 1 kWh per guest night, and that it is feasible to cover this energy demand with renewable energy sources and storage technology. Chumbe Island is thus operational with virtually no emissions, even though boat transfers, visits of experts to maintain or repair the solar system, as well as cooking in the kitchen based on gas do cause some emissions not included in calculations.

Source

Sibylle Riedmiller, Project Director, Chumbe Island Coral Park Ltd., Tanzania
Karlyn Langjahr, Project Manager, Chumbe Island Coral Park Ltd., Tanzania
Preben Byberg, Balslev Consulting Engineers, Denmark

Website

Chumbe Island, www.chumbeisland.com

References

Caterpillar (2009). http://www.cat.com/products/. Accessed 14 November 2009.

Chumbe Grey Water Report (2009). Report on the Grey Water System on Chumbe Island, May 2009, http://www.chumbeisland.com/Accomodation/accomodation.html. Accessed 14 November 2009.

Gössling, S. and Schumacher, K. (2010). Implementing carbon neutral destination policies: issues from the Seychelles. *Journal of Sustainable Tourism* 18(2), in press.

In countries such as Australia, a significant share of accommodation establishments appears to already use renewable energy systems: a survey by Dalton *et al.* (2007) found that more than 9 per cent of polled accommodation establishments in Queensland reported to use renewable energy systems. With regard to future solutions, Dalton *et al.* (2009) conclude that hydrogen fuel cells and storage systems are technically feasible but not as yet economically viable, a result confirmed by Bechrakis *et al.* (2006), who estimate that the costs of wind-hydrogen systems are in the order of US$1.05–1.11 per kWh, i.e. considerably higher than current electricity prices. Renewable energy sources can also be relevant for other uses. For instance, Bermudez-Contreras *et al.* (2008) discuss renewable energy powered desalination systems for water-scarce areas. They conclude that such investments can be profitable in tropical destinations, where amortization horizons can often be in the order of a few years. Overall, studies indicate that in many countries there are government-backed programmes, rebates and tax credits, which help to pay part of the costs for setting up renewable energy systems.

CARBON MANAGEMENT IN FOCUS 6: HOTEL VICTORIA, FREIBURG, GERMANY

Achieving zero-carbon accommodation

The issue

Accommodation establishments account for approximately one fifth of the CO_2 emissions from global tourism. As an emission-intense sector, hotels and other accommodation establishments are thus highly relevant in mitigation efforts, also because there is considerable growth in capacity with a trend towards more luxurious accommodation (UNWTO-UNEP-WMO 2008). Accommodation is, at the same time, highly interesting for emission reductions, because considerable efficiency gains can be achieved at low costs (see Carbon Management in Focus 1). Nevertheless, only few hotels seem to engage in carbon management beyond the 'obvious' measures, such as exchanging conventional light bulbs in favour of energy-efficient ones. While the lack of interest in energy-related issues is generally not well understood, one important restraint might be the lack of an understanding of the costs of retrofitting existing facilities, as well as the perceived effort in reducing energy use.

The solution

Hotel Victoria is located in the heart of Freiburg in the Black Forest in Germany, in a building dating back to 1875. With its 67 rooms and an occupancy rate of 75 per cent, the four star hotel accommodated more than 20,000 guests in 2008. The hotel's environmental strategy evolved over two and a half decades, starting in 1985, when the proprietors Astrid and Bertram Späth decided to reduce the amount of waste caused at breakfast tables, i.e. at a time when pre-packed portions were still a standard in hotels. To change a hotel towards sustainability is a long journey, as Bertram Späth outlines: 'We have transformed Hotel Victoria step by step into a truly sustainable hotel', including measures to reduce energy use and to source energy from renewable sources to become carbon-neutral. In chronological order, Hotel Victoria focused on the following measures:

Since 1985 – Measures to reduce energy use

Installation of low-flow showerheads, flow controls (basins) and ergonomically shaped bathtubs using 30 per cent less water, as well as refitting toilets with stop buttons to reduce water flow (from 9 to 6 litres). Towels are only changed on request. The cost for these measures is not known in detail, but all were economical with short payback times.

2000 – Installation of 7.6 kWpeak of solar PV collectors on rooftop

The cost of setting up solar collectors was in the order of €60.000. The collectors deliver 7,000 kWh per year, leading to avoided costs of about €1,200 per annum (at the current lowest utility price for renewable electricity in Germany at about €0.16 per kWh), with an expected lifetime of 30 years. This measure is thus not cost-neutral, but the German Erneuerbare Energien Gesetz (Renewable Energy Law), which was passed in 2000, is designed to cover the difference in costs over a 20-year period. More specifically, for any kWh fed into the public grid, €0.5 is paid to investors in solar energy (this was recently reduced to €0.4).

2002 – Oil heating system replaced with 300 kW wood pellet furnace

To replace the oil heating system cost €150,000. This saved some 50,000 litres of heating oil per annum, corresponding to avoided costs of about €30,000 and avoided emissions of about 125 t CO_2. The 100 t of wood pellets used per year to replace the oil are sourced from sustainable Black Forest timber production, and cause negligible emissions associated with cutting trees, saw mills, and the production and transport of the wood pellets, which consist of dried and compressed sawdust. Wood pellets are less costly than oil (at current market prices), and can be purchased at €190 per tonne, i.e. running costs are about €19,000 per year. Consequently, the payback time for this measure is highly dependent on oil and pellet prices, but might be in the order of 15 years.

2002 – Installation of 30 m² of solar thermal energy

A total of 30 m² of solar thermal panels were built on the rooftop, in addition to PV panels producing electricity. The cost for this was in the order of €30,000, with unknown savings.

2007 – Cold water air conditioning system

A cold water-based A/C system for the hotel's historical main building was put into operation in 2007, planned by the company Solares Bauen (see Related websites). Cool water at a temperature of 10–13 °C is pumped up from a 16–24 m-deep suction well and fed into a heat exchanger, from where it is pumped back through an injection well at a maximum temperature of 16 °C. All rooms are connected to a cold water circulation system, and convector ventilators distribute cold air in the rooms in summer, when temperatures often climb above 30 °C. The cost for the system amounted to €120,000, but the system reduced energy use for A/C to 2 per cent of a standard system. Notably, integrating a standard A/C system in the hotel would have cost as much, and this measure thus greatly reduced electricity costs for A/C.

2009 – Installation of another 13 kWpeak of solar PV collectors on rooftop

The total cost of installing the solar panels was €100,000. Renewable energy fed into the grid is purchased at €0.40 per kWh, leading to payback of investments after 20 years. As the solar collectors do not deliver enough energy to match the hotel's electricity demand, an investment in a 1.3 MW wind power plant in a location close to Freiburg was also made to generate the remaining energy needed, 70,000 kWh per annum (see Figure 9.7). The investment for this was in the order of €30,000.

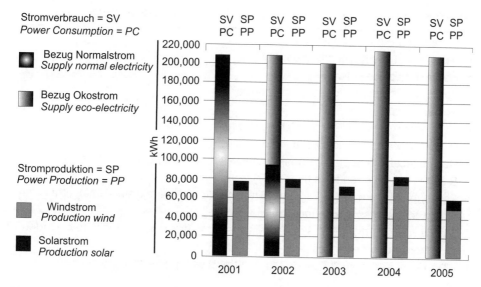

Figure 9.7 *Energy use in Hotel Victoria*
Source: Hotel Victoria 2007

2009 – Installation of four small wind turbines on rooftop

Finally, in 2009, solar power units on the rooftop were complemented with the installation of four small wind power turbines with a combined capacity of 2 kW. While it is uncertain how much energy the wind turbines will yield, Hotel Victoria now has a rooftop 'energy garden', which can be visited by interested guests and groups, and has turned into a popular attraction according to Bertram Späth. The cost for setting up the wind turbines was in the order of €12,000, and it is so far unknown what actual costs per kWh will be.

Energy consumption was also reduced by equipping all rooms with low-energy mini-bars (see Related websites), energy-efficient light bulbs, new windows with thermal insulation glass, and card systems which cut off energy use when the guest leaves the room. Throughout the hotel, motion detectors and dimmers were installed, as well as LED-based lighting. Television sets are switched off completely when rooms are not occupied. Power consumption is also managed by a computer-based energy management system to monitor consumption and costs developed by Energieagentur Freiburg (see Related websites). A display panel prominently positioned at the reception also communicates renewable energy yield to guests.

A wide range of other measures directly or indirectly reducing energy use have been implemented. These are not discussed in further detail, but listed in table 9.6.

Overall, Hotel Victoria currently uses 210,000 kWh of electricity (Figure 9.7)

Table 9.6 *Additional measures leading to reduced energy use and emissions*

- No use of pre-packed portions
- Many foodstuffs regionally sourced
- Waste avoidance policy
- Refillable dispensers for soap and shower gel
- No use of cans
- All paper articles made from high quality recycled paper
- Only recyclable materials used in the office
- Guests receive free public transport passes for the duration of their stay
- Bicycles can be hired from the hotel
- Environmental management plans with specific goals are drawn up together with staff and progress is monitored
- Staff are encouraged to make suggestions for improvement, ideas are rewarded with money or other prizes
- All staff get season tickets for unlimited travel with public transport
- Inner-city errands are run by bike

Source: Hotel Victoria 2007

and the equivalent of 450,000 kWh for heating, corresponding to 33 kWh per guest and even lower values per overnight stay. A future goal is to further reduce energy use by continuously integrating new technologies. Future plans include, for instance, a new ventilation system controlling CO_2 levels and adjusting air exchange dependent on air quality.

The main difficulty in retrofitting Hotel Victoria was the choice of partners, who needed to have experience with the technologies they installed. Bureaucracy was another obstacle. Bertram Späth emphasizes that it takes time to find solutions, particularly when these are highly innovative: 'there are often no competitors for installing new technologies, and that makes it difficult to compare costs'.

Impact

Bertram Späth emphasizes that all measures were taken 'without any loss of comfort for our clients'. Though not all initiatives to become carbon-neutral were cost-neutral, the hotel has gained a reputation as being truly sustainable, and has twice won the award for being 'the most environmentally friendly hotel in the world', a joint award by American Express and the International Hotel and Restaurant Association. Overall, the example shows that it is feasible for hotels to achieve carbon-neutrality, particularly when governmental support programmes exist (cf. Bakos 2009). As outlined by Bertram Späth, it is beneficial to engage in some measures even if a net cost is involved, because of positive media reports and branding effects.

Source

Bertram Späth, Proprietor, Hotel Victoria, Freiburg

Website

Hotel Victoria, www.hotel-victoria.de/

Related websites

Small-scale windpower stations, www.enflo-windtec.ch
Low-energy mini-fridges, www.dometic.com
Energieagentur Freiburg, www.energieagentur-freiburg.de
Solares Bauen, www.solares-bauen.de

References

Bakos, G.C. (2009). Distributed power generation: a case study of small scale PV power plant in Greece. *Applied Energy* 68: 1575–1766.

Bohdanowicz, P. (2009). Theory and Practice of Environmental Management and Monitoring in Hotel Chains. In: Gössling, S., Hall, C.M. and Weaver, D.B. (eds) *Sustainable Tourism Futures: perspectives on systems, restructuring and innovations*. London: Routledge, pp. 102–130.

Hotel Victoria (2007). Environment. Steps for the Future. Available from: http://www.hotel-victoria.de/wsbk/dokumente/Umwelt/Umwelterklaerung2007.pdf. Accessed 3 February 2010.

International Hotel & Restaurant Association (2005). IH-RA Environmental Award. Available from: http://www.ih-ra.com/awards/previous_winners.php. Accessed 5 February 2010.

UNWTO-UNEP-WMO (2008). *Climate Change and Tourism: responding to global challenges*. Madrid: UNWTO.

These, and many other technology-based efficiency measures are documented by various organizations working with energy audits, benchmarking and retrofitting in accommodation (see Related websites in case studies). Note that a full review of technology options to reduce energy use and emissions in accommodation establishments is beyond the scope of this book. More information can be obtained from organizations such as UNWTO, and websites such as Green Hotelier.

RESTAURANTS AND ATTRACTIONS

Most measures in restaurants to reduce energy use are related to management. Regular replacement of old fridges and freezers, for instance, should be a standard for all restaurants. For other measures see Carbon Management in Focus case studies in Chapter 10 'Management'. As for attractions, measures are specific and not discussed in further detail in this book (for examples see e.g. Becken and Hay 2007).

DESTINATIONS

At the most basic level, carbon management is about exchanging light bulbs, at the most complex, it is about restructuring the tourism system. Destinations are at the forefront of such efforts, if they can agree that moving towards low-carbon operations is a desirable goal. This can include entire regions, as demonstrated by South West England (Carbon Management in Focus 27), or companies managing large areas, as in the case of Aspen Skiing Company.

CARBON MANAGEMENT IN FOCUS 7: ASPEN, COLORADO, USA

Achieving CO₂ reductions and building pressure on supply chains

The issue

Ski tourism is particularly vulnerable to climate change (e.g. Scott 2005; Scott *et al.* 2008), and in particular low-lying ski resorts are likely to be among the first tourism sectors to be affected by global warming (UNWTO-UNEP-WMO 2008). The threat of climate change has, however, prompted very different responses by the global ski industry, with many resort managers still ignoring the phenomenon and its anticipated consequences (for an Austrian case study see Wolfsegger *et al.* 2008). At the same time, an increasing number of ski resorts are now at the forefront of companies warning about climate change, influencing political decision-making, and taking action to reduce emissions (e.g. Kelly and Williams 2007). For instance, the National Ski Areas Association (NSAA 2010) reports that 64 resorts in the USA now reduce part or all of their emissions by using electricity from renewable energy sources.

The solution

Aspen Snowmass is a winter resort complex located in Colorado, USA, comprising four ski areas: Aspen Mountain, Aspen Highlands, Buttermilk and Snowmass. It is one of the most popular winter sports areas in the world, with about 1.3 million skier visits per year. The areas' managing company Aspen Skiing Company (ASC) has engaged in pro-environmental activities for more than a decade, and published its first Sustainability Report in 1999 (Aspen Skiing Company 1999). ASC was one of the first destinations in the world to acknowledge climate change and to see it as a challenge for tourism from both adaptation and mitigation points of view.

Aspen Skiing Company has a considerable record of environmental achievements, including compliance with the ISO 14001 standard since 2004, and the joining of the CCX in the same year, committing the company to legally binding

CO_2 reductions. To reduce energy use and emissions, ASC developed a comprehensive energy plan and implemented a wide range of measures, with the goal of cutting emissions by 10 per cent by 2012 and 25 per cent by 2020 from 2000 levels. The company also seeks to achieve carbon-neutrality by 2020 through offsetting (Aspen Skiing Company 2008, 2010a). ASC notes that reducing emissions is not only an environmental issue, as costs of energy have grown by 218 per cent in 2008 over 2000. ASC has published detailed accounts of its fuel and electricity consumption and associated GHG emissions since 2000 (Aspen Skiing Company 2010b). These show that energy costs amounted to almost US$5 million (€3.5 million) in 2007, causing emissions of more than 27,800 t CO_2 (table 9.7).

An important aspect of ASC's activities is also their work in creating networks with other companies acting pro-environmentally, such as Green Mountain Coffee Roasters (see Related websites), a company selling organic and fair-trade coffee. Even more relevant are ASC's efforts to distribute balanced information on climate change and to build up political pressure on non-committed actors. For instance, a section in ASC's (2007a) Sustainability Report 2006–2007 reads:

> When you go home to your family in (New Jersey, Oklahoma, etc.) and talk about climate change around the dinner table, the odds are that someone, Uncle Frank perhaps, will say 'Isn't there some debate on the science there?' That discussion happens not because there is any debate on the science, but because groups like ExxonMobil have funded, to the tune of tens of millions of dollars, one of the most effective marketing campaigns in history, designed entirely to create doubt in the minds of the public on climate change.
>
> (Aspen Skiing Company 2007a: 20)

In responding to what is essentially seen as a marketing challenge, ASC also launched a campaign, SAVESNOW (see Related websites) in 2007, to educate on climate change and to encourage action. Advertisements in special interest media and posters in the ski resorts inform skiers on climate change. Auden Schendler, Executive Director of Sustainability, outlines that 'ASC has long argued that the best and biggest role the ski industry can play in solving global warming is to use its influence as a business to drive policy change'. In this regard, the Sustainability Report 2006–2007 argues:

> the industry needs to look at how it can have the greatest impact on driving broad policy change on climate. We need to find our biggest lever. In Aspen, that lever is influence: because the name carries weight; because the ski industry, as a business, has pull with politicians; and because skiing is a way for people to understand the complex issue of climate change.
>
> (Aspen Skiing Company 2007a: 20)

Two of the most far-reaching initiatives by Aspen Skiing Company included a ban of Kimberly Clark (KC) paper products as well as the support of a filing of a

Table 9.7 2006 and 2007 fuel consumption, costs and emissions, Aspen Skiing

	Media	Cost 2006	Cost 2007	Units 2006	Units 2007	Conversion	CO$_2$ (Tons) 2006	CO$_2$ (Tons) 2007
				2006 and 2007 Baseline				
FUEL (GAS&DIESEL)	Fuel-AH	$111,312.51	$119,792.35	46,420	48,748	B20: 18.87 CO$_2$/GAL	439	461
	Fuel-SM	$453,828.27	$430,174.53	181,137	175,243	Gasoline: 19.59 LBS CO$_2$/GAL	1,726	1,669
	Fuel-BM	$260,617.34	$340,217.78	99,022	113,611		952	1,090
	Fuel-AM	$210,805.48	$187,663.61	84,498	74,991		805	711
	Fuel-SMC	$75,538.19	$61,930.68	27,210	23,909		265	233
	SUB-TOTAL	$1,112,101.78	$1,139,778.95	438,288	436,502		4,184	4,164
SNOWMAKING Gallons	Water-AM	$89,484.00	$96,000.00	44,742,000	48,000,000	.0000006308 tons CO$_2$/gal	28	30
	Water-AH	$8,572.28	$8,394.26	17,144,566	16,788,528		0	0
	Water-BM	$0.00	$0.00	53,610,456	56,502,603		0	0
	Water-SM	$23,910.00	$36,006.75	51,320,000	72,013,504		0	0
	SUB-TOTAL	$121,966.28	$140,401.02	166,817,022	193,304,635	2006: (1.61 lbs CO$_2$/kwh)	28	30
ELECTRICITY kWh	Electric-ASC	$1,800,071.93	$2,013,696.15	18,480,038	19,177,353	2006: (1.61 lbs CO$_2$/kwh)	13,376	13,207
	Electric-SMC	$292,003.77	$303,412.00	3,333,315	3,364,239	2007: (1.57 lbs CO$_2$/kwh)	2,378	2,281
	Elictric-TLN	$292,615.08	$308,562.00	4,248,799	4,435,587		3,117	3,095
	SUB-TOTAL	$2,361,690.78	$2,625,943.15	26,062,152	26,977,179		18,870	18,583
WIND POWER kWh	Direct Wind	$25,920.00	$25,920.00	1,036,800	1,036,800	2006: (−1.61 lbs CO$_2$/kwh) 2007: (−1.57 lbs CO$_2$/kwh)	−835	−814
	SUB-TOTAL	$25,920.00	$25,920.00	1,036,800	1,036,800		−835	−814

MUNICIPAL H₂O Gallons							
Water: Asp. Muni	$33,392.99	$33,662.45	3,809,783	4,887,294	.0000006308 tons CO₂/gal	2	3
Water-TLN	$35,544.47	$37,352.53	15,759,000	15,499,000		10	10
Water-SMC	$68,989.33	$70,050.92	10,120,110	5,658,530		6	4
SM Wat and San	$53,157.40	$50,854.48	4,928,330	4,527,060		3	3
SUB-TOTAL	$191,084.19	$191,920.38	29,688,893	26,044,824		22	19
NATURAL GAS Gallons							
Nat. Gas-ASC	$486,485.95	$246,163.79	27,830	27,653	.059 tons CO₂/MMBTU	1,642	1,632
Nat.Gas-TLN	$400,101.01	$397,898.96	39,565	36,895		2,334	2,177
Nat. Gas-SMC	$228,301.70	$248,242.00	20,838	20,632		1,229	1,217
SUB-TOTAL	$1,114,888.66	$892,304.75	88,233	85,180		5,206	5,026
PROPANE Gallons							
SUB-TOTAL	$3,564.46	$7,774.31	1,696	3,752	.00637 tons/gallon	11	24
TOTAL	$4,905,296.15	$4,998,122.55				28,321	27,847

TOTAL 2006: NUMBER OF SKIERS: 1,444,816/$3.40 PER SKIER/0.020 TONS CO₂ PER SKIER
TOTAL 2007: NUMBER OF SKIERS: 1,444,647/$3.46 PER SKIER/0.019 TONS CO₂ PER SKIER

Source: Aspen Skiing Company (2007a)

Supreme Court brief. KC products were banned in 2006 by ASC, because the company engaged in destructive logging practices, hardly recycled any fibre and was unwilling to meet with environmental advocates. Even though ASC's spending on KC products was only US$25,000 (€17,400) and thus hardly relevant for the US$32 billion (€22.3 billion) turnover company, the move received considerable media attention and initiated change in KC's perspectives on environmental issues: ultimately, the company changed their fibre-sourcing practices.

In 2006, ASC filed an Amicus Brief to the Supreme Court in support of 12 states and three conservation organizations that sued the USA's Environmental Protection Agency (EPA) to regulate CO_2 as a pollutant, a lawsuit known as 'Massachusetts vs. EPA'. The case challenged the 2003 decision by the EPA that CO_2 is not a pollutant – an issue of considerable importance as the EPA has authority under the Clean Air Act to set limits on emissions of pollutants. ASC's Amicus Brief supported the lawsuit, also arguing that climate change is a direct economic threat to the ski industry. In April 2007, the Supreme Court ruled in favour of the plaintiffs, requiring the EPA to regulate CO_2 as a pollutant, a decision that might become an important basis for climate legislation in the USA under the Obama administration.

Impact

ASC shows how far large tourism actors can move in achieving climate sustainability, not only within their own operations, but even with regard to their supply chains. Such efforts are usually rewarded economically, particularly in the North American context, where huge amounts of energy are wasted. Moving towards sustainability also requires significant efforts and overcoming obstacles, however. Auden Schendler has summarized these in his book: *Getting Green Done: hard truths and real solutions from the front lines of the sustainability revolution* (Schendler 2009).

Source

Auden Schendler, Executive Director of Sustainability, Aspen Skiing Company.

Related websites

SAVESNOW, www.savesnow.org (Campaign by ASC to raise climate awareness) Green Mountain Coffee Roasters, www.greenmountaincoffee.com (Coffee roaster with green credentials)

WhistlerBlackcomb, Canada, www.whistlerblackcomb.com (Canadian ski resort engaging in mitigation efforts)

References

Aspen Skiing Company (1999). 1999–2000 Sustainability Report. Available from: http://www.aspensnowmass.com/environment/images/1999–2000_ASC_Sustain-ability_Report.pdf. Accessed 5 February 2010.

Aspen Skiing Company (2007a). 2006–2007 Sustainability Report. Available from: http://www.aspensnowmass.com/environment/images/2006–2007_ASC_Sustain-ability_Report.pdf. Accessed 5 February 2010.

Aspen Skiing Company (2007b). Aspen Skiing Company's Testimony. Available from: http://www.aspensnowmass.com/environment/images/ASC_House_Climate_Testi-mony.pdf. Accessed 5 February 2010.

Aspen Skiing Company (2008). ASC Energy Plan. Available from: http://www.aspens-nowmass.com/environment/policies/Energy_Plan_2008_V7.pdf. Accessed 5 February 2010.

Aspen Skiing Company (2010a). Program Highlights. Available from: http://www.aspens-nowmass.com/environment/highlights/default.cfm. Accessed 4 February 2010.

Aspen Skiing Company (2010b). Sustainability Reports. Available from: http://www.aspensnowmass.com/environment/programs/sustainreport.cfm. Accessed 5 February 2010.

Kelly, J. and Williams, P.W. (2007). Modelling tourism destination energy consumption and greenhouse gas emissions: Whistler, British Columbia, Canada. *Journal of Sustainable Tourism* 15(1): 67–90.

NSAA (2010). Green Power Program Fact Sheet. Available from http://www.nsaa.org/nsaa/press/0708/green-power-fact-sheet.asp. Accessed 5 February 2010.

Schendler, A. (2009). *Getting Green Done: hard truths and real solutions from the front lines of the sustainability revolution*. New York: Public Affairs.

Scott, D. (2005). Global Environmental Change and Mountain Tourism. In: Gössling, S. and Hall, C.M. (eds) *Tourism and Global Environmental Change*. London: Routledge, pp. 54–75.

Scott, D., Dawson, J. and Jones, B. (2008). Climate change vulnerability of the Northeast US winter tourism sector. *Mitigation and Adaptation Strategies to Global Change* 13(5–6): 577–596.

UNWTO-UNEP-WMO (2008). Climate Change and Tourism: responding to global challenges. Madrid: UNWTO, UNEP, WMO.

Wolfsegger, C., Gössling, S. and Scott, D. (2008). Climate change risk appraisal in the Austrian Ski Industry. *Tourism Review International*, 12: 13–23.

In conclusion of the technology section, it is clear that a considerable share of emissions could be avoided through introduction of new technologies. Often, as in the accommodation sector, energy savings are economical. Yet, evidence would indicate that many businesses are not interested in realizing these potentials. A pertinent question with regard to technology is thus under which conditions broader involvement of stakeholders in carbon management based on technology change could be achieved.

10 **Mitigation**
Management

A proactive approach to deal with emissions is still to emerge in large parts of the global tourism industry. In many sectors, such as aviation, there is still considerable resistance to work with climate change mitigation, while more generally the challenge associated with achieving absolute reductions in GHG in pro-growth tourism scenarios appears not to be understood by stakeholders (for analyses of energy and emission scenarios see e.g. Yeoman and McMahon-Beattie (2006) for Scotland; Kelly and Williams (2007) for Whistler, Canada; and Gössling and Schumacher (2010) for the Seychelles). Proactive carbon management often has its starting point in the insight that it is profitable. Case studies as presented in this book also indicate that decisions to move towards low-carbon operations are usually made at the highest company level, i.e. by executive boards, CEOs, directors, sustainability strategists or sustainability managers. In some cases, change borne out of the ambition to engage in more sustainability operations can result in a completely new image for the company, as exemplified by the Scandic chain (cf. Hall and Williams 2008). Furthermore, the recognition many businesses have received for their work with sustainability has often included hundreds of media publications on a global scale as well as industry awards, as exemplified by Aspen Skiing Company, USA; Chumbe Island, Tanzania; or Hotel Victoria, Germany (Carbon Management in Focus 5, 6, 7). These aspects of carbon management also need to be weighed into decisions to engage in climate change mitigation.

AVIATION

The most frequently discussed management measure for airlines to reduce emissions are the Single European Sky and the U.S. NextGen Air Transport System (also an issue of technology development) as part of global airspace management and ATM, also including other measures such as 'green inflights' (for details see IATA 2009a). For airlines, a wide range of other management issues can be relevant. For instance, higher load factors and denser seating in aircraft can reduce per passenger emissions considerably. In June 2009, load factors had fallen to 75.3 per cent, down from 77.6 per cent in June 2008, essentially meaning that one in four seats is flown empty. In comparison, many charter flights reach load factors exceeding 90 per cent, indicating that there is over-capacity among scheduled airlines. In this context, a second relevant factor is the density of the seating, which influences how many people can be carried: even though the weight of the aircraft increases with more people onboard, per capita fuel use declines as the weight of additional people carried adds comparably little to the overall weight of the aircraft.

Seating density can vary substantially. Boeing, for example, offers the 777–300 with a minimum of 368 and up to 500 seats (UNWTO-UNEP-WMO 2008). Low-cost carriers and charter planes typically have the highest seat densities, which can result in fuel reductions per skm of up to 20–30 per cent. Taken together, high load factors and dense seating can considerably reduce specific emissions per pkm: Sweden's TUI Fly Nordic, for instance, reports average fuel use of 0.068 kg CO_2 per pkm (TUI Fly Nordic 2010), i.e. some 47 per cent lower than the global average of 0.129 kg CO_2 per pkm. This can be compared to the global maximum reduction in specific fuel use as outlined by Green (2009), which, considering limits sets by the laws of physics, and combining technological, design and operational measures, could be 65–70 per cent lower per pkm by 2050 relative to 2000, i.e. in the order of 0.045 kg CO_2 per pkm. However, this will also depend on the development of traveller expectations and choices: for instance, business-class travellers use more cabin space, which results in lower passenger densities. A recent study by the French Environment and Energy Agency (ADEME) found that emissions in business and first class are 133 per cent and 250 per cent higher, respectively, than those of economy class passengers (ADEME 2006). There is also a noteworthy recent trend towards small, executive aircraft (hired, shared, or owned), which are even more carbon intense than business- or first-class flights (Cohen 2009). Airlines primarily catering to upscale travellers will thus be less efficient on a per pkm basis.

Yet another issue concerns weight. Aircraft manufacturers have for a long time sought to reduce weight by using light building materials and weight reduction is still high on the airline organization's agenda (cf. IATA 2009a). Weight also refers to tourist baggage, however. There are different approaches to weight management, with many low-cost carriers now regularly charging passengers for baggage taken onboard. While this is primarily a strategy to charge for additional services, such a strategy can nevertheless make a contribution to reducing fuel use and to educate travellers to travel with less baggage. Weight management is also a concern with regard to comparably heavy duty-free objects, such as bottles of alcohol. For instance, transporting an additional bottle of wine onboard a Boeing 747–400 over a typical distance of 7,000 km will increases emissions by roughly half the bottle's weight in CO_2. Such considerations also become important in destination management with, for instance, Australian destinations now selling 'ready-to-roll' six-bottle packs of wine in airports to departing tourists. Many other management issues can be addressed by airlines, such as the fact that return flights can still be cheaper than single flights, or that people have to fly 'backwards' in order to get a connection.

More generally, airlines need to discuss whether they are transport or air-transport service providers. If a consensus could be reached that airlines are transport service providers, they could start to engage in other transport sectors as well. For instance, high-speed trains have become important links between major European cities. Eurostar has proved to be a strong competitor and dominant market player in comparison with airlines on the London–Paris route, and in countries like France or Spain, much of the domestic air traffic between major cities has been replaced in recent years by high-speed train connections. If airlines became engaged in the development of these systems, for instance by using their expertise in electronic boarding and payment systems, they would not have to compete with often more profitable rail systems.

TRAIN SYSTEMS AND COACHES

Rail and coaches can offer many tangible advantages over aircraft and car, such as the convenience of being transported instead of driving (cars), which can be relevant in work-related contexts, as time can be used productively; the knowledge of exact arrival times, in principle to the minute (trains); arrival in city centres, rather than the periphery (trains and usually coaches); the relative spaciousness of train compartments; opportunities to stretch legs while travelling; options to take along considerable amounts of baggage; to buy beverages, snacks or meals at any time (trains); as well as the high speed on major connections, particularly in Europe and Japan (trains). However, worldwide, train travel accounts for only a small share of overall distances travelled (Gilbert and Perl 2008: 66), and innovative service strategies are thus a key in attracting travellers to use train systems and coaches. Carbon Management in Focus 8, 9 and 10 provide insight into the strategies of Swiss Railways, which have, together with Japan Railways, the highest punctuality rates in the world, as well as Avanti Busreisen, a German coach operator attracting customers even on distances exceeding several thousand kilometres. Finally, 9292 in the Netherlands has developed a system to help travellers find their way when using public transport, based on an innovative mobile phone application.

CARBON MANAGEMENT IN FOCUS 8: SBB (SWISS RAILWAYS), SWITZERLAND

Punctuality and customer service to initiate modal shifts from air and car to rail

The issue

Despite the benefits of train travel dicussed above, cars and aircraft still offer perceived advantages over rail transport, including high speeds and low travel costs (aircraft) as well as convenience factors, such as private space or the possibility to move from door to door without changing connections (car) (see e.g. Miller 2001). As there are considerable differences in average per capita train travel between countries with high levels of per capita mobility (cf. UIC 2009), the question arises as to why some countries have managed to attract a greater share of train travellers than others.

The solution

Schweizerische Bundesbahnen (SBB, *Swiss Railways*), the fourth largest employer in Switzerland with 27,800 employees and an annual turnover of CHF8 billion (€5.3 billion), has for many years put emphasis on providing reliable, punctual transport services with a high level of customer service. SBB is now, possibly together with Japan Railways Group, the leading rail transport company in the world when measured in terms of passenger travel relative to the population (UIC 2009).

According to Michael Schürch, Head of the customer punctuality programme, SBB transported more than 322 million passengers in 2008, an increase of 5.2 per cent over 2007. This corresponds to 50 trips per Swiss resident per year, or about 880,000 train trips per day. Calculated in distance, each resident covered 2,422 pkm by train in 2008, which is about 43 per cent more than in any other country in the EU. France is second, with 1,377 pkm per citizen per year, followed by Austria (1,253 pkm), Denmark (1,065 pkm), Belgium (1,000 pkm) and Germany (934 pkm). At the other end of the European statistic, per capita per year travel distances by train are as low as 209 pkm in Estonia, 187 pkm in Greece, and 112 pkm in Lithuania. Worldwide, only the Japanese have similar travel patterns to the Swiss, with 71 journeys per resident per year, and a per person per year travel distance of 2,010 pkm (UIC 2009).

SBB explains inter-European differences in train travel by the high quality of its customer services, particularly with regard to safety, cleanliness and punctuality (SBB 2008, see also Steer Davis Gleave 2006). Swiss railways has maintained a >96 per cent punctuality rate of its trains in recent years, with delays defined as arrival within five minutes of stated time. According to Michael Schürch, more than 90 per cent of trains arrived within three minutes of stated arrival time in 2009. The three-minute threshold is crucial, as most connections can still be reached with such small delays in Switzerland, where connections are optimized with a view to minimizing waiting times. Since 2007, SBB also distinguishes 'customer punctuality', a measure of the share of customers, rather than trains, arriving on time. This measure is important, as trains are more crowded in the morning, when a greater share of people travel to work, and any delay in the morning affects more people. In 2009, SBB achieved 90 per cent customer punctuality within three minutes of stated arrival time.

In comparison, statistics for neighbouring Deutsche Bahn (German Railways) indicate that 21 per cent of long-distance trains, and 15 per cent of regional trains in Germany are more than five minutes late (Stiftung Warentest 2008). SBB has taken some unusual measures to maintain punctuality. One problem for the country, located in the centre of Europe, is delayed incoming foreign trains, which cause irregularities in the Swiss system. In order to reduce the impact of late arrivals on Swiss train punctuality, SBB maintains replacement trains, which continue on time from border stations when foreign trains are delayed.

Other aspects making train travel in Switzerland attractive include, according to Michael Schürch, direct connections; tight intervals between trains (several connections per hour); high travel speed leading to comparably short travel times; clean, modern and comfortable trains; a well-functioning public transport system connected to the train system, such as trams and buses; and easy access. For instance, 300,000 people in Switzerland have a Generalabonnement (general season ticket), allowing them to travel on any train throughout the year. SBB has also focused on providing IT-solutions to make travel easier, for instance through its mobile phone-based journey finder with payment function (SBB 2009a; see also Carbon Management in Focus 10). SBB (2009b) also offers a cost calculation tool to determine the costs of car travel versus train travel for commuters – with train travel regularly being cheaper.

Overall, the case study of SBB shows that train travel can be made more attractive, provided that managers focus on its strategic advantages, and provided that a serious effort is made to reduce inconveniences, as for instance associated with delays or crowded trains. In the period 2003–08, the number of pkm travelled with SBB has grown by 29 per cent, and is estimated to increase by another 16 per cent up to 2014. To match growing demand and to achieve greater speeds on key connections, SBB has planned investments of CHF20 billion (€13.2 billion) up to 2030.

Impact

In terms of avoided emissions, the almost 15.6 billion pkm travelled by passengers on SBB trains might have accounted for 0.11 Mt CO_2 in 2008 (at 0.007 kg CO_2-eq per pkm, a low value due to the fact that 70 per cent of electricity is derived from hydropower; SBB 2008). Had these kilometres been travelled by car instead of train, this would have generated 3.3 Mt CO_2 (at 0.197 kg CO_2-eq per pkm; SBB 2008). SBB estimates that each pkm travelled by SBB causes 20 times lower emissions than one pkm travelled by car (SBB 2009c). SBB consumes 4 per cent of the country's transport-related energy, but manages 16 per cent of the country's passenger traffic and 41 per cent of its freight traffic. Climate-related management in coming years will include further reductions in GHG emissions, with a target of −10 per cent by 2015, compared to 2009. This will primarily be achieved through train operator training (ecodriving), staff environmental training, and energy saving measures in stations. Overall, SBB is thus an example of how public transport needs to be managed in order to attract travellers and to facilitate modal shift.

Source

Michael Schürch, head of customer punctuality programme, Swiss Railways, Switzerland

Website

Schweizerische Bundesbahnen, www.sbb.ch

Related websites

Japan Railways Group, www.japanrail.com

Ecopassenger, www.ecopassenger.org (tool to compare emissions from car and train passenger transport)

Cost calculator, http://mct.sbb.ch/mct/reisemarkt/abos-billette/abonnemente/vergleichsrechner.htm (tool to compare the costs of car and train travel)

References

Gilbert, R. and Perl, A. (2008). *Transport Revolutions: moving people and freight without oil*. London: Earthscan.

Miller, D. (ed.) (2001). *Car Cultures*. Oxford: Berg Publishers.

SBB (2008). Das Umweltmanagement der SBB – Auszug aus dem Geschäftsbericht (Environmental management by SBB – excerpt from the annual financial report). Available from: http://mct.sbb.ch/mct/konzern_gb08_umwelt_d.pdf. Accessed 5 December 2009.

SBB (2009a). Die mobilen Services der SBB (SBB mobile services), Available from: http://www.sbb-mobileworld.ch/. Accessed 5 December 2009.

SBB (2009b). Cost comparison car and train. Available from: http://mct.sbb.ch/mct/reisemarkt/abos-billette/abonnemente/vergleichsrechner.htm. Accessed 5 December 2009.

SBB (2009c). Klimafreundliche Mobilität – treffen Sie Ihre Wahl (climate-friendly mobility: make your choice). Available from: http://mct.sbb.ch/mct/konzern_engagement/konzern_umwelt/konzern_klima/konzern_klima-mobilitaet.htm. Accessed 5 December 2009.

Steer Davis Gleave (2006). Air and Rail Competition and Complementarity (Final Report). Available from: http://ec.europa.eu/transport/rail/studies/doc/2006_08_study_air_rail_competition_en.pdf. Accessed 30 March 2010.

Stiftung Warentest (2008). Wie pünktlich fahren die Züge wirklich? (*Are trains really on time?*). Available from: http://www.test.de/themen/auto-verkehr/test/-Deutsche-Bahn/1617492/1617492/. Accessed 5 December 2009.

UIC (Union Internationale des Chemins de Fer) (2009). Statistics. Available from: http://www.uic.org/spip.php?rubrique1410. Accessed 5 December 2009.

CARBON MANAGEMENT IN FOCUS 9: AVANTI BUS TRAVEL, GERMANY

Modal shift from aircraft to bus

The issue

Coaches have, together with trains, the lowest emissions of all motorized means of transport (UNWTO-UNEP-WMO 2008), but are mostly used for short-distance travel: it is unusual for travellers in many industrial countries to cover distances exceeding 1,000 km by coach, even though there are regular long-distance bus connections in most parts of North and South America, which can serve as models for coach-based transport systems (e.g. Machado-Filho 2009).

The solution

Avanti Busreisen is a medium-sized bus tour operator in Freiburg, Germany, founded in 1991. The company now operates five upscale long-distance buses with 48 seats each, transporting about 8,000 guests per year on its holiday routes. The buses cover distances of up to 2,000 km, with an average occupancy rate of 70 per cent. The company's most successful journey is from Freiburg to Mailand in Italy, with 60–70 return journeys per year and an average load factor of 90 per cent.

Other destinations include Greece, Ukraine and Morocco, all of which are usually reached by aircraft. Tours by bus are attractive, because the comparably slow travel speed allows passengers to develop a sense of distance and to experience landscapes and cultures more closely. Prices for most journeys are comparable to a trip by air and car rental at the destination. In 2008, Avanti received considerable media attention when it offered a 70-day tour to the Olympic Games in Peking by bus from Germany, a trip covering 17,000 km. The journey in an air-conditioned five star bus proved to be a success, and Avanti offered a second, now 74-day long journey to China in 2010, driving from Germany to Switzerland, Italy, Greece, Turkey, following the silk road through Iran and Uzbekistan to Kazakhstan and China. A faster return-route takes 26 days. Alternatively, guests can travel home by Trans-Siberian Railways.

In terms of emissions, the journey makes a far lower contribution to climate change than if covered by air – despite the long journey time of 74 days. Per participant, emissions amount to 0.54 t CO_2, while emissions from a flight would be in the order of about 0.95 t CO_2, not including the impact of non-CO_2 emission on the climate (see Chapter 3). This calculation is based on Avanti's reported emissions of 0.032 kg CO_2 per pkm, which can be compared to about 0.122 kg CO_2 per pkm for travel by air (long-distance flights, global average; cf. UNWTO-UNEP-WMO 2008). It should also be noted that emissions from travel by bus are lower even though the flight route is considerably shorter at 7,850 km (cf. Finnair flight calculator 2010).

Regions such as Europe could also learn from other continents where long-distance travel on a regular basis is more common and better accepted by travellers. For instance, Greyhound Lines, Inc., provides transport between 2,300 destinations with 13,000 daily departures across North America, and into Mexico. The company was founded in 1914, and transports 25 million passengers per year in the USA alone (Greyhound 2010).

As an example for trip length, Greyhound in the USA offers coast-to-coast services with a single transfer. For instance, a trip from Los Angeles to New York takes 2 days 17 hours, with a single transfer in St Louis. Greyhound basically covers all of the US and Canada. Similarly, Greyhound Australia connects all major cities in the continent, where for instance the connection Perth–Darwin can be covered in 62 hours. In many countries, bus services have improved considerably, as bus companies have sought to improve their services: Greyhound in North America now offers wireless Internet access, power outlets and greater leg room.

Impact

Coach-based transport systems are well developed in many areas of the world, and in particular throughout the Americas. Avanti Busreisen is an example of how coaches can also be turned into attractive transport modes for long-distance leisure travel with comparably low per capita emissions.

Source

Hans-Peter Christoph, general manager, Avanti Reisen

Website

Avanti Bus Reisen, www.avantireisen.de
Greyhound USA, www.greyhound.com

Related websites

Estrella Blanca, Mexico, www.estrellablanca.com.mx
Greyhound Australia, www.greyhound.com.au
Greyhound Canada, http://www.greyhound.ca/home/
Greyhound South Africa, www.greyhound.co.za/
National Bus Companies, Chile, www.gochile.cl/info/xporte/bus.asp
Omni Linéas, Argentina, www.omnilineas.com/about/

References

Finnair flight calculator (2010). Distance calculated for flight from Frankfurt, Germany to Beijing, China. Available from: http://www.finnair.com/emissionscalculator/. Accessed 14 January 2010.
Greyhound (2010). About Greyhound. Available from: http://www.greyhound.com/HOME/en/About/About.aspx. Accessed 12 February 2010.
Machado-Filho, H. (2009). Brazilian low-carbon transportation policies: opportunities for international support. *Climate Policy* 9(5): 495–507.
UNWTO-UNEP-WMO (2008). Climate Change and Tourism: Responding to Global Challenges. Madrid: UNWTO, UNEP and WMO.

CARBON MANAGEMENT IN FOCUS 10: 9292, NETHERLANDS

Facilitating public transport through information technology

The issue

One of the greatest obstacles in convincing people to use surface-bound public transport systems is the real or perceived inconvenience in travelling from A to B, which usually involves covering some distance by foot and the use of different transport modes (bus, train, tram, underground, ferries) (e.g. Perrels *et al.* 2008). These require coordination, but information on timetables is often only available from individual operators. As there is usually a need to change transport connections during the trip, there is also an incurred risk of delays, which in the worst case makes travel schedules useless. In contrast, cars are generally seen to provide direct door-to-door connections, and can be easily equipped with advanced navigation systems.

The solution

9292 is a Dutch collaborative initiative involving all public transport companies in the Netherlands. 9292 is a subsidiary of *Reisinformatiegroep bv*, and collects databases with schedules for all Dutch public transportation systems. These databases are interconnected by 9292, allowing the user to find the fastest way to travel by public transport from any given starting point in the Netherlands to any given end point in the country. The service can be accessed by telephone or looked up on the Internet. As outlined by Aarnout Mijling, the PR and PA Manager of 9292, more than 100 million travel requests were processed in 2009.

As an important innovation, the 9292 service has been turned into an iPhone application, which can also be used on other phones. Used on the iPhone, the application automatically recognizes the location of the user, which can be used as the starting point for the planned journey, though any other starting point can be chosen. The destination (as well as the starting point) can be typed in by exact address, and within seconds the application will display suggestions for travel schedules for any given day or time of the day, also including distances walked on foot, for instance to the next bus stop. A map display can be shown to find the way. Importantly, if any connection has been missed, the application can recalculate the trip by pressing just one button. While focusing primarily on public transport, 9292 also allows car drivers to combine car and public transport, for instance by identifying park-and-ride locations.

The service is free of charge for Internet users, the download of the iPhone application costs €2.39 (in 2009). Telephone services are more expensive at €0.70 per minute, with a maximum charge of €14.00. The service is currently only available in the Netherlands, but Aarnout Mijling anticipates that it will soon be available as an Internet-based service throughout the EU.

To create the application, Reiseinformatiegroep has been collecting and coordinating travel databases since 1992. According to Aarnout Mijling, it took only four months to develop the application, which was organized as a competition between student teams. Informatics master students were asked to develop the 'ultimate' public transport navigator. Thirteen teams participated in the project, and the winners were selected based on the criteria innovation, user friendliness and programming. The application can be developed for any country in the world, provided there is data for all transport systems. Even though the costs for developing the application are not recovered from users in the case of 9292, their development should be in the primary interest of all public transport providers, as planning travel schedules is a key obstacle for using public transport.

Impact

The application helps to make the use of public transport systems more convenient and competitive. With interconnected timetables being available at a glance, it becomes far more attractive to travel 'public', particularly because public transport is often faster than individual motorized transport, does not incur problems in finding parking, and can even be cheaper. The application has even greater appeal when a payment function is simultaneously integrated in the software (see Related websites, Swiss Railways).

Source

Aarnout Mijling, PR and PA Manager 9292, Netherlands

Website

9292, www.9292ov.nl

Application download, www.journeyplanner.9292.nl/599/Mobile_service/

Related websites

Swiss Railways, www.sbb-mobileworld.ch/ (Swiss Railways SBB offers a similar service with a 'take me home' function. Travellers can also pay for tickets with their mobile phones)

Reference

Perrels, A., Himanen, V. and Lee-Gosselin, M. (eds) (2008). *Building Blocks for Sustainable Transport: obstacles, trends, solutions*. Bingley: Emerald Group Publishing Limited.

CRUISE SHIPS

Technical and management options to reduce emissions from shipping were discussed in Chapter 9, 'Technology'. However, even if considerable specific emission reductions are achieved, cruise ships will remain high emitters on a per pkm or per passenger night basis. Given the rapid growth in cruise ship holidays, this might ultimately mean that the cruise ship concept has to be reconsidered with a focus on three aspects:

1 the distances travelled, also as a ratio of port to travel times;
2 the speed at which ships travel;
3 the use of alternative ship types that can make use of wind propulsion, such as windjammers or yachts.

With regard to distances travelled as well as travel speeds, passengers often move day and night onboard modern cruise ships, i.e. the very purpose of the journey is movement. In the future, cruise ship trip planners might have to consider shorter routes with more visits to ports to reduce overall travel distances and to overcome the need to move at high speeds, as there is a non-linear relationship between speed and fuel use, i.e. fuel use increases exponentially with speed. Moreover, if alternative ship types were developed, greater use could be made of wind propulsion. As shown in Carbon Management in Focus 11, this can be highly attractive for tourists.

CARBON MANAGEMENT IN FOCUS 11: STAR CLIPPERS, MONACO

Low-carbon cruise experiences

The issue

Cruise ship journeys are very energy intense and cause emissions considerably greater than most other vacations: for instance, Eijgelaar *et al.* (2010) calculate that cruise ships emit on global average 169 kg CO_2 per passenger per day. As there is considerable growth in interest in cruise ship holiday experiences, there is a need to reduce emissions from this highly energy-intense tourism sector.

The solution

Star Clippers, a Monaco-based company founded in 1988, specializes in medium-sized sailboat experiences with three ships carrying 227, 170 and 170 passengers to destinations in the Mediterranean, South-East Asia, the Caribbean, Costa Rica, French Polynesia, the South Pacific, Atlantic and Indian Ocean. The three ships carry about 20,000 passengers per year, mainly relying on sails for propulsion, even though electricity is needed for refrigeration and A/C. When there is wind, only auxiliary engines are used, but in times of calm weather, the ship's main engine is run as well. Fuel consumption of low sulphur gas oil is considerable at 2.5 metric tonnes per day on days without wind, corresponding to about 40 kg CO_2 per day per passenger (calculated for 200 passengers, i.e. at a 90 per cent load factor and consuming the equivalent of 2,500 kg of diesel at a conversion factor of 2.6 kg CO_2 per litre). The figure of 40 kg CO_2 is, however, only one quarter of the emissions caused on global average by cruise ships. When the ship can sail, fuel consumption declines to 1.8 metric tonnes per day for the auxiliary engines, corresponding to about 30 kg CO_2 per passenger per day, i.e. less than one fifth of emissions caused on cruise ships. Passengers appear to be content with the sailing experience, as outlined by Farhat Shamim, Vice President Operations: '65 per cent of our clients return for another journey with our ships'.

Impact

Star Clippers have shown that lower-carbon sailing experiences can be attractive. A wide range of sailing boats is now available for cruising (see Related websites), and further development of these for both cruises as well as passenger transport to replace air travel can consequently be discussed, also with a view on strong growth in cruise ship tourism.

Source

Farhat Shamim, Vice President Operations, Star Clippers, Monaco

Website

Star Clippers, www.starclippers.com

Related websites

Seacloud, www.seacloud.com
Logemann Yacht Charter, www.logemann-yachting.de
Schenk, www.yacht.de/schenk/n003/royal.html
Solar Sailor, www.solarsailor.com.au
Deutscher Bundesverband WindEnergie (German Wind Energy Association), www.windschiffe.de
SkySails, www.skysails.info

Reference

Eijgelaar, E., Thaper, C. and Peeters, P. (2010). Antarctic cruise tourism: the paradoxes of ambassadorship, 'last chance tourism' and GHG emissions. *Journal of Sustainable Tourism* 18(3): in press.

ACCOMMODATION

Accommodation establishments have considerable potential to reduce energy. Ideally, this starts with the construction of new hotels, which can theoretically be built as passive energy structures, or at the very least as low-energy buildings, as it is comparably cheap and cost-effective to consider energy-saving measures when hotels are built. For existing hotels, heating and A/C are the primary factors in energy consumption, and one of the most important management measures is thus to adjust room temperatures to the lowest (heating) and highest (A/C) levels customers will still perceive as comfortable. This also means adjusting temperatures to optimal levels only shortly before rooms are actually used. With regard to ideal temperatures, the Carbon Trust suggests (2010, based on CIBSE 2006), temperatures between 16–18°C for kitchens and laundries, 19–21°C for corridors and guest bedrooms, 20–22°C in bars and lounges, 22–24°C in restaurants and dining rooms, and 26–27°C in guest bathrooms (in the UK).

It seems unclear, however, why temperatures in restaurants would have to exceed those in bars and lounges, and why guest bathrooms would have to have temperatures as high as 26–27°C, given that heat loss is high in bathrooms because of ventilation, while the time spent in bathrooms is comparatively short. Often, lower temperatures, for instance in bathrooms, could be accepted by guests without any loss of comfort. This is an insight also applicable to tropical regions, where temperatures in rooms can be kept considerably higher than assumed by many managers. For instance, the Hilton Seychelles experimented with room temperatures and found that 25°C as the (adjustable) standard temperature was accepted without any complaints by guests (Gössling and Schumacher 2010). As a consequence, A/C electricity use could be considerably reduced. Energy use can also be reduced through other measures, including a reduction in hot water use for showers and baths in all climate zones, as well as freshwater treatment more generally, which can be energy intense. For instance, Bermudez-Contreras *et al.* (2008), report energy requirements of 2.6 kWh to desalinate 1 m³ of seawater. More controversial, yet feasible measures include the phasing out of electrical appliances from hotel rooms (see Carbon Management in Focus 12).

CARBON MANAGEMENT IN FOCUS 12: HOTEL TØRVIS, MARIFJØRA, NORWAY AND NATURHOTEL BALTRUM, GERMANY

Reducing the number of electrical appliances in upscale accommodation

The issue

Electrical appliances in hotel rooms can add considerably to energy use, now including anything from known standards such as TVs, mini-bars, hairdryers, irons, heated towel rails, mini-safes, loudspeakers (radio) and telephones in bathrooms, bathroom scales, to emerging standards including self-cleaning and heated toilet seats, or heated mirrors. Often, the number of appliances in a room is seen as a sign of, or a precondition for, high room and hotel standards: German hotel stars (Hotelsterne 2009), for instance, are awarded on the basis of points allocated for everything from lighted vanity mirrors, heated towel rails, personal care products in one-way packaging, hairdryers, bathroom scales, mini-safes, A/C, CD, DVD, or MP3 players, loudspeakers in the bathroom, Internet-PC in the room, iron, daily change of bed linen, mini-bar, to coffee machines or water boilers (see also www.hotelstars.org, for similar classifications in other European countries). Clearly, the production of electrical appliances, as well as their energy use in the room (standby or running) adds considerably to overall energy use in accommodation establishments, while it is questionable whether, for instance, one-way packaging still is a sign of quality.

The solution

A number of upscale accommodation establishments have more recently started to question the practice of providing electrical appliances. Two hotels that have removed most in-room appliances are Hotel Tørvis, Marifjøra, Norway and Naturhotel Baltrum, on the island of Baltrum, Germany. Naturhotel Baltrum opened in 2008, and has now approximately 5,000 guest nights per year in its 28 rooms. In order to save costs, but also to address a clientele seeking relaxation in a nature-dominated environment, owner Oliver Noppen decided not to have any electronic appliances in the rooms, except hairdryers (rooms do not have telephones either). Hotel Tørvis opened in 2008 as well, and has 27 rooms, currently accounting for 6,000 guest nights per year.

Both hotels cater to an upscale market, with room prices in the order of NOK1,750 (€210, Hotel Tørvis) and €145 (Naturhotel Baltrum) per night per double room, including breakfast. Both hotels have removed electrical appliances because of environmental and/or cost considerations, but also in an effort to 'educate' guests. As Bård Huseby, Hotel director, Hotel Tørvis puts it:

> The reason why we don't have TV sets in the rooms is partially because of the environment, partially because we don't think it is adequate for a hotel like ours. We want our guests to spend time outside in the beautiful environment around us, and in the hotel's guest areas.

Both Naturhotel Baltrum and Hotel Tørvis have spacious guest areas, but also offer a separate TV room, with options to watch DVDs should guests wish. Naturhotel Baltrum offers rental TV sets free of charge, but according to owner Oliver Noppen, there have been few requests in 2008, when the hotel opened, and none in 2009:

> We thought that some people might request TV sets, so we bought a number as a back-up, to hand out to clients if they wished to watch TV in their rooms. However, we hardly ever were asked for a TV set during the first year, and nobody has asked this year.

According to Oliver Noppen, guests enjoy a break from watching TV, instead reading books or engaging in discussions with other guests. Hotel Tørvis also reports that 90 per cent of guests react in a positive way – business travellers sometimes ask for a TV, however, and one of the rooms has thus been equipped with a set. Both hotels also offer a selection of books guests can borrow. Given the success of the concept, the owners of Hotel Tørvis have decided to also skip TV sets and mini-bars in other accommodation establishments they own, including Hotel Mundal and Bed & Breakfast Nigardsbreen, both not far from Hotel Tørvis. Bård Huseby believes that the concept could be used in all hotels not primarily accommodating business travellers. It is important, however, to offer guest areas and to also have special programmes for children.

Impact

Both hotels are very positive about the concept, which helps to reduce costs, and leads to considerable reductions in energy use. Even for the guests, the partially 'enforced' non-TV environment is usually a positive experience, and eventually something that makes the stay particularly memorable. In terms of avoided energy use, a mini-bar consumes between 0.6–1.1 kWh per day, which adds up to more than 13,000 kWh per year (based on a hotel with 45 rooms with mini-bars using 0.8 kWh per day, running 365 days per year; Dometic 2009), corresponding to emissions of between 1.25 t CO_2 (based on the Nordic energy mix of about 0.096 kg CO_2 per kWh; Andersson and Lukaszevicz (2006)) and 7 t CO_2 (grid electricity in the UK: 0.537 kg CO_2 per kWh; Carbon Trust 2008). A TV on standby uses considerably less energy, but 45 TV sets would add another 2,800 kWh per year to electricity use (calculation standby: 0.006 kWh × 365 days × 23.5 hours × 45 TV sets; calculation TV 'on': 0.060 kWh × 365 days × 0.5 hours × 45 TV sets; Energy Star (2009)).

Sources

Bård Huseby, Hotel Director, Hotel Tørvis, Norway
Oliver Noppen, Hotel Director, Naturhotel Baltrum, Baltrum, Germany

Websites

Naturhotel Baltrum, www.naturhotel-baltrum.de
Hotel Tørvis, www.torvis.no

Related websites

Hotel Mundal, Norway, www.hotelmundal.no
Bed and Breakfast Nigardsbreen, http://www.nigardsbreen.com

References

Andersson, E. and Lukaszevicz, P. (2006). *Energy Consumption and Related Air Pollution for Scandinavian Electric Passenger Trains*. Report KTH/AVE 2006: 46. Stockholm: Royal Institute of Technology.

Carbon Trust (2008). Greenhouse Gas Conversion Factors. Available from: http://www.carbontrust.co.uk/resource/conversion_factors/default.htm. Accessed 3 December 2009.

Dometic (2009). HiPro Mini bars. Available from: http://www.dometic.com/FileOrganizer/1-international/hotel/leaflets/HiPro_miniBars_EN.pdf. Accessed 3 December 2009.

Energy Star (2009). Energy Star Television Product List. Available from: http://downloads.energystar.gov/bi/qplist/tv_prod_list.pdf. Accessed 3 December 2009.

Hotelsterne (2009). Criteria 2010–2014. Available from: http://www.hotelsterne.de/uk/downloads/catalogue_of_criteria_2010-2014.pdf. Accessed 3 December 2009.

With regard to branding and image, initiatives to use renewable energy, participation in certification schemes, or the public display of renewable energy harvested (see Carbon Management in Focus 6), can all be used to create a positive image of accommodation establishments, as the use of renewable energy is generally understood as something positive (e.g. Gössling *et al.* 2005; Gössling and Schumacher 2010). Communication of pro-environmental engagement might also allow involvement of tourists, for instance through payments of premiums, and can be an important factor in staff motivation (Carbon Management in Focus 33). Hotel Victoria, Germany, for instance, encourages employees to suggest improvements for energy reductions, and rewards innovative ideas. Accommodation establishments can also make use of their customer preferences of renewable energy systems or carbon-neutrality. For instance, Dalton *et al.* (2008b) found that 49 per cent of Australian tourists were willing to pay extra for renewable energy systems, out of which 92 per cent were willing to pay a premium corresponding to 1–5 per cent above their usual costs. In another study, Gössling and Schumacher (2010) found that 38.5 per cent of a sample of international tourists in the Seychelles expressed positive willingness to pay for carbon-neutrality of their accommodation, out of which 48 per cent stated they would be willing to pay a premium of at least €5 per night. While these values are not representative, they nevertheless indicate that there is considerable potential to involve tourists emotionally and financially in strategies to implement renewable energy schemes.

Advice for energy management in accommodation is available from a range of organizations, including International Tourism Partnership (2008), EUHOFA, IH&RA, UNEP (2001), or South West Tourism (2009). The German Hotel and Restaurant Association (Carbon Management in Focus 13) is an example of an organization seeking to strategically involve its members in energy management.

CARBON MANAGEMENT IN FOCUS 13: GERMAN HOTEL AND RESTAURANT ASSOCIATION

Involving businesses in mitigation

The issue

Tourism is dominated by small- and medium-sized enterprises (SMEs). Philips and Louvieris (2005), for instance, report that 94 per cent of all tourism firms in Europe employ less than 10 persons. Given the diverse and multi-sectorial structure of the tourism industry, a key issue in carbon management is to reach out to millions of stakeholders, in which tourism organizations have a key role.

The solution

In 2006, Dehoga (Deutscher Hotel- und Gaststättenverband (German Hotel and Restaurant Association)), in cooperation with IHA, Hotelverband Deutschland (German Hotel Association) and Bundesumweltministerium (German Federal Ministry for the Environment Nature Conservation and Nuclear Safety) launched a campaign to reduce energy use in hotels and restaurants, predominantly with a view to cutting energy costs, which account for up to 10 per cent of turnover in restaurants and accommodation – a share that is rising (Dehoga 2009). By launching Energiekampagne (energy campaign), Dehoga, IHA and Ministry for the Environment saw an opportunity to reduce operational costs and to make a contribution to climate mitigation. The campaign will run to spring 2011, and discussions about an extension are ongoing.

Dehoga represents 45,227 accommodation businesses, 183,500 restaurants, and 11,067 firms in tenacy and catering, totalling 239,794 firms with more than 1.1 million employees. As such, the organization is thus at the centre of a network involving most accommodation and restaurant businesses in Germany, and has considerable power over the management innovations that could lead to a decline in energy use. 'Energy campaign' was launched with information about a new Internet portal, www.energiekampagne-gastgewerbe.de, which serves as an information platform for interested businesses. The website provides information on various topics, including: Where to save energy?, Energy-savings programme, Financial support and consultancy, Energy forum (questions and answers by firms), Current issues, and Downloads and links. Under 'Where to save energy?', a wide range of information sheets can be accessed and downloaded, explaining energy use in tourism and hospitality firms, together with suggestions for energy savings. For firms signing up to the 'Energy-savings programme', which is free of charge, an energy account is created. The account can be fed with information regarding a business's energy use, which is automatically analysed, and recommendations for energy savings are made. As shown in Figure 10.1 and Table 10.1, participants

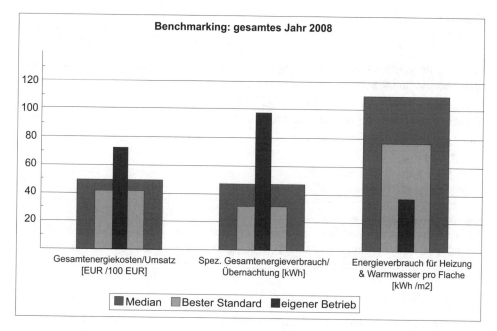

Figure 10.1 *Energy benchmarking, Dehoga*
Columns show: energy cost to turnover ratio; energy use in kWh per guest night; energy use for heating and warm water in kwh per m². Colour schemes: Dark outer space: median; centre space: best practice; column in front: own business.
Source: Energiekampagne (2009)

receive an energy benchmarking, showing them their performance in comparison to others, as well as information about the development of their energy use over time, which allows them to monitor their performance.

All participating firms also receive an energy savings letter (Energiesparblätter) to discuss how energy use can be minimized in specific areas – up to now, 24 energy savings letters have been produced.

The energy campaign is managed by just one person employed part-time, and practically supported by Adelphi Research, a non-profit organization supporting sustainable development strategies. Adelphi Research has staff working on this project which corresponds to 2.5 full-time jobs. However, as outlined by Matthias Meier, Advisor for Marketing and Statistics at Dehoga, more staff would be needed, also to deal with individual information requests. By December 2009, almost 5,000 firms registered for participation in the Energy campaign, including almost 2,000 hotels, 470 bed & breakfast establishments, 163 pensions, and 1,404 pubs. This is seen as a success, as it was anticipated that only 3,000 businesses would have signed up to the campaign after three years.

Table 10.1 *Energy and emissions monitoring*

Energie-Kennzahl	2007	2008
Gesamtenergieverbrauch für Heizung & Warmwasser in kWh	288.000,00	330.000,00 ↑
Gesamtenergiekosten pro Umsatz in €/1000€	55,00	72,00 ↑
Gesamtemergiekosten pro Übernachtung in €	3,99	7,25 ↑
Spez.Gesamtenergieverbrauch pro Übernachtung in kWh	45,38	98,29 ↑
Energieverbrauch für Heizung & Warnwasser pro Fläche in kWh/m²	118,42	36,56 ↓

Source: Energiekampagne (2009)
Key performance indicators (from top): total enery use for heating and warm water in kWh; total energy cost to turnover ratio (in €/1000€), energy cost per guest night in €; total energy use per guest night in kWh; total energy use for heating and warm water in kWh/m².

In this sense, the project has been a huge success, even though in terms of a relative share, this represents only 2 per cent of restaurants and accommodation establishments in Germany (a similar share was reached in campaigns by South West England, see Carbon Management in Focus 27). Even fewer firms (1,000) have registered their energy data, possibly as a result of high workloads in day-to-day operations, and a general disinterest in energy-related issues. Overall, even though energy management can lead to considerable economic savings, this might not be a strong enough argument to convince a significant share of businesses to become interested in energy-related issues. The example shows, however, that tourism networks such as Dehoga can reach out to high business numbers, and initiate carbon management processes. If supported by other measures, such as for instance legal demands on energy reduction or carbon taxes (see Chapter 13), it is likely that approaches such as the energy campaign will receive far greater interest.

Impact

The energy campaign has used economic costs as an avenue to creating interest in saving energy. Key performance indicators address energy use in combination with costs, thus linking an environmental and an economic parameter. This creates knowledge on energy use, and can subsequently lead to further interest in the topic, also including climate change. Furthermore, there is a competitive element in the campaign, as businesses compare each other, which might be one of the most effective means of achieving change (see also Carbon Management in Focus 33).

Source

Matthias Meier, Advisor Marketing and Statistics, Dehoga

Website

Energy campaign, www.energiekampagne-gastgewerbe.de

Related websites

Adelphi Research, www.adelphi-research.de
Dehoga, www.dehoga.de
German Federal Ministry for the Environment, www.bmu.de
Hotelverband Deutschland, www.hotellerie.de

References

Dehoga (2009). Energiekampagne Gastgewerbe. Available from: http://www.dehoga-bundesverband.de/home/page_sta_1433.html. Accessed 9 December 2009.

Energiekampagne (2009) Energiekampagne Aktuell 10–9/2009. Available from: http://www.energiekampagne-gastgewerbe.de/images/stories/Aktuelles/Newsletter/news-letter_10_2009.pdf. Accessed 9 December 2009.

Phillips, P. and Louvieris, P. (2005). Performance measurement systems in tourism, hospitality and leisure small medium-sized enterprises: a balanced scorecard perspective. *Journal of Travel Research* 44: 201–211.

RESTAURANTS

By applying food management practices and making more informed choices about the purchasing, preparation and presentation of their food, restaurants can contribute to considerably reduced GHG emissions. A contribution to these processes has also been made by governments, organizations and retailers seeking to support more climatically sustainable food consumption (cf. Tesco (2009), a UK retailer carbon-labelling selected foods). A number of organizations, in some cases on behalf of governments, have also developed food calculators to help inform customers about the options available to them in choosing low-carbon food (e.g. Food Carbon 2009). Such carbon-labelling approaches have even been used with considerable success in restaurants in Sweden.

CARBON MANAGEMENT IN FOCUS 14: MAX HAMBURGARE, SWEDEN

Informing customer decisions through food carbon-labelling

The issue

One of the greatest challenges in dealing with climate mitigation is to educate people on the abstract concept of GHGs, and to make them understand how various consumption choices contribute to emissions, as well as how relevant these emissions are in terms of sustainable lifestyles. Food is, on a 'farm-to-plate' basis, responsible for an estimated 20 per cent of individual emissions in industrialized countries (for a Norwegian case study see Hille *et al.* 2008). Influencing food choices is thus of great importance in achieving climatically sustainable lifestyles, but this is in reality hampered by many difficulties, including problems with identifying the exact amount of GHG emissions associated with the production and/or consumption of a given meal (for discussion see Gössling *et al.* 2010). Food carbon-labelling has been introduced by companies such as supermarket chain Tesco in the UK (Tesco 2009), but no attempts have so far been made to introduce carbon-labelling in restaurants.

The solution

Max Hamburgare (Max hamburgers) opened in 1968, and there are now 67 restaurants in Sweden. The chain had a turnover of SEK1,050 million (about €100 million) in 2008 and is rapidly expanding: the aim is to operate 120 restaurants by 2012 (Max 2009a). Max Hamburgare has systematically focused on health and climate change in its marketing, and launched various campaigns to communicate its leadership in these issues, including, for instance, 'the world's first bike-in' franchise in Gotland, a lacto-ovo menu, and low-fat cooking practices.

In 2008, the chain decided to become carbon-neutral. In order to achieve this, several measures were carried out, including the measurement of the company's carbon footprint, along with assessments of the GHG-equivalent content of the various foods offered. Max also decided to compensate the company's emissions, including those of suppliers, through tree-planting in Africa. More importantly, the company has implemented a wide range of programmes to reduce emissions, including the sourcing of most vegetables during growing season and from Swedish farms. Beef and chicken are also bought from Swedish farms, all fish is eco-certified and there are no purchases of threatened fish species. Max has also implemented pro-environmental employee training, low-energy LED lighting, and minimization of transports, as well as the use of environmentally friendly cars. Green energy is used in all restaurants, sourced entirely from wind power:

> The use of energy sourced from wind farms in our restaurants reduces our annual carbon emissions by 640 tonnes. Furthermore, our switch to wind power ensures that 56 kilograms less nuclear waste is generated each year.
>
> (Max 2009b)

Based on a calculation by The Natural Step, a consultancy, the chain's total carbon footprint was estimated to be in the order of 27,000t CO_2 per year, about 70 per cent of this associated with the production of beef. Carbon emissions for various meals consequently vary significantly, mostly depending on the use of beef in comparison to alternative meats, fish or vegetables. This led to the most important innovation introduced by Max Hamburgare, i.e. the chain's decision to carbon-label its foods, illustrating the emissions associated with the consumption of each burger or meal-component on the restaurants' illuminated displays as well as in menus (Figure 10.2).

Detailed information on GHG content of all products can also be found on the company's website. As table 10.2 shows, emissions are calculated on a CO_2-eq basis, i.e. considering emissions from NO_x, N_2O and CH_4, which are important GHGs associated with agriculture and livestock breeding. Through this information, customers learn to understand the climate implications of their food choices, and might favour lower carbon meals. For instance, a customer might choose the Max fish menu, which entails emissions of 0.4 kg CO_2-eq, rather than the Max Ultimate Cheese menu causing 1.9 kg CO_2-eq. The difference between the 'best' and the 'worst' menu choice is a considerable factor of 14 (e.g. Fishburger compared to Max de Luxe burger, see Table 10.2).

Table 10.2 also shows that menu add-ons, such as orange juice or milkshakes can also contribute to considerable emissions. This might be relevant, also in terms of comparative choices, as few guests might have known that, for instance, orange juice is 40 per cent more climatically harmful than apple juice. Max has

Figure 10.2 *Carbon-labelling of foods on illuminated displays, Max hamburgare*
Source: Max (2009a)

Table 10.2 *Carbon content of various foods offered at Max*

Food component	CO_2-eq
	(kg)
Cheeseburger	0.9
Hamburger	0.8
Max de Luxe burger	2.9
Green menu (Lacto-ovo)	0.5
Chicken nuggets (9 pieces)	0.4
Chicken menu	0.6
Max menu	1.9
Fishburger	0.2
Falafelburger	0.2
Cheesecake desert	0.1
Ice Sundae	0.2
Orange juice (0,3 l)	0.5
Apple juice (0,3 l)	0.3
Milk	0.3
Milkshake	0.4
Chicken salad	0.5
Veggie salad	0.4
French fries	0.1

Source: Max 2009b

thus assumed an important role in informing customers about the carbon content of various foodstuffs. This is particularly relevant given problems with carbon-labelling of packaged foods, where system boundaries are often difficult to identify (Gössling *et al.* 2010). A chain such as Max is in a better position to calculate the carbon content of their limited number of meals, as they can source their products under the same conditions, and thus provide reliable calculations.

Max's carbon label has been a success. In 2008, 66,850 climate friendly burgers were sold (vegetarian, chicken, or fishburgers), corresponding to 15 per cent of overall sales. Pär Larshans, Max's Director of Sustainability, believes that the high share of these products is almost entirely a result of the carbon-labelling on menus. This is also mirrored in customer reactions, which have been almost entirely positive, or, in Pär Larshans' words: 'it's raining superlatives'. Individual customers might have been uncomfortable with being confronted with the climate change realities of their food choices, but this is outweighed by the branding impact of the carbon-labelling. According to Pär Larshans, there have been reports on Max on Danish TV1 and BBC World News in December 2009, and the chain was earlier awarded the Swedish award of Green Capitalist 2008 (Veckans Affärer 2009).

Impact

Food carbon-labelling is an important measure to inform customers and to facilitate more climatically friendly food choices. Max Hamburgare has shown that it is feasible to introduce carbon-labelling in hamburger chains, and that customers are willing to learn (notably customers of hamburger chains): there is evidence that carbon-labelling actually influences customer choices, and there is a possibility that customers take part of their new knowledge on CO_2 and carbon intensities home. Restaurants can thus succeed in introducing an abstract concept, i.e. GHG intensities, into everyday decision-making.

Source

Pär Larshans, Director of Sustainability, Max Hamburgare, Sweden

Website

Max, www.max.se

Related websites

The Natural Step, www.thenaturalstep.org

References

Gössling, S., Garrod, B., Aall, C., Hille, J. and Peeters, P. (2010). Food management in tourism. Reducing tourism's carbon 'foodprint'. *Tourism Management*, in press.

Hille, J., Sataøen, H.L., Aall, C. and Storm, H.N. (2008). Miljøbelastningen av norsk forbruk og produksjon 1987–2007. Vestlandsforsking, Sogndal. Available from: http://www. vestforsk.no/www/show.do?page=12&articleid=2201. Accessed 10 December 2009.

Max (2009a). Om Max. Utvecklingen. available from: http://www.max.se/max. aspx?page=utveckling. Accessed 11 December 2009.

Max (2009b). Environment. Max Climate Activities. Available from: http://www.max.se/ en/environment.aspx. Accessed 11 December 2009.

Tesco (2009). Our carbon label findings. Available from: http://www.tesco.com/assets/ greenerliving/content/documents/pdfs/carbon_label_findings.pdf. Accessed 20 February 2010.

Veckans Affärer (2009). Han är Årets Gröna Kapitalist Available from: http://www.va.se/ nyheter/2009/01/21/han-blir-arets-grona-kapit/. Accessed 10 December 2009.

As shown in table 10.3, measures to reduce GHG emissions in restaurants can pertain to purchases, preparation and presentation (Gössling *et al.* 2010). With regard to purchases, 'don't buy policies' include vegetables grown in heated greenhouses, foods involving air transport, problematic species such as lobster, imported beef, and environmentally harmful materials such as aluminium foil (for a discussion of 'food miles' see also DEFRA 2005; Xuereb 2005; Saunders *et al.* 2006; Weber and Matthews 2008). 'Buy less policies' would seek to generally reduce the amount of beef, deep-sea and farmed carnivorous fish, rice,

Table 10.3 *Recommendations for climatically sustainable food management*

Purchases	**RED – Buy as little as possible policy**
	• Don't buy vegetables grown in heated greenhouses
	• Don't buy foods involving air transport
	• Don't buy specific species, such as giant, king and tiger prawns, lobster
	• Don't buy imported beef
	• Don't buy aluminium foil
	AMBER – Buy less policy
	• Buy less beef
	• Buy less deep-sea fish (e.g. cod)
	• Buy less farmed carnivorous fish (e.g. salmon)
	• Buy less seasonal foods out of their season/storage time
	GREEN - Buy more policy
	• Buy more locally produced foods, if transported over short distances using CO_2-efficient modes
	• Buy more grains
	• Buy more pelagic fish
	• Buy more pork
	• Buy more chicken
	• Buy more foodstuffs with longer shelf lives
Preparation	• Purchase energy from renewable sources
	• Use more energy-efficient cooking routines
	• Do not prepare energy-intensive foods in-house
	• Put dishes on the menu that use less meat and more vegetables
	• Always offer a vegetarian alternative
	• Prepare meals only after orders have been placed
	• Plan purchases to avoid waste
	• Separate food waste from general waste
Presentation	• Always offer a vegetarian alternative
	• Reduce portion sizes at buffets, with more regular replenishment
	• Reduce plate size at buffets
	• Arrange buffets so that less carbon-intensive foods are at the centre
	• Train staff to recommend less carbon-intensive dishes
	• Avoid single-use packaging

Source: Gössling *et al.* 2010

seasonal foods out of their season time, and foods with high weight-to-calorie or volume-to-calorie ratios. 'Buy more policies' would seek to use greater amounts of locally produced foods (transported over short distances, using CO_2-efficient modes), potatoes and grains, pelagic fish, pork and chicken, as well as foodstuffs with longer shelf lives to reduce wastage. It is unclear whether organic food purchases make a significant contribution to climate change mitigation (for discussion see Gössling *et al.* 2010), but there are other benefits associated with it, such as its role in countering trends of globalization and industrialization, food safety (Vos 2000), large-scale conversion of ecosystems such as rainforests for soybean or palm oil production (Morton *et al.* 2006; Costa *et al.* 2007) or food technology (Chan and Lai 2009). Organic farming systems can also help to maintain landscapes and biodiversity (Norton *et al.* 2009) and to ensure that a greater share of the profits of food production remains with the farmer.

Local sourcing of foodstuffs more generally is of particular importance in tourism in developing countries, where imports over large distances are often associated with high emissions. To this end, Hilton hotels launched the Caribbean Regional Program 'Adopt a Farmer' in cooperation with the World Travel Foundation to strengthen supply chains between farmers and hotels, also advising farmers on quality, desired produce, and funding technology to increase production (Paulina Bohdanowicz, Hilton Sustainability Manager Europe, personal communication 2009). Such strategies appear feasible, and are supported by scientific studies: for instance, Torres (2002) reports that international tourists in Yucatan, Mexico, appear far more amenable to eating local foods than hotel managers seem to believe, while Bélisle (1984) found that the share of imported foodstuffs varied between 5 per cent and 80 per cent in hotels across Jamaica, suggesting that food import choices are, to a large degree, made by hotel managers rather than by tourists.

Preparation could include purchases of energy from renewable sources, energy-efficient cooking routines, purchases of energy-intensive foods such as bread, use of greater shares of vegetables in dishes, preparing meals only after orders have been placed, planning purchases to avoid waste, and separating food waste from general waste (for further discussion see Gössling *et al.* 2010). With regard to the foodstuffs sourced, companies such as SSP Sweden (2009) also claim to have adopted choice-editing policies, for instance by not purchasing fish species identified by the WWF as being threatened. Likewise, Scandic Hotels has edited out giant shrimps and avoids purchases of bottled water (see Carbon Management in Focus 15).

CARBON MANAGEMENT IN FOCUS 15: SCANDIC HOTELS, SWEDEN

Choice-editing food – the case of prawns

The issue

Many foodstuffs used in restaurants or by foodservice providers more generally are environmentally or socially problematic. For instance, farmed prawns or shrimps imported from the tropics are known to lead to mangrove destruction on a massive scale as well as wide-reaching social problems related to land seizures and violence against locals making use of mangrove fisheries (Martinez-Alier 2002). It is estimated that one shrimp farm creates 65 jobs, while displacing 50,000 people through loss of land and fisheries (World Resources Institute (WRI) 2004). Martinez-Alier (2002: 87) also points at the more complex relationships with shrimp production:

In Chakaria Sunderbans [Bangladesh], some 50,000 ha of mangroves have been converted into shrimp ponds since the early 1980s, with initial support from the World Bank. Television reports of flooding and loss of life in Bangladesh are regularly seen in northern homes, but the connection with destroyed mangroves, abandoned shrimp farms and decreased coastal defense against cyclones is not often made.

Global prawn production reached 4.2 million tonnes in 2001, corresponding to an average of 0.7 kg per human being (Worldwatch Institute 2004). Most prawns are caught in the wild (75 per cent), but aquaculture is becoming increasingly important. The Worldwatch Institute (2004) reports that 25 per cent of global mangroves have been lost in the past two decades, mostly for prawn farming. Most prawns are consumed in China, the USA, Japan and Europe, with Japan having the highest per capita consumption. Mangrove destruction leads to emissions of GHGs, with global storage of carbon in mangrove biomass in the order of 4 Gt, and one hectare of mangroves storing 12 t of carbon per year (Twilley *et al.* 1992; see also Nellemann *et al.* 2009). When shrimps are caught in the wild, this entails high fuel use in fisheries (cf. Tyedmers 2001), and shrimps have to be transported deep-frozen to customers in other continents. Shrimps also account for one third of the world fisheries' discarded catches, but less than 2 per cent of the seafood (Worldwatch Institute 2004; for other evaluations of economic benefits and environmental costs see Gunawardena and Rowan 2005; Rönnbäck 1999).

The solution

Scandic Hotels is a European hotel chain that has decided to no longer serve prawns, i.e. any species larger than the common North Sea prawns, in its restaurants. The decision was made by Scandic's former CEO Jean-Paul Hertzog in spring 2006, on suggestion by sustainability manager Jan Peter Bergkvist, who in turn reacted to a request by Naturskyddsföreningen (the Swedish Society for Nature Conservation) to no longer serve prawns in Scandic restaurants. According to an estimate by Jan Peter Bergkvist, some 100,000 kg of prawns were served annually in Scandic restaurants prior to the new no-prawn policy.

Editing out prawns had no effect on Scandic Hotels. Prawns are an exclusive foodstuff that can be sold at comparatively high prices, but they are also expensive to buy and various fish species can serve as suitable substitutes. Moreover, when not on the menu, prawns might not be missed by customers at all. Scandic even chose to set up posters informing customers that prawns had been taken away from the menu for environmental reasons, presupposing positive reactions by customers. It was considered that the no-prawn campaign would reinforce the brand, while simultaneously improving the chain's environmental performance. Scandic also sent out a press release, and yielded considerable positive response with an estimated marketing value of 1.5 million Swedish crowns (€150,000). In retrospect, says Inger Matsson, Manager Sustainable Business, all reactions by customers were indeed positive, indicating that there is considerable room for choice-editing foodstuffs and to proactively communicate such action.

Impact

Scandic Hotels have shown that tourism stakeholders can guide decision-making of customers, proactively communicate their actions, and possibly even foster pro-environmental behaviour at home. Scandic has more recently also started to edit out red-listed fish species, following the WWF's (2008) recommendations. Likewise, foodstuffs based on genetically modified organisms (GMO) are not served in Scandic restaurants. As food volumes purchased by hotels can be substantial, this also has an impact on supply chains and their sourcing of foods.

Source

Inger Mattsson, Manager Sustainable Business, Scandic Hotels, Sweden

Website

Scandic Hotels, www.scandichotels.com/responsibility

Related websites

Marine Stewardship Council, www.msc.org

References

Gunawardena, M. and Rowan, J.S. (2005). Economic valuation of a mangrove ecosystem threatened by shrimp aquaculture in Sri Lanka. *Environmental Management* 36(4): 535–550.

Martinez-Alier, J. (2002). *The Environmentalism of the Poor: a study of ecological conflicts and valuation*. Cheltenham, UK: Edward Elgar.

Nellemann, C., Corcoran, E., Duarte, C.M., Valdés, L., DeYoung, C., Fonseca, L., Grimsditch, G. (Eds) (2009). *Blue Carbon. A Rapid Response Assessment*. United Nations Environment Programme, GRID-Arendal, Norway.

Rönnbäck, P. (1999). The ecological basis for economic value of seafood production supported by mangrove ecosystems. *Ecological Economics* 29: 235–252.

Twilley, R.R., Chen, R.H. and Hargis, T. (1992). Carbon sinks in mangroves and their implications to carbon budget of tropical coastal ecosystems. *Water, Air and Soil Pollution* 64: 265–288.

Tyedmers, P. (2001). Energy consumed by North Atlantic Fisheries. Available from: http://sres.management.dal.ca/Files/Tyedmers/Energy_Tyedmers1.pdf. Accessed 21 October 2009.

World Wide Fund for Nature (WWF) (2008). Sustainable seafood. Consumer guides. Available from: http://www.panda.org/what_we_do/how_we_work/conservation/marine/sustainable_fishing/sustainable_seafood/seafood_guides/. Accessed 5 November 2009.

Finally, 'Presentation' could include reduced portion sizes and plates at buffets, the arrangement of buffets so that less carbon-intensive foods are at the centre, the training of staff to recommend less carbon-intensive meals, and the avoidance of single-use packaging. For instance, Gössling *et al.* (2010) suggest that buffets might encourage customers to eat greater quantities of food, eat a greater proportion of climatically more relevant foods such as meats, and to choose environmentally harmful foods that they would not consume at home such as prawns. Buffet diners also tend to leave more leftovers. Ideally, buffets could however inspire customers to eat only the amount of food they wish to consume. For this, specific management strategies are necessary (see Carbon Management in Focus 17). Again, these strategies are supported by evidence that customer preferences are increasingly turning toward socially and environmentally responsible products (Mitchell 2001; Klein and Dawar 2004), with perceptions of value having considerable importance (Gallastegui and Spain 2002; McCarty and Shrum 1994; Gilg *et al.* 2005). Importantly, 'value' can refer to various aspects of the food, including perceived quality, taste, health benefits, animal welfare and responsibilities to future generations. Marketing referring to any of these is more likely to yield emotional responses by customers, creating linkages between sustainability issues (Ilbery and Kneafsey 2000; Harper and Makatouni 2002).

CARBON MANAGEMENT IN FOCUS 16: MARITIM PRO ARTE HOTEL, BERLIN, GERMANY

Reducing wastage from buffets involving social marketing

The issue

Hotel restaurants prepare considerable amounts of food, which are often offered as buffets. Observational evidence suggests that compared to table service, buffets might encourage customers to fill plates with greater quantities of food than are eaten, and to choose a greater proportion of energy-intense and thus more climatically problematic foods than are eaten at home, such as meats, milk products, or fruit juices (cf. Gössling *et al.* 2010). When customers have eaten, considerable amounts of food from the buffet itself might have to be discarded, in addition to leftovers on plates. Even though not representative, chef Ingrid Fjellestad (Hotel Alexandra, Loen, Norway, unpublished interview 7 September 2009) estimates, for example, that 5–10 per cent of the food served on the hotel's buffets is thrown away.

The solution

Buffets could theoretically inspire customers to only eat the amount of food they wish to consume, and to make more ecological food choices. Ideally, more sustainable eating patterns 'learned' in restaurants could later on inform everyday food-related decision-making. The Maritim pro Arte Hotel in Berlin supports customer choices in this direction. The hotel serves about 140,000 breakfast guests and another 300,000 lunch, dinner and banquet guests per year in its three restaurants. The hotel has a strong focus on providing sustainable foods, and offers both a 'conventional four-star' breakfast buffet with about 100 food components, and an alternative organic breakfast buffet with 52 food components. By offering the two buffets side by side, the organic breakfast buffet, which can be identified by customers through signs with the German 'BIO' label for organic food, is implicitly marketed as a healthier and high-quality choice compared to the conventional buffet.

According to the hotel's food and beverage manager, Marcell Kästner, guests show strong interest in the organic buffet, with 25–30 per cent of overall food purchases of the hotel now being organic. The Maritim pro Arte restaurants also offer organic menus, starters and main courses for lunch and dinner guests. There are seven organic wines on the wine list, and the hotel offers other organic beverages as well as an organic coffee list. While organic food is not necessarily more climate friendly, there is consensus that it offers a wide range of other sustainability benefits (for discussion see Gössling et al. 2010). More important from a climate mitigation perspective, Maritim pro Arte uses seasonal foods only in season, with for instance asparagus or strawberries only being served from late April to the end of June, even though they could easily be imported at any time of the year. This would entail higher emissions for transport, however.

The Maritim pro Arte also seeks to reduce wastage from buffets by providing comparably small plates with a diameter of 26 cm. Deep dishes on the buffet have a diameter of only 18–26 cm, and are filled with a maximum of 10 portions. This helps to avoid the 'overloading' of plates with food that diners do not actually eat. Moreover, carbon-intense foods such as meats are displayed on the periphery of the buffet table, while low-carbon foods are placed at the centre. All items of food are provided in small portions, again with the intention to avoid wastage. Taken together, such measures can be significant in influencing consumer choices and have a particular relevance in reducing waste.

Customers perceive these efforts in a very positive light: Marcell Kästner reports that the most negative comment ever encountered in discussions with banquet customers, i.e. when Maritim pro Arte functions as a caterer, is that they 'do not care'. Most customers perceive the organic component as a significant add-on. Consequently, more sustainable food provisions can be seen to create tangible benefits for customers, such as perceived healthiness and higher food quality.

The idea to engage in pro-environmental food management was born out of Marcell Kästner's insight that business-as-usual operations should not be continued because of their negative environmental consequences, growing environmental awareness among customers, trends towards more healthy lifestyles and concomitant changes in consumer demand. However, a key obstacle was the high costs of organic food purchases, which are on average 10–15 per cent more expensive compared to conventional foods. These expenses could not be passed on to guests for fear of negative price increase perceptions. As a result, profit margins declined when organic food purchases commenced. This was accepted, however, as the Maritim pro Arte expected to profit from the branding effect of organic food offers. The fact that the hotel would be one of the first to engage in pro-environmental food management was even seen as a particular advantage, helping them to stand out against competitors. As Marcell Kästner outlines, there is massive competition in large cities and a need to be distinguishable from competitors. Organic foodstuffs however also opened up new opportunities from a gastronomic point of view, as retailers occasionally offer rare vegetable varieties.

Problems encountered in the implementation phase were the size of trading units of organic food, which are too small for large consumers such as the Maritim pro Arte, and the price difference for some foods, with for instance organic poultry being up to 300 per cent more expensive than conventional poultry. Other problems include temporary shortages of some foodstuffs, the fact that only few retailers can offer the full assortment of organic foods, and additional costs for being certified as 'BIO' (after the EU organic standard for foods). Being 'BIO' certified also entails additional demands on accounting, as organic purchases have to be documented. Implementation also required cooperation with certifier Agro-Öko-Consult Berlin GmbH (see Related websites). Total certification costs of €2,600 are reported by Marcell Kästner, including €600 for certification and €2,000 for 70 hours of working time by various members of staff. An annual control costs €400, which is required to remain certified.

In order to even out additional costs, Maritim pro Arte developed a number of strategies. First of all, a decision was made to subsequently introduce organic foodstuffs, and to increase their share continuously to avoid sudden increases in overall costs. Moreover, meals were designed to primarily use moderately more expensive organic foodstuffs, and to steer customers towards choices with higher profit margins. For instance, comparably expensive poultry is predominantly used to complement comparably cheap salads, with the result that a reasonable profit margin can be maintained. Such strategic planning could help to use considerably greater amounts of organic food in the future, with only moderate increases in costs, and wide-reaching advantages in marketing and climate change mitigation.

Impact

Hotel Maritim pro Arte has shown that it is possible to serve more sustainable and climatically unproblematic food at moderate cost increases, particularly if organic food is served with a strategy to address costs of cheap/expensive food components in meals. Importantly, serving organic food is perceived favourably by customers and reinforces brand image and customer loyalty.

Source

Ingrid Fjellestad, Chef, Hotel Alexandra, Loen, Norway
Marcell Kästner, Food and Beverage Manager, Maritim pro Arte hotel, Berlin, Germany

Website

Hotel Maritim pro Arte, http://www.maritim.de/de/hotels/deutschland/proarte-hotel-berlin

Related websites

BIO (German national eco label for food), www.bio-siegel.de/english/homepage/
Agro-Öko Consult (BIO certifier), www.aoec.de/

References

Gössling, S., Garrod, B., Aall, C., Hille, J. and Peeters, P. (2010). Food management in tourism. Reducing tourism's carbon 'foodprint'. *Tourism Management*, in press.

Overall, Gössling *et al.* (2010) estimate that compared to business-as-usual food purchasing, preparation and presentation practices, these measures could save an estimated 50–80 per cent of GHG emissions, indicating that there is considerable scope for food management to make a significant contribution to climate mitigation.

TOUR OPERATORS AND TRAVEL AGENTS

Tour operators and travel agents, both those with offices and those that are Internet-based, have considerable influence on the tourists' choice of destinations, and could become far more important agents in fostering low-carbon holiday choices. For instance, the greatest amount of carbon can be saved by promoting closer destinations, with emission savings being proportional to the reduction in flying distance. Convincing customers to focus on closer destinations can be based on social marketing emphasizing shorter flight times or lower transport costs, as well as carbon-labelling facilitating more climate-friendly destinations or transport choices. As outlined by Peeters *et al.* (2009a), Global Distribution Systems (GDS) have become key platforms in facilitating comparisons between competing choices, with for instance three systems – Amadeus, Sabre, and Galileo – sharing two-thirds of global air booking. GDS usually compare offers made by airlines or hotels based on standard (e.g. first class, economy class), routes (direct, stop-over), travel time (hours from departure to destination), departure time (convenient?), as well as costs, which is probably the most important parameter in decision-making. A simple measure to facilitate pro-environmental choices is the inclusion of yet another parameter, i.e. emissions of GHG, in GDS, which could have considerable impact on the choices made by travellers (see Carbon Management in Focus 17).

CARBON MANAGEMENT IN FOCUS 17: CHEAPTICKETS, THE NETHERLANDS

Customer-friendly carbon-labelling for online booking services

The issue

An increasing number of people use Internet platforms to compare flight or accommodation prices in order to find the cheapest travel options. In particular with regard to air travel, there can be considerable price differences for flying between a given city-pair, depending on airline and connection, with 'odd' connections involving detours often being the cheapest travel options. Booking services for air travel usually structure travel options by cost, travel time, departure time and number of stopovers. As the cost of a journey is an important factor in decision-making (Schafer 2000), and in particular with regard to the frequency of air travel and the use of low-cost airlines (Nilsson 2009), travellers will be tempted to choose less convenient, cheaper flights with stopovers in order to save money. However, these flights will usually also involve greater emissions, as flights involving stopovers on short- to medium-distance routes are more energy intense than direct flights, also covering greater distances. Consequently, opportunities to compare prices for travel will often lead to less environmentally friendly travel choices.

The solution

Cheaptickets is a Dutch online booking agent for air travel. Besides information on price, departure time, flight times and stopovers, Cheaptickets also provides information on emissions, expressed as 'eco value'. 'Eco value' is a customer-friendly approach to a climate impact indicator. It is related to the EU's energy label for white appliances, which uses a colour scheme from green to red to indicate environmental performance, with green being the most energy-efficient choice, and thus the least environmentally harmful.

Cheaptravel calculates the 'eco value' of flights by considering the distance flown as well as the number of stopovers on a given route. If stopovers are made, these are calculated as an additional 100 miles flown, as the aircraft's take-off is particularly energy intense. Travellers can also find out about total travel distance by pointing their mouse at the 'eco value'. As shown in figure 10.3 for a return flight from Frankfurt to New York, the flight to New York is a direct flight and thus ranks 'A' (the most environmentally friendly option). The return flight involves a stopover in Detroit, thus increasing emissions because of a greater flight distance, and an additional take-off. The resulting 'eco value' is 'E' (least environmentally friendly option). Travellers are offered this return flight along with a range of other travel options, including return flights ranked 'A'. They can thus make a

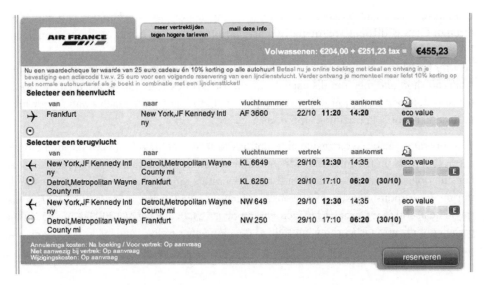

Figure 10.3 *Example of booking information provided by Cheaptickets*

decision to either choose the cheapest flight, to choose the most climatically friendly option, or to return on another day, when price and environmental performance are in better balance.

Impact

The 'eco value' indicator educates travellers on relative environmental harmfulness of flights and raises awareness of climate change, which might be an important precondition for introducing travellers subsequently to more abstract indicators such as CO_2 (see also Carbon Management in Focus 32). Even though there are no studies to confirm this hypothesis, at least some air travellers are likely to choose more environmentally friendly travel options when provided with information on environmental performance.

Website

Cheap Tickets, www.cheaptickets.nl

References

Nilsson, J.H. (2009). Low-cost Aviation. In: Gössling, S. and Upham, P. (eds) *Climate Change and Aviation: issues, challenges and solutions*. London: Earthscan, pp. 113–129.
Schafer, A. (2000). Regularities in travel demand: an international perspective. *Journal of Transportation and Statistics* 3(3): 1–31.

GDS have other characteristics that could be changed. For instance, booking complex trips through GDS is difficult, particularly when various transport modes are to be combined. Peeters *et al.* (2009a) thus suggest that 'carbon optimization' needs to become a key concept for travel agents, and propose that travel agents (1) favour direct flights wherever possible (on short and medium distances), (2) choose airlines with comparatively new fleets, (3) substitute part of the journey with a trip by train, for instance to reach a hub from which to fly, and (4) offset remaining emissions.

Tour operators also have considerable options to influence travel choices through advice given to clients on the Internet, in travel catalogues and brochures, as well as in personal consultations. An important element for tour operators might be to develop an understanding of the carbon-intensity of various products, for which newly developed CSR-tools might be useful (see Carbon Management in Focus 18). Peeters *et al.* (2009a) conclude that carbon optimization is a promising field to develop new services, and eventually even new business models for tourism.

CARBON MANAGEMENT IN FOCUS 18: FORUMANDERSREISEN, GERMANY

CO_2-benchmarking of tour operators

The issue

Tour operators are key actors in the development of sustainable tourism because they have considerable influence on the destinations chosen, as well as the average length of stay of tourists. Both are key factors in average per tourist per trip emissions. So far, the engagement of tour operators in contributing to sustainable tourism has however remained limited (van Wijk and Persson 2006), while it has been suggested that tour operators are, in fact, responsible for the observed growth in travel distances by marketing cheap mass holidays based on air travel (cf. Timothy and Ioannides 2002) – often in developing countries where profit margins are comparatively high (e.g. Gössling 2003). The role of tour operators in creating change towards more or less climatically friendly holidays is thus considerable. For instance, in 2008, Swedish Fritidsresor (part of Touristik Union International (TUI) group) marketed the Maldives in billboard campaigns with the slogan 'the dream is just 9 hours away'. However, a year earlier, in 2007, Swedish Fritidsresor had launched the 'Blue Train' campaign, which took travellers from Sweden all the way to Lake Garda or Cinque Terre in northern Italy, involving journeys over more than 20 hours by train, and covering distances of up 1,500 km (see Carbon Management in Focus 20). In terms of their contribution to emissions, the two concepts make a considerable difference: while Blue Train emissions are in the order of 80 kg per return trip per traveller, a return trip to the Maldives will cause per capita emissions of about 1,780 kg (trip only), i.e. emissions vary by a factor >20 on a per trip basis. The calculation is based on an average emissions factor of 0.027 kg CO_2 per pkm for rail and 0.111 kg CO_2 per pkm for air (UNWTO-UNEP-WMO 2008); a journey to Italy will cause emissions of about 80 kg CO_2, while a return-flight to the Maldives over 7,800 pkm (one-way Stockholm-Male) will lead to emissions of about 1,730 kg CO_2. Adding non-CO_2 effects of aviation or accommodation (hotels in the Maldives are run with inefficient diesel-driven generators) would affect this ratio even further.

The solution

Forumandersreisen, an association of about 140 small tour operators seeking to provide sustainable travel offers (see also Carbon Management in Focus 20) developed a new label Corporate Social Responsibility (CSR) Tourism Certified, in cooperation with Kontaktstelle für Umwelt & Entwicklung (Center for Ecology and Development; KATE). The certification has the goals of measuring the sustainability performance of tour operators, making performance transparent to the customer, and allowing for a benchmarking of various novel parameters, including local value added (the share of money paid for the trip that will stay within the visited country), average length of stay, average flight distance, and average emissions per traveller per day. The overall goal is to include all parts of the value chain in the evaluation process to ensure that sustainability is considered in a holistic way.

In March 2009, the first 15 tour operators went through the process and became certified, a process that will be repeated after two years (second certification), and every third year thereafter. The usefulness of the certification with regard to benchmarking is apparent in a comparison of the various tour operators (Figure 10.4 and 10.5). For instance, with regard to 'average per tourist flight distances', the benchmarking reveals considerable differences between tour operators, from a low of 48 pkm per traveller per trip to a maximum of 18,402 pkm. These differences are a result of the packages offered: tour operators focusing on long-distance destinations have considerably higher values than those focusing on packages not involving flights. However, as figure 10.5 shows, average per capita per day emissions are also influenced by average length of stay and the energy-intensity of the non-flight part of the holiday, i.e. other transport, accommodation and activities. Differences are considerable even here, with the 'best' tour operator causing emissions of just 15 kg of CO_2-eq per tourist per day (forumandersreisen uses a RF index for calculations, which is a multiplier of CO_2 emissions at flight altitude), which can be compared to almost half a tonne of CO_2-eq per day for the 'worst' performing tour operator. Benchmarking can reveal such differences and automatically becomes an incentive to change the tour operator's strategy in favour of lower-carbon packages.

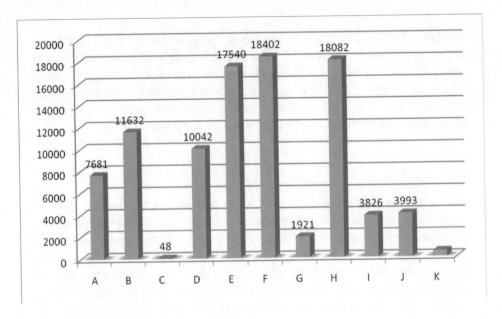

Figure 10.4 *Average per customer flight distance in km*

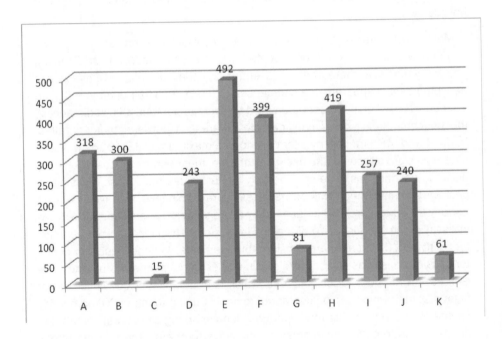

Figure 10.5 *Emissions per customer per day in kg CO_2-eq*

Impact

According to Rolf Pfeifer, the CSR Project Manager, results of the certification process have already influenced operations. For instance, one tour operator decided to no longer offer a number of trips with particularly high emissions. Even though the certification process was time-consuming, virtually all participants were positive about it as they, for the first time, learned about key sustainability parameters in their companies as well as the performance of their competitors. This provides an incentive to improve operations from a climate change point of view. Importantly, participating companies also learned about other elements of their packages, which helped to improve quality management.

Source

Rolf Pfeifer, Project Manager CSR, forumandersreisen

Website

Forumandersreisen CSR reports, www.forumandersreisen.de/downloads/CSR_Nachhaltigkeitsbericht.pdf (in German)

Related websites

Kontaktstelle für Umwelt & Entwicklung (Center for Ecology and Development), www.kate-stuttgart.org

Arkadia Yachtcharter & Segelreisen (Hamburg), http://www.arkadia-segelreisen.de/

Auf und Davon Reisen GmbH (Gummersbach), http://www.auf-und-davon-reisen.de/

avenTOURa GmbH (Freiburg), http://www.aventoura.de/

Demeter-Reisen (Nürnberg), http://www.demeter-reisen.de/

INTI Tours e.K. (Deggingen), http://www.inti-tours.de/

Neue Wege Seminare & Reisen GmbH (Euskirchen), http://www.neuewege.com/

Nomad. Reisen zu den Menschen (Gerolstein), http://www.nomad-reisen.de/index/

One World – Reisen mit Sinnen (Dortmund), http://www.reisenmitsinnen.de/

Radissimo GmbH (Karlsruhe), http://www.radissimo.de/

ReNatour (Nürnberg), http://www.renatour.de/

Rucksack Reisen (Münster), http://www.rucksack-reisen.de/

travel-to-nature GmbH (Ballrechten), http://www.travel-to-nature.de/

Urlaub & Natur (Karlsruhe), http://www.urlaubundnatur.de/

Weltweitwandern GmbH (Graz), http://www.weltweitwandern.at

Windbeutel Reisen (Köln), http://www.windbeutel-reisen.de/

References

Gössling, S. (ed.) (2003). *Tourism and Development in Tropical Islands: political ecology perspectives*. Cheltenham: Edward Elgar Publishing.

Timothy, D.J. and Ioannides, D. (2002). Tour Operator Hegemony: dependency and oligopoly in insular destinations. In: Apostolopoulos, Y. and Gayle, D.J. (eds) *Island Tourism and Sustainable Development: Caribbean, Pacific, and Mediterranean Experiences*. Westport: Praeger.

UNWTO-UNEP-WMO (2008). *Climate Change and Tourism: responding to global challenges*. Madrid: UNWTO, UNEP and WMO.

van Wijk, J. and Persson, W. (2006). A long-haul destination: sustainability reporting among tour operators. *European Management Journal* 24(6): 381–395.

Tour operators also have considerable power to engage in de-marketing and social marketing, i.e. marketing principles to influence travel choices and to change tourism-related consumption patterns. Peeters *et al.* (2009a) conclude that such marketing techniques have remained rarely used in tourism, even though they have considerable power to influence behaviour. While de-marketing can work on the basis of simply no longer targeting certain markets (see Carbon Management in Focus 19), social marketing techniques need to be based on an understanding of what motivates each market segment, possibly addressing non-environmental motivations. Such an approach has, for instance, been a major success in the case of the Swedish Ecotourism Society, which has in recent years marketed ecotourism packages by small operators as unique, unforgettable experiences rather than environmentally and socially benign holiday choices (Gössling 2006).

CARBON MANAGEMENT IN FOCUS 19: ECOTOURISM NORWAY

Attracting visitors from close markets, involving de-marketing

The issue

Growth in tourism is usually warranted and unquestioned (e.g. Gössling *et al.* 2010), but there are situations where growth in certain market segments is not necessarily welcome. Peeters *et al.* (2009a) discuss a number of such situations, where attempts were actually made to actively reduce demand from certain tourist segments, including young, often drunk tourists in Cyprus in the 1980s (cf. Clements 1989), or college and high school students on spring break in Fort Lauderdale, Florida. Techniques to reduce demand are based on de-marketing, first discussed by Kotler and Levy (1971) (for a more recent review of demand management and de-marketing see Beeton and Benfield 2002).

De-marketing effectively seeks to reduce demand from certain market segments, which could be an important strategy for destinations whose emissions are linked predominantly to long-haul travellers (UNWTO-UNEP-WMO 2008; Gössling et al. 2009, 2010). Currently, many countries might focus on long-haul markets to increase international arrival numbers, i.e. a strategy that is likely to lead to growing emissions. Norway, Sweden and Denmark, for instance, are countries with a considerable seasonality in demand in the summer months. One strategy by Scandinavian incoming tourism marketing organizations has thus been to attract tourists from Asia, who appear to be less susceptible to specific climate conditions, and interested in experiencing Scandinavia even in spring or autumn. China in particular is seen as a huge emerging market, with an expected number of 100 million international outbound trips by 2020 (cf. Lew 2000). In order to attract a share of them, Denmark, Sweden and Norway have established a Scandinavian Tourist Board with offices in Beijing and Guangzhou (Innovation Norway 2009). Should these efforts result in a significant increase in traveller arrivals from China, emissions from incoming tourism to Scandinavia are likely to grow considerably (cf. Gössling and Hall 2008).

The solution

Peeters et al. (2009a: 247) note that de-marketing 'is often heavily dependent on the public sector creating consensus and partnership approaches. ... It can be useful at local and sub-regional level; but its economic and political consequences make it almost impossible to implement at regional or national levels'. This is also the case in Norway, but the concept of de-marketing can nevertheless be applied by companies and organizations.

Ecotourism Norway is a certification scheme for Norwegian ecotourism businesses. The brand is owned by Innovation Norway (www.innovasjonnorge.no), an agency to promote industrial development including tourism. The Ecotourism Norway certification scheme was developed over a three-year period in cooperation with tourism companies and destinations, and funded by the Norwegian government. The certification scheme was presented in January 2008. There are currently (November 2009) 13 certified companies, but more are expected to join in 2010. With regard to marketing, Ecotourism Norway has chosen to add a number of specific certification requirements. These include several which are of relevance in terms of de-marketing and reducing emissions (Ecotourism Norway 2009: 23–24):

Addressing environmentally conscious target groups

The business works actively to sell to organisations (tour operators, travel agencies, companies) that have an environmental profile and a clearly stated goal concerning the reduction of their own environmental and climate pressures. The business priori- tises the ethical and environmentally conscious user in its active marketing.

Packages offered in marketing are organised for longer stays

The business offers 'ecotourism-experiences', either alone, or together with other operators, organised for longer stays in the area. Length of stay: By the second approval [of being certified; author's explanation], at least 75 per cent of packages offered to markets dependent on air transport are of a minimum length of one week or more. This is in accordance with the company's own marketing.

Own marketing activities and climate challenges

The company's marketing is directed towards closer markets, limited to Europe, as an active contribution to reducing the climate pressures.

The climate promise

The business has given 'Klimaløftet' (the Climate Promise: Norwegian Government's campaign on reducing GHG emissions: http://www.grip.no/Klima/klimaloftet.htm)

In the context of this case study it is important to note that Ecotourism Norway also puts pressure on certified businesses in terms of the use of motorized vehi- cles for leisure activities, including the use of snowmobiles, safaris by car, as well as zodiacs and other rafting boats (Ecotourism Norway 2009).

Several aspects of these marketing rules are of interest: first, there is a focus on climatically aware partners and tourist groups, with the intention to create 'green' networks. According to Lone Lamark, Initiator of Ecotourism Norway, the principle was established to push certified businesses to make use of opportuni- ties to specifically target the growing segment of environmentally aware tourists, a market many companies are not fully aware of. Secondly, certified companies should seek to make clients arriving by air stay longer, a criterion also used by forumandersreisen (see Carbon Management in Focus 32). The idea is to move away from short trips, and to organize and market packages in a way to make cli- ents stay longer. Certified Ecotourism Norway companies do, for instance, reduce the price for accommodation if guests stay for more than three days. Third, active marketing by certified companies is limited to Europe, with the general recom- mendation to focus on close markets, i.e. Norway itself, Denmark, UK, France, Germany, as well as Belgium, Netherlands and Luxemburg. This is the major de- marketing measure used by Norwegian Ecotourism to reduce travel distances and emissions related to arrivals, and means that certified companies cannot support marketing campaigns taking place outside Europe. Lone Lamark reports that this criterion has had a major awareness-creating effect. Some businesses had to stop their marketing activities in the USA, but according to Lone Lamark, all seem proud to now seriously address climate change as an issue. Lone Lamark also points at the importance of the integration of a 'Europe only' criterion in the certification process:

Norwegian Ecotourism takes the climate change challenge seriously, and we are meeting the criticism that has been forwarded to ecotourism in this regard. We have integrated this criterion because we can influence travel length through marketing, and by actively choosing the 'right' guests. By this we also say that, yes, we do in fact have a responsibility for the trip that is made by the guest to visit us, even if the trip is not part of our product.

Yet another relevant criterion is the 'climate promise', a Norwegian initiative for companies to commit themselves to active emission measurements and reductions. To make this promise means that companies have to work with climate change and emissions, and this is thus an important step in generating awareness and knowledge.

Impact

Ecotourism Norway is the first organization not seeking to actively develop any market that might be lucrative, thus implementing principles addressing the important question of travel distances. To reduce the average distance travelled by incoming tourists is the most relevant single measure to reduce emissions at the destination level, and Ecotourism Norway shows that such de-marketing is feasible. Furthermore, the organization establishes guidelines for length of stay, and asks its members to engage in active mitigation. Together, these constitute a progressive package of carbon management measures.

Source

Lone Lamark, Initiator and consultant, Ecotourism Norway

Website

Ecotourism Norway, www.ecotourismnorway.org

Related websites

Ecotourism Norway certified companies:
Alaskan Husky Tour, http://www.huskytour.no/
Spydspissen Villmarksopplevelser, http://www.spydspissen.no/
Bjåen Fjellsove, http://www.bjaen.no/
Ypsøy Kustgard, http://www.kystgard.no/
Svalbard Villmarkssenter, http://www.svalbardvillmarkssenter.no/
Lofoten Kajakk, http://www.lofoten-aktiv.no/
Havnomaden Kajakksenter, http://www.havnomaden.no/
Romsdal Aktiv, http://www.romsdalaktiv.com/
Turgleder, http://www.turgleder.com/
Hardangervidda Fjellguiding, http://www.fjellguiding.no/
Matsafari, http://www.matsafari.no/

Ekkerøy Feriehus, http://www.horisontvaranger.no/
Høve Støtt, http://www.hovestott.no/

References

Beeton, S. and Benfield, R. (2002). Demand control: the case for demarketing as a visitor and environmental management tool. *Journal of Sustainable Tourism* 10(6): 497–513.
Clements, M.A. (1989). Selecting tourist traffic by demarketing. *Tourism Management* 10(2): 89–94.
Ecotourism Norway (2009). Norwegian Ecotourism Certification, available from: http://ekstranett.innovasjonnorge.no/Felles_fs/Ecotourism/Dokumenter/Norwegian%20Ecotourism%20Certification09.pdf. Accessed 25 November 2009.
Gössling, S. and Hall, C.M. (2008). Swedish tourism and climate change mitigation: an emerging conflict? *Scandinavian Journal of Hospitality and Tourism* 8(2): 141–158.
Gössling, S., Ceron, J.-P., Dubois, G. and Hall, C.M. (2009). Hypermobile Travellers. In: Gössling, S. and Upham, P. (eds) *Climate Change and Aviation: issues, challenges and solutions*. London: Earthscan, pp. 131–149.
Gössling, S., Hall, C.M., Peeters, P. and Scott, D. (2010). The future of tourism: can tourism growth and climate policy be reconciled? A climate change mitigation perspective. *Tourism Recreation Research* 35(2), in press.
Innovation Norway 2009. Aktiviteter per marked. Available from: http://www.innovasjonnorge.no/Satsinger/Reiseliv/markedsforing/Aktiviteter-per-marked/. Accessed 25 November 2009.
Kotler, P. and Levy, S.J. (1971). Demarketing? Yes, demarketing! *Harvard Business Review* 49(6): 74–80.
Lew, A.A. (2000). China: a growth engine for Asian tourism. In: Hall, C.M. and Page, S. (eds) *Tourism in South and South East Asia: issues and cases*. Oxford: Butterworth-Heinemann, pp. 268–285.
Peeters, P., Gössling, S. and Lane, B. (2008). Moving Towards Low-carbon Tourism: new opportunities for destinations and tour operators. In: Gössling, S., Hall, C.M. and Weaver, D. (eds) *Sustainable Tourism Futures: perspectives on systems, restructuring and innovations*. London: Routledge, pp. 240–257.
UNWTO-UNEP-WMO (2008). *Climate Change and Tourism: responding to global challenges*. Madrid: UNWTO, UNEP and WMO.

More generally, tour operators can influence destination choices (travel distances), transport choices (high-carbon vs. low-carbon), and length of stay, i.e. all the key parameters influencing overall emissions associated with a holiday. A successful example is Fritidsresor, Sweden, who have succeeded in creating an attractive train-based product (Carbon Management in Focus 20). With respect to length of stay, Peeters *et al.* (2009a) suggest, for instance, that packages be sold on a 'per day' basis, i.e. with the price of a holiday package averaged over the number of days. As the price of a package is largely the cost of transport plus the length of stay multiplied by, the cost per night, staying an additional day or two becomes comparatively cheap. This could encourage customers to stay longer. Even for tour operators, such an approach would have advantages, as revenues and, in particular, profits would increase. This is because transport yields the lowest profits, and longer stays entailing more (profitable) guest nights would lead to higher profit margins. Notably, this would also lead to lower costs at the destination, for instance with regard to cleaning, house-keeping, washing linen, check-in and check-out, or welcome drinks. Tour operators with such an approach to marketing might even have a comparative advantage, as prices in travel cata-logues will appear to be lower than those of competitors. Tour operators could also engage in other marketing measures to increase average length of stay, such as 'buy 6 nights, stay another night for free' (Peeters *et al.* 2009a; see also Alegre and Pou 2006; Artal Tur *et al.* 2008).

CARBON MANAGEMENT IN FOCUS 20: FRITIDSRESOR, SWEDEN

Modal shift from air to train

The issue

The question of how travellers can be convinced to change environmentally harm-ful transport modes in favour of more environmentally friendly ones is complex (see also Carbon Management in Focus 23). Marketing appealing to behavioural change has usually been met with only limited success (e.g. Holding and Kreut-ner 1998; see also Jackson 2005; Steg and Vlek 2009), and when air travel is involved, a 'distance decay' function can be postulated with regard to willingness to change transport modes, i.e. the longer the journey, the less likely are travel-lers to use slower transport modes. More innovative strategies thus have to be developed to achieve modal shift towards more environmentally friendly means of transport over longer distances (see also Carbon Management in Focus 8, 9).

The solution

Fritidsresor belongs to the Swedish group Fritidsresegruppen (Fritidsresor Group Nordic), which again is part of the world's largest travel company, TUI Travel Plc, with 30 million customers per year. Fritidsresor started to offer train charter as an alternative to air charter flights in summer 2007, in cooperation with Swedish Railways. The idea was born out of discussions of how to create more climatically friendly tourism, and the first train packages offered by Fritidsresor went all the way from Sweden to Italy. The marketing of the new train charter product was initiated with a press release on 28 March 2007, and no significant demand was expected: reservations had been made for just 20 train seats on four departures, i.e. totalling 80 seats. However, the 80 seats were sold out within a few days, and after additional capacity was created, a total of 800 train charter tourists were finally sent on the trip to Lake Garda and the opera festival in Verona (both Italy), a journey taking 21 hours (Malmö–Berlin–Munich–Verona). In 2008, Fritid-sresor developed further train charter offers, with traveller numbers increasing to 5,000. However, in 2009, traveller numbers declined again to 2,500, which Lottie Knutson, the company's Director of Marketing, Communications and CSR, explains by a growing number of (direct) flight connections, and hard-to-compete prices of low-cost carriers. Another negative factor is train changes, as travellers from Stockholm have to change connections in Lund or Malmö in southern Sweden, and again in Munich in southern Germany.

Despite considerable interest, train charter is thus a niche product, even though this might be seen as a result of the current market situation (competition from low-cost carriers) as well as the role of train charter in comparison to flight-based packages and associated marketing efforts: Fritidsresor sells more than 500,000 package journeys involving air travel, i.e. train packages were just 1 per cent of sales in 2008, and marketing is consequently focused on – more profitable – air-travel packages. Fritidsresor continues to offer a range of packages by train, however, now including summer and winter trips, and involving car rental at the destination as well as attractive stopovers on the way (for instance in Berlin). Lottie Knutson also believes that 'train charter has come to stay': the expectation is that train charter could account for as much as 50 per cent of Fritidsresor's trips to the Mediterranean by 2030, provided that high-speed infrastructure is developed and that direct trains are available. By then, it could be possible to board the train in the morning in Stockholm or Gothenburg and to arrive in the evening in the Mediterranean. Lottie Knutson believes that price will be a key component in this development, however, and suggests that there have to be special facilities onboard the trains, including restaurants and play areas for children.

Fritidsresor differentiates three customer groups interested in train charter: the 'Stones generation' (55+ years of age), the 'Interrail generation', and the 'Afraid-to-fly's'. Families with children are also a relevant group of travellers. Even though no systematic studies have been carried out, Lottie Knutson suggests that train charter is popular because a train journey provides time for what has become known in Sweden as the 'inner journey', after a campaign by Swedish Railways in the mid-2000s with the slogan 'Upplev den inre resan' (experience the inner journey). Train journeys are considered slow travel, allowing one to relax and reflect upon life, and to move at a speed different from everyday life (see also Ehn and Löfgren 2007). Train travel is also seen to lead to interesting encounters with other people, and to provide another kind of travel experience.

Environmental benefits, such as lower emissions, might be a travel motive for a share of travellers, but rather an add-on to other benefits than a critical argument in itself (for another viewpoint, however, see Carbon Management in Focus 21). As a matter of fact, Lottie Knutson emphasizes that any reference to environmental issues was consciously omitted in marketing, and that tangible advantages of train charter trips were underlined:

> Holidays are the most important time of the year. ... That's why environmentally friendly tourism alternatives have to be positive and attractive – we simply do not put our holidays or money on things that are 'musts'.

In light of this, the success of the train charter concept might predominantly lie in Fritidsresor's communication strategy and packaging, which for instance allows for stopovers at interesting sights on the way – sights that air travellers cannot see (cf. Peeters et al. 2009a).

In terms of CO_2, train journeys help to avoid considerable amounts of emissions. For a rough calculation, a traveller using the train from Stockholm to Lake Garda (3,400 km return) will cause emissions of roughly 73 kg CO_2 for transport only, including ferry (Table 10.4; SJ 2009), while the same traveller arriving by air will cause emissions of 346 kg CO_2 (Scandinavian Airlines 2009; return flight Stockholm Arlanda to Verona, 3,286 pkm). Air emissions are thus more than 350 per cent larger, notably not including additional RF from aviation's non-CO_2 emissions. Moreover, when flying, people might choose more distant destinations, as the high speed of the aircraft shrinks perceived distance. As it is unknown which destinations would have been chosen by travellers in the absence of opportunities to use the train, the avoided amount of >250 kg CO_2 per traveller is, arguably, a conservative assumption.

Impact

Fritidsresor has shown that through the creation of new products it is possible to achieve modal shifts, considerably reducing emissions associated with transport. Moreover, it is anticipated that the future potential of such offers is far greater than current uptake. Train travel over distances covering up to 2,000 km have considerable potential to be made attractive to tourists, but the train product has to be improved for this, including faster and more direct connections, as well as special amenities, such as play areas for children, or family compartments with shower and toilet onboard the train – all of this at competitive prices. This again points at the importance of air transport becoming more expensive, given current competitive distortions of transport systems (see Chapter 13).

Table 10.4 *Emissions caused by various train trips from Sweden*

Destination	kg CO_2 per traveller, one way
Desenzano (Lake Garda)	36,8
Venedig	38,3
Schüttdorf/Zell am See	30,7
Tremezzo (Lake Como)	33,2
Siófok (Lake Balaton)	34,2

Source: SJ 2009
Source: Kelly and Williams (2007)

Source

Lottie Knutson, Director of Marketing, Communications and CSR, Fritidsresor Group Nordic

Marie Malmros, communications officer, Fritidsresor Group Nordic

Website

Fritidsresor (charter train), available at: http://www.fritidsresor.se/resor/Resa-med-tag/

Related websites

Swedish Railways Carbon Calculator, available at: http://www.sj.se/sj/jsp/polopoly.jsp?d=280&l=en&intcmp=13196

References

Ehn, B. and Löfgren, O. (2007). *När ingenting särskilt hander: nya kulturanalyser (When nothing special happens: new cultural analyses)*. Stockholm: Symposium.

Holding, D.M. and Kreutner, M. (1998). Achieving a balance between 'carrots' and 'sticks' for traffic in national parks: the Bayerischer Wald project. *Transport Policy* 5: 175–183.

Jackson, T. (2005). Motivating sustainable consumption. A review of evidence on consumer behaviour and behavioural change. A report to the Sustainable Development ResearchNetwork. Available from: http://www.sd-research.org.uk/post.php?p=126. Accessed 30 March 2010.

Peeters, P., Gössling, S. and Lane, B. (2009). Moving Towards Low-carbon Tourism: new opportunities for destinations and tour operators. In: Gössling, S., Hall, C.M. and Weaver, D. (eds) *Sustainable Tourism Futures: perspectives on systems, restructuring and innovations*. London: Routledge, pp. 240–257.

Scandinavian Airlines (2009). Emission calculator. Available from: http://www.sasems.port.se/EmissionCalc.cfm?lang=1&utbryt=0&sid=simple&left=simple. Accessed 5 December 2009.

SJ (Swedish Railways) (2009). Koldioxidutsläpp tågcharter (CO_2 emissions train charter) Available from: http://www.sj.se/sj/jsp/polopoly.jsp?d=260&a=109423&l=sv. Accessed 5 December 2009.

Steg, L. and Vlek, C. (2009). Encouraging pro-environmental behaviour: an integrative review and research agenda. *Journal of Environmental Psychology* 29: 309–317.

UNWTO-UNEP-WMO (2008). *Climate Change and Tourism: responding to global challenges*. Madrid: UNWTO, UNEP and WMO.

As the example of Fritidsresor shows, rail (and coach) travel might be attractive on distances of up to 1,500 km, and could be an alternative to air transport. However, rail and coach use will depend on travel speed and transport cultures. For instance, the market share of train passenger transport (measured in distances covered) is about 20 per cent in Japan and Switzerland, but only 0.3 per cent in the USA (UNWTO-UNEP-WMO 2008).

DESTINATIONS

Destinations are key units in climate change mitigation, as they can mobilize large stake-holder numbers, which together can achieve significant change. Many destinations are now increasingly aware of the consequences of climate change for their tourism industries. For instance, Australian tourism stakeholders have recognized climate change as a challenge, stating that:

> Climate change has a range of potential implications for the sustainability of the Australian tourism industry. A change in the Earth's climate has the potential to alter Australia's unique set of environmental resources, affect economic growth, and jeopardise the future viability of the tourism industry. ... While there is a need for adaption, in the future the focus will be on mitigation for the long-term benefits it can provide. Simply off-setting the carbon footprint does not tackle the cause of the issue and the environment will continue to be detrimentally impacted. Long-term mitigation strategies should focus on investing in technological development and finding new fuel types (particularly in transport). ... The industry needs incentives to uptake tools provided to help them reduce their environmental impact (e.g. emissions calculator and climate action certification). ... A paradox of tourism is that visitors are aware of environmental issues but to the present their behaviour remains unchanged as they expect the industry to solve the problem.
>
> (STCRC 2009: 12)

Among key actions, STCRC (2009) mentions a voluntary emission reduction goal in line with other sectors, the development of mitigation strategies, a carbon management pro-gramme, an ETS that includes aviation, a long-term strategic focus for the industry, and the definition of key messages to industry on climate change. These measures would make Australia leaders in efforts to address climate change, but it is unclear whether and when action will be taken: the current reality rather appears to follow a business-as-usual path-way focused on volume growth.

In destinations, there is increasing recognition of the role of 'soft' measures to encour-age a modal shift towards sustainable forms of transport. Initiatives can range from des-tination-wide transport management (e.g. car-free resorts) to travel restrictions on certain routes, encouragement of public transport use, establishment of cycle paths or networks, and other benefits offered at tourist attractions or accommodation to non-car users. Soft measures also involve improved information systems (see Carbon Management in Focus 10), better reliability of public transport systems (see Carbon Management in Focus 8), increased personal security, and improved transfer facilities to connect different types of public transport.

Various destinations have started to proactively work with carbon management in this direction. These include, large ski resorts such as Whistler Blackcomb, Canada, or Aspen Snowmass, USA (see Carbon Management in Focus 7), tourist regions such as Davos or South West England, networks covering several countries such as the Alpine Pearls (see Carbon Management in Focus 21), or even entire countries such as New Zealand or Nor-way, though the latter has had mixed results. Notably, carbon management can also turn communities into destinations, as exemplified by Mohrbach, Germany (Carbon Manage-ment in Focus 26).

CARBON MANAGEMENT IN FOCUS 21: ALPINE PEARLS, EUROPE

Creating networks for sustainable mobility

The issue

In the Alps, car travel as the predominant mode of tourism mobility has increased considerably in recent decades, with the latest available figures for the region suggesting that an estimated 80 per cent of all tourist trips are based on the car (in 1997) (European Environment Agency (EEA) 2003). As a response to increasing pressure from car use, including crowding in alpine villages as well as air and noise pollution (see e.g. Krippendorf 1987), a number of communities in Switzerland decided to become car-free as early as in 1988, founding the Gemeinschaft Autofreier Schweizer Tourismusorte (GAST; *Community of Vehicle-Free Swiss Tourist Resorts*). The concept has worked well for the involved communities, with for instance guest nights in Saas-Fee developing at 'three times the Swiss average' (Holding 2001: 412). The nine Swiss car-free communities are still organized in GAST, but little has been done over the past 10 years to actively market the concept. A new Internet presentation is however planned for 2010 (see Related websites).

Most measures to achieve modal shifts from the car to alternative transport modes have, in the past, been based on incentives or 'carrots' (Holding 2001). However, as Holding points out, incentives have generally had only limited success, while disincentives ('sticks') have attracted public and political opposition, and thus generally been deemed unacceptable. This raises the question of how modal shifts from cars to trains or buses can be achieved more systematically. Possibly, this should include measures to also address origin–destination mobility, which accounts for the majority of emissions caused by a holiday, and not just the destination itself.

The solution

In 1996/1997, 11 destinations in the Alps became involved in a programme supported by the EU Tourism Directorate (DG XXIII) called 'Sanfte Mobilität' (*sustainable mobility*), with the goal of optimizing transport systems in tourism regions (ÖAR Regionalberatung 1997). Subsequent projects included Alps Mobility and Alps Mobility II – Alpine Pearls (from 2000–06), which led to the foundation of the Alpine Pearls network. The network is now well established and offers a range of advantages to its members, including a strong brand, marketing under the Alpine Pearls umbrella, cooperation with three media agencies, and marketing materials in five languages. The Alpine Pearls now include 21 communities in six countries – Austria, Germany, France, Italy, Switzerland, and Slovenia – accounting for about 10 million bed nights. The network's marketing focus is on soft mobility, which is communicated to guests through the association's website:

Alpine Nature and Culture – Up Close and Personal

The Alpine Pearls is a network of 21 communities that offer easy, yet comfortable ways to enjoy holidays in environmentally conscious fashion. Climate protection and nature conservation via soft mobility are part and parcel of the Alpine Pearl association's focus.

[...]

Mobility Without a Car – Holiday Pure

The Alpine Pearls offer soft mobility throughout your entire holiday: From the time you arrive here by bus or train to the time you leave, your mobility is guaranteed. Softly mobile offers abound and we are always happy to help and consult. To make sure you can rest and relax, all of our Alpine Pearls have car-free areas. Take your time to explore the streets and alleys of the villages and towns – by foot or electric bicycle. Enjoy the mountains on a traditional hike, on horseback or, even more actively, on a mountain bike.

(Alpine Pearls 2009a: no page)

An interesting difference to communication strategies by other tour operators and organizations presented in this book (see e.g. Carbon Management in Focus 20) is that the Alpine Pearls make direct reference to environmental issues – possibly, because they cater more directly to tourists wishing to escape car-based lifestyles, enjoying quiet areas, and exploration of the local on foot, by bike or on horseback, as well as by means of e-mobility (see also Carbon Management in Focus 23, for a discussion of tourist attitudes). Communities wishing to join the Alpine Pearls consequently have to fulfil a list of criteria centred around sustainable mobility, including (1) basic mobility, i.e. mobility offers connected to arrival and departure, mobility within the region and within the Alpine Pearls; (2) fun mobility, i.e. offers of e-mobility; and (3) service quality for mobility, i.e. information and service regarding mobility (the full list of criteria can be downloaded from the Alpine Pearls (2009b)). Slow mobility is thus at the heart of the marketing strategy, as also mirrored in the Alpine Pearls (2009c) 'quality promise':

The Pearls of the Alps promise to provide a new quality for your holidays:

1 Our 'Pearls' co-operate all across the Alps and offer eco-friendly tourism at top quality.
2 We guarantee a comfortable and relaxed trip to one of our 'Pearls' via bus or train.
3 Once you are here, you don't need your car to get to places. All locations are easily accessible the 'softly mobile' way.
4 Fun leisure activities abound, including hiking, Nordic walking, mountain biking, horseback riding, electric vehicles, water sports, cross-country skiing, snow-shoeing, and much more ...

5 We keep expanding the areas where you can be safe on foot, without the annoy-ance of traffic, exhaust fumes, or car noise. This includes parks, carfree valleys, and walking trails within easy reach.

6 We are at your service to ensure your vacation mobility. Let us take care of any necessary reservations and bookings. We are also happy to consult you personally.

7 Check out our special 'Alpine Pearls' packages, which can help you make your 'softly mobile' experience even simpler and more comfortable.

8 Rest assured: From our active involvement in nature conservancy to alternative energy supply, we do not leave any stone unturned to protect both nature and people.

9 Diversity is our goal, and that does not stop at the local culture and cuisine. In fact, we support Alpine culture, traditions and cooking.

10 The 'Pearls' conserve the aesthetic character and local beauty of our Alpine villages.

The focus on sustainable mobility by the Alpine Pearls appears to have been a success, even though no statistics on arrival numbers are collected (see, how-ever, Carbon Management in Focus 23). As outlined by Karmen Mentil, Project Director Alpine Pearls, safe, quiet, healthy alpine environments are an attraction in themselves, and the market for this type of holiday is growing. The marketing message that can be distributed through the network and under the Alpine Pearls brand is that there already exist options to engage in climate-sensitive holidays. The success of the concept is also reflected in the growth of the network, with expectations for 4–5 new communities joining the Alpine Pearls by 2012. A total of 35 Pearls is possible, according to Karmen Mentil.

Impact

The Alpine Pearls have shown that it is possible to address mobility, and to make it attractive to arrive by public transport at the destination. This also includes per-spectives on marketing and branding with, for instance, pristine alpine environ-ments being highly attractive for tourism, thus allowing for intercontextualization of pro-environmental behaviour.

Source

Karmen Mentil, Project Director Alpine Pearls, ÖeAR Regionalberatung GmbH, Austria.

Websites

Alpine Pearls, www.alpinepearls.com

Alpine Pearls Carbon Calculator, www.alpine-pearls.com/alpine_pearls/live/ flash/ KR_AlpinePearls_en.html

Related websites

OeAR Regionalberatung GmbH, www.oear.at

Gemeinschaft Autofreier Schweizer Tourismusorte (GAST), www.gast.org, www. auto-frei.ch

Car-free islands, www.autofrei-wohnen.de/UrlaubIslands.html

Car-free network, www.worldcarfree.net

References

Alpine Pearls (2009a). The Alpine Pearls – enjoy holidays with true awareness. Available at: http://www.alpine-pearls.com/alpine_pearls/live/ap_navi/show.php3?id=38&nodeid= 38&_language=en#. Accessed 1 December 2009.

Alpine Pearls (2009b). Criteria. Available at: http://www.alpine-pearls.com/alpine_pearls/ live/ap_navi/powerslave,id,35,nodeid,35,_language,en.html.

European Environment Agency (2003). Europe's Environment: the third assessment. http://www.eea.europa.eu/publications/environmental_assessment_report_2003_10. Accessed 1 December 2009.

Holding, D.M. (2001). The Sanfte Mobilitaet project: achieving reduced car-dependence in European resort areas. *Tourism Management* 22: 411–417.

Krippendorf, J. (1987). *The Holiday Makers: understanding the impact of leisure and travel.* Oxford: Heinemann.

ÖAR Regionalberatung (1997). EU-Projekt 'Sanfte Mobilität in Tourismusorten und –regionen' Endbericht. ÖAR Regionalberatung GmbH, Wien.

For any destination, work with carbon management has to begin with an inventory of energy consumption and associated emissions, followed by an identification of strategies to reduce emissions, and the monitoring of progress towards a specific goal. This can be exemplified based on the study of Whistler, one of the largest North American mountain resort areas with about 2 million visitors per year. In order to assess emissions in the resort area and to develop abatement strategies, Kelly and Williams (2007) developed a methodology: in a first step, system boundaries were defined to include (1) internal destination energy consumption (including buildings, infrastructure, and transportation), (2) employees commuting to and from the destination and (3) visitor travel to and from the destination (Figure 10.6). This approach goes beyond system boundaries as identified by e.g. Aspen Skiing Company (see Carbon Management in Focus 7), and is in line with recommendations for system boundaries in Gössling (2009).

Kelly and Williams (2007) also discuss direct, indirect and induced effects, concluding that direct and indirect energy consumption and associated emissions, including for instance energy consumed by hotels in providing accommodation as well as energy consumed by businesses providing associated services, should be included, while induced effects, such as domestic energy use by resort employees and their families, should not be included. While this is in line with calculations by Aspen Skiing Company (Carbon Management in Focus 7), it does not include energy use on a lifecycle basis, such as emissions associated

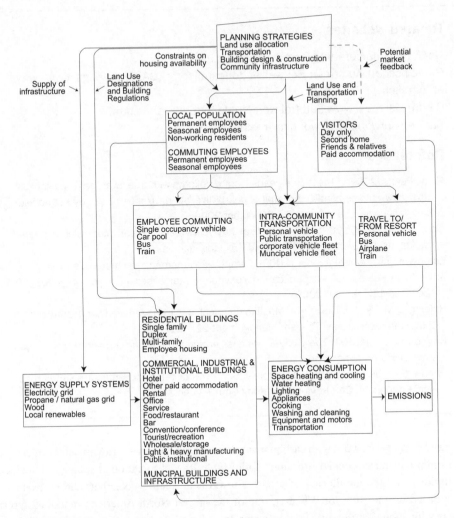

Figure 10.6 *Resort destination energy consumption and emission model*
Source: Kelly and Williams 2007

with the construction of hotels and other infrastructure (cf. UNWTO-UNEP-WMO 2008; Gössling 2009), and calculations thus need to be seen as conservative. Tables 10.5 and 10.6 show emissions by sub-sector for the years 2000 and 2020. Table 10.5 includes destination emissions, while Table 10.6 also includes transportation of employees and visitor travel to and from Whistler. Results indicate that visitor travel to and from Whistler is responsible for 86 per cent of emissions (note that it is unclear how CO_2-equivalents for aviation were calculated). One important finding is that even in the Year 2020 Energy Efficiency Scenario there is an increase in absolute emissions, pointing at the difficulty of achieving absolute emission reductions.

Based on these findings, Kelly and Williams (2007: 86) suggest implementation of various strategies to reduce emissions, focusing on transportation, building design and construction, energy supply systems, as well as external energy consumption.

Table **10.5** *Energy and greenhouse gas projections*

Sector	Year 2000		Year 2020: Business-as-Usual Scenario		Year 2020: Energy Efficient Scenario	
	Energy consumption (GJ)	GHG E=emissions (tCO$_2$e)	Energy consumption (GJ)	GHG Emissions (tCO$_2$e)	Energy consumption (GJ)	GHG emissions (tCO$_2$e)
Residential	792,335	17,256	1,020,479	21,112	924,947	17,022
Passenger Transportation	892,707	62,596	1,247,090	87,446	997,672	69,957
Commercial, Industrial and Institutional	1,129,499	40,229	1,366,768	49,060	1,275,681	39,956
Municipal Buildings and Infrastructure	50,465	1,498	58,550	1,642	53,495	1,231
Public Transportation	25,239	1,802	85,766	6,124	68,613	4,899
Solid Waste Disposal		8,243		12,236		12,236
TOTAL	**2,890,245**	**131,625**	**3,778,653**	**177,620**	**3,320,408**	**145,301**
					12.1% decrease from BAU	18.2% decrease from BAU

Source: Kelly and Williams (2007)

Table 10.6 Energy and greenhouse gas emissions including transportation

Sector	Year 2000		Year 2020: Business-as-Usual Scenario		Year 2020: Energy Efficient Scenario	
	Energy consumption (GJ)	GHG E= emissions (tCO₂e)	Energy consumption (GJ)	GHG Emissions (tCO₂e)	Energy consumption (GJ)	GHG emissions (tCO₂e)
All Internal Uses	2,890,245	131,625	3,778,653	177,620	3,320,408	145,301
Employee Commuting	133,551	9,366	110,736	7,782	110,736	7,782
Visitor Travel To/from Whistler	11,838,744	858,947	17,693,607	1,283,399	17,693,607	1,283,399
TOTAL	**14,862,541**	**999,938**	**21,582,995**	**1,468,801**	**21,124,751**	**1,436,482**
					2.1% decrease from BAU	2.2% decrease from BAU

Source: Kelly and Williams (2007)

In another study seeking to assess the emissions of Davos, Switzerland, CO_2 fluxes are calculated by including emissions from energy consumption including buildings and transport, 'CO_2 stocks and sequestration in natural materials, and further direct emissions within the region' (Walz *et al.* 2008: 814). Davos is estimated to emit 109,300t of CO_2, but the authors deduct 14,800t CO_2 which is sequestered in ecosystems and buildings (wood) per year, leading to emissions of 94,500t CO_2 per year. Of the total, 79.3 per cent are from heating, 17.9 per cent from mobility, 2.8 per cent from machines, and 0.1 per cent from further activities. Walz *et al.* (2008) conclude that Davos' residents are responsible for emissions 25 per cent greater than the Swiss annual per capita average, noting that:

> The reduction aim of −15 per cent until 2015 (compared to 2004), as set by the municipality itself, could be easily reached through better building insulation and the use of renewable energy sources. More ambitious aims, ... however, will not be realised without major drawbacks in living standards.
>
> (Walz *et al.* 2008: 811)

Notably, the calculation by Walz *et al.* (2008) does not include emissions on a lifecycle basis, nor those associated with RF impacts or GHG other than CO_2. It is also unclear on which basis aviation has been considered or not (for details on the calculations and emission sectors see Walz *et al.* 2008).

In the light of the omission of a considerable share of emissions in most tourism-related studies discussed in this book, a framework for emission inventories for destinations is suggested in the following, covering all emissions 'embedded' in a tourism system. This is necessary to develop an understanding of the 'true' size of the emissions associated with tourism activities. First of all, the framework should consider CO_2 as well as other major GHGs as identified in the UNFCCC framework, i.e. CH_4, N_2O, PFCs, HFCs, and SF_6. However, non-CO_2 emissions from aviation also need to be considered. As shown in table 10.7, direct, indirect and lifecycle emissions of these GHGs can be distinguished in a simplified and comprehensive framework. A simplified assessment would look at energy throughput and associated emissions from all tourist transports, accommodation and activities, which can be multiplied with a factor (Gössling 2009 suggests 1.15 to account for lifecycle emissions). Such an analysis is comparatively simple when focusing on CO_2, but more difficult to accomplish when other GHGs are considered as well. Simplified emission inventories might be a good starting point for destinations engaging in measurements for the first time, and can be accomplished by any destination with some basic understanding of markets (share of tourists arriving from which countries), travel modes (air, car, rail, coach), the number of guest nights spent in the destination, possibly by category, as well as the activities carried out. Missing data can be complemented with assumptions on average emission values.

A more comprehensive assessment would seek to include food, which can make a considerable contribution to emissions, and also include indirect emissions, i.e. those associated with services needed to book the journey, commuting of employees, or Internet-based information services, the latter being of growing importance as an emission source. Finally, lifecycle emissions refer to the production of aircraft, cars, trains, railways, roads, construction of accommodation, computers and office buildings, all of which are part of the tourism system. Again, as it will often be difficult to identify these emissions, factors can be used to account for energy and emissions embedded in these categories. For instance, with regard to aviation, a factor 2 can be used to account for non-CO_2 emissions (for discussion see Gössling 2009). While this is not scientifically correct, it provides a proxy value so that the climatic impact of these emissions is not omitted.

Table 10.7 *Matrix emission inventory*

	Direct	Indirect	Lifecycle
Simplified	• Transports to/from destination • Transports at destination • Accommodation • Activities		• Production of aircraft, cars, etc. • Construction of accommodation
Comprehensive	• Food	• Services (e.g. tour operator, travel agent) • Commuting by employees • Internet-based information	• Production of computers • Construction of office buildings

Once emission inventories are set up and major emission sources identified, destinations can start to strategically work with climate change mitigation. This will primarily include a focus on emissions from transports to and from the destination, the most important source of emissions. Becken (2008) suggests 10 indicators for destinations to assess transport emissions on various levels, and to make informed decisions on how to reduce these. More comprehensive approaches would seek to combine the focus on emissions with economic indicators, such as the eco-efficiency concept (Gössling *et al.* 2005). Yet another concept is 'Sustainable Yield', a framework also seeking to integrate a social sustainability dimension (Becken and Simmons 2008). These, and other concepts, can help to strategically reduce emissions without disrupting the economy.

Any destination seeking to reduce transports will have to provide public transport options. Werfenweng, Austria (Carbon Management in Focus 23) has, for instance, succeeded in providing a local transport and 'pleasure mobility' infrastructure, making it attractive to arrive by train. Many destinations have also discovered the positive effects of dedicated bicycle lanes and bicycle rentals, often free of charge, which can have a considerable impact on mobility patterns. For instance, Gilbert and Perl (2008) report that the percentage share of local trips made by bike was, in 2001, 10 per cent in Berlin, 12 per cent in Hamburg, 14 per cent in Ghent, 15 per cent in Zurich, 19 per cent in Rotterdam, 20 per cent in Copenhagen and 26 per cent in Amsterdam. In contrast, car or motorcycle shares are 68 per cent in Manchester, 76 per cent in Melbourne, 77 per cent in Dubai and 88 per cent in Chicago. These shares can be explained with the development of local, regional or national transport cultures, which in turn are a result of the infrastructure provided. Dutch cities, for instance, usually offer bicycle lanes throughout the city, and there are hundreds of locations where bicycles can be rented with minimum effort and at low prices (see Carbon Management in Focus 22). European cities also increasingly offer dedicated bicycle roads where motorized traffic has been restricted or prohibited (see e.g. Copenhagen Free Bike Program (Denmark) or UK National Cycling Network). Werfenweng, Austria, is an example of a destination that has successfully offered 'mobility guarantees' (Carbon Management in Focus 23).

CARBON MANAGEMENT IN FOCUS 22: OV-FIETS, THE NETHERLANDS

Facilitating low-carbon transport through bicycle rentals at train stations

The issue

When public transport systems are used, there is often the question of how to cover the last section of the trip, for instance from the train or bus station to the final destination. Taxis are convenient, but costly and less environmentally friendly. Buses are usually available, but there might be long waiting times, and/ or the need to change connections on route. If no significant baggage has to be carried, bicycles can be a comparatively fast and convenient option, particularly in cities without hills and with reserved bicycle lanes, as is the case everywhere in the Netherlands.

The solution

OV-fiets (*Openbaar Vervoer fiets*, i.e. 'Public Transport Bicycles') is a service by the Nederlandse Spoorwegen (*Dutch Railways*, NS) started in January 2002, which offers rental bicycles in 200 locations throughout the Netherlands, close to train, metro and bus stations, park & ride areas, and in city centres. Anyone who wants to rent a bicycle has to register through a website and to subscribe to the service at an annual cost of €9.50. Participants receive either a swipe card, which allows them to enter all bicycle stations, take a bike and leave again, or they can, once a year, register their rail annual, season or discount passes – all of this within less than a minute. The daily rent for the bicycle is €2.85 (20 hours), and payment is automatically drawn from the subscriber's bank account. Bicycles are solid standard bikes, equipped with lights, baggage-holder, and a quick release to adjust the saddle. Alternatively, electric scooters can be rented at a price of €7.50 per hour, or €15 per day (20 hours). Additional fees apply for damage caused by the user, as well as theft (OV-fiets 2009). As an important service, there are repair shops integrated in the rental stations, where for instance flat tyres can be quickly fixed. OV-fiets quickly increased in popularity with 5,600 rentals per month by the end of 2003. The number of journeys made with the bicycles reached 480,000 in 2008, with 51,000 registered subscribers (Nederlandse Spoorwegen 2009).

OV-fiets helps people to maintain mobility when arriving by train, while also facilitating healthy, sustainable lifestyles. Emissions saved by bicycle locations are moderate, as travel involves only shorter distances, but can add up to considerable values if multiplied by user numbers.

Based on the simple calculation of riding 10 km by bicycle instead of using a car this reduces emissions by 1.3 kg CO_2, while choosing a scooter would still reduce emissions by 1.1 kg CO_2. Multiplied by the number of trips made in 2008 (480,000), this would correspond to emission savings of more than 0.6 Mt CO_2. Additional emission savings can be added if trips made by environmentally friendly scooter are included.

Table 10.8 Emissions associated with different transport choices

Transport choice	Emissions per pkm (kg CO_2)
Bicycle	<0.001
NS scooters (Novox C20)	0.020
Car	0.130 (small car, one passenger)

Source: European Commission 2009; Paul Peeters, personal communication, January 2010

Website

OV-fiets, www.ovfiets.nl

Related websites

Bycyklen Copenhagen, www.bycyklen.dk/english/thecitybikeandcopenhagen.aspx
Velib' bicycles Paris, www.velib.paris.fr/
Call a bike, Germany, www.callabike-interaktiv.de/kundenbuchung/ (in German)

References

European Commission (2009). Reducing CO_2 emissions from light-duty vehicles. Available from: http://ec.europa.eu/environment/air/transport/co$_2$/co$_2$_home.htm. Accessed 10 January 2010.

Nederlandse Spoorwegen (2009). Spectaculaire groei OV-fiets in 2008 (Spectacular growth in OV-bicycles in 2008). Available from: http://www.ov-fiets.nl/NSPoort_C01/ShowDocument.asp?OriginCode=H&OriginComID=22&OriginModID=295&OriginItemID=4609&CustID=673&ComID=22&DocID=5&SessionID=73499276037670328377 16311548&Ext=.pdf. Accessed 7 January 2010.

OV-fiets (2009). OV-fiets in het kort (OV-bicycles in short). Available from: www.ov-fiets.nl. Accessed 18 December 2009.

CARBON MANAGEMENT IN FOCUS 23: WERFENWENG, AUSTRIA

Modal shift from car to train based on mobility guarantees and pleasure mobility offers

The issue

Transports are the major factor in generating tourism-related emissions, with air travel being responsible for 40 per cent of CO_2 emissions from global tourism, and car travel for another 38 per cent (in 2005) (UNWTO-UNEP-WMO 2008). Calculated on a per holiday basis, travel to the destination consequently generates the largest share of emissions; in the case of holidays involving air travel, the flight will typically account for 60–90 per cent of the overall energy footprint (Gössling et al. 2005). As outlined by UNWTO-UNEP-WMO (2008), achieving a modal shift from aircraft or car to train is thus essential. However, air or car travel is, in many situations, a self-evident and emotionally deeply rooted mobility choice (e.g. Miller 2001; Randles and Mander 2009). Convincing car or air travellers to favour other means of transport is, consequently, difficult.

The solution

Werfenweng, a small alpine village with 850 inhabitants (in 2005) in Austria, was one of the first destinations to systematically develop a holistic Sanfte Mobilität (*sustainable mobility*) concept. In 1994, a meeting was held to develop a new destination model for Werfenweng, a highly tourism-dependent community that had seen declining tourist arrivals over a number of years. In the brainstorming process to identify key values for the new destination concept, the suggestion to become car-free to attract new visitors was made half-jokingly, according to Manfred Kojan, one of the consultants in the process, even though a community of car-free tourism destinations had in fact existed since 1988 in Switzerland (Gemeinschaft Autofreier Schweizer Tourismusorte, GAST, originally translated as the *Community of Vehicle-Free Swiss Tourist Resorts*). The proposition was nevertheless accepted after discussions with tourism businesses in Werfenweng.

In the period 1996–2007, the village developed into a model community for 'sustainable mobility – car-free tourism', with financial support from various ministries, Salzburger Landesregierung (provincial government) and the EU, and based on models developed by Thaler et al. (1993). In 2006, this also resulted in the foundation of the Alpine Pearls, a network of soft-mobility communities building on the success of the concept in Werfenweng (see Carbon Management in Focus 21): tourist arrivals in Werfenweng reached 36,000 in 2008, with 210,000 guest nights being spent in the village, corresponding to a 20 per cent increase in guest nights over 1996 (175,000 guest nights). Moreover, the share of train traveller arrivals grew from 6–7 per cent in 1999 to 25 per cent in 2005 – notably representing an even greater increase in train travellers in absolute arrival numbers.

Emissions avoided because of the higher share of train traveller arrivals were quantified at more than 450t CO_2 per year (travel origin–destination), which corresponds to an average reduction in per visitor emissions of 15 per cent in winter and 5 per cent in summer (Trafico 2001). Within Werfenweng, the sustainable mobility focus and pleasure mobility offers led to a decline in average per tourist emissions by 27 per cent in winter and 14 per cent in summer – the higher reduction in emissions in winter reflecting greater difficulties in making summer guests use public transport. Werfenweng also seeks to become carbon-neutral by compensating emissions caused by the origin–destination travel of all guests, irrespective of the mode of transport used. All guests are asked where they have come from and which means of transport they have used, a basis on which total emissions can be calculated.

The overall idea of sustainable mobility communities is that visitors remain mobile, even when they do not arrive by car. According to Dr Peter Brandauer, the mayor of Werfenweng, this is a key perceptual issue, as people travelling by aircraft never seem to think about their mobility at the destination, while the main concern of car and train travellers is 'how do I remain mobile?' Visitors arriving by train are thus picked up by a shuttle service at the train station in Bischof-shofen, 12 km from Werfenweng. Once in Werfenweng, train travellers can buy the 'Vorteils-Pass SAnfte MObilität' (SAMO, short for 'sustainable mobility pass-port'). The passport is available for €6 per person, including car travellers leav-ing their car keys at the tourist information, and allows its owner to use various 'pleasure mobility' vehicles, most of which are electricity powered. These include Segway, Flyer, Arrow, Biga, E-fun Rider, E-Scooter, but also conventional mountain bikes (see Related websites). Electric vehicles are powered by a solar park built in 2008, which generates almost 0.3 MWh of electricity per year – more than the amount used for e-mobility. Other services include rental mobile phones to place shuttle service orders or to call 'Elois', a taxi service to take tourists anywhere in the village area between 9 a.m. and 10 p.m. There is also a night taxi service up to 4 a.m. All services are free of charge. Likewise, various excursions in the area are also offered free of charge. The overall costs of the concept are in the order of €95,000 per year (excluding the shuttle service Werfenweng–Bischofshofen), and financed through sales of SAMO passports (at €6 per person, adding up to €25,000), and a fee of €0.5 per guest night in the 40 accommodation establish-ments supporting the concept, collecting another €70,000.

In order to better understand sustainable mobility perceptions by Werfenweng visitors, Gössling (2008, unpublished) interviewed a convenience sample of 15 visitors to Werfenweng, all of them families (with children 0–10), or elderly peo-ple, who seemed to represent the greater tourist population. Travellers provided a wide range of motivations for using the train, ranging from convenience ('It is more comfortable, the children can run around, and you don't end up in a traffic jam') to green values ('We don't have a car'). Travellers also had in common that they all were very positive about the sustainable mobility concept, despite experi-ences including delayed, missed, or cancelled trains as well as crowding onboard trains. Interviews also indicated that tourists chose Werfenweng as a destination because of the sustainable mobility concept, and that they were willing to adapt to slow-mobility preconditions, such as planning in time, low flexibility, or waiting times if shuttles or excursions were over-booked. Offers of free pleasure mobil-ity were highly appreciated by tourists. Overall, the sustainable mobility concept is attractive to many travellers, both with regard to origin–destination mobility and mobility at the destination, but it is the very combination of car-free travel, mobility guarantees and pleasure mobility offers that appears to be at the heart of positive tourist perceptions.

In most contexts, ambitions to make even a small village 'car-free' will arouse emotions. In the case of Werfenweng, the 'car-free' concept was implemented against considerable resistance in the local population: a political party was founded to prevent the concept, which held, in 2005, still one third of the vote. However, according to Dr Peter Brandauer, acceptance of the concept is grow-ing with its economic success and the opportunities it brings to the locals, such as the possibility to use the free shuttle service to Bischofshofen. Werfenweng also struggles with external problems over which it has no power, such as those encountered in the form of delays, crowded or cancelled trains in the German and Austrian railway systems. Financing the sustainable mobility concept is a permanent struggle (see also Holding 2001).

In the future, Werfenweng plans to attract a greater share of people within the range of 500–700 km to come by train. It will offer guests more services at the destination, so that people can travel light. Hybrid and e-cars will be increasingly used for transport of goods, also including the use of horse-drawn carriages. Locals will be involved in sustainable mobility through 'Advantage packages', designed for various groups, such as commuters, children, youths, families with children, and people agreeing to use their car less (Mentil 2008). For these target groups, special offers are made if car-dependent mobility is reduced by a given degree, including such diverse incentives as a free e-motorbike and cinema tickets for youths (for agreeing not to buy a 'real' motorcycle with combustion engine), or a free electric bicycle for a family agreeing not to use their car over one consecutive week. Werfenweng will also build an underground parking lot to make cars vanish from the streets.

Impact

The sustainable mobility concept as explored and developed by Werfenweng appears to have considerable potential to attract travellers by train, leading to new jobs, and having a wide range of associated advantages, such as fewer traffic jams, reduced air pollution, fewer accidents, and an increased attractiveness of the destination leading to growing tourist arrival numbers. It also addresses the travel patterns by the locals, and encourages changes in transport patterns through incentives. It is thus an option worth exploring by more destinations.

Sources

Dr Peter Brandauer, Mayor Werfenweng, Austria
Dr Romain Molitor, Consultant, Komobile, Austria
Manfred Kojan, Consultant, ÖeAR Regionalberatung GmbH, Austria
Susi Zentner, General manager, Braunwald-Klausenpass Tourismus AG, Austria

Websites

Werfenweng Tourismusverband (tourism association), www.werfenweng.org, see also www.werfenweng-austria.com and www.klimaneu.at

Related websites

Gemeinschaft Autofreier Schweizer Tourismusorte (GAST), www.gast.org; www.auto-frei.ch

OeAR Regionalberatung GmbH, www.oear.at

Komobile, Austria, www.komobile.at

Segway, www.segway.com/

Flyer, www.swissflyer.de/

Other e-mobility offers: www.tourismus-werfenweng.at/de/fun-e-fahrzeuge/

References

Gössling, S., Peeters, P.M., Ceron, J.-P., Dubois, G., Patterson, T. and Richardson, R.B. (2005). The eco-efficiency of tourism. *Ecological Economics* 54(4): 417–434.

Holding, D.M. (2001). The Sanfte Mobilitaet project: achieving reduced car-dependence in European resort areas. *Tourism Management* 22: 411–417.

Mentil, K. (2008). Werfenweng mobil +. Förderung der lokalen Akzeptanz für die sanfte Mobilität (*Werfenweng mobile +. Supporting local willingness to accept sustainable mobility*). ÖAR Regionalberatung GmbH, Wien.

Miller, D. (ed.) (2001). *Car Cultures*. Oxford: Berg Publishers.

Randles, S. and Mander, S. (2009). Aviation, consumption and the climate change debate: 'Are you going to tell me off for flying?' *Technology Analysis & Strategic Management* 21(1): 93–113.

Thaler, R., Frosch, W., Kien, B., Glasl, P., Robatsch, K., Stadlhuber, C. and Wagner E. (1993). *Wege zum Autofreien Tourismus. Handbuch im Auftrag von Bundesministerium für Umwelt, Jugend und Familie und Wissenschaft und Forschung* (*Avenues to car-free tourism. Handbook on behalf of the Ministry of Environment, Youth, Family, Science and Research*). Verkehrsclub Österreich, Wien.

Trafico (2001). *Umweltwirkungen des Modell-Projektes 'Autofreier Tourismus' in der Gemeinde Werfenweng 1998–2001 (Environmental effects of the model project 'car-free tourism' in Werfenweng 1998–2001)*. Gmunden: Trafico.

UNWTO-UNEP-WMO (2008). *Climate Change and Tourism: responding to global challenges*. Madrid: UNWTO, UNDP and WMO.

As Carbon Management in Focus 22 and 23 indicate, slow mobility planning in destinations with a focus on bicycles and public transport is generally attractive for tourists, not least because averaged speed levels decline, and noise and air pollution are reduced. When cities become attractive for walks and bicycle tours, this can also open up the way for new tourism products, such as guided tours by bicycle or inline skates, as now offered in many major European cities. For studies investigating resident/tourist perceptions of restructuring transport systems, the acceptance and potential of alternative transport systems, planning and tourist spending see Dickinson *et al.* (2009), Dickinson and Dickinson (2006), Dickinson and Robbins (2007, 2008), Downward *et al.* (2009), Guiver *et al.* (2007), Lumsdon (2006), Lumsdon *et al.* (2004). Carbon Management in Focus 24 and 25 also provide perspectives on the importance, acceptability and financing mechanisms of regional public transport systems.

CARBON MANAGEMENT IN PRACTICE 24: EUREGIO BODENSEE, SWITZERLAND, GERMANY, AUSTRIA

Facilitating trans-border mobility by means of public transport

The issue

Many regions of the world are attractive because they comprise several countries, allowing visitors to experience various cultures, sites, or to engage in cross-border shopping (e.g. Timothy and Butler 1995). Trans-border tourism also generates mobility, however, and creating effective systems for sustainable transport is thus paramount in avoiding emissions from tourist travel. This poses challenges in terms of connecting public transport modes, changes between various transport systems, and payments, which might have to be made in different currencies and for different sections of the journey.

The solution

Euregio Bodensee, which comprises the German, Swiss and Austrian parts of Lake Constance, accounted for more than 34.5 million guest nights in 2003 (Statistik Euregio Bodensee 2007). In order to facilitate travel in the region, a trans-border day card was developed, allowing families, small groups or individual travellers to cross borders with a single ticket within the Lake Constance region. The ticket was offered for the first time in 2002, and can be bought to cover one or several 'Euregios' with more than 5,000 km of route networks (Figure 10.7).

The day card Euregio Bodensee is the first trilateral public transport offer in Europe, and was developed within the context of an Interreg IIIA project of the EU, in a cooperation of tourism organizations, transport providers, and regional government (Maurer 2003). As such, Edgar Meier, Head of Marketing, points out, the Euregio card is a 'political product', i.e. it has been the political will of the different countries involved to create a trans-border public transport system, which might otherwise not have been perceived as a feasible project. Cardholders can use all regional trains, buses, mountain cable cars and ferries. The card also entitles the holder to discounts at various attractions. Across the categories adults, children and small groups, 30,588 cards were sold in 2009, making the card economically feasible with a turnover of €807,000 in this year. Travelling throughout the Bodensee region (zones 1–4) costs, for instance, €28 per day for an individual, €21 for children aged 6–15, or €56 for small groups (up to 2 adults and 4 children) (Euregio Bodensee 2009b).

Impact

Facilitating public transport is a key challenge in achieving low-carbon tourism. Mobility by public transport can be particularly interesting for tourists in border

Figure 10.7 *Lake Constance and surrounding regions*
Source: Euregio Bodensee (2009a)

regions, as it is often more difficult to cross borders by private car, which can also involve insurance issues. However, trans-border mobility by means of public transport could be particularly difficult because of different currencies or different sales systems for tickets. The Euregio Bodensee card overcomes these problems and can thus serve as a role model to using synergies between tourist interests and climatically sustainable transport choices, while at the same time stimulating regional tourism.

Source

Edgar Meier, Head of Marketing, Euroregio Bodensee, Switzerland

Website

Euregio Bodensee, www.euregiokarte.ch

Related websites

Travel schedules Germany, www.efa-bw.de, www.bahn.de
Travel schedules Austria, www.vmobil.at, www.oebb.at
Travel schedules Switzerland, www.sbb.ch

References

Euregio Bodensee (2009a). Euregio 1–4. Available from: http://www.euregiokarte.ch/index.php?id=29. Accessed 11 December 2009.

Euregio Bodensee (2009b). Preise Tageskarte. Available from: http://www.euregiokarte.ch/index.php?id=28. Accessed 11 December 2009.

Maurer, S. (2003). ÖV-Angebote für Freizeitwirtschaft und Tourismus (Public transport offers for leisure businesses and tourism). Mobilitätszentrale Pongau GesmbH, Bischofshofen, Austria.

Statistik Euregio Bodensee (2007). Im Fokus. Die Regio Bodensee. Available from: http://www.statistik.euregiobodensee.org/pdfs/imfokus.pdf. Accessed 11 December 2009.

Timothy, D.T. and Butler, R.W. (1995). Cross-border shopping: a North American perspective. *Annals of Tourism Research* 22(1): 16–34.

CARBON MANAGEMENT IN FOCUS 25: KONUS-GÄSTEKARTE BADEN-WÜRTTEMBERG, GERMANY

Mandatory public transport support from tourists

The issue

In most destinations, a majority of tourists arrive by car, and there are considerable difficulties in convincing them to use alternative modes of transport, such as bus or train (see, however, Carbon Management in Focus 21, 23). Modal shift is not only hindered by irregular and infrequent departure times, but also made inconvenient because of the need to buy various tickets, for instance when using different transport modes.

The solution

The KONUS guest card allows its holder to use any public transport, i.e. all buses and trains, free of charge (Figure 10.9). The card covers the Black Forest region in Germany, with nine different linked transport systems covering an area of 11,000 km². Throughout Europe, there are many different forms of guest cards giving access to a region's or city's public transport system for a given period of time (cf. Maurer 2003). The KONUS guest card is unique, however, because its purchase is mandatory in the 120 municipalities (2009) that have signed up to be part of the system: from the tourist tax charged on every guest night, a fixed sum of €0.30 is paid by the municipalities to the transport authorities to co-finance the public transport system, and €0.01 to finance marketing of the guest card. Importantly, this implies that tourists cannot choose whether they want to buy the card or not – all they can decide is whether to use it or not. As public transport is consequently pre-paid, many tourists take the opportunity to use trains or buses to explore the area – also because popular city break destinations such as Freiburg make it increasingly difficult for individual motorized transport to enter. On the other hand, tourists still preferring to travel by car subsidize the Black Forest's low-carbon public transport system. The German high-speed trains Intercity and Intercity Express as well as mountain cable cars are not included, but the card also offers discounted entrance fees for the region's attractions.

The KONUS guest card is provided to tourists in more than 6,000 accommodation establishments in the Black Forest area. In 2008, the roughly 3 million guests in the then 108 KONUS-municipalities in the Black Forest supported the public transport system with €2.7 million (at an average length of stay of three days corresponding to 9 million 'KONUS' guest nights). For comparison, the entire Black Forest region receives 6.5 million visitors accounting for 19 million guest nights.

Impact

The KONUS guest card is an advanced model of internalizing the environmental costs of individual motorized transport, by making all visitors to the KONUS Black Forest municipalities pay for the public transport system – irrespective of use. This not only helps to finance the public transport system and to potentially provide more frequent departures of e.g. buses and trains, but also stimulates interest in the use of the system, which becomes a cost-free transport option as it is pre-paid. The system has thus great potential to be implemented by tourist destinations throughout the world.

Source

Isabel Wolf, Project Management, Schwarzwald Tourismus GmbH

Website

KONUS guest card, www.konus-schwarzwald.info
Black Forest Tourism, www.blackforest-tourism.com

References

Maurer, S. (2003). ÖV-Angebote für Freizeitwirtschaft und Tourismus (Public transport offers for leisure businesses and tourism). Mobilitätszentrale Pongau GesmbH, Bischofshofen, Austria.

Schwarzwald Tourismus (2009). Die KONUS-Gästekarte gibt freie Fahrt mit Bus und Bahn (Free travel by bus and train with KONUS guest card). Available from: http://www.schwarzwald-tourismus.info/service/konus/was_ist_konus. Accessed 10 December 2009.

Ultimately, destinations may even seek to become carbon-neutral, a goal that has for instance been announced by Costa Rica and the Maldives (Gössling 2009). In particular small destinations seeking to achieve carbon-neutrality might profit from such approaches, as exemplified by the Danish island of Samsø, which turned within a few years from an energy importer (mostly oil) into an energy exporter (electricity), also becoming a major 'energy attraction'. A case study of another area turning into a 'renewable energy destination' is Energielandschaft Mohrbach, Germany (Carbon Management in Focus 26). How destinations can involve residents more broadly to move towards carbon-neutrality is illustrated in Carbon Management in Focus 27, discussing the example of South West England.

CARBON MANAGEMENT IN FOCUS 26: ENERGIELANDSCHAFT MORBACH, GERMANY

Renewable energy as a tourist attraction

The issue

Many governments have ambitions to reduce emissions of GHGs by increasing the share of renewable energy sources, including wind, solar, biomass, or micro-hydro. Wind farms often have the greatest potential to contribute significantly to power generation, but their expansion can lead to conflict, as these are sometimes perceived as disturbing elements in otherwise pristine landscapes. Conflicts over wind energy have occurred in many countries including the UK and Norway, where tourism stakeholders have expressed fears that wind farms will deter tourists or lead to a decline in landscape qualities (The Scottish Government 2008; Tveit et al. 2009).

However, the perception of renewable energies appears to be usually positive in society (e.g. Gössling et al. 2005; Dalton et al. 2008), and perceptions of wind farms are highly dependent on factors such as structure, distribution and density. Studies indicate that visitors to wind power areas generally have no specific opinion on this renewable energy, and only a small share might be holding explicitly negative views (for a review of studies see The Scottish Government 2008). Studies seeking to understand the impact of future wind power development indicate that an even smaller share of visitors would not return should wind farms be realized (see The Scottish Government 2008). Conversely, wind farms have a considerable potential to become tourist attractions, and 'visit a wind farm' is encouraged in many countries (e.g. Bakos and Soursos 2002; New Zealand Wind Energy Association 2009). Sites can be particularly attractive if various forms of renewable energy can be visited in 'energy landscapes'.

The solution

Morbach Municipality, a small community with 11,000 inhabitants in Rheinland Pfalz, Germany, hosted the largest ammunition deposit of the US air force in

Europe, a 145 ha area, until 1995. When the area was returned to the municipality, the question arose of how the area could be used in the future. Early plans included a leisure park, an adventure park, a sports hotel, and a resort, but no investors could be found for these concepts. In 2000, wind power operators started to write contracts with farmers for plots of land all over the municipality (121 km^2), and the administration was forced to stop developments in order to develop a structured land-use plan. It was decided that the former ammunition deposit was best suited for the development of a wind farm. At that time, the University of Trier published a survey on sunshine hours and solar radiation in the wider region, showing that the area around Morbach had the highest values and thus the best conditions for developing solar energy.

In light of this, the Head of the building authority, Alfons Gorges, and the authority's engineer Michael Grehl made the suggestion to not only develop wind power in the area, but to focus on solar and biomass renewable energy production as well. The idea was favourably received by the mayor, Gregor Eibes, and unanimously approved by the building committee and local council. Several town hall meetings were organized to give everyone the opportunity to pronounce their opinions, and the plans were widely discussed in the media, with the overall outcome of a largely favourable public opinion.

In 2001 it was decided to create an 'energy landscape'. The community's land-use plan was changed, and in 2002, 14 wind power stations (each 2 MW) and an area of 10,000 m^2 of PV modules were built and connected to the grid. A biogas plant was added in 2006, which is now also used to dry wood chips for pellet production. The energy landscape already produces more energy than the 11,000 inhabitants of Morbach use themselves and the community has consequently become a net energy producer.

The costs for the project were shared by different stakeholders. The planning process was partially paid by the community, partially by the federal state (*Bundesland*) Rheinland Pfalz. Renewable energy infrastructure was financed by limited partners coordinated by Juwi, a company planning, implementing and managing renewable energy infrastructure. More specifically, the 14 wind power stations were built at a cost of €40 million, and paid for by 100 limited partners. Notably, one of the wind power stations was financed by 34 citizens paying a minimum of €2,500: financing renewable energy in such limited partner approaches involving interested laypeople is now becoming common in Germany. When projects run as planned, annual rates of return of 9–10 per cent are not uncommon – this is facilitated by German law guaranteeing a fixed amount of money for every kWh produced from new renewable power stations and fed into the grid (currently €0.06–0.09 per kWh for wind power stations built inland, and €0.40 per kWh of solar energy; see also Carbon Management in Focus 6). The PV modules cost €3.3 million to build, and the biogas plant €3 million, a joint project with Ökobit, a company developing biogas plants. The annual energy output of the energy landscape is equivalent to 50 million kWh.

Energielandschaft Morbach has become an important tourist attraction, with more than 3,350 visitors per year participating in guided tours. Since 2003, some 20,000 visitors from 62 countries have been guided through the energy landscape. Recently, energy landscape Morbach has also become part of networks such as the Austrian 'Energy Road' (*Energieschaustrasse*), which seeks to connect sites with renewable energy projects in different countries. The energy landscape has also won various national prizes for energy innovation. A key to success has been the broad support of the local population. For guidelines and advice to develop regions with renewable energy autarky see e.g. Tischer *et al.* (2006).

Impact

Energielandschaft Morbach combines renewable energy development with tourist interest in renewable energies. This increases the acceptability of renewable energy, and creates knowledge, awareness and further interest in energy and climate change.

Source

Michael Grehl, Engineer, Municipal Administration Morbach, Germany
Stefanie Hidde, Project Manager Public Affairs, Juwi, Germany

Website

Energielandschaft Morbach, www.energielandschaft.de/

Related websites

Juwi, www.juwi.com/

Ökobit, www.oekobit-biogas.com/en/home.html

Energieschaustrasse, www.energieschaustrasse.at

'Energy island' Samsø, Denmark, www.energiakademiet.dk/front_uk.asp?id=55

Travel guide renewable energies Wendland, Germany, www.wendenenergie.de/Projekte/reisefuehrer/reisefuehrer.html

References

Bakos, G.C. and Soursos, M. (2002). Techno-economic assessment of a stand-alone PV/hybrid installation for low-cost electrification of a tourist resort in Greece. *Applied Energy* 73: 183–193.

Dalton, G.J., Lockington, D.A. and Baldock, T.E. (2008). A survey of tourist attitudes to renewable energy supply in Australian hotel accommodation. *Renewable Energy* 33: 2174–2185.

Gössling, S., Kunkel, T., Schumacher, K., Birkemeyer, J., Froese, J., Heck, N., Naber, N. and Schliermann, E. (2005). A target-group specific approach to 'green' power retailing: students as consumers of renewable energy. *Renewable & Sustainable Energy Reviews* 9(1): 69–83.

New Zealand Wind Energy Association 2009. Visit a Wind Farm. Available at: http://www.windenergy.org.nz/nz-wind-farms/visit. Accessed 15 October 2009.

The Scottish Government (2008). The economic impacts of wind farms on Scottish tourism. Available at: http:/www.scotland.gov.uk/Publications/2008/03/07113554/0. Accessed 6 October 2009.

Tischer, M., Stöhr, M., Lurz, M. and Karg, L. (2006). *Auf dem Weg zur 100% Region. Handbuch für eine nachhaltige Energieversorgung von Regionen (Towards the 100% region. Handbook for a sustainable energy supply of regions)*. Munich: B.A.U.M. Consult GmbH.

Tveit, E.-M., Aall, C. and Heiberg, E. (2009). Vindkraft, reiseliv og miljø – en konfliktanalyse. Available from: http://www.vestforsk.no/www/show.do?page=12&articleid=2469. Accessed 6 October 2009.

CARBON MANAGEMENT IN FOCUS 27: SOUTH WEST ENGLAND

Implementing low-carbon destinations

The issue

One of the greatest difficulties in achieving sustainable tourism, and low-carbon tourism in particular, is to mobilize stakeholders to achieve significant change at the destination level. This is important, as the scale of change necessary to deal with climate change means that high stakeholder numbers need to become involved over a short period of time to achieve significant results (cf. Gössling 2009). Given the structure of the tourism industry, which mostly consists of small and medium-sized enterprises (e.g. Phillips and Louvieris 2005), reaching out to hundreds or thousands of stakeholders simultaneously and convincing them to engage in restructuring and retrofitting is thus one of the key challenges that have to be addressed (see also Carbon Management in Focus 13). A precondition for change at the destination level is consensus that a low-carbon tourism system is desirable and feasible. Once there is agreement, the challenge is to develop strategies for implementing sustainable, low-carbon tourism. This involves guiding stakeholders and providing practical, comprehensible advice on how to adjust and restructure the tourism system.

The solution

The South West is the UK's foremost holiday destination, receiving 96 million day visitors and some 20 million domestic and 2 million international tourists staying for at least one night, which together support about 260,000 jobs (South West Tourism 2009). South West Tourism (SWT) initiated a process towards sustainable tourism development through publication of its regional strategy 'Towards 2015' in January 2005, which put sustainability at the heart of its tourism vision (South West Tourism 2005). To actually implement the strategy, SWT started to recruit expert staff, in partnership with tourism businesses, visitors, and decision-makers. In the period 2005–08, several programmes were developed in this respect. Key actions included an awareness campaign for businesses, 'Action of the Year', which focused on one theme per year, such as 'saving energy'. Within the 'Action of the Year' campaign, presentations to about 4,000 businesses were made. Furthermore, a green certification scheme already operating in Scotland and South East England was rolled out in South West England and, over three years, was joined by 500 businesses out of about 20,000 accommodation and attraction providers in the South West.

SWT also worked to integrate sustainability indicators in national quality standards for tourism businesses, as well as tourism training courses, and produced a number of introductory publications on sustainability issues for tourism businesses. These were backed up with workshops and assistance schemes for sub-regional destination managers. A communication strategy for visitors was developed in partnership with Sustainability South West, an awareness-raising charity, including room cards with sustainability messages. SWT also started to offer a wide range of documents on its website, helping businesses to reduce energy and resource use. Emma Whittlesea, Sustainability Strategist for SWT, points out that it is paramount to actively promote these resources to stakeholders, emphasizing that they are provided free of charge. All costs act as a significant barrier to progress, which is for instance a significant constraint for interest in certification schemes, even though costs are comparatively low. Emma Whittlesea adds that for tourists, green credentials of a business are not necessarily influencing choices, but are seen as an important add-on:

> There are real difficulties in tracking the impact [of work towards sustainability] on visitor numbers. This is because visitor surveys show that it is part of the overall decision making process rather than something that is the top decision making factor. ... However, there is starting to be evidence that those with green certification have higher occupancy levels than those of the same quality grading. ... for most visitors [green certification] is considered as an expectation, added bonus or an element of quality ...

More recently, SWT has focused on calculating and monitoring progress towards sustainability. Specifically, this includes scenario planning as a tool to understand the environmental consequences of various development paths (South West Tourism 2005), and the development and dissemination of tools to help stakeholders make sustainable decisions. In cooperation with the Stockholm Environment Institute (SEI), SWT developed the Resource, Energy and Analysis Program (REAP) for Tourism, a tool to assess the environmental impact of visitor and tourism activities. REAP Tourism is a software tool designed for destinations and was launched in February 2009 (South West Tourism 2009).

REAP is based on national GHG accounts, which are broken down by industrial sector. Using input-output analysis, the environmental impact associated with a unit of final demand (e.g. an additional visitor day) can be calculated. This impact takes into account the full supply chain of manufacturing a product or supplying a service. In effect, this allows comparison of impact (measured in t CO_2) with spending (in pounds sterling) on goods and services. The model can be used to calculate how tourist spending on different goods and services translates into emissions of CO_2, also allowing for a calculation of the carbon footprint of individual activities or tourism products. As a crucial step, results are then compared to sustainable emissions. For this purpose, global sustainable emissions per year are defined by the SEI at 2 t CO_2 per capita per year, or 5.5 kg CO_2 per day (South West Tourism 2009).

To estimate the carbon footprint of visitors to the South West, emissions data for transport, accommodation, food and catering, shopping, attractions, events, services and activities was assessed and fed into the software tool REAP Tourism (REAP Tourism 2009). The tool allows quantification on the basis of CO_2 and for GHGs uses CO_2-eq, but also considers three other environmental measures, the ecological footprint in global ha (gha), kg waste, and litres of water used, as alternative parameters. The impact can be displayed as a total of all tourism, or on a 'per tourist per day' basis. The tool also allows investigation of various scenarios for tourism development by changing visitor spending patterns or tourism travel (distance/mode), accommodation choices and activities. Changes in terms of emissions and spending growth/decline can thus be compared to different development options – essentially a form of scenario planning (cf. Page *et al.* 2009).

Results for 2006, the base year for calculations, show that emissions from tourism in the South West are considerable (almost 7 Mt CO_2), with significant differences between the counties in the South West (Figure 10.8). However, as these results could be attributed to various factors, such as visitor numbers or their travel patterns, further information is needed for strategic change. Figure 10.9 provides an understanding of emissions on a 'per visitor day carbon footprint' basis, i.e. the total emissions divided by the number of visitor days. Results also indicate that it is meaningful to distinguish 'staying visitors' (tourists) and 'day visitors', as these have different emission profiles and account for unequal shares of overall emissions. In Figure 10.10, these results are further split up by emission sub-sector, including transport, accommodation, food and catering, shopping, attractions, events, services and activities. It can also be seen how the results compare to sustainable emission levels, i.e. 5.5 kg CO_2 per capita per day.

Results indicate that calculated on a per visitor day basis, tourists in Gloucestershire and Wiltshire have considerably greater footprints than those in, for instance, Devon, a result of a greater share of overseas arrivals by air. For tourists ('staying visitors'), the travel component is thus most relevant for emissions, followed by accommodation and food, while for day visitors, shopping is most relevant, followed by food. Figure 10.10 also shows emissions per tourist per day have been compared to sustainable emissions (5.5 kg CO_2 per day). Results show that in order for tourism to become sustainable, average carbon footprints would have to be reduced considerably. Figure 10.10 also indicates where priorities for emission reductions might lie – for tourists, travel to and from the destination is most relevant, and efforts could be made to reduce the share of long-haul arrivals in favour of closer markets (see also Carbon Management in Focus 19). For day visitors, shopping has the greatest impact, an issue that can only be addressed through more complex analyses. Finally, food is relevant for both visitor groups and is clearly an issue that can be strategically addressed (see Carbon Management in Focus 15, 16). Insights as revealed through REAP are extremely

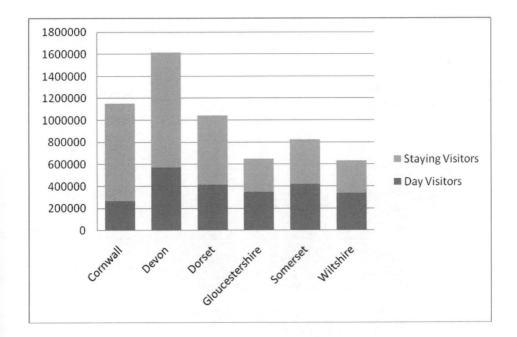

Figure 10.8 *Total carbon footprint for counties in the South West of England, 2006 (t CO_2)*
Source: REAP Tourism 2009

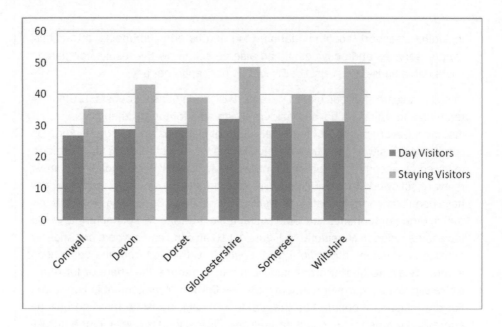

Figure 10.9 *Per visitor day carbon footprint for counties in the South West of England, 2006 (kg CO$_2$)*
Source: REAP Tourism 2009

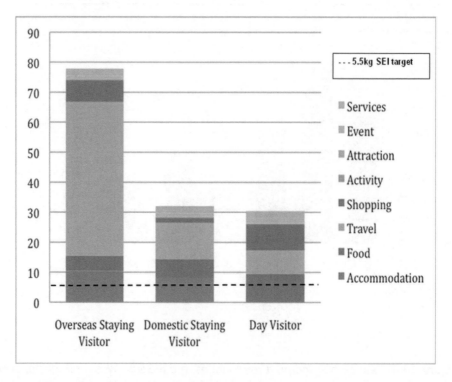

Figure 10.10 *South West England carbon footprint per visitor day (kg CO$_2$)*
Source: REAP Tourism 2009

valuable in guiding strategies to reduce emissions, particularly when connected to economic considerations.

Impact

South West England is probably the region in the world with the best-developed carbon monitoring system on the destination level, combining environmental indicators (CO_2 emissions) with economic indicators for the various sub-sectors of the tourism system. This allows the region to systematically identify and implement low-carbon strategies. Simultaneously, the region has succeeded in involving a considerable share of businesses in mitigation, through raising awareness and providing hands-on advice of how to restructure and retrofit the tourism system. Notably, South West England is also a case study of adaptation, in the sense that the British government has turned significant national emission reductions into a law, and strategies for decarbonization thus have to be explored by all tourism actors (for UK carbon budgets and monitoring see the Committee on Climate Change, www.theccc.org.uk).

Source

Emma Whittlesea, Sustainability Strategist, South West Tourism, UK

Website

South West Tourism, www.swtourism.org.uk/

Documents with advice of how to minimize resource use, www.swtourism.org.uk/business-support/save-money-go-green/

Documents with advice of how to save energy, http://www.swtourism.org.uk/documents/q/category/business-support-documents/green-downloads/energy-download-folder/

Related websites

Green holidays in South West England, feelgood.visitsouthwest.co.uk/

Sustainability South West, http://www.sustainabilitysouthwest.org.uk/

REAP Tourism Tool, www.resource-accounting.org.uk/reap-tourism

KUNTIKUM, Klimatrends und nachhaltige Tourismusentwicklung in Küsten- und Mittelgebirgsregionen (KUNTIKUM; *Climate trends and sustainable tourism development in coastal- and Central German Uplands*), German pilot adaptation programme for destinations vulnerable to climate change, www.klimatrends.de

References

Gössling, S. (2009). Carbon neutral destinations: a conceptual analysis. *Journal of Sustainable Tourism* 17(1): 17–37.

Page, S., Yeoman, I. and Greenwood, C. (2009). Transport and Tourism in Scotland: a case of scenario planning at Visit Scotland. In: Gössling, S., Hall, C.M. and Weaver, D.B. (eds) *Sustainable Tourism Futures: perspectives on systems, restructuring and innovations.* London: Routledge, pp. 58–83.

Phillips, P. and Louvieris, P. (2005). Performance measurement systems in tourism, hospitality and leisure small medium-sized enterprises: a balanced scorecard perspective. *Journal of Travel Research* 44: 201–211.

REAP Tourism (2009). Introducing REAP Tourism. Available from: http://www.resource-accounting.org.uk/reap-tourism. Accessed 14 December 2009.

South West Tourism (2005). Towards 2015. Shaping tomorrow's tourism. Available from: http://towards2015.co.uk/. Accessed 14 December 2009.

South West Tourism (2009). REAP – Resource and Energy Analysis Program. Available from: http://www.swtourism.org.uk/our-strategic-work/sustainability-work/reap-resource-and-energy-analysis-program/. Accessed 14 December 2009.

The above sections indicate that destinations now have a wide range of options to reduce emissions and to engage proactively in carbon management. This should include efforts to closely cooperate with destination marketers. Marketing campaigns could take issues such as energy use and GHG emissions into account. For instance, Sweden currently seeks to establish a massive inflow of Chinese tourists, despite strong growth in incoming tourism from European countries. This will substantially increase national emissions in both Sweden and China, indicating the need for a better understanding of the consequences of various development pathways. An important tool for this could be scenario planning, a technique so far primarily employed for crisis management in tourism (e.g. Glaesser 2003), but recently also used to develop an understanding of various development pathways and their consequences for economy and environment.

For instance, VisitScotland used scenario planning to discuss various goals for tourism development, as well as preconditions for achieving these goals and/or possible trade-offs such as increasing emissions associated with volume growth in arrival numbers (Page *et al.* 2009). A similar approach to scenario planning is currently being developed by the Western Norway Research Institute to better understand how tourism development goals will affect the sustainability of the tourism system as well as economic development in Norway by 2030. The major goals of this project are to understand the dynamics of the tourism system, to involve stakeholders in decision-making and to achieve consensus on government policy needed to steer the tourism system. Scenario planning is however also expected to create interest in longer-term planning, and to stimulate debate about various development pathways, not least with regard to sustainability implications. With regard to carbon management, the scenario planning exercise is also expected to identify tourism development paths that can combine economic growth with mitigation.

As shown in Figure 10.11, the core of the project is a system dynamics model, which simulates changes in dependent, independent and interdependent variables characterizing the tourism system, with key output parameters including arrival numbers, revenues, or emissions. The model is based on various information sources, including (1) external factor scenarios, reflecting the overall global economic and environmental development; (2) policy scenarios, i.e. the policies adopted by the Norwegian government to steer tourism development; (3) historical data for Norwegian tourism, i.e. the state of tourism as a result of past developments; and (4) qualitative data, i.e. the perspectives of stakeholder groups on development. These are fed into the system dynamics model, which shows, depending on input, how Norwegian tourism will develop with regard to various parameters. Input to the model can then be changed to reflect desired development goals for 2030 including, for instance, (6) sustainability (emissions) or economic development. In this regard, stakeholders can make recommendations for policies to support goal orientation (7). Finally, a number of policy scenarios are derived, which can be used by government for decision-making. Models such as this are likely to be increasingly used in tourism, where development and innovation have so far taken place more on an ad hoc basis, rather than based on informed choices. The relevance of scenario planning for policy makers is that they can focus their decisions on long-term planning and justify eventually less popular decisions with a view on longer-term benefits. This also allows disjunctures between climate science

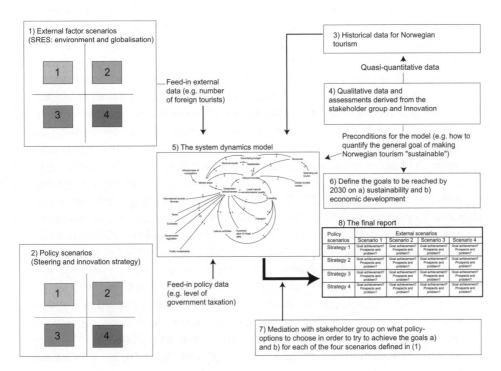

Figure 10.11 *System dynamics model and input data*
Source: Carlo Aall, Western Norway Research Institute, 2010 (unpublished)

(longer timeframes >20 years) and policy making (timeframes 5–10 years) to be overcome. See also the UK Climate Impacts Programme (www.ukcip.org.uk/).

EVENTS

Events and festivals become ever more important in tourism, often attracting thousands or tens of thousands of visitors. As visitors often arrive over considerable distances, for instance in the case of sports competitions or championships, emissions associated with events and festivals are considerable. As yet, not much attention has been paid to green event management, but there is evidence that there is growing interest in sustainable event planning (Laing and Frost 2010; see also Hede 2008; Getz 2009).

CARBON MANAGEMENT IN FOCUS 28: BEST FOOD FORWARD, UK

Avoiding emissions from festivals

The issue

Festivals and events can attract thousands, and often tens of thousands of visitors, often over great distances. In the UK alone, the 85 major festivals in 2007 are estimated to have had an audience of more than 2 million (Upham et al. 2009a, b). Such festivals are usually associated with significant traffic flows: Glastonbury festivals in Somerset, UK, for instance, attract between 28,500 and 42,700 vehicles (Robbins et al. 2007). Transport generated by such festivals leads to considerable emissions, even in the context of smaller festivals. A number of recent calculations carried out to assess the carbon footprint with associated with festivals confirms this: in Werfenweng, Austria (see also Carbon Management in Focus 23), for instance, car transports to the 2009 husky world championship caused emissions of almost 560 t CO_2, corresponding to more than 3 million pkm driven by car (Peter Brandauer, Mayor of Werfenweng, personal communication 2009). Total emissions (including accommodation) caused by the annual Futuresonic event in Manchester, UK, are estimated to be in the order of 300 t CO_2 (10,000 participants; Upham et al. 2009a, b). Even though small on a per visitor basis, festivals and events can thus add considerably to emissions, and there is growing interest in creating green, climatically sustainable events (Laing and Frost 2010; see also Hede 2008; Getz 2009). In the past, there have been various attempts to offset emissions caused by festivals and events. For instance, the soccer World Championship in Germany in 2006 was managed to be a 'carbon-neutral' event (Öko-Institut 2006). Even various bands have sought to 'neutralize' emissions (Broderick 2009), but efforts have been met with mixed success.

The solution

In the light of problems incurred in offsetting (see Chapter 4), it is interesting to study options to avoid emissions associated with events and festivals, rather than to offset these. Measuring is still an important first step to understanding the emissions problem, and efforts to address emissions are usually directly linked to action taken by bands or organizers. An illustration is the band Radiohead, who commissioned a report on the carbon footprint of two concert tours in the USA, one an out of town 'amphitheatre tour', the other a small 'theatre tour' in city centres. The report, written by Best Foot Forward (2007), suggests that the theatre tour caused emissions of 2.295t CO_2 (70,000 fans), while the amphitheatre tour caused 9,073t CO_2 (240,000 fans). Adjusted on a 'per fan' basis, the amphitheatre tour caused emissions in the order of 38 kg CO_2 per fan, i.e. 10–12 per cent more than the theatre tour at 33 kg CO_2 per fan. Best Foot Forward explains higher emissions during the amphitheatre tour mainly by high-emission car travel to the theatre locations. Fan travel is consequently the primary factor generating emissions, while the band's 'own' emissions amounted to 317t CO_2 (theatre tour) and 300t CO_2 (amphitheatre tour), mostly associated with air travel, also in chartered planes, and the transportation of equipment by air.

Best Foot Forward (2007) notes that the breakdown of emission statistics will help to identify priority areas for action:

- Fan travel has by far the largest impact at 86 per cent (2006 tour) and 97 per cent (2003 tour), of overall CO_2 emissions.
- International air travel by the band accounts for about 78t CO_2 (2006 and 2003).
- Air freight accounts for about 20t CO_2 to cover the distance UK–USA (east coast) and 26t to cover the distance USA (west coast)–UK.
- The chartered planes from New York to Nashville, then to Chicago, and on to San Francisco added a further 64t CO_2.
- Trucks carrying equipment account for 62t CO_2 (2006) and 73t CO_2 (2003).
- Beer for the theatre tour, estimated at 2 bottles per fan, accounts for 50t CO_2 while the bottles and plastic glasses account for a further 16t CO_2 (2006). Catering, waste and merchandise result in 1.1 kg CO_2 per fan.
- Beer accounts for nearly 160t CO_2, and food for an estimated 215t CO_2, for the amphitheatre tour in 2003. Catering, waste and merchandise work out at 2.7 kg CO_2 per fan (amphitheatre tour).

Even though these results are not likely to be comparable to most other countries due to the specific characteristics of urban infrastructure in the USA, a number of lessons can be learned. First, the band's own emissions for travel, transport of gear and instruments, as well as electricity used during the concert are the single largest source of emissions, but visitor travel is most relevant in absolute terms. Choosing a central concert location that can be reached easily by public transport is thus a key management issue. A problem specific for concerts is that some fans might travel over long distances to attend a concert, with air travel in particular pushing up overall emissions considerably. Steering attendees to use public transport might consequently be easier where events and festivals are more local in character.

With regard to car travel in the US, Best Foot Forward (2007) suggests that 10–20 per cent of emissions could be avoided by encouraging fans to share cars to achieve higher load factors. This would constitute by far the most important measure to reduce overall emissions. However, even the band's emissions are relevant. As both tours began on the west coast and continued on the east coast of the USA, band members and equipment were flown. Best Foot Forward (2007) estimates that travelling by train across the US would have reduced the band's emissions by about 26 per cent, while transporting equipment by rail instead of truck would have saved another 20 per cent. Shipping equipment from the UK instead of air-freighting would have saved another 47 tonnes, or 15 per cent, of the band's CO_2 emissions.

The Best Foot Forward report written for Radiohead induced a number of changes. First of all, the band started to understand their emissions, realizing that both the band's and fans' travel patterns made a crucial contribution to the overall impact: 'One of the big hidden factors that we hadn't looked at was the way people travel to the shows' (lead singer Thom Yorke, cited in McLean 2008). Radiohead also made headlines when they announced they would not play at Glastonbury: 'Radiohead say they will not play at Glastonbury this summer because poor public transport to the festival has a negative impact on the environment' (BBC News 2008). Instead, Radiohead would seek smaller, city-centred theatres in the future: 'What we're trying to do now is only play in areas that have a public transport infrastructure in place' (lead singer Thom Yorke, cited in BBC News 2008). The band also communicated their carbon footprint on their website (Radiohead 2008), thus engaging in a broader communication process of environmental impacts associated with events.

Best Foot Forward has recently audited a number of events, with reports commissioned by Radiohead (2007), the Forestry Commission (2008), the UK Public Health Association (2008), the Welsh Assembly Government (2009), the London Organising Committee for the Olympic Games (2009); see Best Foot Forward (2009). According to Paul Cooper, Best Foot Forward's Managing Director, event-related carbon assessments are becoming more popular, and the organization has thus designed online tools for carbon assessments, with a free basic version being available at www.footprinter.com, and an events-specific version available at www.event.footprinter.com.

Impact

Carbon audits of events show that these cause considerable emissions, but they also allow identification of mitigation strategies, for instance by choosing locations with public transport connections or in city centres. Furthermore, emission inventories can help bands to understand emissions and to plan accordingly. In the case of Radiohead, this even resulted in pressure on organizers to improve public transport options.

Source

Paul Cooper, Managing Director, Best Foot Forward, UK

Website

Best Foot Forward, www.bestfootforward.com

Related websites

Event Footprinter, www.event.footprinter.com

Emission calculator for organizations, www.footprinter.com

Tyndall Centre Carbon Pilot, www.futuresonic.com/07/eco2.html

Event ecological footprint calculator, www.resource-accounting.org.uk/reap-tourism

References

BBC News (2008). Green Radiohead avoid Glastonbury, 28 February 2008, available at: http://news.bbc.co.uk/2/hi/entertainment/7268916.stm. Accessed 28 November 2009.

Best Foot Forward (2007). Ecological footprint & carbon audit of Radiohead North American tours, 2003 & 2006. Available from: http://www.bestfootforward.com/media/upload/report/BFF_Radiohead_Final.pdf. Accessed 8 December 2009.

Best Foot Forward (2009). Clients and case studies. Available from: http://www.bestfootforward.com/case_study/focus/event/. Accessed 8 December 2009.

Broderick, J. (2009). Voluntary Carbon Offsets: a contribution to sustainable tourism? In: Gössling, S., Hall, C.M. and Weaver, D.B. (eds) *Sustainable Tourism Futures: perspectives on systems, restructuring and innovations*. London: Routledge, pp. 169–199.

Getz, D. (2009). Policy for sustainable and responsible festivals and events: institutionalization of a new paradigm. *Journal of Policy Research in Tourism, Leisure and Events* 1(1): 61–78.

Hede, A.-M. (2008). Managing special events in the new era of the triple bottom line. *Event Management* 11(1–2): 13–22.

Laing, J. and Frost, W. (2010). How green was my festival: exploring challenges and opportunities associated with staging green events. *International Journal of Hospitality Management* 29: 261–267.

McLean, C. (2008). Radiohead: the band who rewrote the rules. *Telegraph*, 1 April 2008. Available from: http://www.telegraph.co.uk/culture/music/3672236/Radiohead-the-band-who-rewrote-the-rules.html. Accessed 28 November 2009.

Öko-Institut (2006). Green goal. Legacy report. Available from: http://www.oeko.de/oeko-doc/292/2006-011-en.pdf. Accessed 8 December 2009.

Radiohead (2008). Dead air space. Available from: http://www.radiohead.com/deadairspace/index.php?a=310. Accessed 8 December 2009.

Robbins, D., Dickinson, J. and Calver, S. (2007). Planning transport for special events: a conceptual framework and future agenda for research. *International Journal of Tourism Research* 9: 303–314.

Upham, P., Boucher, P. and Hemment, D. (2009). Piloting a Carbon Emissions Audit for an International Arts Festival under Tight Resource Constraints: methods, issues and results. In: Gössling, S., Hall, C.M. and Weaver, D.B. (eds) *Sustainable Tourism Futures: perspectives on systems, restructuring and innovations*. London: Routledge, pp. 152–168.

VOLUNTARY CARBON OFFSETTING

Voluntary carbon offsetting is a management strategy that can be potentially relevant for all tourism actors, and in particular airlines, accommodation businesses, as well as entire destinations. There is also evidence of considerable support from tourists willing to pay premiums for mitigating or compensating the climate impact of their travel (e.g. Brouwer *et al.* 2008; Gössling *et al.* 2009c; Gössling and Schumacher 2010). However, in a review of the voluntary carbon market for aviation, Gössling *et al.* (2007) concluded that there were considerable differences between offset providers with regard to the calculation of emissions caused by identical flights, the reliability of credits sold, and the share of administrative costs compared to project costs, indicating little consistency in the approaches chosen and low degrees of credibility with regard to most actors. The survey also found that most organizations focused partially or entirely on forestry projects, an ambiguous offset strategy (for discussion see e.g. Gössling *et al.* 2007; Broderick 2009). While it is clear that afforestation and halting deforestation need to be part of strategies to address climate change (cf. Palmer and Engel 2009), the role of afforestation/deforestation projects as offsets is more difficult to assess, for instance because of the need to guarantee that carbon stored in biomass can be maintained over decades and centuries (for discussion see Gössling *et al.* 2007). It should also be noted that there is no political consensus yet regarding the role of, and mechanisms for, 'reducing emissions from deforestation and degradation' (REDD) in a global emission reduction framework. In their analysis of deforestation, van den Werf *et al.* (2009) conclude:

> The combined contribution of deforestation, forest degradation and peatland emissions to total anthropogenic CO_2 emissions is about 15 per cent (range 8–20 per cent). ... Therefore, reducing fossil fuel emissions remains the key element for stabilizing atmospheric CO_2 concentrations. Nevertheless, efforts to mitigate emissions from tropical forests and peatlands, and maintaining existing terrestrial carbon stocks, remain critical for the negotiation of a post-Kyoto agreement. ... For about 30 developing countries, ... deforestation and forest degradation are the largest source of CO_2.

While surveys indicate substantial willingness to pay for carbon offsets (see Table 10.9), there appears to be a considerable gap with regard to actual payments. The share of travellers stating that they have paid for offsetting their flight is generally less than 5 per cent and even lower uptake figures have been reported by airlines and tour operators (cf. Gössling *et al.* 2009b). There might be various reasons for this. For instance, Becken (2007) found that some travellers were unwilling to pay for offsets because other passengers were not, i.e. a problem referring to altruistic behaviour. In a survey conducted at Landvetter airport (Gothenburg, Sweden), Gössling *et al.* (2009c) also found that a broad majority of travellers did not feel responsible for emissions, asking that airlines, aircraft manufacturers or governments solve the problem. In this study, travellers also indicated that they were confused about whether flying was making a significant contribution to climate change or that their payments would have a significant benefit to solving the problem, as transport provider Scandinavian Airlines simultaneously communicated that flying was not environmentally harmful. Finally, it has been argued that there might be a 'rebound effect' in traveller behaviour, i.e. air travellers might not perceive it as necessary to change travel patterns as they have offset their emissions. Further research is however needed to confirm this hypothesis.

Table 10.9 Willingness to take personal action to reduce the environmental impact of air travel

---

Britain

(World Environmental Review 2007)
- 18% claim to have cut back on air travel in the last year
- 13% say they would be willing to cut back on air travel in the future

(Taylor Nelson Sofres 2007)
- Majority of holidaymakers would be unwilling to change their travel plans to a more environmentally-friendly alternative
- 7% of tourists said they would be 'quite likely' to choose a green destination; 2% are "very likely" to do so
- 14% said they would opt for a tour or holiday tour operator which is involved in a carbon offsetting scheme
- Only 4% reported to make a payment to offset their travel over the last year

(Travel Insurance Web 2007)
- 61% of tourists would pay a 'green tax' (of an unspecified amount) to help balance impact air travel has on the environment

(National Statistics Omnibus Survey – 2006)
- Respondents who believed air travel harms the environment (70%) were asked whether they agreed in principle with the price of a plan ticket reflecting environmental damage caused by air travel and how much extra they would be prepared to pay:
  - 63% agreed the price should reflect even if this makes air travel a bit more expensive
  - 47% agreed the price should reflect even if it makes air travel much more expensive

Table 10.9 Continued

   ° Older people were more likely to support additional payments
   ° Managerial/professional and intermediate occupations were more likely to support an increase in the price of a ticket
   ° Those who had flown were less likely to support price increases than those who had not
- Respondents who agreed air travel harms the environment were asked if they would be willing to pay extra on the price of their ticket or nothing extra at all:
   ° 2006 – 24% would not be willing to personally pay any more for a plane ticket to reflect environmental damage caused by flying; 55% willing to pay 15% more, 35% willing to pay 20% more
      ▪ Female travellers willing to pay more than males (56% would pay more, 40% pay an additional 20%) and the male figures were (43% and 31% respectively)
   ° 2002 – 82% believed that a 5% increase would be acceptable, 56% believed a 10% increase would be acceptable, 29% agreed with a 15% increase

USA
   (Travel Horizons Survey 2007)
- More than 50% said they were more likely to select an airline, rental car or hotel that uses more environmentally friendly products
- 50% said they would be more likely to use an airline if they knew it took the initiative to offset carbon emissions
- 13% said they would be willing to pay higher rates for demonstrated environmental responsibility (56% said they might)
- 76% said they would pay less than 10% extra per usage (flight, night)

Canada
   (Conference Board of Canada/ Canadian Tourism Research Institute 2007)
- 70% said they would pay US$10 or more for every US$1,000 (~1%) of a flight cost, if the funds were collected to develop sustainable resources of energy and reduce GHG emissions

   (Innovative Research Group, 2007)
- 44% of Canadians say carbon-offset programs will make minor differences towards improving the environment; 39% feel such programs will make no difference at all
   ° Albertans (61%) are most likely to feel offsets have no effect on the environment;
   ° Quebeckers (12%) most likely to think they will make a difference
- 23% said they are likely to pay an extra US$10 for carbon offsets when buying an airline ticket; drops to 14% for US$20 extra and 8% for US$50 extra
- People who are not convinced offsets work will not buy at any price

(Dawson *et al.* 2007)
- 12% willing to pay a carbon offset/carbon tax in addition to the price of an airline ticket
- Reasons why not willing to participate in air travel carbon offset schemes included a lack of understanding of what a carbon tax is (20%) and what the money would be used for (33%), not knowing what company to trust (19%), and a perception that it would be too expensive (6%)
- Of those willing to pay more to offset their carbon emissions from air travel, the majority would pay 5-10% of the price of their airline ticket on top of the ticket price

Australia
(Totaltravel.com 2007)
- 18% said they would give up air travel as it caused irreparable harm to the environment
- 32% said they would not stop flying on planes because it was quick and convenient for travel
- 16% said they did not care about climate change and it would not affect their travel choices
- 35% are looking at voluntary carbon-offsets for future flights taken

(Dalton *et al.* 2009)
- 45% of Australian tourists are willing to pay premiums in the order of 1–5% of trip cost for renewable energy systems.

Multi-national
(Poverty Reduction and Environmental Management Program 2007)
- 75% were willing to pay a carbon tax on air travel (80% of Europeans, 75% of North Americans and 59% of Asians)
- For those willing to pay, the average amount ranged from €0.2 per 100km (Asian travellers) to €1.0 per 100km (European travellers)

Source: Simpson *et al.* (2008) updated

Based on these findings, a number of conclusions can be drawn. First of all, the choice of a suitable offset provider should be made by the tour operator, airline or hotel seeking to offer carbon-neutrality, as this requires information on offsetting standards. A simple rule might be that offset providers offering Gold Standard Certified Emission Reductions (GS CER) are generally more credible than others, because the combination of the Gold Standard, a quality label developed by NGOs and recognized by UNFCCC, and the CER standard controlled and registered by the UN guarantee that emissions offsets have been independently verified and certified (see Chapter 4 and Carbon Management in Focus 29). Another important aspect is that the offset provider considers non-carbon effects from aviation, and that the focus is not only on CO_2. This is because a focus on CO_2 would underestimate the effect of flights on the climate, and an 'uplift' factor should consequently be used by offset providers (cf. DEFRA 2008).

CARBON MANAGEMENT IN FOCUS 29: ATMOSFAIR, GERMANY

Offsetting emissions from air travel that cannot be avoided

The issue

A considerable share of air travel is unnecessary in the sense that it is either induced (low-cost carriers, cf. Nilsson 2009), avoidable because other means of transport are available, or made for other reasons, such as status in frequent-flyer programmes and the associated collection of bonus points (cf. Gössling and Nilsson 2010). However, many flights might be considered 'necessary', including various motives related to business, leisure or visiting friends and relations (VFR). As technological options to reduce emissions from aviation are limited, while measures to 'neutralize' emissions through the replacement of fossil fuels with biofuels are not technically feasible or will be outpaced by growth in aviation, there is a need to address emissions through other means such as carbon offsetting.

The solution

While not contributing to the 'neutralization' of emissions from aviation (for a discussion of terms see Gössling 2009), voluntary carbon offsets can be seen as a mechanism to deal with 'unavoidable' emissions as a form of compensation. Carbon offsetting refers to payments made for emission reductions in other sectors, where this might be more feasible or less costly (Broderick 2009; see also Chapter 4). There are now about 100 offsetting agencies, but these have widely varying standards, particularly when offering offsets for aviation. Key aspects to be considered when purchasing carbon offsets regard principles of additionality, i.e. the question as to whether an emissions reduction would not have occurred in the absence of the offsetting project, as well as the calculation process of the amount of CO_2-eq to be offset (cf. Gössling et al. 2007).

A key problem in offsetting emissions from aviation pertains to non-CO_2 emissions (Lee et al. 2009). CO_2 emissions are most relevant for all surface-bound transport modes, but aviation also releases emissions at flight altitude, where they are injected in the lower stratosphere and upper stratosphere. Here, emissions including NO_x, water vapour, and soot particles cause additional RF. However, these effects are short-lived and not directly comparable to the long-term RF caused by CO_2. Consequently, it is not correct to compare non-CO_2 emissions with CO_2 on the basis of CO_2-eq, but omitting the RF caused by non-CO_2 emissions would mean that a major part of the impact of aviation on global warming remains unaccounted for. As a precautionary principle, compensation should thus consider a factor for non-CO_2 emissions by which CO_2 emissions are multiplied (for discussion see Gössling 2009). Currently, most offsetting agencies only consider CO_2 when offsetting emissions from aviation, but some use 'uplift' factors with values of up to 3.0 (Gössling et al. 2007).

Atmosfair was founded in 2004 within the framework of a research project of the German Federal Ministry for the Environment to develop standards for voluntary CO_2 compensation, and is often seen as the leading agency in the voluntary offsetting market. Customers and industry partners include, for instance, Munich Re Group, TuiNordic, Thomas Cook, German government, Food and Agriculture Organization (FAO), UNDP, EEA, and Greenpeace. Atmosfair is a not-for-profit organization, and offers a transparent annual report, detailing all donations and expenses.

Atmosfair sells only Clean Development Mechanism Gold Standard credits (GS-CERs). This means that all offset projects are established in developing countries and emission reductions are calculated and monitored based on UN guidelines. Emission reductions are qualified and approved by Designated Operational Entities (DoEs), i.e. UN-approved assessors, who must accept liability. This means that the DoE has responsibility for emission reductions – should it later on turn out that emissions have not been avoided as calculated, the DoE becomes responsible for finding alternative offsets. Documentation of CERs, the unit of offsets generated within the CDM, is guaranteed through the website of the Climate Change Secretariat of the United Nations. The GS means that no afforestation projects are accepted; rather, all projects have a focus on renewable energies and energy efficiency. The GS, developed by environmental NGOs and development agencies, sharpens and details many criteria of the CDM, for instance with regard to additionality, stakeholder involvement and additional benefits such as employment.

For its calculations of emissions caused by a given flight, Atmosfair uses an uplift factor of 2.7, based upon a recommendation of the German Environmental Agency (2008). The factor is only applied to emissions in altitudes of 9 km and above and thus not to emissions caused by take-off, climb and descent. In order to determine the exact amount of emissions injected into the atmosphere at different flight levels, Atmosfair has developed an advanced emissions calculator, which also considers aircraft types and load factors. Customers can consequently calculate the amount of emissions (and their approximate RF impact) associated with any flight between three-letter coded airports, as shown in figure 10.12 for a flight from New York to Tokyo.

Importantly, the presentation of the amount of emissions caused by the flight also provides an understanding of the magnitude of these emissions by way of comparison with emissions caused by, for example, a refrigerator running over one year, annual emissions of an average Indian, one year of car driving, and the average climate-compatible budget of one person over one year. Such comparisons are important to help travellers understand the impact of their flight. Customers are also informed about flight distance and flight altitude.

Compensation projects carried out by Atmosfair include the distribution of solar lamps in India replacing kerosene lamps, a biomass power plant in Burkina Faso, hydraulic rams in China, and a small hydropower plant in Honduras. In 2009,

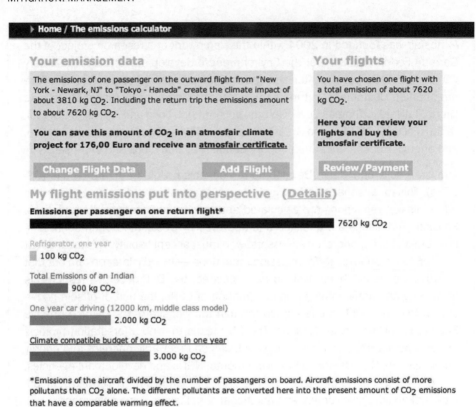

Figure 10.12 *Emissions caused by a flight from New York to Toyko*
Source: Website Atmosfair (2009)

Atmosfair's projects have reduced global emissions of CO_2 by 120,000 t, with the expectation that this amount will grow to more than 220,000 t CO_2 in 2010 (Atmosfair 2009).

With regard to turnover and expenses, Atmosfair collected €2.1 million in 2008. Only 8 per cent of the money has been used for administration, including everything from salaries to IT, office rent and credit card fees. The current price for offsetting 1 t of CO_2 is in the order of €25, with considerably lower prices for customers developing their own projects through Atmosfair. The organization also offers a range of associated services, such as carbon auditing and software solutions to integrate offset purchases in existing management systems – this is of relevance, for instance, for tour operators, seeking to involve customers in the problem-solving process.

Impact

Carbon offsetting can make an important contribution to education on climate change, as air travellers become aware of the environmental costs of flying.

Projects help to reduce emissions, often generating employment in innovative projects, which might also serve as role models in broader development contexts. According to Dietrich Brockhagen, the Managing Director, Atmosfair is the only offset provider worldwide with a 100 per cent GS-CERs portfolio.

Source

Dietrich Brockhagen, Managing Director, Atmosfair, Germany

Website

www.atmosfair.org

Related websites

Gold Standard Certified Emission Reductions (GS-CERs) can also be bought from:

- Climact, Belgien, www.climact.com
- My Climate, Switzerland, www.myclimate.org
- Tricorona, Sweden, www.tricoronagreen.com

References

Atmosfair (2009). Annual Report 2008. Available from: http://www.atmosfair.de/fileadmin/user_upload/Medien/AnnualReport2008_En_Website.pdf. Accessed 6 December 2009.

Broderick, J. (2009). Voluntary Carbon Offsetting for Air Travel. In: Gössling, S. and Upham, P. (eds) *Climate Change and Aviation: issues, challenges and solutions*. London: Earthscan, pp. 329–346.

Gössling, S. (2009). Carbon neutral destinations: a conceptual analysis. *Journal of Sustainable Tourism* 17(1): 17–37.

Gössling, S. and Nilsson, J.H. (2010). Frequent flyer programmes and the reproduction of mobility. *Environment and Planning A*, in press.

Gössling, S. and Peeters, P. (2007). 'It does not harm the environment!' – An analysis of discourses on tourism, air travel and the environment. *Journal of Sustainable Tourism* 15(4): 402–417.

Lee, D.S., Fahey, D.W., Forster, P.M., Newton, P.J., Wit, R.C.N., Lim, L.L., Owen, B. and Sausen, R. (2009). Aviation and global climate change in the 21st century. *Atmospheric Environment*, 43: 3520–3537.

Nilsson, J.H. (2009). Low Cost Aviation. In: Gössling, S. and Upham, P. (eds) *Climate Change and Aviation: issues, challenges and solutions*. London: Earthscan, pp. 113–129.

Finally, when offsets are offered, these should be made compulsory rather than voluntary. For instance, UK-based tour operator Explore! introduced mandatory offsets, reporting no negative customer reactions (Gössling *et al.* 2009b). Likewise, French 'Voyageurs du Monde' and German 'Demeter Reisen' include offsetting in all of its packages. Other tour operators have chosen to share costs with customers, with for instance German Neue Wege Reisen paying 50 per cent of the offsetting costs. Overall, new approaches to carbon offsetting services based on sound communication strategies and mandatory or matching approaches could thus be seen as basic strategies to improve customer interest in offsetting schemes.

The USA-based Tufts Climate Initiative (2006) evaluated 13 offset companies with regard to the quality of offsets, standards and verification, the quality of air travel calculator parameters and their accuracy with available science, price per tonne of carbon offset, transparency, company profile (for profit/not for profit), as well as the overhead percentage used to cover operating costs. Four offset companies were recommended without reservation, including Atmosfair, Climate Friendly, MyClimate, and Native Energy. Table 10.10 compares these companies with regard to the reduction units sold, the factors used to include non-carbon emissions from aviation, cost per ton of CO_2, the sustainable development/innovation character of these offsets, and whether credits are cancelled in the UN registry.

Atmosfair and MyClimate offer registered, UNFCCC-acknowledged credits, but Atmosfair is the only provider exclusively offering GS-CERs, which are cancelled from the UN registry after purchase in order not to interfere with national reduction goals/mandatory markets. With regard to 'uplift' factors, all offset providers use acceptable factors between 2.0–2.7. Costs per offset unit vary greatly, between €20–72, depending on whether emission reductions are generated in Switzerland or China (MyClimate). With regard to Sustainable Development benefits and innovation, Atmosfair and Native Energy seem to focus on small to medium-sized projects, and both Atmosfair and MyClimate also consider projects with a high degree of innovation. For alternative assessments see, for example, IATA (2008c, 2010b), Kollmuss *et al.* (2008) or David Suzuki Foundation (2009).

Table 10.10 Offset providers and key criteria, 2008

Offset provider	Reduction units sold	'Uplift' factor for aviation	Cost per t CO_2	CERs/ ERUs/ GS CERs: cancelled in UN registry?
Atmosfair www.atmosfair.de Germany	GS CERs	2.7	€23*	Yes
Climate Friendly www.climatefriendly.com Australia	VERs GS VERs	2.7	€20	Not applicable
MyClimate www.myclimate.org Switzerland	CERs, GS VERs GS CERs	2.0	€24–72 (discount >1000 t)	Yes
Native Energy www.nativeenergy.com USA	VERs	unclear	€22 (estimate)	Not applicable

* Atmosfair reports that for projects specifically developed for a client, prices for GS CERs can be as low as €10/tCO_2.

11 Mitigation

Education

Education on climate change and carbon management is a prerequisite for raising awareness and generating interest in climate change mitigation. Knowledge is however also a key resource for efficient carbon management and of particular relevance for five groups, i.e. academics and students, tourism managers, staff, tourists and journalists; the latter because they are important mediators of information, with a considerable role in the creation of travel trends.

Table 11.1 shows how residents in various countries currently perceive tourism and air travel with regard to their environmental impact. It appears that in most countries, tourism and air travel in particular are now understood as being harmful for the environment, with some surveys (e.g. Germany, Sweden) indicating that air travel is even perceived as one of the major contributing factors to climate change. Overall, there is thus a heightened awareness with regard to tourism and the environment.

Depending on target groups, a working knowledge of climate change mitigation can be developed through a wide range of measures. Aspen Skiing Company (Carbon Management in Focus 7), for instance, initiated various awareness raising campaigns to educate travellers on climate change. Hilton Worldwide introduced training courses as well as eLearning tools to raise awareness and to establish a working knowledge base for staff members (see Carbon Management in Focus 33). Zoos, which attract high visitor numbers, might be less obvious as agents in the distribution of knowledge, but they have considerable options to emotionally involve people in the topic of climate change, for example by linking the loss of charismatic species with rainforest destruction, an important factor in global climate change (see Carbon Management in Focus 30). Specific climate exhibitions, such as Klimahaus® Bremerhaven 8° Ost, Germany, can also play important roles in educating the broader public, particularly as the Klimahaus is an attraction in itself (Carbon Management in Focus 31). More broadly, awareness of energy use and emissions is now coming into existence through media, certification schemes and energy labels, as well as a range of online carbon measurement tools. These are discussed in the following.

Table 11.1 *Perceptions of environmental impact of (air) travel and tourism*

Britain

(DEFRA 2001)
- 65% agree transport in general is a contributor to climate change

(National Statistics Omnibus Surveys – 2002, 2006)
- 2002–62% believed air travel harmed the environment
- 2006–70% believe air travel harmed the environment
  ○ Those who flew more frequently were more likely to consider air travel harmful to the environment than those who had not flown at all in the last year or had flown once
  ○ Those in managerial/professional occupations and with higher income levels were particularly likely to strongly agree air travel harms the environment
- 64% agreed that 'the current level of air travel has a serious effect on climate change'

(Nunwood 2007)
- UK consumers in general overestimated carbon dioxide emissions from aviation (as % of UK emissions)

Germany
(BMU 2008)
- 83% believe that aviation is a main contributor to climate change

Sweden
(Naturvårdsverket 2009)
- 89% believe that aviation and surface bound transports are the main contributor to climate change

France
(Dubois and Ceron 2009, reporting on The Association for Corporate Travel Executives 2008)
- 45% of business travelers state that climate change has influence on travel decision-making.

Canada
(Dawson *et al.* 2007)
- 69% believed that '*air travel is a contributor to climate change*'

Source: based on Simpson *et al.* (2008), updated.

ENERGY AND CARBON LABELS

There is a growing number of ecolabels worldwide. For instance, Font (2002) identified over 100 ecolabels for tourism, hospitality and ecotourism worldwide, a number that is likely to have grown in recent years. Most ecolabels focus on environmental issues, even though energy use or GHG emissions are not usually considered as yet. This might partially

CARBON MANAGEMENT IN FOCUS 30: ZOO ZÜRICH, SWITZERLAND AND ZOO MÜNSTER, GERMANY

Visitor information to raise awareness of rainforest and species loss

The issue

Increasing the knowledge and understanding of climate change is an essential prerequisite for achieving behavioural change towards more climate-friendly consumption choices. Education on climate change is however difficult (see also Carbon Management in Focus 31), as the concept of GHGs is abstract in time and space, and consequently difficult to grasp. Zoos can play an important role in educating visitors (e.g. Weiler and Smith 2009), because they create an emotional basis for the visitors' interest through animals and, in particular, charismatic megafauna, while there are various linkages between species loss through deforestation and climate change: deforestation is now the second largest anthropogenic source of CO_2 to the atmosphere after fossil fuel combustion, contributing about 12 per cent of total anthropogenic CO_2 emissions (with an uncertainty range of 6–17 per cent; van der Werf *et al.* 2009).

The solution

Zoo Zürich (opened in 1929) hosts 360 species, while Allwetterzoo Münster (opened in 1974) hosts 346 species. Both zoos are dedicated to the protection of species and habitat, and have created exhibitions to emotionally involve visitors. Allwetterzoo Münster, for instance, has created a short film in collaboration with the WWF, showing how global warming affects polar bears, a key charismatic species associated with climate change. As visitors can experience and see polar bears in the zoo, the effect of this short film might be different from other TV-mediated information. Allwetterzoo Münster also refers to species extinction through habitat loss, in particular through deforestation, in various other parts of the zoo, emotionally linking threatened animal species with habitat loss and climate change. In Münster, a permanent exhibition 'biocity' has also been set up at the zoo's entrance, inviting visitors to participate in experiments and to learn about human actions that threaten species diversity.

Zoo Zürich developed the exhibition 'Shopping for the Rainforest: Hints and tips on how to keep the monkeys in the forest' (Zoo Zürich 2010a; see also Graf *et al.* 2009), which is currently set up at Allwetterzoo Münster as well, though comprising fewer themes than the one in Zürich. The exhibition consists of five different sections showing how the consumption of various goods affects biodiversity and habitat, including soybeans (used for instance for intensive livestock breeding), tropical wood (used for garden furniture), gold (jewellery) and coltan (mobile phones), palm oil (margarine), rubber (tyres), and giant shrimps (now served as a delicacy in many restaurants). Visitors are encouraged to reflect upon their consumption patterns and to choose alternatives. Visitors can also take with them a detailed document, outlining why various goods consumed in industrialized countries have directly and indirectly contributed to the destruction of rainforests (Zoo Zürich 2010a). As rainforests are not only the host of the majority of the world's species (e.g. Lawton and May 1995), but also of significant importance in the global carbon cycle, visitors learn that species loss and climate change are interconnected, and that their individual choices can make a difference in preserving habitat and carbon stored in biomass.

It is through such exhibitions that interest in tropical rainforests could increase, and it can be speculated that the emotional bonds people develop with rainforests and tropical species will lead to a growing interest in climate change. According to Roger Graf, Head of Zoo Information and Education at Zoo Zürich, no earlier exhibition at the zoo has ever been met with such strong, and mostly positive, reactions. Negative reactions included a number of companies, which felt that their environmentally harmful activities were exposed. However, as shown by the example of Aspen Skiing Company, USA (Carbon Management in Focus 7), initiatives building pressure on such companies can often be the only way to make them change. Notably, visitors to the exhibition felt upset to discover that the zoo's restaurant offered environmentally destructive food choices, such as farmed prawns (see also Carbon Management in Focus 15), and lobbied for change: today, these foodstuffs are no longer available, and the restaurant has started to increasingly purchase regional produce.

Both zoos also engage actively in climate change mitigation. Zoo Zürich recently exchanged its oil-based heating system with a system burning regionally sourced wood pellets, saving 550,000 litres of heating oil per year, and reducing emissions by 1,450t CO_2 per year. All electricity is sourced entirely from renewable energy sources. Visitors are encouraged to use public transport, with 40 per cent of the 1.7 million visitors arriving by bus or tram (Zoo Zürich 2010b). Allwetterzoo Münster also reduced energy use by replacing its outdated oil heating system with a system burning gas, and, to a limited degree, oil. Various energy-saving measures were also implemented. This reduced energy use to 7.2 MWh per year, corresponding to about 7.25 kWh energy per visitor (at roughly 992,000 visitors per year). Through the new system, emissions declined by 1,400t CO_2 to 1,600t CO_2, or about 1.6 kg CO_2 per visitor, according to Dirk Heese, Chief of Engineering Management. Allwetterzoo Münster also cooperates with Stadtwerke Münster, the city's energy provider, to sell natural gas to private customers, who pay an additional €0.0025 per kWh to finance rainforest protection in Vietnam (Allwetterzoo Münster 2009).

Impact

Zoos are visitor magnets, and have considerable potential to inform about environmental problems including climate change. Information provided in zoo environments can be particularly relevant in affecting perceptions because emotional bonds are created through animals. This can ultimately foster greater interest in climate change and its drivers, and possibly lead to altered consumption patterns.

Source

Roger Graf, Head of Zoo Information and Education, Zoo Zürich, Switzerland
Jörg Adler, Director, Allwetterzoo Münster, Germany
Dirk Heese, Chief of Engineering Management, Allwetterzoo Münster, Germany
Dr Dirk Wewers, Curator, Allwetterzoo Münster, Germany

Website

Zoo Zürich, www.zoo.ch
Allwetterzoo Münster, www.allwetterzoo.de

Related websites

Biocity Münster, www.biocity-muenster.de

References

Allwetterzoo Münster (2009). Pilotprojekt in Münster: Bürger heizen dem Klima ein! (Pilot project in Münster: citizens heat up the climate!) Available from: http://www.allwetterzoo.de/fotos/news2009/klimaschutz.php. Accessed 12 February 2010.

Graf, R., Schnyder, N. and Rübel, A. (2009). Shopping for the rain forest – hints and proposals, how the forest stays full of apes. *Der Zoologische Garten* 78 (2–3): 132–140.

Lawton, J.H. and May, R.M. (1995). *Extinction Rates.* Oxford: Oxford University Press.

Van der Werf, G.R., Morton, D.C., DeFries, R.S., Olivier, J.G.J., Kasibhatla, P.S., Jackson, R.B., Collatz, G.J. and Randerson, J.T. (2009). CO_2 emissions from forest loss. *Nature Geoscience* 2: 737–738.

Weiler, B. and Smith, L. (2009). Does more interpretation lead to greater outcomes? An assessment of the impacts of multiple layers of interpretation in a zoo context. *Journal of Sustainable Tourism* 17(1): 91–105.

Zoo Zürich (2010a). Shopping for the Rainforest: Hints and tips on how to keep the monkeys in the forest. Zürich: Zoo Zürich.

Zoo Zürich (2010b). Zoo Zürich nimmt Rücksicht auf die Umwelt. Available from: http://www.zoo.ch/xml_1/internet/de/application/d297/f302.cfm. Accessed 12 February 2010.

be a result of the perception that energy and emissions are less relevant indicators for tourism. For instance, based on a Delphi technique, Choi and Sirakaya (2006) asked a panel of 38 academics to suggest indicators. Out of 125 consensus indicators, 32 were political, 28 social, 25 ecological, 25 economic, 3 technological, and 13 cultural. However, only one referred to energy ('Per capita water/energy consumption'), and none to GHG emissions.

CARBON MANAGEMENT IN FOCUS 31: KLIMAHAUS® BREMERHAVEN 8 ° OST

Building awareness and interest in climate change

The issue

Climate change is one of the most difficult issues for humans to understand and act upon, because it is perceived by most people as a global problem the worst impacts of which will occur in the more distant future, while responsibility for climate change is usually ascribed to major polluting industrial plants, and not the individual. Education on climate change is thus a key challenge to build knowledge and awareness, which in turn can lead to pro-climate attitudes and behavioural change (see Chapter 12 for a more comprehensive discussion, as well as Jackson (2005) and Steg and Vlek (2009)).

The solution

The Klimahaus® Bremerhaven 8 ° Ost (Climate House Bremerhaven 8 ° East) is a new tourist attraction in northern Germany designed to educate its visitors on climate change. Klimahaus was planned in cooperation with scientific partners including the Alfred Wegner Institute for Polar and Marine Research and the Max Planck Institute for Meteorology. The Klimahaus cost €100 million to plan and build, and was officially opened on 27 June 2009, hosting an exhibition area of 11,500 m². In the first six months after inauguration, Klimahaus was already visited by more than 460,000 visitors.

To attract visitors, planners of the Klimahaus chose to create emotional experiences. Michael Liebert, Scientific Exhibition Manager, explains that the guiding theme through the Klimahaus is a journey through eight different countries along 8 ° longitude, i.e. following the meridian on which Bremerhaven is located. By walking from exhibition to exhibition, visitors move from Isenthal in Switzerland to Seneghe in Sardinia, Kanak in Niger, Ikenge in Cameroon, Queen-Maud-Land in Antarctica, Satitoa in Samoa, Gambell in Alaska, and Hallig Langeneß in Germany to finally 'return' to Bremerhaven. Moving through the Klimahaus thus means moving through different climate zones (with below-zero temperatures in the Antarctica exhibition and elevated temperatures at a sandy beach in Samoa), learning about the climate in these zones and becoming acquainted with the people living in them. Michael Liebert outlines that the journey is meant to create positive identification with the Earth, also creating emotional bonds with the people met during the journey. Rather than just being informed about climate, visitors experience climates, and learn about the living conditions in various climate zones. These experiences are complemented with options to participate in a wide range of climate-related experiments, further enhancing the visitors' knowledge, awareness and understanding.

A separate part of the exhibition informs on climate change, where visitors learn about the climatic history of the Earth system, and the role of GHGs and their heat-trapping properties in changing temperatures. The origins of fossil fuels are explained, as well as their contribution to anthropogenic global warming. From there the exhibition moves on to the future climate of the world, asking specifically how the eight countries visited will change by 2050. Michael Liebert argues that 'because visitors have met various people in these countries, they don't see how for instance Niger will be affected by climate change, but the kind of world the girl Mariam and her family from Niger will be living in by 2050'. Interest and emotions are created through identification with different environments and specific people living in these environments. Through this, the initiators of the exhibition hope to create lasting and growing interest in climate change.

In its final part, the exhibition moves on to the individual's role in global warming and action that can be taken to mitigate climate change. Visitors can use 14 computer terminals to assess their personal CO_2 emissions. Moving through eight different sections comprising Heating/insulating, Hot water, Electricity, Living/ household, Motoring, Travelling, Food and 'My new flat' visitors assess how their respective lifestyles contribute to global warming. The terminals are based on a simplified version of a carbon calculator created by German Umweltbundesamt (The Federal Environment Agency). By opening a 'climate account' visitors start to understand how different parts of their consumption patterns affect their overall emissions, which is, for instance, of great importance in correctly understanding the role of transport and in particular air travel in holiday-making. Once visitors have finished feeding in their answers, they are provided with a 'climate account statement', showing their personal emissions (Figure 11.1).

Michael Liebert points out that in order for people to understand emissions, 'CO_2 has to have a value', and the account statement helps to build an understanding of how emissions can be measured, compared and monitored, and where average emissions will be exceeded. Visitors can also send the carbon account statement to their email address. Currently, about 8.5 per cent of all visitors use the option to create personal climate accounts.

Impact

Klimahaus® Bremerhaven 8 ° Ost features an exhibition appealing to emotions, which is an innovative way of mediating information, creating awareness and interest in climate change. Through the exhibition, and in particular the option to assess their personal carbon footprints, visitors are likely to become more interested in the topic, and might begin to get involved in climate change mitigation.

Source

Michael Liebert, Scientific Exhibition Manager, Klimahaus® Bremerhaven 8 ° Ost

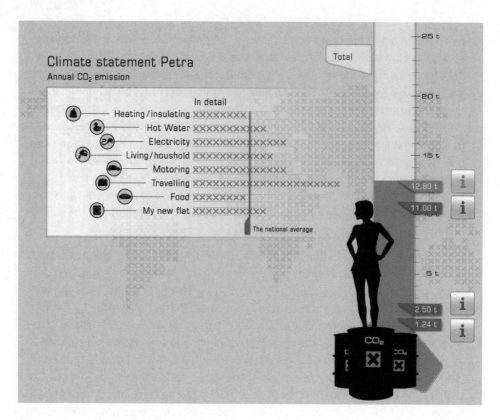

Figure 11.1 *Climate account statement*
Source: Klimahaus® Bremerhaven 8° Ost

Website

Klimahaus Bremerhaven, www.klimahaus-bremerhaven.de

Related websites

Carbon calculator by German Umweltbundesamt (The Federal Environment Agency), http://uba.klima-aktiv.de/umleitung_uba.html (in German)

References

Jackson, T. (2005). Motivating Sustainable Consumption. A review of evidence on consumer behaviour and behavioural change. A report to the Sustainable Development Research Network. Available from: http://www.sd-research.org.uk/post.php?p=126. Accessed 30 March 2010.

Steg, L. and Vlek, C. (2009). Encouraging pro-environmental behaviour: an integrative review and research. *Journal of Environmental Psychology* 29: 309–317.

Nevertheless, a number of energy- and GHG-related indicators are already in use. The best known might be the EU energy label. In the EU, most white appliances, including light bulbs, refrigerators, freezers, washing machines, tumble dryers, dishwashers, ovens, air conditioners, water heaters, and TV sets must be rated by energy efficiency class. The most efficient appliances are rated A, the least efficient G, with grades A+ and A++ more recently introduced for refrigerators and freezers to keep up with energy efficiency developments (cf. EC 2009). The energy label also exists for cars, but displays emissions of CO_2 per pkm, rather than energy use. Figure 11.2 shows the energy label for white appliances (left hand side, an example from Sweden), and cars (right hand side, an example from Ireland). The label is easy to understand even for people with no previous knowledge of energy and emissions, with green bars representing low energy use/emissions, and red bars representing high energy use/emissions. A variation of the EU energy label is also used by Cheaptickets, an online air ticket service, to inform travellers about environmentally more favourable choices (see Carbon Management in Focus 17).

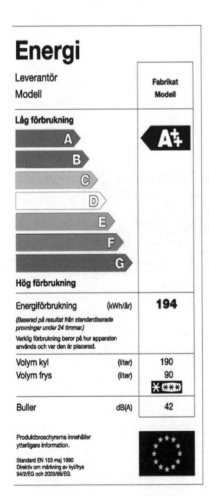

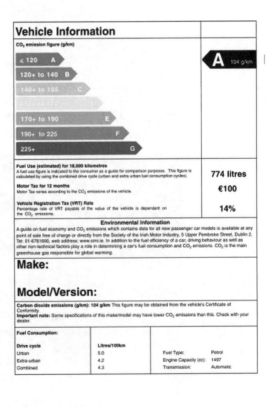

Figure 11.2 *Energy label for white appliances (left-hand side, from Sweden) and an emission label for cars (right-hand side, from Ireland)*

A variation of the European approach is the Energy Rating Label used in Australia for domestic appliances (Figure 11.3). The label was first introduced in 1986 in New South Wales and Victoria and is now mandatory in all states and territories for refrigerators, freezers, clothes washers, clothes dryers, dishwashers and air-conditioners. Customers less engaged in energy-related issues can easily judge an appliance's energy rating from the star rating, while more specific information on power consumption (kWh energy use per year) is also provided for customers better informed about energy-use values (Energy Rating Australia 2010). Similar labels exist in other countries: in the USA, for instance, Energy Star is a joint programme of the EPA and the US Department of Energy to help identify energy-efficient products and practices (Energy Star 2010).

While the above labels are relevant for tourism, some carbon labels have been developed more specifically for tourism. The light bulb has been used as an indicator in the UK's DEFRA project on sustainable tourism (Miller *et al.* 2007). The carbon label provides

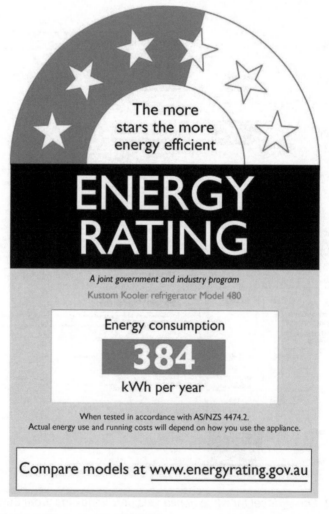

Figure 11.3 *Energy rating used in Australia*

Example: London to Cornwall by car

- Emissions: 0.16 tonnes CO_2
- Equivalent to one 100W light bulb on non-stop for 22 weeks

Figure 11.4 *Lightbulb energy indicator*
Source: Miller *et al.* (2007)

information on the environmental impact of travel in t CO_2 and 'light bulb weeks', i.e. the time a 100 W light bulb would have to be left burning to emit the same amount of CO_2 as the journey, based on the electricity mix in the UK (given in the report at about 0.430 kg CO_2 per kWh; for a higher value see the Carbon Trust 2008).

Another indicator used by forumandersreisen, an association of German tour operators committed to pro-environmental practices, is CO_2-eq. The association labels all journeys offered by member tour operators in its catalogue, detailing emissions of CO_2-eq associated with each of the journeys.

CARBON MANAGEMENT IN FOCUS 32: FORUMANDERSREISEN, GERMANY

Carbon-labelling and offsetting

The issue

It is essential for customers to understand the environmental impact of their trip in order to adjust decisions regarding destination choice, transport mode, travel frequency or length of stay. When such information is provided, tourists might choose climatically less harmful journeys and reduce the impact of their holiday by offsetting emissions (see also Gössling *et al.* 2009; Carbon Management in Focus 17). Information on environmental performance is thus a basic prerequisite for decision-making, but not often provided by tour operators or other stakeholders, and in particular not with regard to climate change.

The solution

Forumandersreisen (*Forum travel differently*) is an association of about 160 tour operators (November 2009) committed to sustainable tourism. With regard to ecological sustainability, forumandersreisen states, for instance, that 'length of stay, travel time and distance should be in appropriate relation'. The association offers a wide range of different holiday packages, from bicycle tours in Europe to long-distance travel to South America, but no package should involve flights to destinations less than 700 km away, flights between 700–2,000 km with a length of stay of less than eight days, or flights to destinations more than 2,000 km away with a length of stay of less than 14 days. When tour packages are offered to destinations that can only or predominantly be reached by air, the respective tour operator has to specify the GHG emissions caused by the flight.

Flying customers are offered voluntary compensation, a service that offers 'neutralization' of emissions caused by the flight through compensation in another sector, for instance by investing in renewable energy or energy efficiency projects (see also Chapter 4). Flights are offset by Atmosfair, a not-for profit organization forumandersreisen helped to launch (see Carbon Management in Focus 29). As shown in figure 11.5, tour package information includes information on emissions, measured in kg CO_2-eq. For this, forumandersreisen uses a RF index of 2.7, i.e. stratospheric emissions of CO_2 are multiplied by a factor 2.7 to account for the RF caused by non-CO_2 emissions at flight altitude. For example, a flight to Spain from Germany would cause emissions equivalent to 920 kg CO_2, which can be offset on a voluntary basis for €23. A trip to Costa Rica from Germany would cause emissions of 6,680 kg CO_2, and entail costs of €157 for offsetting.

Companies associated with forumandersreisen have experienced consistent growth in client numbers in recent years (totalling 118,200 in 2008, up from 11,000 in 1998). According to Ute Linsbauer, forumandersreisen's press officer, tourist numbers continued to grow even during crises including 11 September 2001, SARS in 2003, and the financial crisis in 2008. This is seen to mirror

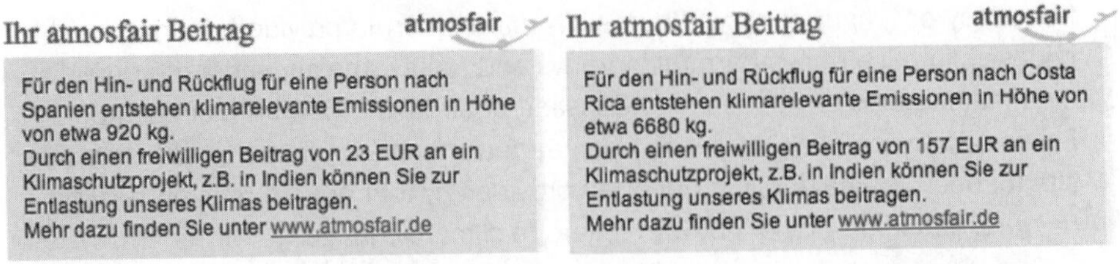

Ihr atmosfair Beitrag   atmosfair

Für den Hin- und Rückflug für eine Person nach Spanien entstehen klimarelevante Emissionen in Höhe von etwa 920 kg.
Durch einen freiwilligen Beitrag von 23 EUR an ein Klimaschutzprojekt, z.B. in Indien können Sie zur Entlastung unseres Klimas beitragen.
Mehr dazu finden Sie unter www.atmosfair.de

Ihr atmosfair Beitrag   atmosfair

Für den Hin- und Rückflug für eine Person nach Costa Rica entstehen klimarelevante Emissionen in Höhe von etwa 6680 kg.
Durch einen freiwilligen Beitrag von 157 EUR an ein Klimaschutzprojekt, z.B. in Indien können Sie zur Entlastung unseres Klimas beitragen.
Mehr dazu finden Sie unter www.atmosfair.de

Text: The return flight to Spain/Costa Rica causes emissions of 920kg/6,680kg CO_2-equivalent per person. By voluntarily paying €23/€157 for a climate protection project, for instance in India, you can make a contribution to climate mitigation. More information can be found on www. atmosfair.de.

Figure 11.5 Emissions caused by flights from Germany to Spain/Costa Rica

growing awareness of environmental and social issues among travellers. For companies associated with forumandersreisen, the success of the concept has also meant that average turnover per company grew from €350,000 in 1998 to €1.68 million in 2008.

With regard to offsetting, it is not known which percentage of travellers have actually offset their flights, but estimates by individual tour operators point at rather low percentages (<5 per cent). However, offsetting forumandersreisen customers have, on average, paid €80 per journey, an amount more than twice as high as the average paid by other Atmosfair customers, according to Ute Linsbauer. This would indicate that forumandersreisen customers are more aware of environmental issues, and more willing to contribute financially to solutions, even though they also participate in longer and more carbon-intense journeys.

Impact

The importance of the forumandersreisen approach is that customers are informed on the emissions they are causing, an important prerequisite for more environmentally friendly destination choices. Moreover, customers are given the opportunity to act on the climate-related problems their travel is causing. Notably, wider sustainability issues are already addressed within the packages sold. In principle, the forumandersreisen approach could be incorporated by any tour operator or airline: offset provider Atmosfair offers, for instance, the incorporation of its database containing information on emissions from any three-letter code flight into any tour operators' booking software. Once this is done, online customers can, with one click, choose to offset their emissions. Overall, forumandersreisen shows that it is possible to involve customers in pro-climate action through information and the provision of options to act.

Source

Ute Linsbauer, press officer, forum anders reisen
Rolf Pfeifer, Project manager CSR, forum anders reisen

Website

Forumandersreisen, http://forumandersreisen.de/

Related websites

International Civil Aviation Organization (ICAO), Carbon Emissions Calculator, available from: http://www2.icao.int/en/carbonoffset/Pages/default.aspx.

Scandinavian Airlines, Carbon calculator for SAS flights available from: http://www.flysas.com/en/Travel_info/CO2-emissions2/ (also provides information on emissions other than CO_2).

Lufthansa, Carbon calculator for Lufthansa flights available from: http://lufthansa.myclimate.org/EN (CO_2 emissions only).

Finnair, Carbon calculator for Finnair flights available from: http://www.finnair.com/emissionscalculator/ (CO_2 emissions only).

References

Gössling, S., Hultman, J., Haglund, L., Källgren, H. and Revahl, M. (2009). Voluntary carbon offsetting by Swedish Air travellers: towards the co-creation of environmental value? *Current Issues in Tourism* 12(1): 1–19.

British low-cost carrier Flybe recently introduced a suggestion for a carbon label for aircraft, also based on the energy label for white appliances in the EU. The label allows comparison of different aircraft models and their efficiency (Figure 11.6). It features noise most prominently, however, and is thus focused on local environmental aspects, rather than emissions more specifically. Information provided on take-off and landing emissions might also be confusing for air travellers, and is not as relevant as overall emissions from the journey, which are provided both on a 'total aircraft fuel consumption by journey length' and on a 'per seat by journey length' basis, again potentially confusing travellers. Clearly, the most relevant aspect of a label should be the emissions caused by the transport of one traveller over a given distance, including occupancy rate. This, however, can only be calculated in retrospect, but competition for higher rankings, for instance valid for the full following year, would be an important incentive for airlines to actually increase load factors while also using efficient aircraft. Nevertheless, Flybe's initiative to develop an environment label is a good starting point for a competitive efficiency approach between airlines.

Finally, though not discussed in further detail in this book, there are also energy labels emerging in other tourism-related contexts, such as food. Tesco, a supermarket chain in the UK, has started to develop a programme, in which the CO_2-eq content of 100 of its own-brand products is indicated on their packaging (Tesco 2009). Overall, there is considerable scope for energy and emission indicators and labels in tourism. It is important, however, to ensure that an energy or emissions label is understandable, while simultaneously providing sufficient information for people with a more fundamental knowledge of these issues. As indicated in the discussion of the above labels, this might however be difficult.

Figure 11.7, originally developed on behalf of a Swedish newspaper, provides an example of how an energy label might be designed for holiday packages. It builds on a survey of student perceptions of 11 different energy labels (Gössling 2008, unpublished). Based on the EU energy label, the label considers emissions from transport, accommodation and

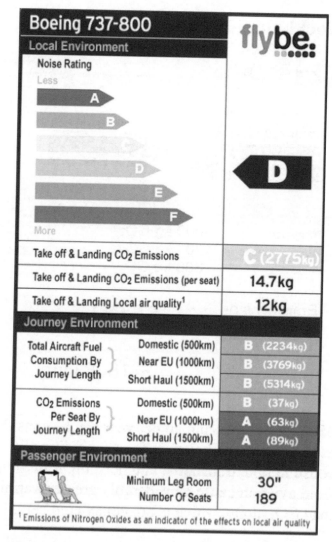

Figure 11.6 *Flybe environment label*
Source: Flybe 2010

activities. A summary of total GHG emissions is provided together with a corresponding measure in fuel use, i.e. a unit most people are most likely to be familiar with. Finally, a short text compares emissions caused by the respective journey with sustainable emissions per year to allow for comparison. Energy and carbon labels such as this, if introduced in travel catalogues or on websites, could help educate the traveller and influence holiday decision-making.

Another emerging educative tool are carbon calculators, which are now available on the Internet for different aspects of consumption, and sometimes specifically for tourism or transports. Carbon calculators are helpful in understanding CO_2, as they quantify and

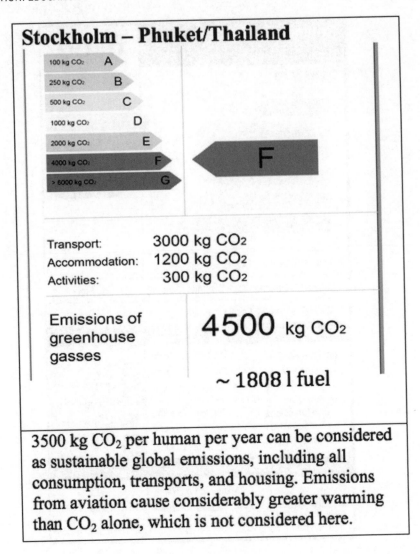

Figure 11.7 *Optimized carbon label (proximate values)*

illustrate, often on the basis of comparisons (see Figure 11.8; Carbon Management in Focus 17, 31).

Table 11.1 provides an overview of carbon calculators, but it should be noted that the list is not exhaustive, with IATA (2010b: no page) suggesting that 'over 30 airlines run offset programs with different methodologies for calculating emissions and different criteria for offset projects'. Further emission calculators are available on the websites of virtually all voluntary carbon offset providers. Note that most calculators are based on specific methodologies and results are thus not comparable. Particularly with regard to offsetting, it is thus of importance to have a basic understanding of what is included or omitted in calculations (see e.g. Jardine 2009).

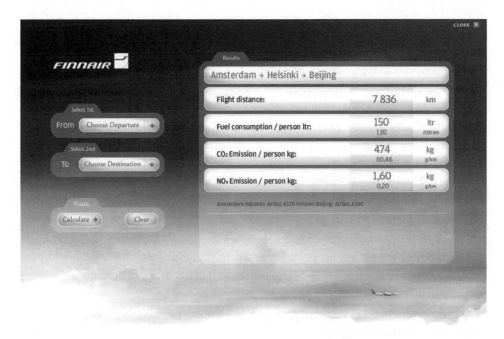

Figure 11.8 *Screenshot of Finnair's carbon calculator*
Source: Finnair 2009

Table 11.2 *Examples of carbon calculators*

Comprehensive calculators

Nature Protection Agency, Germany, www.uba.klima-aktiv.de/umleitung_uba.html (includes transport, food, housing, other consumption in CO_2-eq, in German only)

New Energy Foundation, UK, http://www.nef.org.uk/greencompany/co2calculator. htm (includes housing and transport, in CO_2)

Government, UK, http://carboncalculator.direct.gov.uk/index.html (per individual or household, CO_2)

Environmental Protection Agency, USA, http://www.epa.gov/climatechange/emissions/ ind_calculator.html (considers CO_2, including vehicles, home energy and waste)

CO_2 Balance, UK, http://www.co2balance.uk.com/co2calculators/ (considers CO_2, including flights, home energy, car, and rail)

Emissions Zero, China, http://www.emissionszero.com/calculator/ (CO_2, includes vehicles, aircraft, electricity and gas)

World Resources Institute, USA, http://www.safeclimate.net/calculator/ (for individuals in various countries, including vehicles and home energy)

Sustainable Travel International, USA, http://www.sustainabletravelinternational.org/ offset/index.php?c=1 (considers air travel, car travel, gifts, home energy and accommodation)

Klimatløftet, Norway, http://klimakalkulatoren.no/klimakalkulatoren/personer.aspx (considers transports, home energy, food, and other consumption)

Table 11.2 *Continued*

Air travel

International Civil Aviation Organization (ICAO), www2.icao.int/en/carbonoffset/ Pages/default.aspx (considers CO_2)

Finnair, Finland, www.finnair.com/emissionscalculator (considers CO_2)

KLM, Netherlands, http://www.klm.com/travel/nl_en/about/co2/together/co2_ calculator.htm (considers CO_2)

Scandinavian Airlines, Scandinavia, http://www.flysas.com/en/Travel_info/CO2- emissions2/ (considers CO_2, also provides information on NO_x, CO, HC, H_2O and SO_2)

French government, www.aviation-civile.gouv.fr/eco-calculateur (considers CO_2, includes load factors, freight, in French only)

Air France, http://corporate.airfrance.com/fr/developpement-durable/calculateur- de-co2/calculez-vos-emissions-de-co2 (considers CO_2, in French only)

Delta Air Lines, USA, https://gozero.conservationfund.org/delta/home (CO_2 only, including home energy, car, and air travel)

Atmosfair, www.atmosfair.de (considers non-CO_2 effects by using RF factor of 2.7 for stratospheric share of flights)

Railways (incl. comparison to other transport)

Svenska Järnvägen, Sweden, www.sj.se/sj/jsp/polopoly.jsp?d=6765&l=sv&intcmp=1 41286

(compares train, bus, car, aircraft, including CO_2, VOC, NO_x, soot, in Swedish only)

SNCF, France, ecocomparateur.voyages-sncf.com/ (compares price, travel time and CO_2 emissions of rail, car, regular- and low-fare airline, in French only)

Deutsche Bahn, Germany, www.bahn.de/umweltmobilcheck (compares travel time, 'usa- ble time', travel cost and fuel use in litres for train, aircraft and car, in German only).

Ecopassenger, http://www.ecopassenger.com/ (compares emissions and energy use for various transport modes)

BENCHMARKING TOOLS

There are now various benchmarking tools, in particular for accommodation businesses, which can help to assess energy and emission performances. Among benchmarking tools, Bohdanowicz (2009) distinguishes performance reports, regional league tables, hotel profiles, benchmark reports, balance score cards and energy indicators. Tools such as these can help to illustrate energy consumption, while they are simultaneously strate- gic management tools allowing for comparison of the performance of hotels within the same chain, as well as individual hotels with the same standard. Notably, benchmarking tools can also include parameters other than energy use or emissions, which can also be weighed against economic parameters (e.g. energy use per turnover). Figure 11.9 shows an example a benchmarking tool (for a comprehensive discussion of these in accommo- dation see Bohdanowicz 2009).

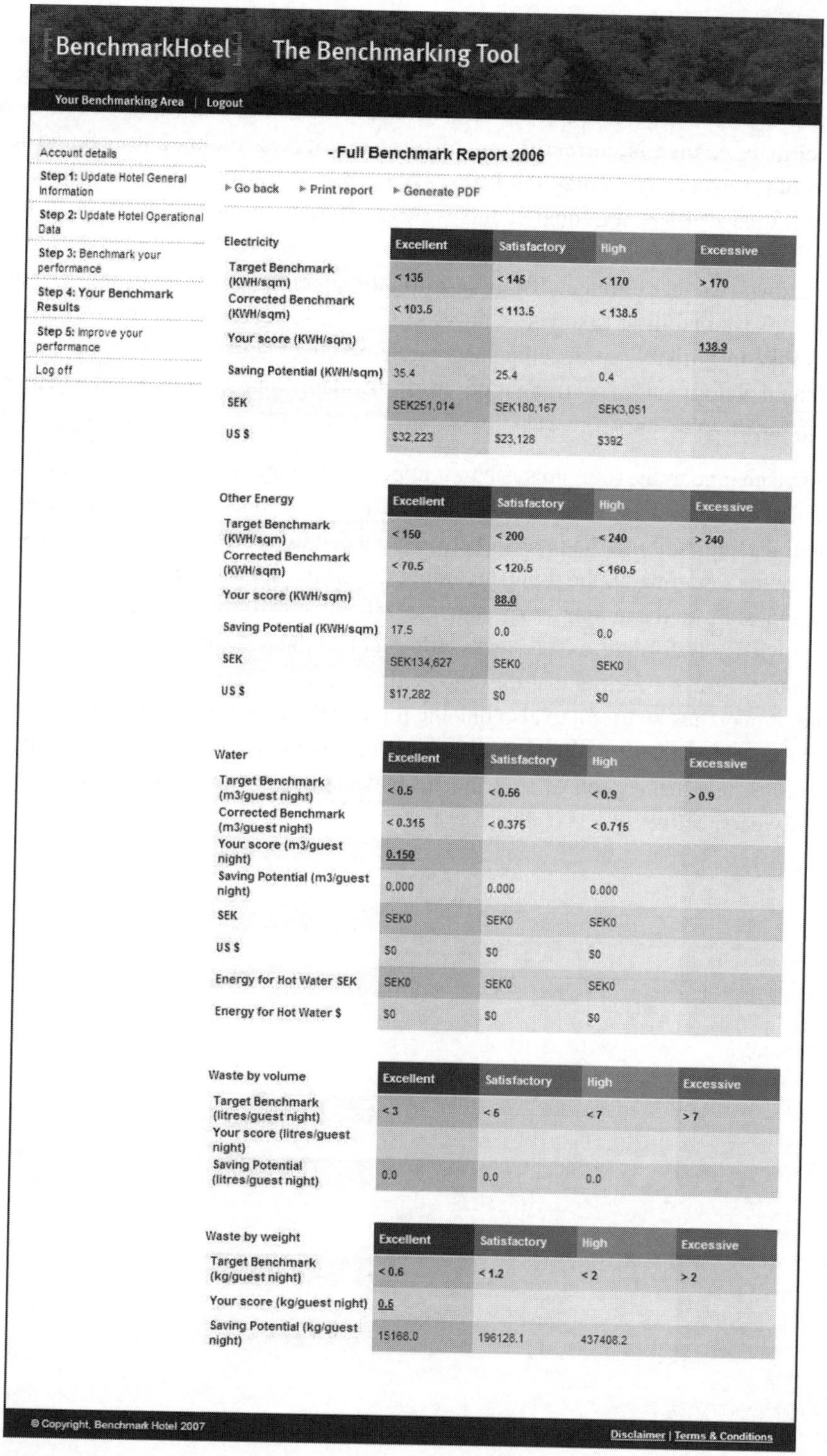

BenchmarkHotel The Benchmarking Tool

Your Benchmarking Area | Logout

- Account details
- Step 1: Update Hotel General Information
- Step 2: Update Hotel Operational Data
- Step 3: Benchmark your performance
- Step 4: Your Benchmark Results
- Step 5: Improve your performance
- Log off

- Full Benchmark Report 2006

▸ Go back ▸ Print report ▸ Generate PDF

Electricity	Excellent	Satisfactory	High	Excessive
Target Benchmark (KWH/sqm)	< 135	< 145	< 170	> 170
Corrected Benchmark (KWH/sqm)	< 103.5	< 113.5	< 138.5	
Your score (KWH/sqm)				138.9
Saving Potential (KWH/sqm)	35.4	25.4	0.4	
SEK	SEK251,014	SEK180,167	SEK3,051	
US $	$32,223	$23,128	$392	

Other Energy	Excellent	Satisfactory	High	Excessive
Target Benchmark (KWH/sqm)	< 150	< 200	< 240	> 240
Corrected Benchmark (KWH/sqm)	< 70.5	< 120.5	< 160.5	
Your score (KWH/sqm)		88.0		
Saving Potential (KWH/sqm)	17.5	0.0	0.0	
SEK	SEK134,627	SEK0	SEK0	
US $	$17,282	$0	$0	

Water	Excellent	Satisfactory	High	Excessive
Target Benchmark (m3/guest night)	< 0.5	< 0.56	< 0.9	> 0.9
Corrected Benchmark (m3/guest night)	< 0.315	< 0.375	< 0.715	
Your score (m3/guest night)	0.150			
Saving Potential (m3/guest night)	0.000	0.000	0.000	
SEK	SEK0	SEK0	SEK0	
US $	$0	$0	$0	
Energy for Hot Water SEK	SEK0	SEK0	SEK0	
Energy for Hot Water $	$0	$0	$0	

Waste by volume	Excellent	Satisfactory	High	Excessive
Target Benchmark (litres/guest night)	< 3	< 5	< 7	> 7
Your score (litres/guest night)				
Saving Potential (litres/guest night)	0.0	0.0	0.0	

Waste by weight	Excellent	Satisfactory	High	Excessive
Target Benchmark (kg/guest night)	< 0.6	< 1.2	< 2	> 2
Your score (kg/guest night)	0.5			
Saving Potential (kg/guest night)	15168.0	196128.1	437408.2	

© Copyright, Benchmark Hotel 2007 Disclaimer | Terms & Conditions

Figure 11.9 *Facility performance report generated by IBLF/ITP BenchmarkHotel*
Source: BenchmarkHotel (2007)

TOURISM CURRICULA

Tourism academics have an important role in developing curricula incorporating sustainability and CSR issues, including climate change. It is not known, however, to what extent climate change is currently part of tourism courses. Flohr (2001) found in her analysis of tourism programmes and courses offered in 1999/2000 at 42 British universities that a total of 81 postgraduate courses were offered, out of which six incorporated sustainability or environmental issues. The analysis only considered course titles, and it is unknown whether climate change or mitigation were part of any of the six courses addressing sustainability. Likewise, Jurowski (2002), in reporting on the second BEST Think Tank, an initiative to develop sustainable practices for the tourism industry, suggested the development of learning modules for students, but it is unknown whether this has been taken up by universities.

To achieve change in the tourism system, it appears paramount to establish a basic understanding of climate change, adaptation and mitigation in tourism among students, also including the capability to distinguish between persisting uncertainties in climate science and the media reporting on the topic, including the propaganda spread by professional climate sceptics. From the author's experience, teachers must be aware that developing such basic knowledge is difficult, as there is usually a lack of interest among students, eventually also because there is a feeling that this knowledge requires a reconsideration of one's own lifestyle. It may thus be useful to also link the topic to the enormous energy-dependency of industrial societies, the geopolitics of oil production, potential cost savings, rising customer expectations and other aspects of relevance from economic and/or service management and hospitality perspectives.

12 Mitigation

Behavioural change

> To a psychologist, climate change looks as if it was designed to be ignored. It is a global problem, with no obvious villains and no one-step solution, whose worst effects seem as if they'll befall somebody else at some other time. In short, if someone set out to draw up a problem that people would not care about ..., it would look exactly like climate change.
>
> (Fahrenthold 2009: 32).

This quote from the newspaper *The Guardian* indicates why climate change and mitigation are so difficult to deal with: not only is climate change a phenomenon that human senses are not capable of grasping, it also confronts people in industrialized countries with the necessity to change lifestyles, particularly with regard to mobility patterns. However, there appear to be various mechanisms supporting and justifying non-action. Three of these, the perception of mobility as a human right, the presentation and prevalence of technology-to-solve-the-problem discourses, and the questioning of climate science can be seen as central to the problem of mitigation.

THE 'RIGHT' TO BE MOBILE

With regard to mobility, the need to mitigate climate change appears to cut deep into the cultural fabric of Western democracies, where the right to rest from work has been extended to include a perceived 'right' to be mobile – notably including all private and public motorized transport modes – essentially in line with other human rights as listed in the Universal Declaration of Human Rights by the United Nations. In Europe and North America, the entitlement to be mobile might have its roots in the 1950s, when individual motorized transport became a norm and average per capita distances driven by car grew exponentially (cf. Gilbert and Perl 2008), a process now also observable in India and China.

To understand how the opportunity to be mobile subsequently turned into a perceived right to be mobile, it might be necessary to trace mobility discourses, which appear to have been implemented, maintained and controlled by industry and lobby organizations. Even though any review of this issue is beyond the scope of this book, some evidence can be found in Germany, where the 1970s' slogan 'Freie Fahrt für Freie Bürger' (Free Movement for Free Citizens) has sought to interlink individual automobility with a constitutionally granted personal freedom and right to mobility, and has since been used in political campaigns by liberal and conservative parties and automobile lobby organizations. In 2008, the president of German Allgemeiner Deutscher Automobil Club (ADAC, General German Automobile Club), postulated, for instance, that 'Mobilität ist ein Grundrecht' (Mobility is a fundamental right), stating that:

> It makes sense and is necessary that our constitutional law protects the fundamental rights of car drivers and their mobility. Article 2 guarantees the free development of the individual – and thus individual choices of being mobile. Furthermore, the constitutional right of freedom of profession (Article 12) protects people being dependent on their vehicle for work.
>
> (Peter Meyer, president ADAC, 2008; author's translation)

This example shows how mobility – and in particular individual motorized mobility – is discursively interlinked with constitutional rights, and extended to cover all aspects of mobility, i.e. the choice of motorized transport mode (train, bus, car, aircraft, cruise ship), the energy intensity of the transport mode chosen (small or large cars, scheduled air traffic or private jets), as well as the distances covered (i.e. how mobile one can be within a given period of time). Any attempt to curb emissions from transport through taxes or fees is consequently perceived as a threat to freedom, as for instance expressed in the reaction of bloggers to plans in the EU to reduce emissions from aviation: 'I don't know why I continue to be amazed at the willingness of Europe, including the UK, to curtail freedoms as they see fit. They are considering rationing air travel to combat global warming' (Riehl World View 2010).

Lobby organizations and industry have simultaneously pointed out that technological innovation will solve environmental problems. For instance, in an analysis of statements spread by the aviation industry and its organizations on the environmental performance of the sector, it was found that 'statements often use "scientific" language, presenting indisputable "facts", coupled with enthusiasm about technological progress. Comparisons are selected carefully, ... pointing out that aviation is not more environmentally harmful than cars (not trains), that fuel is "saved"' (not used), etc.' (Peeters and Gössling 2008: 198). Khisty and Zeitler (2001: 602) found similar mechanisms in the context of cars, stating that: 'the automobile-industrial complex, through advertising, lobbying and other influences on public discourse, helps to sustain an "auto culture", cleverly masking its problematic and costly features'. The mechanisms encouraging climatically problematic behaviour might often be complex, as exemplified by Scandinavian Airlines. The airline, often portrayed as one of the environmentally most proactive (e.g. Lynes and Dredge 2006), even though in reality operating an old, inefficient fleet, distributed leaflets in spring 2009, asking 'Can you fly with a clear environmental conscience? Yes, you can!', thus encouraging aeromobility while simultaneously masking its environmental impacts through discourses based on (future) technology and relative efficiency gains.

TRUST IN TECHNOLOGY: ENVIRONMENTAL VALUES

Given the dominance and power of trust in technology to solve environmental problems, most recently embedded in emerging discussions about geo-engineering to mitigate climate change, it is necessary to understand the role of values out of which truth systems defining how 'the world really is' are constructed. Gilg *et al.* (2005) conceptualize altruistic-egoistic, biocentric-anthropocentric and ecocentric-technocentric value dimensions. The values associated with these dimensions range from notions of 'nature as being in a delicate balance' to 'no limits to growth' and 'technology will solve problems'. Based on these values, individuals design belief systems of how problems such as climate change can or should be addressed, with a potential continuum between the extremes of 'living with nature' to 'geo-engineering'. If indeed such values and corresponding truth systems are foundations for the arguments of various societal groups and organizations, addressing the emergence and dominance of technocentric belief systems might be one of the key issues in achieving more objective discussions on climate change mitigation. For this it will be necessary to gain a better understanding of how certain values come into existence, and how different pathways to deal with climate change are rationalized within the framework of these value systems.

Another powerful mechanism contradicting individual action to mitigate climate change might be media reports, which have often outlined conflicting views, rather than the broad scientific consensus on climate change (Boykoff and Boykoff 2004, 2007), including, in 2009/2010, exaggerated or unsubstantiated reports on 'climategate' and other 'gates' (see also Chapter 3; for ongoing debates see www.realclimate.org). Overall, these mechanisms, i.e. the construction of individual motorized mobility as a fundamental human right, the presentation of technology-fix discourses, and the questioning of climate science might all be factors reducing the willingness of individuals to take action or to support climate policy. Further insights into the complexity of these issues can be gained from the psychology literature.

THE PSYCHOLOGY OF DENIAL

Generally speaking, non-action on climate change has been discussed on the basis of the 'psychology of denial', a concept developed by Stoll-Kleemann et al. (2001). In interviews with Swiss respondents, Stoll-Kleemann et al. (2001) revealed that respondents were alarmed about climate change, yet erected psychological barriers to justify individual and collective non-action. Material comfort needs and high energy dependence justified the impossibility of behavioural change, with 'excuses' as originally outlined by Schahn (1993: 59–60):

1 Metaphor of displaced commitment: 'I protect the environment in other ways'.
2 To condemn the accuser: 'You have no right to challenge me'.
3 Denial of responsibility: 'I am not the main cause of this problem'.
4 Rejection of blame: 'I have done nothing so wrong as to be destructive'.
5 Ignorance: 'I simply don't know the consequences of my actions'.
6 Powerlessness: 'I am only an infinitesimal being in the order of things'.
7 Fabricated constraints: 'There are too many impediments'.
8 After the flood: 'What is the future doing for me?'
9 Comfort: 'It is too difficult for me to change my behaviour'.

Stoll-Kleemann et al. (2001: 112) suggest that these nine categories can be integrated in four overarching themes, including 'comfort', 'tragedy-of-the-commons', 'managerial fix' and 'government distrust':

1 Comfort: an unwillingness to give up customary habits and favoured lifestyles, which are closely associated with a sense of self-identity.
2 Tragedy of the commons: the construction of attitude and behaviour connections that regard any costs to the self as greater than the benefits to others.
3 Managerial fix: a lack of acceptance that the climate problem is as serious as made out, and a belief that, in any case, it can be resolved by recourse to technological and regulatory innovation.
4 Government distrust: an underlying lack of faith in the capacity of government to deliver its side of the bargain over climate change mitigation.

Socio-psychological denial mechanisms thus represent obstacles to changing comfortable lifestyles, based on blame for inaction on others, including governments, and emphasis on doubts about the immediacy of action. Stoll-Kleemann *et al.* (2001) emphasize that 'more attention needs to be given to the social and psychological motivations to why individuals erect barriers to their personal commitment to climate change mitigation, even when professing anxiety over climate futures'. Overall, these findings suggest that climate change mitigation is faced with multiple complexities, including various processes working against individual responsibility and action.

THE PSYCHOLOGY OF BEHAVIOURAL CHANGE: A REVIEW

More generally, difficulties of changing behaviour in favour of more environmentally friendly patterns have also been discussed in the environmental psychology literature. In a recent review, Steg and Vlek (2009; see also Jackson 2005) suggest that to change behaviour, it is necessary to understand the factors underlying the behaviour, and to then design and apply interventions. Factors determining behaviour include (1) perceived costs and benefits, (2) moral and normative concerns, (3) affect, (4) contextual factors and (5) habits.

Perceived costs and benefits

Steg and Vlek (2009) present Ajzen's (1991) theory of planned behaviour as one framework to explain environmental behaviour – including travel mode choice – based on variables such as money, effort and/or social approval. Of importance in the light of the above discussion on values, moral and normative concerns refer to the role of values in behaviour, i.e. the more 'self-transcendent, prosocial, altruistic or biospheric' a person's values are, the more likely is this person to engage in pro-environmental behaviour. A higher degree of environmental concern is also associated with more pro-environmental behaviour. Steg and Vlek (2009) point out that relationships are not generally strong, however (see also Stoll-Kleemann *et al.* 2001), and there is evidence from the tourism literature that climate change awareness is not a factor affecting tourism consumption significantly (e.g. Anable *et al.* 2006; Dickinson 2009; Hares *et al.* 2009; Eijgelaar *et al.* 2010; McKercher *et al.* 2010). Conversely, perceived benefits are an explanatory variable for pro-environmental behaviour. Badland *et al.* (2010), for instance, found that for commuters, lack of worksite car park access, or limited car access as well as the proximity to public transport stops, were important factors in perceiving public transport as beneficial.

Moral and normative concerns

With regard to moral and normative concerns, the norm-activation model (Schwartz 1977) as well as the value-belief-norm of environmentalism (Stern *et al.* 1999) are cited by Steg and Vlek (2009) as relevant theories, postulating that moral obligations will lead to pro-environmental behaviour. Both can explain 'low-cost' environmental behaviour, but have less explanatory power in situations where there is a 'high cost', as in the case of reduced car use. Likewise, social norms can influence behaviour. The theory of normative conduct (Cialdini *et al.* 1990), distinguishes behaviour that is seen to be commonly approved of or disapproved of, as well as behaviour that is perceived as common. In the context of tourism consumption, this theory would be of relevance with regard to, for instance, car use, long-distance travel by air, or holiday 'trends' as depicted by the media.

Affect

Studies have also shown the role of affective and symbolic factors in behaviour, for instance with regard to car use (Gatersleben 2007). Steg and Vlek (2009) suggest goal-framing theory (originally proposed by Lindenberg 2001a, b, 2006) as an integrative theory for environmental behaviour, i.e. considering that behaviour is based on multiple motivations, with hedonic goal-frames ('to feel better right now') being generally stronger than gain goal-frames ('to guard and improve one's resources') or normative goal-frames ('to act appropriately'). Within the framework of this theory, changing behaviour consequently has to move from instrumental motives to embracing affective and symbolic factors.

Contextual factors

Moreover, it needs to be considered that contextual factors are important in changing behaviour, because even if motivations are in favour of pro-environmental behaviour, preconditions for changing behaviour have to be acceptable: 'it is not only important to consider inter-personal factors such as attitudes, norms and habits, but also contextual factors such as physical infrastructure, technical facilities, the availability of products and product characteristics' (Steg and Vlek 2009: 312). These findings would be relevant for tourism because of the need to provide appropriate infrastructure to encourage modal shifts (e.g. Lumsdon 2006; Guiver *et al.* 2007), or, alternatively, politics for urban and regional planning that focus on public transport rather than private mobility (see also Badland *et al.* 2010), always with a focus on different mobility groups and their specific expectations and perceptions (Hunecke and Haustein 2007).

Habits are another factor to be considered in behavioural change:

> When people frequently act in the same way in a particular situation, that situation will be mentally associated with the relevant goal-directed behaviour. The more frequently this occurs, the stronger and more accessible the association becomes, and the more likely it is that an individual acts accordingly. Thus, habitual behaviour is triggered by a cognitive structure that is learned, stored in, and retrieved from memory when individuals perceive a particular situation.
>
> (Steg and Vlek 2009: 312)

These findings are highly relevant for tourism, also because they would indicate that habits learned early in life become relevant for choices throughout life. This might be considered for instance in the context of frequent-flyer programmes targeting children (Gössling and Nilsson 2010). Steg and Vlek (2009: 312) also emphasize that 'Habitual behaviour may involve misperceptions and selective attention: people tend to focus on information that confirms their choices, and neglect information that is not in line with their habitual behaviour'.

Habits

Two general strategies can be developed based on these findings, including informational strategies, which are aimed at changing 'perceptions, motivations, knowledge, and norms', as well as structural strategies aimed at reducing the barriers for action (Steg and Vlek 2009: 313). With regard to informational strategies, knowledge of environmental problems and behavioural alternatives is a precondition for changing behaviour. Initiatives for environmental learning such as those initiated by Hilton Worldwide (Carbon Management in Focus 33) are thus of great importance. Steg and Vlek (2009: 313) add that the most promising results are achieved with 'individualised social marketing approaches, in which information is tailored to the needs, wants and perceived barriers of individual segments of the population'. These can be aided by 'social support and role models' to inform about the perceptions, efficacy and behaviour of others. Overall, informational strategies could work well when pro-environmental behaviour is not costly with regard to money, time, effort and/or social disapproval. Again, the Hilton Worldwide campaign to reduce water and energy use appears to incorporate these insights successfully, also rewarding pro-environmental behaviour.

CARBON MANAGEMENT IN FOCUS 33: HILTON WORLDWIDE, USA

Building staff knowledge and creating awareness

The issue

Knowledge about climate change and awareness of its consequences are prerequisites for changing behaviour (Steg and Vlek 2009). In tourism, education about climate change is thus of relevance for tourists, for instance to influence their travel choices, as well as for those working in tourism, i.e. managers as well as staff, particularly in larger companies where daily behaviour has a direct influence on resource use.

The solution

Under the umbrella of Hilton Worldwide, there are 10 brands comprising more than 3,400 hotels in 79 countries. The chain is committed to reducing resource use, also with a view on side effects such as financial savings, heightened guest and employee loyalty, new revenue opportunities, marketing and public relations coverage, and the pre-empting of governmental regulations. In 2008, Hilton Worldwide's CEO Christopher Nassetta announced the chain's global goal of reducing waste, energy consumption, and CO_2 emissions by 20 per cent, as well as water consumption by 10 per cent by 2014 compared to 2008 levels, as part of the Hilton Worldwide Global Sustainability Initiative. Earlier, Hilton hotels in continental Europe had already initiated the 'we care!' environmental programme, running between 2006 and 2008. The principal idea of the programme was to empower Hilton employees (called team members) to act pro-environmentally at work and at home, focusing on four key issues: energy efficiency, waste reduction, water efficiency and reduced use of chemicals. To measure success, targets were set and performance measured, with the goal of creating a pro-environmental team culture. The results of the campaign exceeded expectations, with energy consumption declining by 15 per cent and normalized water consumption by 8 per cent compared to 2005. The programme was based on five pillars: (1) environmental policy, supported by the top management; (2) the consideration of the guidelines for 'Sustainable hotel siting, design and construction' (see CI and IBLF 2005); (3) workshops and 'ecoLearning'; (4) Hilton Environmental Reporting (HER), a performance monitoring tool; and (5) HiWay, an intranet communication tool. Workshops, ecoLearning and HER are presented in the following in more detail.

Environmental workshops were organized at all hotels and a total of 16,000 team members were trained in 'we care!' sessions across Europe. Employees were encouraged to further develop their knowledge and understanding of environmental issues by participating in ecoLearning courses available in eight language versions on the company's intranet. Courses aim at explaining global environmental issues and provide advice on how to act more responsibly. Each session includes a series of quizzes, games, advice specific for certain areas (e.g. kitchen or cleaning), as well as 'take-it-home' advice. In February 2010, 8,000 team members in 54 countries had attended the online ecoLearning sessions, and received certificates after successful completion. These courses are the first step in environmental education, which can later be developed at meetings and seminars/events organized by the Green Team. The benefit of online training is, according to Paulina Bohdanowicz, Sustainability Manager Europe, that team members can progress with the course at their own pace. Figures 12.1, 12.2 and 12.3 illustrate ecoLearning sessions.

To encourage team members to actively reduce resource use, competitions were organized over three years, with each team member in the best performing hotel in each operational region receiving a mountain bike. Between 2006 and 2008, over 3,000 mountain bikes were awarded. Also with a view to facilitate competition, the HER tool was designed to communicate progress in

What can you do with 50 litres of water?

Two minutes in a water-efficient shower = 18 litres
Three toilet flushes = 18 litres
Brushing teeth (with tap turned off) = 0.5 litre
Drinking = 0.5 litre
Cooking = 3 litres
Washing hands = 2 litres
Remaining = 8 litres

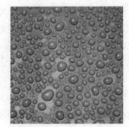

Figure 12.1 *Information on water use*
Source: From Hilton ecoLearning 1

Living according to the eco principles

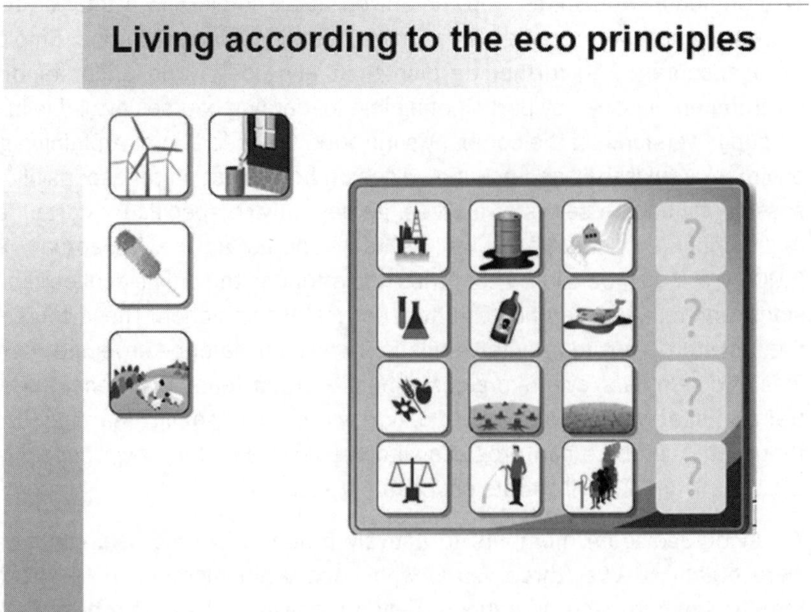

Figure 12.2 *Quiz based on principles by The Natural Step*
Source: From Hilton ecoLearning 1

Housekeeping

- Check that the lights are turned off when you leave the guestroom
- Close open windows
- Sort out all waste at your workplace
- Avoid disposable items
- Use cloth towels instead of paper ones
- Use concentrated products to reduce packaging and transport
- Use eco-labelled cleaning products
- Use the right dosages
- Use toilet paper that has not been chlorine bleached
- Don't throw waste that contains environmentally hazardous chemicals down the drain or in the bin – put them in the chemicals bank
- Alternative methods such as bread, erasers, knives, cooking oil or vinegar are often just as good at removing dirty marks

Figure 12.3 *Tips for responsible housekeeping*
Source: From Hilton ecoLearning 1

resource-efficiency to all team members, providing online information on the development in key performance indicators such as CO_2 emissions, energy per guest night and energy use per m² (see Figure 12.4: Hotels on top of the list perform best, those at the end of the list worst).

In the period 2005–08, these measures helped Hilton hotels in continental Europe to reduce energy use by 15 per cent and water use by 8 per cent, corresponding to 28,600 t CO_2 of 'saved' emissions, and avoided energy and water costs of US$16 million (€11.1 million), of which US$9.6 million (€6.7 million) could be attributed to behavioural change of staff members, and US$ 6.4 million (€4.5 million) to the installation of energy- and water-efficient equipment and control systems.

As outlined by Paulina Bohdanowicz, Hilton in continental Europe sees the success of the programme mostly in the challenge to staff and its competitive element (mountain bike awards), combined with a fun element, the focus on resource-use reductions, not cost savings, committed team members and the continuous support from the top management. A number of lessons can be learned as well: on the management side, the programme should be well planned, have achievable goals, provide training and support throughout, empower team members, be a continuous effort, be kept fresh and alive, and be fun and competitive.

Hotel	No of Mon	Energy/GN				Energy/m²				Energy/Corr 2008	Energy/Corr 2008	Overall % Change 2005-2008	CO₂/GN Corr 2008
		2005	2006	2007	2008	2005	2006	2007	2008				
Hilton Tel Aviv	2.0	156.1	112.8	95.5	91.4	470.7	425.0	361.8	442.8	56.9	391.4	-40.2%	13.1
Hilton Amsterdam Airport Schiphol	2.0	76.0	68.7	39.2	48.6	576.0	620.7	365.6	440.0	40.7	477.7	-31.7%	6.4
Hilton Luxembourg	2.0	170.9	208.3	163.6	122.5	485.3	492.0	377.8	396.1	107.5	465.7	-20.6%	23.6
Hilton Royal Parc Soestduinen	2.0	171.8	142.7	118.2	125.6	710.2	668.6	529.8	594.6	109.7	675.5	-20.5%	19.2
Hilton Copenhagen Airport	2.0	94.5	94.4	81.5	83.6	343.3	372.5	322.5	329.7	77.1	369.0	-5.5%	13.6
Hilton Malmö City	2.0	121.9	128.3	109.8	110.0	362.3	375.5	321.0	313.7	114.7	344.3	-5.4%	3.0
Hilton Stockholm Slussen	2.0	81.7	79.3	91.0	75.2	287.2	304.4	324.6	240.6	82.5	256.5	-4.9%	0.9
Hilton Rotterdam	3.0	118.1	126.4	88.8	110.4	340.6	385.1	300.1	337.0	104.3	367.8	-1.8%	25.3
Hilton Brussels	2.0	127.4	164.0	164.8	119.4	547.7	605.1	560.9	564.5	108.5	618.6	-0.9%	17.3
Hilton Amsterdam	3.0	149.9	135.3	126.3	152.8	601.5	676.9	491.6	544.3	172.2	589.3	6.4%	20.8
Hilton Eilat Queen of Sheba Resort	2.0	74.4	83.0	79.5	94.7	299.8	315.3	294.8	361.0	100.1	342.9	24.5%	10.3
Hilton Brussels City	2.0	56.8	64.6	47.3	70.8	382.1	436.8	371.7	445.7	75.5	491.8	30.3%	10.9
Hilton Antwerp	3.0	97.9	94.4	87.8	237.4	179.1	186.9	157.7	399.3	258.2	418.6	148.7%	38.0

Figure 12.4 *Energy key performance indicator table, Hilton Hotels*
Source: from Hilton Environmental Reporting tool (August 2008)

Impact

Educational campaigns by Hilton Worldwide have shown that education of employees pays off financially, while also having a wide range of positive side effects, from higher employee and guest loyalty to positive media attention. Importantly, education of staff is likely to lead to behavioural change even at home, as the 'challenge' of resource-use reductions is packaged as a competitive fun exercise. As ecoLearning courses are available in eight languages, with participation in 54 countries, there are considerable educational benefits with global coverage associated with Hilton's various campaigns.

Source

Paulina Bohdanowicz, Sustainability Manager Europe, Hilton

Website

Hilton, www.hilton.com, www.hiltonworldwide.com

Related websites

The Natural Step, http://www.naturalstep.org/

References

CI & IBLF (Conservation International & the Prince of Wales International Business Leaders Forum) (2005). *Sustainable Hotel Siting, Design and Construction*. Abingdon: Nuffield Press.

Steg, L. and Vlek, C. (2009). Encouraging pro-environmental behaviour: an integrative review and research agenda. *Journal of Environmental Psychology* 29: 309–317.

INFORMATIONAL AND STRUCTURAL STRATEGIES

Informational strategies can be seen as important building blocks of structural strategies, for instance in terms of creating political support for measures forcing individuals to change behaviour. It could be argued that this is particularly relevant in tourism and leisure contexts, where behaviour might not be changed voluntarily because 'costs' are perceived as being too high. As outlined by Steg and Vlek (2009), structural strategies seek to change contextual factors by changing the availability and quality of products and services, through legal interventions, or pricing. This would result in environmentally harmful behaviour becoming less feasible, more expensive or prohibited. At the same time, structural strategies would also seek to reward 'correct' behaviour, as exemplified in the bonus/malus system for new cars in France. Steg and Vlek (2009) outline that rewards are more effective than punishments (but only if they succeed in making pro-environmental behaviour more attractive), and that their effect in time will be dependent on the continuation of rewards. These insights could be used more systematically in tourism, where new low-carbon products could be developed and promoted by focusing not on their carbon properties but, rather, their unique character or the experiences that can be gained through their consumption. For instance, such a marketing focus on enjoyable, unique experiences can be assumed to be the major reason for the success of ecotourism in Sweden (Gössling 2006). More generally, strategies to encourage pro-environmental behaviour will have to be context-specific, with multiple, combined measures being most successful.

Changing behaviour in tourism can make use of many of these insights. For instance, Kelly *et al.* (2007a) found that parking fees and fuel costs influenced the propensity of visitors to Whistler, Canada to favour public over private transport. In other studies, it has been outlined that changing behavioural patterns of tourists on a voluntary basis might be more difficult (see e.g. Becken and Wilson 2007 for an experiment seeking to influence self-drive tourists in New Zealand). In order to involve tourists in destination planning and to find out about their preferred options to reduce resource use, Kelly *et al.* (2007b) suggest a stated preferences methodology; results can then be used to design mitigation strategies. However, findings by Steg and Vlek (2009) also indicate many obstacles. For instance, broad media reporting following the publication of the IPCCs (2007b) AR4 is likely to have been useful in creating a common identification with the topic (see e.g. Naturvårdsverket 2009 for Sweden). Common approval of the notion that action is needed to deal with climate change might have helped people to feel that they are part of a broad movement, i.e. overcoming the 'psychology of denial'. The current questioning of climate science in the media could have the opposite effect, however, with surveys indicating that belief in climate change is already declining (e.g. *Washington Post* 2009).

Overall, voluntary behavioural change in tourism is, however, not likely to become significant, even if strategies to achieve change are optimized based on insights from psychology. As outlined by Peeters *et al.* (2009a: 248): 'Many people have a powerful belief in their personal right and need to travel, coupled at the same time with a contradictory powerful belief that others should be denied that right for the good of the planet'. Such insights are confirmed by studies such as Barr *et al.* (2010) or McKercher *et al.* (2010), who find that the most environmentally aware tourists might not be more willing to alter travel behaviour:

The public generally has strong awareness of and reasonable knowledge about both local and global environmental issues but is generally unwilling to make voluntary changes. Resistance to change in tourist behaviour must be placed within a larger context of an overall thicket of unsustainability that most of the developed world finds itself in and overall resistance to making needed changes to address this issue.

(McKercher *et al.* 2010: 17)

These somewhat paradoxical findings would be explained by recent psychological research indicating that where people engage in pro-environmental behaviour in one area, this might license selfish and unethical behaviour in other arenas (Barr *et al.* 2010; Mazar and Zhong 2010). As there are studies providing evidence that the most climatically aware tourists might also be the most active travellers (e.g. Barr *et al.* 2010; Gössling *et al.* 2009a), there might be a particular need to address the uneven distribution of emissions between individuals (e.g. Chakravarti *et al.* 2009; Gössling *et al.* 2009b), also with a view on avoiding a larger share of human beings entering GHG-intense mobile lifestyles (Gössling and Nilsson 2010). Climate policy is thus the most important arena to achieve change, while considering insights from environmental psychology as outlined above.

13 Mitigation

Politics and research

There is general consensus that climate policy has a key role to play in the transformation of tourism towards sustainability, not least because technological innovation and behavioural change will demand strong regulatory environments (e.g. Chapman 2007; Hickman and Banister 2007; Bows *et al.* 2009a, b; Barr *et al.* 2010; Gössling *et al.* 2010; Peeters and Dubois 2010b; see also Giddens 2009). For instance, in a recent modelling exercise to identify prerequisites for a transition to a sustainable surface-based mobility system, Köhler *et al.* (2009: 2994) concluded that:

> a large-scale shift in the preferences – and therefore choices – of consumers and also strong and lasting policy action is a prerequisite for a transition to a sustainable mobility system. ... this shift must be maintained for a long time (20–30 years), or indeed permanently ... radical institutional and behavioural change will probably be harder to achieve than technological change. The challenge for policy makers is to inspire and connect to grassroots support for social change in order to effectively introduce potentially unpopular changes (e.g., fuel tax increases, parking restrictions), and to demonstrate the wider benefits of such changes (e.g., reduced air pollution, more reliable public transport) to garner this support.

Tourism is largely a private sector activity, but it has close relationships with the public sector at supranational central, regional and local government levels (Hall and Jenkins 1995). Governments are involved in regulating the industry, stimulating tourism development – for instance in foreign aid or through national marketing campaigns – and in creating infrastructure such as airports, roads or railways. On the other hand, governments are responsible for ensuring that emissions reductions within the Kyoto Protocol are achieved, which in some cases might mean that new infrastructure projects should not be carried out because they would mean interference with national climate politics. This could, in reality, often be difficult, as exemplified by the construction of a third runway at Heathrow airport in the UK or Förbifart Stockholm, a national highway project in Sweden, which both caused major public and political debates in their respective countries in 2009/2010.

Nevertheless, there appears to be support for regulatory action on the side of tourism organizations such as WTTC (2009), airline organizations (IATA 2009a), airlines (AGD 2009) and associated business organizations such as WEF (2009), but it is less clear how organizations within this consensus look at the potential to achieve emission reductions, tourism's carbon 'allowance' compared to other sectors, the burden sharing between tourism sub-sectors, countries, and individual travellers, and suitable strategies to achieve emission reductions. Most notably, perhaps, is that despite calls for emission reductions, notions of growth remain unchallenged, ubiquitous, and positive (Gössling et al. 2010; see also Yeoman and McMahon-Beattie 2006; Yeoman et al. 2007), and business leaders and politicians appear set to return to the same routes of economic development that led to economic crisis in 2008 (cf. Hall 2009b), i.e. a system based on the notion that growth can be reconciled with reductions in emissions and even be a precondition for climate action (see Daley 2009). Scott and Becken (2010; see also Schilcher 2007) remark that:

> It becomes clear that organisations such as UNWTO, WTTC, ICAO and IATA are firmly anchored in a neoliberal view of the world where ongoing economic growth is paramount and largely without physical limits. Such views are increasingly questioned (e.g. Lloyd 2007) and might be at the heart of the failure of Copenhagen. ... These questions challenge the very existence of tourism as a means to achieving sustainability (Hunter 1997) and the underlying paradigms of neoliberalism and capitalism in which tourism operates.
>
> (Scott and Becken 2010, no page)

Overall, evidence suggests that significant structural change towards lower mobility as well as altered tourism consumption patterns are required to achieve absolute emission reductions within the sector by 2020, demanding 'serious' climate policy (Scott et al. 2010; see also Peeters et al. 2007a; Gössling et al. 2008; Pentalow and Scott 2009). Notably, 'serious' would include the endorsement of national and international mitigation policies by tourism, global closed ETS for aviation and shipping, the introduction of significant and constantly rising carbon taxes on fossil fuels, incentives for low-carbon technologies and transport infrastructure, and, ultimately, the development of a vision for a fundamentally different global tourism economy (cf. Scott et al. 2010). All of these aspects of a low-carbon tourism system are principally embraced by business organizations. For instance, the WEF (2009) suggests as mechanisms to achieve emission reductions: (1) a carbon tax on non-renewable fuels, (2) economic incentives for low-carbon technologies, (3) a cap-and-trade system for developing and developed countries, and (4) the further development of carbon trading markets. Furthermore, evidence from countries seeking to implement low-carbon policies suggests that the tourism businesses themselves also call for the implementation of legislation to curb emissions, a result of the wish for 'rules for all', with, in particular, pro-climate-oriented businesses demanding regulation (cf. Global Focus 2008).

AVIATION

Aviation, which accounts for 40 per cent of CO_2 emissions from tourism and a considerably greater share of the sector's contribution to RF, is the most important sector that needs to be addressed in climate policy, as it is impossible to achieve absolute reductions in emissions in tourism without reducing growth rates in aviation. As discussed by Scott et al. (2010), if aviation emissions continue to grow by 100 per cent by 2035 as portrayed by AGD group, or even by only 10 to 20 per cent as portrayed in the best case by IATA, it is impossible to see how absolute emission reductions could occur in the tourism sector by 2020 or even 2035: 'Indeed, using the UNWTO-UNEP-WMO (2008) emission scenarios, even if all surface transport, accommodation and activities sub-sectors no longer contributed to GHG emissions by 2035 ... tourism emissions would still increase by 40 per cent' (Scott *et al.* 2010).

Emissions of environmentally harmful substances are usually addressed through economic instruments. Currently, aviation does not pay any VAT, in contrast to virtually all other means of transport. For instance, in Sweden, a litre of Jet A fuel costs about €0.40, while a litre of diesel costs €1.20. VAT on international flights is 0 per cent, and for domestic flights 6 per cent, while all other services and goods (except food) incur 25 per cent VAT. Deutsche Bahn (German railways) calculates that the difference between a flight and train travel from Berlin to Munich and back is €50 per traveller in favour of air travel (Deutsche Bahn 2009). These examples explain why aviation, i.e. the most emission-intense transport mode on a per pkm basis, can be significantly cheaper than the train, i.e. the least emission-intense transport mode (with coaches). Notably, competitive differences in the EU will be further emphasized through the EU ETS, where aviation will receive 85 per cent of its emission rights for free, while the train system will have to buy 100 per cent of its quota through auctioning (Deutsche Bahn 2009).

With regard to policy to curb emissions from aviation, the EU is currently the only region in the world that foresees including aviation in an ETS (see Chapter 4). An open-trading scheme is favoured, as it is assumed that this will guarantee the greatest efficiency in reducing emissions, i.e. the lowest cost reductions can be made first throughout all sectors. However, as emission reductions by further improving fuel efficiency in aviation are comparatively costly, airlines will probably not reduce absolute emissions but, rather, will purchase emission permits from the market. This is economically feasible, as the cost of flying will increase by just about €3 per 1,000 pkm at permit prices of €25 per tonne of CO_2 (Scott *et al.* 2010). Similar findings are presented by Mayor and Tol (2010b), who find that a price of €23/t CO_2 per permit will have a negligible effect on emissions. Furthermore, the trading scheme would have three distorting effects, including a decline in non-EU visitors travelling elsewhere, 'equal to a reduction of 1.1 per cent in the EU, and an increase of 0.8 per cent elsewhere' (Mayor and Tol 2010b: 29), a tendency for EU citizens to spend their holiday in the EU more often, though at a modest level of 0.1 per cent, and a redistribution of tourists within the EU. All effects are minor, though.

Further insights can be gained from research on elasticities in aviation, i.e. changes in demand because of increasing ticket prices. For instance, Tol (2007) presents the results of a simulation model of international tourist flows for the year 2010 under global taxes of $10, $100 and $1,000 per t carbon (C), concluding that CO_2 from international aviation would decline by 0.8 per cent if a tax of $1,000 per t C was introduced (see also Mayor and Tol 2008, 2009 for a simulation of falling fares). Results thus indicate high elasticities of air travellers to increasing costs for air travel. Mayor and Tol (2008) note that one effect of a trading system could be that medium-distance flights might become more attractive relative to short trips because cost increases would be proportionally lower. This confirms Mayor and Tol's (2007) earlier research for the UK which found that doubling the UK's 2001 Air Passenger Duty – charged on a per flight basis – would even slightly increase CO_2 emissions because the relative price difference between closer and more distant air-based holidays would be distorted, causing people to choose more distant destinations. The analysis is based on the assumption that domestic and foreign holidays are not substitutable, but it is conceivable that UK tourists would not consider a domestic holiday as a substitute for a foreign holiday. On the other hand, Mayor and Tol (2007) find that abolishing the current Passenger Duty in the UK would result in lower emissions, because the price of short-haul flights falls relative to the price of long-haul flights. Similar findings are presented by Mayor and Tol (2010b) for the Netherlands.

These results indicate that a duty or tax on a per flight basis might not be the most effective instrument to reduce emissions from aviation, at least in the UK. Mayor and Tol (2007) conclude that 'a simple carbon tax ... would be far superior' to Passenger Duties. In an analysis of the consequences of a carbon tax, Tol (2007) finds that in particular long-haul flights (because of high emissions) and short-haul flights (because of emissions during take-off and landing) would be affected. However, this would actually support the argument for a carbon tax, because long-haul and short-haul flights are the most important sectors to target. Long-haul flights are important because even though they account for just a few per cent of flights, they are responsible for the majority of overall emissions (see Chapter 8). On the other hand, short-haul flights are problematic because they create an understanding that aviation is a comparably cheap means of transportation, leading to self-evident transport choices in favour of air travel (Becken 2007).

While this supports the argument of a carbon tax, it is important to note that this tax also needs to be comparably high to have a significant effect. Mayor and Tol (2010a, in press) also outline legal difficulties:

> Surprisingly the most direct way of taxing emissions, a kerosene tax, has only been implemented on a domestic level in a few countries. Existing bilateral air services agreements, which preclude the introduction of fuel taxes, would need to be renegotiated if a kerosene tax were to be implemented on an international level.

This points at legal problems incurred in policy making: the most efficient system, a tax on fuel, would be the best approach to reduce emissions. This, however, is not legally feasible, even though it might be possible to introduce a tax on emissions (Peeters *et al.* 2007b). The only system that is clearly legally feasible, a fee on tickets, has distorting effects (Mayor and Tol 2010a), but it might be discussed if fees can be designed in a way to consider distances, i.e. be made proportional to emissions. In summary, it could be concluded that taxes on emissions of CO_2 (as well as NO_x to reduce non-CO_2 RF) would be preferable in policy making, and that these could be combined with a closed emission trading system for aviation to guarantee an overall cap on emissions from this sector and to reduce the risk of price-shocks in the system:

> An open-trading scheme will thus mean that aviation can continue to grow its emissions, as anticipated by the AGD group (Aviation Global Deal group 2009), which foresees that the sector's emissions will more than double by 2035. This scenario has inherent problems. For some years emissions would continue to increase rapidly, thus increasing climatic risks. As cheap credits become exhausted and multiple sectors compete for increasingly expensive emission credits, there could be a sudden dramatic change in cost structures within the aviation sector; putting large investments in air transport and destinations at risk. In order to avoid such a potential

price-shock and the detrimental impact on international tourism, it thus seems advisable to establish a closed emission-trading scheme for aviation, or to include aviation in an open-trading scheme with a gradually tightening cap on the amount of permits than can be bought from other sectors.

(Scott *et al.* 2010, in press)

As shown in Table 13.1, there is general support for taxation in society, though not necessarily among air travellers (e.g. Barr *et al.* 2010). Business organizations (e.g. IATA 2009a; AGD group 2009; WEF 2009) and scientists (e.g. Sterner 2007; Walz *et al.* 2008; Gössling *et al.* 2010) also support taxation, and there would thus be strong support for a renegotiation of bilateral agreements to allow introduction of a carbon tax. It is likely, however, that such negotiations will meet the resistance of airlines in the USA, which have old, inefficient fleets. In this case, alternative approaches focusing on emissions need to be developed. The approach chosen should also be monitored to assess whether real progress towards decarbonization is made.

Table 13.1 *Support for policies to reduce the environmental impact of air travel*

Britain

(World Environmental Review 2007)

46% think the government should impose a carbon tax on all domestic and international flights

(National Statistics Omnibus Survey – 2003, 2005)

2003–78% agreed people should be able to travel by plane as much as they want to

Agreement fell to 17% if 'air travel harms the environment', then 59% were against unrestricted air travel

More frequent travellers are more likely to support unrestricted travel even when potential environmental consequences are considered

2005 – agreement that 'people should be able to travel by plane as much as they like' fell to 70% (from 78% in 2003)

(Ipsos MORI 2006)

Between 37% and 58% support policies aimed at slowing down growth in air travel

Support was higher for airlines paying higher taxes (55% to 65%) to reflect the environmental damage done by aircraft than higher passenger duties (47% to 57%)

Support for passenger taxes on air travel was highest when the revenues would go toward improving the environment (71% to 74%).

Sweden

(Naturvardsverket 2009)

85 % believe that it is important to act to mitigate climate change, and 63% support higher taxes to steer consumption. The share of the population demanding a clear role of the state in addressing climate change has increased to 41%.

Source: Simpson et al. (2008)

In summary, there is a clear need to address emissions from aviation, because if these cannot be reduced – in absolute terms – then emissions from tourism as a sector will continue to grow. However, while there is consensus on an absolute mitigation goal among political, business and academic stakeholders, there are vastly different positions on how emission reduction can or should be achieved. With regard to global policy, the academic position is that the simplest mechanism to reduce emissions is taxation of fuel use or emissions, and efforts should eventually be focused on this goal, even if this means that hundreds of bilateral agreements have to be renegotiated. The alternative, a global agreement on emission trading in an open trading scheme, as favoured by industry, is not likely to lead to significant mitigation. Rather, emerging policy documents by supranational organizations such as IATA, ICAO or UNWTO on the allocation of emissions between countries and exemptions to be granted, all indicate that success will be hampered by negotiations where each stakeholder's position is characterized by the quest for strategic advantages in the design of increasingly complex policy documents.

CARS

Cars account for 32 per cent of emissions from tourism, and there is strong growth in worldwide car ownership. In a discussion of policy packages to reduce emission from cars, Hickman and Banister (2007) suggest that the introduction of more fuel-efficient cars and the use of alternative fuels are most promising. These, however, might be risky options, because of global growth in car ownership, outpacing efficiency gains, and the rebound effect of efficient cars, i.e. increased travel due to the perception of low costs (cf. OECD 1996). Primarily, there might thus be a need to prevent car ownership (Gilbert and Perl 2008), as well as to introduce taxes to maintain stable fuel costs for people switching to more efficient cars. Moreover, it might be necessary to consider elasticities, as there is evidence that the owners of large and less efficient cars are not susceptible to taxation due to disproportionally higher incomes and/or private wealth. In this context, Hickman and Banister (2007) suggest one policy package that focuses on carbon rationing, i.e. annual carbon budgets for individuals, which are distributed on an equitable basis and tradable in a market. Assuming that price elasticities of, in particular, the major individual emitters are huge – with, for instance, the wealthiest 10 per cent of the German population owning 61 per cent of the country's residents' private wealth (in 2007, Hans Böckler Stiftung 2009) – individual carbon budgets might indeed be the only solution to deal with mitigation (see e.g. Roberts and Thumim 2006).

The importance of taxation has also been outlined by Sterner (2007), who found that taxes have been an important factor in restraining growth in fuel demand and emissions. Even though demand is elastic at a high level, modelling shows that if Europe had fuel taxes as low as the USA, demand for fuel would have been twice as high. Sterner (2007: 3194) concludes that: 'fuel taxes are the single most powerful climate policy instrument implemented to date'. Notably, there are considerable differences in current tax levels, showing that there is potential for most countries to increase taxes on fuel (cf. Sterner 2007).

Increases in fuel taxes would have to be significant in order to have an impact. For instance, Morrow et al. (2010) outline that reducing CO_2 emissions from the transportation sector in the US by 14 per cent below 2005 levels by 2020 will require fuel prices greater than US$7/gallon by 2020 (€1,17/litre). Notably, this corresponds to current prices in most European countries, but is almost three times higher than fuel prices in the USA in March 2010 (about US$2.80/gallon; cf. www.gasbuddy.com). Notably, Morrow *et al.* (2010: 2) also remark that:

> A fundamental insight from this study is that if one wishes to reduce U.S. CO_2 emissions or net petroleum imports from the transportation sector during 2010–2030, consumers cannot continue to drive more and more each year. The EIA currently projects that vehicle-miles traveled will grow more than 30% between 2010 and 2030 as a result of the increase in household incomes and population. In this study, higher fuel prices are the mechanism to reduce vehicle-miles traveled. Higher transportation costs are also closely linked to land-use policy and development of mass-transit systems.

In summary, the most efficient policy to reduce emissions from car travel might be a fuel tax, supporting findings as already outlined for aviation, even though this might have to be combined with the improvement of surface-bound public transport infrastructures as well as specific incentives. Notably, the IEA (2009) also supports higher fuel prices, even though it does not explicitly mention taxation. These findings apply for other tourism sub-sectors more generally, calling for a policy focus on higher fuel prices, which could be combined with other measures, such as incentives for owners of small cars, or the users of alternative transport modes including trains and buses.

TRAINS

Countries seeking to curb emissions from aviation have often focused on the expansion of railway systems, including, for instance, Sweden, France, USA and China. Neiberger (2009) outlines that railways have been neglected in Chinese politics for decades, with a net density of 0.74 km/100 km², compared to, for instance, 1.9 km/100 km² in India, or 10 km/100 km² in Germany. Realizing the deficit in transport capacity and enormous growth in transport capacity needs in China, a considerable extension of railway tracks by 37 per cent (to 100,000 km) was announced in 2004 (see Figure 13.1). The plan considers specific tracks for passenger and cargo traffic, as well as 'coal lines'. Plans foresee simultaneously increasing the speed of trains, with high-speed tracks for passenger trains between Peking and Shanghai at 200 km/h. Building costs are estimated to be in the order of US$240 million, financed by the Chinese government, Worldbank and Asian Development Bank. The example shows that the political will to develop high-speed train systems can lead to far-reaching restructuring. Even though this is not even discussed internationally, this might in the future also include high-speed railway systems across continents, for instance connecting Europe and Asia through rail linkages.

DESTINATIONS

Destinations are key in achieving absolute emission reductions in tourism. However, one of the implications of climate change for tourism destinations is the potential impact mitigation policy could have on travel costs and tourist mobility, which is particularly relevant

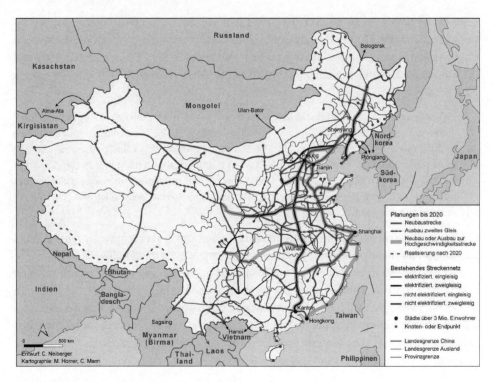

Figure 13.1 *Plans for extensions of the Chinese train system to 2020*
Source: Neiberger 2009

for long-haul destinations. Tourism organizations have also expressed concern that avia-
tion-focused mitigation policies in wealthy nations that are the major international tourism outbound markets, will negatively affect tourism development and wealth transfers
to tourism-dependent developing nations. While this is debatable (see e.g. Gössling *et al.*
2008), there is undoubtedly a need for destinations to plan for low-carbon futures, including engagement in emission audits, definition of mitigation needs, and identification of
decarbonization strategies.

As the situation of developing countries is of particular importance in this context (e.g. Hall
et al. 2009), the situation of destinations is illustrated in the following based on the example of the Caribbean, one of the most tourism-dependent regions in the world. Caribbean
states have frequently outlined that their contribution to global emissions of GHG is minor,
and tourism organizations have demanded that the islands should not be 'penalized' by the
industrialized countries' ambitions to curb emissions (e.g. Caribbean Hotel and Tourism
Association 2007). This claim would be justified by statistics showing that the Caribbean
accounts for 0.2 per cent of global emissions of CO_2, even though its population of 40
million (Dulal *et al.* 2009) corresponds to 0.6 per cent of the world's population. A more
detailed analysis reveals, however, that in many Caribbean countries, and in particular
those that have developed their tourism systems, per capita emissions are already exceeding levels that can be considered sustainable at the global level.

Countries such as Aruba (21 t CO_2 per capita/year), Antigua and Barbuda (5 t CO_2 per capita/year), or the Bahamas (6 t CO_2 per capita/year) (UNSD 2009) all have per capita emission levels that are close to, or even exceed, those in developed countries, and many exceed the current global average of about 4.2 t CO_2 per capita per year (IPCC 2007b). If the Caribbean's contribution to global emissions of CO_2 is currently still comparably low on a regional basis, this is largely because of populous islands such as Cuba and Haiti and their comparatively low per capita emission levels. If all Caribbean countries had emission levels such as the Bahamas, the region would considerably exceed its emission share to population ratio, i.e. turn into an 'above average' contributor to climate change (Hall *et al.* 2009). Notably, given global emission reduction targets, this would imply emission cuts even in countries like Aruba, Trinidad & Tobago, Bahamas, Cayman Islands or Antigua and Barbuda, all of which exceed global average per capita emissions (Figure 13.2).

Many islands in the Caribbean seek to further develop their tourism systems by increasing arrival numbers, and there is evidence that some of the countries with already the most well-developed tourism systems are also the most eager to grow further. Notably, a considerable share of national fuel imports can already now be linked to tourism (cf. Gössling *et al.* 2008; Hall 2010), and a growing tourism system will thus mean growing emissions from these countries. Table 13.2 illustrates this for a sample of island states, showing that each arrival will increase emissions by in between 0.635 t CO_2 and 1.873 t CO_2, of which half, on a bunker fuel allocation basis, would be associated with the host country (cf. Hall *et al.* 2009; see also Daley 2009).

In summary, it appears likely that further growth in the Caribbean or other island nations dependent on long-haul incoming tourism would be in conflict with global climate policy

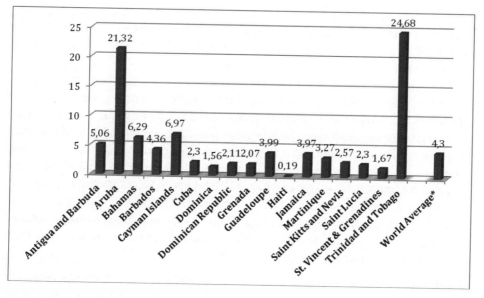

Figure 13.2 *Per capita emissions in Caribbean islands*
Source: Hall *et al.* 2009

Table 13.2 *Energy characteristics of island tourism, 2005*

Country	Av. Weighted emissions per tourist, air travel (return flight; kg CO_2) [1]	Intern. tourist arrivals (2005)*	Total emissions, air travel (1,000t CO_2)	Emissions per tourist, main market (return flight; kg CO_2) Percentage: share of total arrivals [1]
Anguilla	750	62,084	47	672 (USA; 67%)
Bonaire	1,302	62,550	81	803 (USA; 41%)
Comoros	1,734	**17,603	31	1,929 (France; 54%)
Cuba	1,344	2,319,334	3,117	556 (Canada; 26%)
Jamaica	635	1,478,663	939	635 (USA: 72%)
Madagascar	1,829	277,422	507	2,159 (France; 52%)
Saint Lucia	1,076	317,939	342	811(USA; 35%)
Samoa	658	101,807	67	824 (New Zealand; 36%)
Seychelles	1,873	128,654	241	1,935(France; 21%)
Sri Lanka	1,327	549,309	729	606 (India; 21%)

* UNWTO 2007 b,c; **2004
Source: Gössling et al. 2008
1) Calculation of emissions is based on the main national markets only, using a main airport to main airport approach (in the USA: New York; Canada: Toronto; Australia: Brisbane).

(cf. Gössling *et al.* 2008). Nevertheless, destinations can engage in 'carbon smart' tourism market restructuring to reduce the emissions intensity of tourism and market risk to climate policy changes. To this end, a simple indicator is the arrival to emission ratio, based on a comparison of the percentage of arrivals from one market to the emissions caused by this market. For instance, as shown in table 13.3, tourists from the USA account for 67 per cent of arrivals in Anguilla, but cause only 55 per cent of overall emissions. The resultant ratio is 0.82 (55 per cent divided by 67 per cent). The lower the ratio, the better this market is for the destination, with ratios <1 indicating that the market is causing lower emissions per tourist than the average tourist (and vice versa). Arrivals from source markets with a ratio <1 should thus be increased in comparison to the overall composition of the market in order to decrease emissions, while arrivals from markets with a ratio >1 should ideally decline. In the case of Anguilla, the replacement of a tourist with a ratio >1 in favour of one tourist from the USA (ratio: 0.82) would thus, from a GHG emissions point of view, be beneficial. However, as arrivals from the USA already dominate overall arrivals, it might be relevant to also discuss the diversity of markets. Ideally, this is also combined with expenditure data to calculate eco-efficiencies, as well as a leakage factor, i.e. the share of money actually staying within the economy (Gössling *et al.* 2008).

Notably, such a focus on energy issues by destinations is also relevant from an oil-dependency viewpoint. For instance, Miller *et al.* (2008: 273) remark that 'one of the great-est sources of economic leakage for Cuba, like most of its smaller Caribbean competitors,

Table **13.3** *Market structure and emissions ratio*

Emissions ratio[1]	Anguilla	Comorosc	Cuba	Jamaica	Madagascar	Saint Lucia	Samoa	Seychelles
1. market	USA 0.8	France 1.4	Canada 0.4	USA 0.8	France 1.2	USA 0.9	New Z. 0.7	France 1.2
2. market	UK 2.5	Reun. 0.3	UK 1.8	—	Reunion 0.1	UK 2.0	A. Samoa 0.1	Italy 1.0
3. market	—	—	Spain 1.9	—	Italy 1.0	Barbados 0.1	Austral. 1.1	Germany 1.2
4. market	—	—	Italy 2.1	—	—	Canada 1.0	—	UK 1.2
5. market	—	—	France 2.0	—	—	—	—	—
6. market	—	—	Germany 2.6	—	—	—	—	—

The table includes only markets with shares of at least 5% of total tourist arrivals. 1) the arrivals/emission ratio is a measure of the share of tourists from one market compared to these tourists' share in overall emissions.

Source: Gössling et al. (2008)

remains energy', and there are lessons to be learned from the energy crises in the 1970s. Wilkinson's (2003: 92) account of St Lucia's situation in the 1970s is one such example:

> Just as tourism was becoming a central feature in the economy, the ... 'energy crisis' in 1973 ... resulted in disruption of all sectors of the economy, rapid inflation and a growing balance of payments problem. ... In 1979, ... growth was again curtailed by world recession, rapid inflation, rising energy costs and the closing of several industries. ... The problem was exacerbated by Hurricane Allen in August 1980 which severely damaged several hotels, some of which were not fully operational for over a year. ... Despite the serious curtailment of foreign income for nearly a year, the energy import bill continued to rise. There were delays in shipments of gasoline, diesel fuel and propane, causing gasoline shortages, electricity outages and cold water in hotels – and increased deforestation resulting from increased local demand for wood and charcoal, as petroleum-based energy prices rose ...

Overall, it is essential for destination planners to understand that absolute emission reductions in tourism can only be achieved if there are considerable changes in the aviation sector, i.e. a reduction in long-haul travel (Scott *et al.* 2010). This insight is equally relevant for all countries: as the example of the Caribbean shows, as there might be a false understanding that there is room to expand in emissions in line with the CBDR principle. Many countries in the Caribbean, and often the ones that most aggressively pursue a growth strategy, have little room to further grow in per capita emissions. For insights regarding strategies to decarbonize tourism systems, see also South West England (Carbon Management in Focus 27).

On a more regional level, destination planning can also focus on innovative approaches. For instance, Ghent in Belgium declared Thursdays to be meat-free days. 'Meatless Day' (Veggiedag in Flemish) received global media attention, thus representing a major marketing campaign. The day, a voluntary event, has the goal of reducing GHGs related to the consumption of meat. According to the website Veggiedag (2010), cities including São Paulo (Brazil) and Bremen (Germany) have also introduced Meatless Thursdays.

RESEARCH

On the most basic level, research is needed to assess the economic and sociocultural consequences of mitigation for tourism on global, national, regional and local scales, and with regard to the various stakeholders involved. As outlined in various studies, radical shifts in T&T are required to change the global tourism system in a way consistent with emission reduction demands (Peeters and Dubois 2010a), with the consequence that tourism stakeholders have to prepare for a fundamentally changing tourism economy (Scott *et al.* 2010). Research can facilitate this restructuring process. In this book, several areas were identified with a notable lack of research.

First, there is, among the case studies, a notable absence of examples from continents including North and Latin America, Africa and Asia, with most of the change towards low-carbon tourism currently taking place in Europe. This might be partially explained by the fact that Europe is a carbon-intense region hoping to enter another boom and bust economic cycle through its focus on developing a green, low-carbon economy.

There is also a population aware of environmental issues in Europe, looking beyond the rhetoric of climate sceptics and large corporations. Further research into the perceptions and understanding of climate change and climate change mitigation, the identification of best practices approaches to mitigation, and the challenges of low-carbon tourism for these countries should thus be explored in particular for Asia and India, i.e. the regions that will dominate world tourism in the medium-term future (cf. Mayor and Tol 2010a).

Second, the review of the literature has revealed that most studies of changing transport systems have focused on industrialized countries, discussing, for instance, how politics should be designed to reduce air travel, foster purchases of fuel-efficient cars, achieve modal shift, or create preconditions for low-carbon transport systems more generally. There is a notable absence of research, however, with regard to the developments in India, China and other countries, where largely sustainable transport systems have existed for long periods of time, which are now subsequently transformed in favour of individual motorized transport by car and mass participation in air travel. Paradoxically, China and India might thus be engaged in converting the very transport systems urban planners seek to establish in European cities, i.e. systems with high shares of bicycle traffic and efficient public transport systems. Yet, rickshaw services are being made more difficult in Indian cities (Burke 2010) while pre-financial crisis aviation growth rates of 33 per cent per annum have been recorded in this country (Vasedua 2008). In both India and China, the bicycle has now become a dangerous transport mode from both traffic safety and air pollution viewpoints. Research needs to address these developments.

Finally, the psychology of tourism consumption is a research area that has remained little addressed. Many studies have discussed when and why people travel, but few appear to have looked beyond the proximate reasons for travel, such as seeking sun, relaxation or maintaining social relations. It becomes increasing clear, however, that important social and psychological functions are associated with travel, including social status (Randles and Bows 2009; Gössling and Nilsson 2010). More research is thus needed to understand sociocultural and psychological drivers of the 'consumption of distance'.

14 Planning for change, exploring innovation

The chapters in this book have outlined the considerable climate change mitigation challenges ahead, which perhaps becomes most obvious when expressed as the annual rate at which GHG emissions have to be reduced globally to keep climate change at a level not risking 'dangerous interference with the climate system', i.e. 3 per cent per year, notably corresponding to efficiency gains of at least twice this rate given observed growth rates in tourism-related emissions (cf. IPCC 2007b; Anderson and Bows 2008; UNWTO-UNEP-WMO 2008). Furthermore, this 3 per cent is the rate if emissions peak in the very near future: the challenge becomes significantly greater should emissions peak by 2020 or later. As various authors have outlined, a 3 per cent per year cut in emissions is already a very ambitious goal, and is not likely to leave room for any economic sector not to make a contribution to this target.

However, global tourism stakeholders such as WTTC (2009) have outlined that they are willing to commit the tourism system to emission cuts equal to those in other economic sectors. This, again, means that a considerable restructuring of the sector is necessary, particularly with regard to transport and aviation. As Peeters and Dubois (2010: 455) have outlined: 'without radical shifts [in travel patterns], it seems impossible to find a future tourist travel system consistent with the strong CO_2 emission reductions required to avoid dangerous climate change'. In the light of the findings presented in this book, 'radical' would refer to all dimensions of the tourism system, including such major changes as the development of high-speed train systems connecting countries and continents; the abolition of national tourist offices and marketing efforts in other continents; social marketing of closer destinations in travel media, rather than advertising and promoting long-haul destinations; as well as the abolition of frequent-flyer programmes and low-cost travel.

While this will appear like a major threat for global tourism, it is, rather, about restructuring the tourism system to accommodate the travel aspirations of a growing number of humans in a contracting carbon economy. Notably, this could have advantages from many viewpoints, including the ethics of climate change, i.e. the growing number of humans to suffer or die from global warming every year; the vulnerability of the global tourism industry to climate change; energy scarcity leading to rising energy costs as an increasingly important factor in operational costs; emerging climate policy frameworks seeking to curb GHG emissions, also leading to growing operational costs; growing public awareness of climate change and expectations on businesses to engage in mitigation; and the importance of an understanding of climate change and its consequences for longer-term strategic planning. The most important argument arising out of the findings of this book, however, is that virtually all tourism businesses appear to waste significant amounts of energy and that measures to increase their energy efficiency would directly lead to significant savings. Finally, a point could be made about the profitability of some tourism sectors, and in particular aviation, where it does not seem economically meaningful that ever-declining profit margins are compensated for with volume growth in passenger numbers. Here, stakeholders need to develop new perspectives on how financial resources can either contribute to stimulate sustainable economic growth, or the wasting of finite resources.

Carbon management is about strategic approaches to emission reductions in tourism, both to be efficient in identifying economic savings potentials and to maintain the sector's credibility in mitigation efforts. As discussed by Scott *et al.* (2010), 'aspirational' goals as formulated by supra-national tourism organizations are in line with recommendations by the IPCC, but highly unlikely to be achieved. In particular, there is a lack of detailed plans or strategies of how declining emission pathways could be credibly achieved, and even supposedly 'scientific' assessments (e.g. Lawrence 2009) fail to provide any kind of model convincingly showing how absolute emission reductions can be achieved. Likewise, in international politics arenas, the role of tourism, including aviation, is at best discussed in side-events, as for instance during the last COP in Copenhagen in December 2010. Scott and Becken (2010: in press) comment:

> So, what do the outcomes of Copenhagen really mean for tourism? It depends on your perspective and whether you choose to see the glass half empty or half full. Geoffrey Lipman (Vision on Sustainable Travel 2009) from UNWTO is optimistic, pointing out that the Copenhagen Accord achieved the creation of a framework that contains critical lines relating to global temperature stabilisation, carbon reduction levels, verification aspirations, an agreement in principle to develop a mechanism for technology transfer and the Copenhagen Green Climate Fund for the poorest States. While Lipman's piece succeeds to spread optimism, his introduction of the newly (and UNWTO endorsed) launched campaign 'Live the Deal' as a key vehicle to achieve needed change in the tourism sector leaves the reader wondering about the actual mechanisms of the campaign.

The lack of a measurable, credible commitment by the global tourism industry is lamentable, but stakeholders do not need to wait for supranational organizations to provide frameworks – the evidence is in favour of independent action, irrespective of what other stakeholders might or might not do. To achieve emission reductions it has been suggested to follow the general guidelines of eliminating, reducing, substituting and offsetting, as outlined by UNEP-Oxford University-UNWTO-WMO (2008). This book has added a number of strategic dimensions on the systemic level, i.e. the need to redirect tourism flows from distant to closer markets/destinations; to move tourists with low-energy transport modes, rather than high-energy ones; to increase average length of stay and to reverse the current trend towards shorter holidays; to engage tourists in low-carbon spending rather than high-carbon spending; and to move towards higher profits in tourism more generally and in aviation in particular. Again, these systemic changes could be realized through technology change and technological innovation; changes in management practices; education; behavioural change; climate change policy or research. Notably, these dimensions are primarily of relevance to companies, who could also, through their choices of supply-chain partners as well as their influence on consumer choices, achieve emission reductions.

Aspen Skiing Company (Carbon Management in Focus 7) is an example of a tourism stakeholder that has not only improved its operations through the choice of supply-chain partners with green credentials, but has also exerted great pressure on companies refusing to comply with such standards. Many lessons can be learned from innovators such as Aspen Skiing Company:

> Meanwhile, after six years of using clean, renewable biodiesel in our snowcats, federal diesel standards changed, meaning the pollution reduction from biodiesel was negated. Simultaneously, concerns have arisen about the use of food crops to create fuel when people are starving, even in America. As a result, we discontinued the use of biodiesel in the fall of 2008. All this makes people – internally and externally – wonder if we know what we're doing. The short story is this: pursuing sustainability is dynamic, and we're learning as we go. We'll never continue to spend money on something that doesn't have environmental value, just for the image. Time is too short, and the problems too great. So bear with us. Think of the field of sustainability as a teenager: messy, unpredictable, but learning quickly and growing every day.
>
> (Auden Schendler, Executive Director of Sustainability, in ASC 2010: 15)

This touches upon a key challenge in carbon management, the need to implement change swiftly, and to identify role models. As this book has shown, there are now many businesses that can serve as highly innovative leaders in low-carbon tourism, showing that carbon management is feasible for virtually all businesses. Yet, despite considerable achievements in emission reductions by some businesses, emissions have risen steeply on a global level, and more stakeholders have to be involved quickly. It would follow that carbon management has to address two crucial dimensions: (1) the barriers that have to be overcome to involve a greater number of actors rapidly, ultimately demanding better knowledge, understanding and awareness of climate change and its consequences among tourism stakeholders and tourists alike, and (2) the distribution of practical knowledge of how to restructure the tourism system and retrofit businesses, as well as to involve employees, supply-chain partners and tourists in change. To this end, the book suggests a development in line with three steps:

1 KNOWLEDGE AND AWARENESS

Various mechanisms have been identified in this book that prevent individuals, organizations, companies, and politicians from being more climatically proactive. On the most fundamental level, this concerns issues such as the ubiquitous focus on volume growth, neoliberal perspectives on economic systems, belief in technological fixes, lack of knowledge of climate change, and unwillingness to change habitual behaviour. Tourism organizations on global, national, regional and local levels all have to play a role in generating a better understanding of climate change and the distribution of practical advice to engage in mitigation. Evidence presented in this book from Dehoga (Carbon Management in Focus 13) and South West England (Carbon Management in Focus 27) shows that pro-climate action on a voluntary basis is promising, but that involving a significant share of stakeholders will demand regulatory approaches as well.

2 MOTIVATION AND ENGAGEMENT ROOTED IN ECONOMICS

One of the most important findings of this book is that climate change mitigation can be profitable for businesses, with rewards in cost avoidance, employee and customer loyalty, and positive media attention, or industry awards. Emission reductions of 10–20 per cent can be achieved at no cost, with payback times <5 years. On the business level, this should enable tourism stakeholders to decarbonize in line with the EU's emission reduction target of 25 per cent by 2020. This scenario is likely to be cost-neutral for most actors if payback times for investments in low-carbon technology of up to 10 years are accepted, and possibly faster if energy prices increase. Aviation is a notable exception to this rule, however, and new business models have to be developed for this sector.

3 IMPLEMENTATION

Any company, organization or destination seeking to engage in carbon management needs to understand the size and structure of its emissions. A carbon audit should thus be the first step towards an understanding of emissions by company sub-sector. Based on this profile, businesses can move on to implement specific measures to reduce emissions, with a view to primarily targeting major emission sources. Often this can include various dimensions of carbon management. Tour operators, for instance, can decarbonize by carbon-labelling their packages or travel offers to help customers make pro-environmental choices. Changes in the packaging and pricing of products as well as social marketing can reinforce these choices. Changing the destination portfolio and transport modes offered could provide a framework for these changes.

However, even if every single tourism company in the world engaged in climate change mitigation, it will remain unlikely that absolute emission reductions in tourism can be achieved. This is because of the rapid growth in global tourism and, in particular, air travel. To achieve absolute emission reductions in global emissions is thus dependent on policy intervention, focusing on air transport, cruise ships and cars. With regard to aviation and cruise ships, closed ETSs might be the only viable option to reduce emissions in the short-term future, as renegotiations of bilateral agreements on tax exemptions in aviation will be difficult to achieve. For shipping, taxes proportional to emissions might, however, be an option. Cars can be taxed according to their fuel use, and bonus/malus systems could be introduced to provide incentives for low-emission cars.

Implementing these measures will lead to fundamental changes in the global tourism system, which should be anticipated by industry, national tourism organizations and communities with tourism-dependent economies. Specifically, new regulatory and taxation regimes will increase air transport costs and, to some extent, car usage costs, and thus initiate shifts between transport modes and destination choices. Long-haul destinations are likely to be particularly affected and need to rethink their tourism development strategies, particularly if these involve continued volume growth in tourism from distant markets. More generally, the profitability of energy-intense forms of tourism (long-haul air transport-based, some forms of high energy-using accommodation, cruises) will decline and the profitability of low-carbon forms of tourism (rail- or coach-based, short- to medium-haul, longer stays, domestic, low-carbon accommodation) will improve. Adaptation to climate policy and concomitant changes in transport systems is thus vital for destinations, also calling for new business models. For instance, if airlines came to understand themselves as transport service providers, they could get involved in alternative transport systems as well. Domestic air travel has declined in many countries with the establishment of high-speed rail connections. Airlines can anticipate these changes and become involved in developing such systems, rather than seeking to prevent them.

The result of such changes would be a fundamentally altered global tourism economy, focusing on longer stays, shorter travel distances, the greater use of trains and coaches, and tourism consumption with better eco-efficiency and higher profit margins more generally. This means no less than a major departure from business-as-usual tourism development models, which probably needs to go along with a number of radical changes, such as the abolition of frequent-flyer programmes, travel pages in newspapers marketing long-haul destinations, or national tourist offices in long-haul markets.

Much of the tourism community appears to remain unaware of the implications of the proposed emission reduction targets for the sector and the consequences of the transition toward a low-carbon tourism system. As outlined by Scott *et al.* (2010), proactive restructuring by design will be more advantageous for long-term tourism development than reactive restructuring forced by potentially rapid changes in transportation cost structures and attendant diminished access to destinations that are highly dependent on the tourism economy.

Glossary

Common but differentiated responsibility UNFCCC adopts a principle of 'common but differentiated responsibilities'. The parties agreed that: the largest share of historical and current global emissions of GHGs originated in developed countries; per capita emissions in developing countries are still relatively low; the share of global emissions originating in developing countries will grow to meet social and development needs.

Abrupt climate change The nonlinearity of the climate system might lead to abrupt climate change, sometimes called *rapid climate change, abrupt events* or even *surprises*. The term *abrupt* often refers to time scales faster than the typical time scale of the responsible forcing. However, not all abrupt climate changes need be externally forced. Some possible abrupt events that have been proposed include a dramatic reorganization of the thermohaline circulation, rapid deglaciation and massive melting of permafrost or increases in soil respiration leading to fast changes in the carbon cycle. Others could be truly unexpected, resulting from a strong, rapidly changing, forcing of a non-linear system.

Activities Implemented Jointly (AIJ) The pilot phase for Joint Implementation, as defined in Article 4.2(a) of the UNFCCC that allows for project activity among developed countries (and their companies) and between developed and developing countries (and their companies). AIJ is intended to allow parties to the UNFCCC to gain experience in jointly implemented projects. There is no credit for AIJ during the pilot phase. A decision remains to be made on the future of AIJ projects and how they might relate to the Kyoto Mechanisms. As a simple form of tradable permits, AIJ and other market-based schemes represent potential mechanisms for stimulating additional resource flows for reducing emissions. See also Clean Development Mechanism, and Emissions Trading.

Adaptation Initiatives and measures to reduce the vulnerability of natural and human systems against actual or expected climate change effects. Various types of adaptation exist, e.g. *anticipatory* and *reactive*, *private* and *public*, and *autonomous* and *planned*. Examples are raising river or coastal dykes, the substitution of more temperature-shock resistant plants in place of sensitive ones, etc.

Adaptive capacity The whole selection of capabilities, resources and institutions a country or region has to implement effective adaptation measures.

Aerosols   A collection of airborne solid or liquid particles, with a typical size between 0.01 and 10 micrometres (a millionth of a metre) that reside in the atmosphere for at least several hours. Aerosols can be of either natural or anthropogenic origin. Aerosols can influence climate in several ways: directly through scattering and absorbing radiation, and indirectly through acting as cloud condensation nuclei or modifying the optical properties and lifetime of clouds.

Afforestation   Planting of new forests on lands that historically have not contained forests (for at least 50 years).

Aggregate impacts   Total impacts integrated across sectors and/or regions. The aggregation of impacts requires knowledge of (or assumptions about) the relative importance of impacts in different sectors and regions. Measures of aggregate impacts include, for example, the total number of people affected, or the total economic costs.

Albedo   The fraction of solar radiation reflected by a surface or object, often expressed as a percentage. Snow-covered surfaces have a high albedo, the surface albedo of soils ranges from high to low, and vegetation-covered surfaces and oceans have a low albedo. The Earth's planetary albedo varies mainly through varying cloudiness, snow, ice, leaf area and land cover changes.

Annex I countries   The group of countries included in Annex I (as amended in 1998) to the UNFCCC, including all the OECD countries in the year 1990 and countries with economies in transition. Under Articles 4.2 (a) and 4.2 (b) of the Convention, Annex I countries committed themselves specifically to the aim of returning individually or jointly to their 1990 levels of GHG emissions by the year 2000. By default, the other countries are referred to as *non-Annex I countries*. For a list of Annex I countries, see http://unfccc.int.

Annex II countries   The group of countries included in Annex II to the UNFCCC, including all OECD countries in the year 1990. Under Article 4.2 (g) of the Convention, these countries are expected to provide financial resources to assist developing countries to comply with their obligations, such as preparing national reports. Annex II countries are also expected to promote the transfer of environmentally sound technologies to developing countries. For a list of Annex II countries, see http://unfccc.int.

Annex B countries   The countries included in Annex B to the Kyoto Protocol that have agreed to a target for their GHG emissions, including all the Annex I countries (as amended in 1998) except for Turkey and Belarus. For a list of Annex I countries, see http://unfccc.int.

Anthropogenic emissions   Emissions of GHGs, GHG precursors and aerosols associated with human activities, including the burning of fossil fuels, deforestation, land-use changes, livestock, fertilizers, etc.

Atmosphere   The gaseous envelope surrounding the Earth. The dry atmosphere consists almost entirely of nitrogen (78.1 per cent volume mixing ratio) and oxygen (20.9 per cent volume mixing ratio), together with a number of trace gases, such as argon (0.93 per cent volume mixing ratio), helium and radiatively active GHGs such as carbon dioxide (0.035 per cent volume mixing ratio) and ozone. In addition, the atmosphere contains the GHG water vapour, whose amounts are highly variable but typically around 1 per cent volume mixing ratio. The atmosphere also contains clouds and aerosols.

Barrier   Any obstacle to reaching a goal, adaptation or mitigation potential that can be overcome or attenuated by a policy, programme, or measure. *Barrier removal* includes correcting market failures directly or reducing the transaction costs in the public and private sectors by e.g. improving institutional capacity, reducing risk and uncertainty, facilitating market transactions, and enforcing regulatory policies.

Baseline   Reference for measurable quantities from which an alternative outcome can be measured, e.g. a non-intervention scenario used as a reference in the analysis of intervention scenarios.

Biofuel   A fuel produced from organic matter or combustible oils produced by plants. Examples of biofuel include alcohol, black liquor from the paper-manufacturing process, wood and soybean oil.

Biomass   The total mass of living organisms in a given area or volume; recently dead plant material is often included as dead biomass. The quantity of biomass is expressed as a dry weight or as the energy, carbon or nitrogen content.

Bottom-up models   Bottom-up models represent reality by aggregating characteristics of specific activities and processes, considering technological, engineering and cost details. See also Top-down models.

Carbon dioxide (CO_2)   A naturally occurring gas, also a by-product of burning fossil fuels from fossil carbon deposits, such as oil, gas and coal, of burning biomass, and of land-use changes and other industrial processes. It is the principal anthropogenic GHG that affects the Earth's radiative balance. It is the reference gas against which other GHGs are measured and therefore has a Global Warming Potential of 1.

Carbon (dioxide) Capture and Storage (CCS)   A process consisting of separation of carbon dioxide from industrial and energy-related sources, transport to a storage location, and long-term isolation from the atmosphere.

Carbon leakage   The part of emissions reductions in Annex B countries that may be offset by an increase of the emissions in the non-constrained countries above their baseline levels. This can occur through (1) relocation of energy-intensive production in non-constrained regions; (2) increased consumption of fossil fuels in these regions through decline in the international price of oil and gas triggered by lower demand for these energies; and (3) changes in incomes (thus in energy demand) because of better terms of trade.

Clean Development Mechanism (CDM)   Defined in Article 12 of the Kyoto Protocol, the CDM is intended to meet two objectives: (1) to assist parties not included in Annex I in achieving sustainable development and in contributing to the ultimate objective of the convention; and (2) to assist parties included in Annex I in achieving compliance with their quantified emission limitation and reduction commitments. CERUs from CDM projects undertaken in non-Annex I countries that limit or reduce GHG emissions, when certified by operational entities designated by COP/Meeting of the Parties, can be accrued to the investor (government or industry) from parties in Annex B. A share of the proceeds from the certified project activities is used to cover administrative expenses as well as to assist developing country parties that are particularly vulnerable to the adverse effects of climate change to meet the costs of adaptation.

Climate   Climate in a narrow sense is usually defined as the average weather, or more rigorously, as the statistical description in terms of the mean and variability of relevant quantities over a period of time ranging from months to thousands or millions of years. The classical period for averaging these variables is 30 years, as defined by the WMO. The relevant quantities are most often surface variables such as temperature, precipitation and wind. Climate in a wider sense is the state, including a statistical description, of the climate system. In various parts of this report different averaging periods, such as a period of 20 years, are also used.

Climate change   Climate change refers to a change in the state of the climate that can be identified (e.g. by using statistical tests) by changes in the mean and/or the variability of its properties, and that persists for an extended period, typically decades or longer. Climate change might be due to natural internal processes or external forcings, or to persistent anthropogenic changes in the composition of the atmosphere or in land use. Note that the UNFCCC, in its Article 1, defines climate change as: 'a change of climate which is attributed directly or indirectly to human activity that alters the composition of the global atmosphere and which is in addition to natural climate variability observed over comparable time periods'. The UNFCCC thus makes a distinction between climate change attributable to human activities altering the atmospheric composition, and climate variability attributable to natural causes. See also Climate variability; Detection and Attribution.

Climate feedback   An interaction mechanism between processes in the climate system is called a climate feedback when the result of an initial process triggers changes in a second process that in turn influences the initial one. A positive feedback intensifies the original process, and a negative feedback reduces it.

Climate model   A numerical representation of the climate system based on the physical, chemical and biological properties of its components, their interactions and feedback processes, and accounting for all or some of its known properties. The climate system can be represented by models of varying complexity, that is, for any one component or combination of components a spectrum or hierarchy of models can be identified, differing in such aspects as the number of spatial dimensions, the extent to which physical, chemical or biological processes are explicitly represented, or the level at which empirical parameterizations are involved. *Coupled Atmosphere-Ocean General Circulation Models (AOGCMs)* provide a representation of the climate system that is near the most comprehensive end of the spectrum currently available. There is an evolution towards more complex models with interactive chemistry and biology. Climate models are applied as a research tool to study and simulate the climate, and for operational purposes, including monthly, seasonal and interannual climate *predictions*.

Climate scenario   A plausible and often simplified representation of the future climate, based on an internally consistent set of climatological relationships that has been constructed for explicit use in investigating the potential consequences of anthropogenic climate change, often serving as input to impact models. Climate projections often serve as the raw material for constructing climate scenarios, but climate scenarios usually require additional information about, for instance, the observed current climate. A *climate change scenario* is the difference between a climate scenario and the current climate.

Climate system The climate system is the highly complex system consisting of five major components – the atmosphere, the hydrosphere, the cryosphere, the land surface and the biosphere – and the interactions between them. The climate system evolves in time under the influence of its own internal dynamics and because of external forcings such as volcanic eruptions, solar variations and anthropogenic forcings such as the changing composition of the atmosphere and land-use change.

Climate variability Climate variability refers to variations in the mean state and other statistics (such as standard deviations, the occurrence of extremes, etc.) of the climate on all spatial and temporal scales beyond that of individual weather events. Variability might be due to natural internal processes within the climate system (*internal variability*), or to variations in natural or anthropogenic external forcing (*external variability*). See also Climate change.

Compliance Compliance is whether, and to what extent, countries do adhere to the provisions of an accord. Compliance depends on implementing policies ordered, and on whether measures follow up the policies. Compliance is the degree to which the actors whose behaviour is targeted by the agreement, local government units, corporations, organizations, or individuals, conform to the implementing obligations. See also Implementation.

Confidence The level of confidence in the correctness of a result is expressed in this report, using a standard terminology defined as follows:

Terminology	Degree of confidence in being correct
Very high confidence	At least 9 out of 10 chance of being correct
High confidence	About 8 out of 10 chance
Medium confidence	About 5 out of 10 chance
Low confidence	About 2 out of 10 chance
Very low confidence	Less than 1 out of 10 chance

See also Likelihood; Uncertainty

Cost The consumption of resources such as labour time, capital, materials, fuels, etc. as a consequence of an action. In economics all resources are valued at their *opportunity cost*, being the value of the most valuable alternative use of the resources. Costs are defined in a variety of ways and under a variety of assumptions that affect their value. Cost types include: *administrative costs*, *damage costs* (to ecosystems, people and economies due to negative effects from climate change), and *implementation costs* of changing existing rules and regulations, capacity-building efforts, information, training and education, etc. *Private costs* are carried by individuals, companies or other private entities that undertake the action, whereas *social costs* include also the external costs on the environment and on society as a whole. The reverse of costs are *benefits* (also sometimes called *negative costs*). Costs minus benefits are *net costs*.

Deforestation   Conversion of forest to non-forest.

Development path or pathway   An evolution based on an array of technological, economic, social, institutional, cultural, and biophysical characteristics that determine the interactions between natural and human systems, including production and consumption patterns in all countries, over time at a particular scale. *Alternative development paths* refer to different possible trajectories of development, the continuation of current trends being just one of the many paths.

Ecosystem   A system of living organisms interacting with each other and their physical environment. The boundaries of what could be called an ecosystem are somewhat arbitrary, depending on the focus of interest or study. Thus, the extent of an ecosystem can range from very small spatial scales to, ultimately, the entire Earth.

El Niño-Southern Oscillation (ENSO)   The term *El Niño* was initially used to describe a warm-water current that periodically flows along the coast of Ecuador and Peru, disrupting the local fishing. It has since become identified with a basin-wide warming of the tropical Pacific east of the dateline. This oceanic event is associated with a fluctuation of a global-scale tropical and sub-tropical surface pressure pattern called the *Southern Oscillation*. This coupled atmosphere–ocean phenomenon, with preferred time scales of two to about seven years, is collectively known as *El Niño-Southern Oscillation*, or *ENSO*. It is often measured by the surface pressure anomaly difference between Darwin and Tahiti and the sea surface temperatures in the central and eastern equatorial Pacific. During an ENSO event, the prevailing trade winds weaken, reducing upwelling and altering ocean currents such that the sea surface temperatures warm, further weakening the trade winds. This event has a great impact on the wind, sea surface temperature and precipitation patterns in the tropical Pacific. It has climatic effects throughout the Pacific region and in many other parts of the world, through global teleconnections. The cold phase of ENSO is called *La Niña*.

Emission scenario   A plausible representation of the future development of emissions of substances that are potentially radiatively active (e.g. GHGs, aerosols), based on a coherent and internally consistent set of assumptions about driving forces (such as demographic and socioeconomic development, technological change) and their key relationships. *Concentration scenarios*, derived from emission scenarios, are used as input to a climate model to compute climate projections. In 1992 the IPCC presented a set of emission scenarios which were used as a basis for their climate projections in 1996. These emission scenarios are referred to as the *IS92 scenarios*. In the IPCC Special Report on Emission Scenarios new emission scenarios, the so-called SRES scenarios, were published. For the meaning of some terms related to these scenarios, see SRES scenarios.

Emission(s) trading   A market-based approach to achieving environmental objectives. It allows those reducing GHG emissions below their emission cap to use or trade the excess reductions to offset emissions at another source inside or outside the country. In general, trading can occur at the intra-company, domestic, and international levels. The Second Assessment Report by the IPCC adopted the convention of using permits for domestic trading systems and quotas for international trading systems. Emissions trading under Article 17 of the Kyoto Protocol is a tradable quota system based on the assigned amounts calculated from the emission reduction and limitation commitments listed in Annex B of the Protocol.

Energy   The amount of work or heat delivered. Energy is classified in a variety of types and becomes useful to human ends when it flows from one place to another or is converted from one type into another. *Primary energy* (also referred to as *energy sources*) is the energy embodied in natural resources (e.g. coal, crude oil, natural gas, uranium) that has not undergone any anthropogenic conversion. This primary energy needs to be converted and transported to become *usable energy* (e.g. light). *Renewable energy* is obtained from the continuing or repetitive currents of energy occurring in the natural environment, and includes non-carbon technologies such as solar energy, hydropower, wind, tide and waves, and geothermal heat, as well as carbon-neutral technologies such as biomass. *Embodied energy* is the energy used to produce a material substance (such as processed metals, or building materials), taking into account energy used at the manufacturing facility (zero order), energy used in producing the materials that are used in the manufacturing facility (first order), and so on.

Energy efficiency   Ratio of useful energy output of a system, conversion process or activity, to its energy input.

Energy intensity   Energy intensity is the ratio of energy use to economic or physical output. At the national level, energy intensity is the ratio of total primary energy use or final energy use to Gross Domestic Product. At the activity level, one can also use physical quantities in the denominator, e.g. litre fuel/vehicle km.

Evapotranspiration   The combined process of water evaporation from the Earth's surface and transpiration from vegetation.

External forcing   External forcing refers to a forcing agent outside the climate system causing a change in the climate system. Volcanic eruptions, solar variations and anthropogenic changes in the composition of the atmosphere and land-use change are external forcings.

Extinction   The complete disappearance of an entire biological species.

Extreme weather event   An event that is rare at a particular place and time of year. Definitions of 'rare' vary, but an extreme weather event would normally be as rare as or rarer than the 10th or 90th percentile of the observed probability density function. By definition, the characteristics of what is called *extreme weather* might vary from place to place in an absolute sense. Single extreme events cannot be simply and directly attributed to anthropogenic climate change, as there is always a finite chance the event in question might have occurred naturally. When a pattern of extreme weather persists for some time, such as a season, it can be classed as an *extreme climate event*, especially if it yields an average or total that is itself extreme (e.g. drought or heavy rainfall over a season).

F-gases   This term refers to the groups of gases hydrofluorocarbons, perfluorocarbons, and sulphurhexafluoride, which are covered under the Kyoto Protocol.

Forest   A vegetation type dominated by trees. Many definitions of the term forest are in use throughout the world, reflecting wide differences in biogeophysical conditions, social structure and economics. Particular criteria apply under the Kyoto Protocol.

Fossil fuels   Carbon-based fuels from fossil hydrocarbon deposits, including coal, peat, oil and natural gas.

Global surface temperature   The global surface temperature is an estimate of the global mean surface air temperature. However, for changes over time, only anomalies, as departures from a climatology, are used, most commonly based on the area-weighted global average of the sea surface temperature anomaly and land surface air temperature anomaly.

Global Warming Potential (GWP)   An index, based upon radiative properties of well mixed GHGs, measuring the RF of a unit mass of a given well-mixed GHG in today's atmosphere integrated over a chosen time horizon, relative to that of carbon dioxide. The GWP represents the combined effect of the differing times these gases remain in the atmosphere and their relative effectiveness in absorbing outgoing thermal infrared radiation. The Kyoto Protocol is based on GWPs from pulse emissions over a 100-year time frame.

Greenhouse effect   GHGs effectively absorb thermal infrared radiation, emitted by the Earth's surface, by the atmosphere itself due to the same gases, and by clouds. Atmospheric radiation is emitted to all sides, including downward to the Earth's surface. Thus GHGs trap heat within the surface-troposphere system. This is called the *greenhouse effect*. Thermal infrared radiation in the troposphere is strongly coupled to the temperature of the atmosphere at the altitude at which it is emitted. In the troposphere, the temperature generally decreases with height. Effectively, infrared radiation emitted to space originates from an altitude with a temperature of, on average, $-19\,°C$, in balance with the net incoming solar radiation, whereas the Earth's surface is kept at a much higher temperature of, on average, $+14\,°C$. An increase in the concentration of GHGs leads to an increased infrared opacity of the atmosphere, and therefore to an effective radiation into space from a higher altitude at a lower temperature. This causes an RF that leads to an enhancement of the greenhouse effect, the so-called *enhanced greenhouse effect*.

Greenhouse gas (GHG)   GHGs are those gaseous constituents of the atmosphere, both natural and anthropogenic, that absorb and emit radiation at specific wavelengths within the spectrum of thermal infrared radiation emitted by the Earth's surface, the atmosphere itself, and by clouds. This property causes the greenhouse effect. Water vapour (H_2O), carbon dioxide (CO_2), nitrous oxide (N_2O), methane (CH_4) and ozone (O_3) are the primary GHGs in the Earth's atmosphere. Moreover, there are a number of entirely human-made GHGs in the atmosphere, such as the halocarbons and other chlorine- and bromine-containing substances, dealt with under the Montreal Protocol. Beside CO_2, N_2O and CH_4, the Kyoto Protocol deals with the GHGs sulphur hexafluoride (SF_6), hydrofluorocarbons (HFCs) and perfluorocarbons (PFCs).

Halocarbons   A collective term for the group of partially halogenated organic species, including the chlorofluorocarbons (CFCs), hydrochlorofluorocarbons (HCFCs), hydrofluorocarbons (HFCs), halons, methyl chloride, methyl bromide, etc. Many of the halocarbons have large GWPs. The chlorine- and bromine-containing halocarbons are also involved in the depletion of the ozone layer.

Hydrofluorocarbons (HFCs)   One of the six GHGs or groups of GHGs to be curbed under the Kyoto Protocol. They are produced commercially as a substitute for chlorofluorocarbons. HFCs largely are used in refrigeration and semiconductor manufacturing. See Halocarbons.

(Climate change) Impacts   The effects of climate change on natural and human systems. Depending on the consideration of adaptation, one can distinguish between potential impacts and residual impacts:

- *Potential impacts*: all impacts that may occur given a projected change in climate, without considering adaptation.
- *Residual impacts*: the impacts of climate change that would occur after adaptation.

See also aggregate impacts, market impacts, and non-market impacts.

Implementation   Implementation describes the actions taken to meet commitments under a treaty and encompasses legal and effective phases.

- *Legal implementation* refers to legislation, regulations, judicial decrees, including other actions such as efforts to administer actions which governments take to translate international accords into domestic law and policy.
- *Effective implementation* needs policies and programmes that induce changes in the behaviour and decisions of target groups. Target groups then take effective measures of mitigation and adaptation.

Industrial Revolution   A period of rapid industrial growth with far-reaching social and economic consequences, beginning in Britain during the second half of the eighteenth century and spreading to Europe and later to other countries including the USA. The invention of the steam engine was an important trigger of this development. The Industrial Revolution marks the beginning of a strong increase in the use of fossil fuels and emission of, in particular, fossil carbon dioxide. In this Report the terms *pre-industrial* and *industrial* refer, somewhat arbitrarily, to the periods before and after 1750, respectively.

Integrated assessment   A method of analysis that combines results and models from the physical, biological, economic and social sciences, and the interactions between these components in a consistent framework to evaluate the status and the consequences of environmental change and the policy responses to it. Models used to carry out such analysis are called *Integrated Assessment Models*.

Joint Implementation (JI)   A market-based implementation mechanism defined in Article 6 of the Kyoto Protocol, allowing Annex I countries or companies from these countries to implement projects jointly that limit or reduce emissions or enhance sinks, and to share the ERUs. JI activity is also permitted in Article 4.2(a) of the UNFCCC. See also Kyoto Mechanisms; Activities Implemented Jointly.

Kyoto Mechanisms (also called Flexibility Mechanisms)   Economic mechanisms based on market principles that parties to the Kyoto Protocol can use in an attempt to lessen the potential economic impacts of GHG emission-reduction requirements. They include Joint Implementation (Article 6), Clean Development Mechanism (Article 12), and Emissions Trading (Article 17).

Kyoto Protocol   The Kyoto Protocol to the UNFCCC was adopted in 1997 in Kyoto,

Japan, at the Third Session of the Conference of the Parties (COP) to the UNFCCC. It contains legally binding commitments, in addition to those included in the UNFCCC. Countries included in Annex B of the Protocol (most OECD countries and countries with economies in transition) agreed to reduce their anthropogenic GHG emissions (carbon dioxide, methane, nitrous oxide, hydrofluorocarbons, perfluorocarbons, and sulphur hexafluoride) by at least 5 per cent below 1990 levels in the commitment period 2008 to 2012. The Kyoto Protocol entered into force on 16 February 2005.

Land use and Land-use change   *Land use* refers to the total of arrangements, activities and inputs undertaken in a certain land cover type (a set of human actions). The term *land use* is also used in the sense of the social and economic purposes for which land is managed (e.g. grazing, timber extraction, and conservation).

Land-use change refers to a change in the use or management of land by humans, which might lead to a change in land cover. Land cover and land-use change can have an impact on the surface albedo, evapotranspiration, sources and sinks of GHGs, or other properties of the climate system and might thus have an RF and/or other impact on climate, locally or globally.

Level of Scientific Understanding (LOSU)   This is an index on a 5-step scale (high, medium, medium-low, low and very low) designed to characterize the degree of scientific understanding of the RF agents that affect climate change. For each agent, the index represents a subjective judgement about the evidence for the physical/chemical mechanisms determining the forcing and the consensus surrounding the quantitative estimate and its uncertainty.

Likelihood   The likelihood of an occurrence, an outcome or a result, where this can be estimated probabilistically, is expressed in IPCC reports using a standard terminology defined as follows:

Terminology	Likelihood of the occurrence/outcome
Virtually certain	>99% probability of occurrence
Very likely	>90% probability
Likely	>66% probability
More likely than not	>50% probability
About as likely as not	33 to 66% probability
Unlikely	<33% probability
Very unlikely	<10% probability
Exceptionally unlikely	<1% probability

Methane (CH_4)   Methane is one of the six GHGs to be mitigated under the Kyoto Protocol. It is the major component of natural gas and is associated with all hydrocarbon fuels, animal husbandry and agriculture. *Coal-bed methane* is the gas found in coal seams.

Millennium Development Goals (MDGs)   A set of time-bound and measurable goals for combating poverty, hunger, disease, illiteracy, discrimination against women and environmental degradation, agreed at the UN Millennium Summit in 2000.

Mitigation   Technological change and substitution that reduces resource inputs and emissions per unit of output. Although several social, economic and technological policies would produce an emission reduction, with respect to Climate Change, mitigation means implementing policies to reduce GHG emissions and enhance sinks.

Mitigative capacity   This is a country's ability to reduce anthropogenic GHG emissions or to enhance natural sinks, where ability refers to skills, competencies, fitness and proficiencies that a country has attained, and depends on technology, institutions, wealth, equity, infrastructure and information. Mitigative capacity is rooted in a country's sustainable development path.

Mitigation potential   In the context of climate change mitigation, the mitigation potential is the amount of mitigation that could be – but is not yet – realized over time.

Market potential is the mitigation potential based on private costs and private discount rates, which might be expected to occur under forecast market conditions, including policies and measures currently in place, noting that barriers limit actual uptake. Private costs and discount rates reflect the perspective of private consumers and companies.

Economic potential is the mitigation potential that takes into account social costs and benefits and social discount rates, assuming that market efficiency is improved by policies and measures and barriers are removed. Social costs and discount rates reflect the perspective of society. Social discount rates are lower than those used by private investors.

Studies of market potential can be used to inform policy makers about mitigation potential with existing policies and barriers, while studies of economic potential show what might be achieved if appropriate new and additional policies were put into place to remove barriers and include social costs and benefits. The economic potential is therefore generally greater than the market potential.

Technical potential is the amount by which it is possible to reduce GHG emissions or improve energy efficiency by implementing a technology or practice that has already been demonstrated. No explicit reference to costs is made but adopting 'practical constraints' might take implicit economic considerations into account.

Nitrous oxide (N_2O)   One of the six types of GHG to be curbed under the Kyoto Protocol. The main anthropogenic source of nitrous oxide is agriculture (soil and animal manure management), but important contributions also come from sewage treatment, combustion of fossil fuel, and chemical industrial processes. Nitrous oxide is also produced naturally from a wide variety of biological sources in soil and water, particularly microbial action in wet tropical forests.

Patterns of climate variability   Natural variability of the climate system, in particular on seasonal and longer time scales, predominantly occurs with preferred spatial patterns and time scales, through the dynamical characteristics of the atmospheric circulation and through interactions with the land and ocean surfaces. Such patterns are often called *regimes, modes* or *teleconnections*. Examples are the North Atlantic Oscillation (NAO), the Pacific-North American pattern (PNA), the El Niño-Southern Oscillation (ENSO), the Northern Annular Mode (NAM; previously called Arctic Oscillation, AO) and the Southern Annular Mode (SAM; previously called the Antarctic Oscillation, AAO).

Policies In UNFCCC parlance, policies are taken and/or mandated by a government – often in conjunction with business and industry within its own country, or with other countries – to accelerate mitigation and adaptation measures. Examples of policies are carbon or other energy taxes, fuel efficiency standards for automobiles, etc. *Common and coordinated or harmonized policies* refer to those adopted jointly by parties.

Radiative forcing Radiative forcing (RF) is the change in the net, downward minus upward, irradiance (expressed in watts per square metre, W/m^2) at the tropopause due to a change in an external driver of climate change, such as, for example, a change in the concentration of carbon dioxide or the output of the Sun. RF is computed with all tropospheric properties held fixed at their unperturbed values, and after allowing for stratospheric temperatures, if perturbed, to readjust to radiative-dynamical equilibrium. RF is called *instantaneous* if no change in stratospheric temperature is accounted for. For the purposes of this report, RF is further defined as the change relative to the year 1750 and, unless otherwise noted, refers to a global and annual average value.

Reforestation Planting of forests on lands that have previously contained forests but that have been converted to some other use. For a discussion of the term forest and related terms such as afforestation, reforestation and deforestation, see the IPCC Report on Land Use, Land-Use Change and Forestry.

Resilience The ability of a social or ecological system to absorb disturbances while retaining the same basic structure and ways of functioning, the capacity for self-organization, and the capacity to adapt to stress and change.

Retrofitting Retrofitting means to install new or modified parts or equipment, or undertake structural modifications, to existing infrastructure that were either not available or not considered necessary at the time of construction. The purpose of retrofitting in the context of climate change is generally to ensure that existing infrastructure meets new design specifications that might be required under altered climate conditions.

Scenario A plausible and often simplified description of how the future might develop, based on a coherent and internally consistent set of assumptions about driving forces and key relationships. Scenarios might be derived from projections, but are often based on additional information from other sources, sometimes combined with a *narrative storyline*. See also SRES scenarios; Climate scenario; Emission scenarios.

Sea-level change/sea-level rise Sea level can change, both globally and locally, due to (1) changes in the shape of the ocean basins, (2) changes in the total mass of water and (3) changes in water density. Factors leading to sea level rise under global warming include both increases in the total mass of water from the melting of land-based snow and ice, and changes in water density from an increase in ocean water temperatures and salinity changes. *Relative sea level rise* occurs where there is a local increase in the level of the ocean relative to the land, which might be due to ocean rise and/or land level subsidence.

Sink Any process, activity or mechanism which removes a GHG, an aerosol or a precursor of a GHG or aerosol from the atmosphere.

Solar radiation   Electromagnetic radiation emitted by the sun. It is also referred to as *shortwave radiation*. Solar radiation has a distinctive range of wavelengths (spectrum) determined by the temperature of the sun, peaking in visible wavelengths. See also Thermal infrared radiation; Total Solar Irradiance

Spatial and temporal scales   Climate can vary on a large range of spatial and temporal scales. *Spatial scales* can range from local (less than 100,000 km²), through regional (100,000 to 10 million km²) to continental (10 to 100 million km²). *Temporal scales* can range from seasonal to geological (up to hundreds of millions of years).

SRES scenarios   SRES scenarios are emission scenarios developed as a basis for some of the climate projections used in the Fourth Assessment Report. The following terms are relevant for a better understanding of the structure and use of the set of SRES scenarios:

- *Scenario family*: Scenarios that have a similar demographic, societal, economic and technical-change storyline. Four scenario families comprise the SRES scenario set: A1, A2, B1 and B2.
- *Illustrative scenario*: A scenario that is illustrative for each of the six scenario groups reflected in the Summary for Policymakers. They include four revised 'scenario markers' for the scenario groups A1B, A2, B1, B2, and two additional scenarios for the A1FI and A1T groups. All scenario groups are equally sound.
- *Marker scenario*: A scenario that was originally posted in draft form on the SRES website to represent a given scenario family. The choice of markers was based on which of the initial quantifications best reflected the storyline, and the features of specific models. Markers are no more likely than other scenarios, but are considered by the SRES writing team as illustrative of a particular storyline. These scenarios received the closest scrutiny of the entire writing team and via the SRES open process. Scenarios were also selected to illustrate the other two scenario groups.
- *Storyline*: A narrative description of a scenario (or family of scenarios), highlighting the main scenario characteristics, relationships between key driving forces and the dynamics of their evolution.

Stabilization   Keeping constant the atmospheric concentrations of one or more GHGs (e.g. carbon dioxide) or of a CO_2-equivalent basket of GHGs. Stabilization analyses or scenarios address the stabilization of the concentration of GHGs in the atmosphere.

Stakeholder   A person or an organization that has a legitimate interest in a project or entity, or would be affected by a particular action or policy.

Storm surge   The temporary increase, at a particular locality, in the height of the sea due to extreme meteorological conditions (low atmospheric pressure and/or strong winds). The storm surge is defined as being the excess above the level expected from the tidal variation alone at that time and place.

Stratosphere   The highly stratified region of the atmosphere above the troposphere extending from about 10 km (ranging from 9 km in high latitudes to 16 km in the tropics on average) to about 50 km altitude.

Structural change   Changes, for example, in the relative share of Gross Domestic Product produced by the industrial, agricultural, or services sectors of an economy; or more generally, systems transformations whereby some components are either replaced or potentially substituted by others.

Sulphurhexafluoride (SF$_6$)   One of the six GHGs to be curbed under the Kyoto Protocol. It is largely used in heavy industry to insulate high-voltage equipment and to assist in the manufacturing of cable-cooling systems and semi-conductors.

Sustainable development (SD)   The concept of sustainable development was introduced in the World Conservation Strategy (IUCN 1980) and had its roots in the concept of a sustainable society and in the management of renewable resources. It was adopted by the World Commission on Environment and Development (WCED) in 1987 and by the Rio Conference in 1992 as a process of change in which the exploitation of resources, the direction of investments, the orientation of technological development, and institutional change are all in harmony and enhance both current and future potential to meet human needs and aspirations. SD integrates the political, social, economic and environmental dimensions.

Tax   A *carbon tax* is a levy on the carbon content of fossil fuels. Because virtually all of the carbon in fossil fuels is ultimately emitted as carbon dioxide, a carbon tax is equivalent to an emission tax on each unit of CO_2-equivalent emissions. An *energy tax* – a levy on the energy content of fuels – reduces demand for energy and so reduces carbon dioxide emissions from fossil fuel use. An *eco-tax* is designed to influence human behaviour (specifically economic behaviour) to follow an ecologically benign path. An *international carbon/emission/energy tax* is a tax imposed on specified sources in participating countries by an international agreement. A *harmonized tax* commits participating countries to impose a tax at a common rate on the same sources. A *tax credit* is a reduction of tax in order to stimulate purchasing of or investment in a certain product, such as GHG emission-reducing technologies. A *carbon charge* is the same as a carbon tax.

Technological change   Mostly considered as technological *improvement*, i.e. more or better goods and services can be provided from a given amount of resources (production factors). Economic models distinguish autonomous (exogenous), endogenous and induced technological change. *Autonomous (exogenous) technological change* is imposed from outside the model, usually in the form of a time trend affecting energy demand or world output growth. *Endogenous technological change* is the outcome of economic activity *within* the model, i.e. the choice of technologies is included within the model and affects energy demand and/or economic growth. *Induced technological change* implies endogenous technological change but adds further changes induced by policies and measures, such as carbon taxes triggering R&D efforts.

Technology   The practical application of knowledge to achieve particular tasks that employs both technical artefacts (hardware, equipment) and (social) information ('software', know-how for production and use of artefacts).

Technology transfer   The exchange of knowledge, hardware and associated software, money and goods among stakeholders that leads to the spreading of technology for

adaptation or mitigation. The term encompasses both diffusion of technologies and technological cooperation across and within countries.

Thermal infrared radiation   Radiation emitted by the Earth's surface, the atmosphere
and the clouds. It is also known as *terrestrial* or *longwave radiation*, and is to be distinguished from the near-infrared radiation that is part of the solar spectrum. Infrared radiation,
in general, has a distinctive range of wavelengths (*spectrum*) longer than the wavelength of
the red colour in the visible part of the spectrum. The spectrum of thermal infrared radiation
is practically distinct from that of shortwave or solar radiation because of the difference in
temperature between the sun and the Earth-atmosphere system.

Top-down models   Top-down models apply macroeconomic theory, econometric and
optimization techniques to aggregate economic variables. Using historical data on consumption, prices, incomes and factor costs, top-down models assess final demand for goods
and services, and supply from main sectors, such as the energy sector, transportation, agriculture and industry. Some top-down models incorporate technology data, narrowing the
gap to bottom-up models.

Tradable permit   A tradable permit is an economic policy instrument under which rights
to discharge pollution – in this case an amount of GHG emissions – can be exchanged
through either a free or a controlled permit-market. An *emission permit* is a non-transfer-
able or tradable entitlement allocated by a government to a legal entity (company or other
emitter) to emit a specified amount of a substance.

Tropopause   The boundary between the troposphere and the stratosphere.

Troposphere   The lowest part of the atmosphere, from the surface to about 10 km in
altitude in mid-latitudes (ranging from 9 km in high latitudes to 16 km in the tropics on
average), where clouds and weather phenomena occur. In the troposphere, temperatures
generally decrease with height.

Uncertainty   An expression of the degree to which a value (e.g. the future state of the
climate system) is unknown. Uncertainty can result from lack of information or from disagreement about what is known or even knowable. It might have many types of sources,
from quantifiable errors in the data to ambiguously defined concepts or terminology, or
uncertain projections of human behaviour. Uncertainty can, therefore, be represented by
quantitative measures, for example, a range of values calculated by various models, or by
qualitative statements, for example, reflecting the judgement of a team of experts.

United Nations Framework Convention on Climate Change (UNFCCC)   The Convention was adopted on 9 May 1992 in New York and signed at the 1992 Earth Summit
in Rio de Janeiro by more than 150 countries and the European Community. Its ultimate
objective is the 'stabilization of greenhouse gas concentrations in the atmosphere at a level
that would prevent dangerous anthropogenic interference with the climate system'. It contains commitments for all Parties. Under the Convention, Parties included in Annex I (all
OECD member countries in the year 1990 and countries with economies in transition) aim
to return GHG emissions not controlled by the Montreal Protocol to 1990 levels by the year
2000. The Convention entered into force in March 1994. See Kyoto Protocol.

Voluntary action   Informal programmes, self-commitments and declarations, where the parties (individual companies or groups of companies) entering into the action set their own targets and often do their own monitoring and reporting.

Voluntary agreement   An agreement between a government authority and one or more private parties to achieve environmental objectives or to improve environmental performance beyond compliance to regulated obligations. Not all voluntary agreements are truly voluntary; some include rewards and/or penalties associated with joining or achieving commitments.

Vulnerability   Vulnerability is the degree to which a system is susceptible to, and unable to cope with, adverse effects of climate change, including climate variability and extremes. Vulnerability is a function of the character, magnitude and rate of climate change and variation to which a system is exposed, its sensitivity, and its adaptive capacity.

Water stress   A country is water stressed if the available freshwater supply relative to water withdrawals acts as an important constraint on development. In global-scale assessments, basins with water stress are often defined as having a per capita water availability below 1,000 m^3/yr (based on long-term average runoff). Withdrawals exceeding 20 per cent of renewable water supply have also been used as an indicator of water stress. A crop is water stressed if soil available water, and thus actual evapotranspiration, is less than potential evapotranspiration demands.

Source: IPCC (2007c)

References

Aall, C. (2010). The environmental impacts of leisure consumption. *Journal of Sustainable Tourism*, submitted.

ADEME (2006). Bilan carbone. Calcul des facteurs d'émissions et sources bibliographiques utilisées, (version 4.0). Paris: ADEME, MIES.

Air Berlin (2010). More miles, more advantages. Available from: http://www.airberlin.com/site/tb/program/advantagesoverview.php?LANG=eng. Accessed 16 February 2010.

Air New Zealand (2008). World-first biofuel test flight. Available from: http://www.airnewzealand.co.nz/aboutus/biofuel-test/default.htm. Accessed 2 March 2010.

Airbus (2009). Global market forecast 2009–2028. Available from: http://www.airbus.com/en/corporate/gmf/. Accessed 30 March 2010.

Ajzen (1991). The theory of planned behavior. *Organizational Behavior and Human Decision Processes* 50: 179–211.

Åkerman, J. (2005). Sustainable air transport – on track in 2050. *Transportation Research – D* 10(2): 111–126.

Alegre, J. and Pou, L. (2006). Length of stay in the demand for tourism. *Tourism Management* 27: 1343–1355.

Allen, M.R., Frame, D.J., Huntingford, C., Jones, C.D., Lowe, J.A., Meinshausen, M. and Meinshausen, N. (2009). Warming caused by cumulative carbon emissions towards the trillionth tonne. *Nature* 458(7242): 1163–1166.

Amelung, B., Moreno, A. and Scott, D. (2008). The place of tourism in the IPCC Fourth Assessment Report: a review. *Tourism Review International* 12(1): 5–12.

American Express Business Travel (2009). American Express business travel monitor shows signs travellers are returning to the road. Available from: http://home3.americanexpress.com/corp/pc/2009/road.asp. Accessed 16 February 2010.

Anable, J., Lane, B. and Kelay, T. (2006). An evidence base review of public attitudes to climate change and transport. UK: The Department for Transport.

Andersen, O., Gössling, S., Simonsen, M., Walnum, H.J., Peeters, P. and Neiberger, C. (2010). CO_2-emissions from the transport of China's exported goods. *Energy Policy*, submitted.

Anderson, K. and Bows, A. (2008). Reframing the climate change challenge in light of post-2000 emission trends. *Philosophical Transactions of the Royal Society* 366(1882): 3863–3882.

Andersson, E. and Lukaszevicz, P. (2006). Energy Consumption and Related Air Pollution for Scandinavian Electric Passenger Trains. Report KTH/AVE 2006: 46. Stockholm: Royal Institute of Technology.

AOSIS (2009). Alliance of small island states (AOSIS) declaration on climate change. Available from: www.sidsnet.org/.../AOSIS%20Summit%20Declaration%20Sept%2021%20FINAL.pdf.

Artal Tur, A., García Sánchez, A. and Sánchez García, J.F. (2008). The length of stay determinants for sun-and-sand tourism: an application for the region of Murcia. Available from: http://www.uv.es/asepuma/XVI/801.pdf. Accessed 30 March 2010.

ASC (2010). Sustainability Reports. Available from: http://www.aspensnowmass.com/environment/programs/sustainreport.cfm Accessed 5 February 2010.

Asian Development Bank (2009). *The Economics of Climate Change in Southeast Asia: a regional review*. Asian Development Bank.

Aumann, H.H., Ruzmaikin, A. and Teixeira, J. (2008). Frequency of severe storms and global warming. *Geophysical Research Letters* 35, L19805.

ATA (2007). Airlines and pilots oppose Lieberman-Warner Climate Change Bill. Air Transport Association Press Release, 6 December. Available from: www.airlines.org/news /releases/2007/news_12-6-07. Accessed 15 March 2010.

ATA (2009). Climate change. Available at: http://www.airlines.org/. Accessed 20 February 2010.

Aviation Global Deal Group (2009). A sectoral approach to addressing international aviation emissions. Discussion Note 2.0 09 June 2009. Available from: http://www.agdgroup.org/pdfs/090609_AGD_Discussion_Note_2.0.pdf. Accessed 22 December 2009.

Bach, W. and Gössling, S. (1996). Klimaökologische Auswirkungen des Flugverkehrs, *Geographische Rundschau* 48: 54–59.

Badland, H.M., Garrett, N. and Schofield, (2010). How does parking availability and public transport accessibility influence work-related travel behaviour? *Sustainability* 2: 576–590.

Bakos, G.C. and Soursos, M. (2003). Techno-economic assessment of a stand-alone PV/hybrid installation for low-cost electrification of a tourist resort in Greece. *Applied Energy* 73: 183–193.

Bang, H.-K., Ellinger, A.E., Hadjimarcou, J. and Traichal, P.A. (2000). Consumer concern, knowledge, belief, and attitude toward renewable energy: an application of the reasoned action theory. *Psychology and Marketing* 17(6): 449–468.

Barr, S., Shaw, G., Coles, T. and Prillwitz, J. (2010). 'A holiday is a holiday': practicing sustainability, home and away. *Journal of Transport Geography* 18: 474–481.

Beccali, M., La Gennusa, M., Lo Coco, L. and Rizzo, G. (2009). An empirical approach for ranking environmental and energy saving measures in the hotel sector. *Renewable Energy* 34: 82–90.

Bechrakis, D.A., McKeogh, E.J. and Gallagher, P.D. (2006). Simulation and operational assessment for a small autonomous wind-hydrogen energy system. *Energy Conversion and Management* 47: 46–59.

Becken, S. (2002). Analysing international tourist flows to estimate energy use associated with air travel. *Journal of Sustainable Tourism* 10(2): 114–131.

Becken, S. (2004). How tourists and tourism experts perceived climate change and carbon-offsetting schemes. *Journal of Sustainable Tourism* 12(4): 332–345.

Becken, S. (2007). Tourists' perception of international air travel's impact on the global climate and potential climate change policies. *Journal of Sustainable Tourism* 15(4): 351–368.

Becken, S. (2008). Developing indicators for managing tourism in the face of peak oil. *Tourism Management* 29: 695–705.

Becken, S. and Simmons, D.G. (2002). Understanding energy consumption patterns of tourist attractions and activities in New Zealand. *Tourism Management* 23: 343–354.

Becken, S. and Patterson, M. (2006). Measuring national carbon dioxide emissions from tourism as a key step towards achieving sustainable tourism. *Journal of Sustainable Tourism* 14(4): 323–338.

Becken, S. and Hay, J. (2007). *Tourism and Climate Change – risks and opportunities*. Clevedon: Channel View Publications.

Becken, S. and Simmons, D. (2008). Using the concept of yield to assess the sustainability of different tourist types. *Ecological Economics* 67: 420–429.

Becken, S., Frampton, C. and Simmons, D. (2001). Energy consumption patterns in the accommodation sector – the New Zealand case. *Ecological Economics* 39: 371–386.

Bélisle, F.J. (1984). Tourism and food imports: the case of Jamaica. *Economic Development and Cultural Change* 32(4): 819–842.

BenchmarkHotel (2007). Hotel benchmarking software developed by The Prince of Wales International Business Leaders Forum International Tourism Partnership. Available from: www.benchmarkhotel.com.

Bermudez-Contreras, A., Thomson, M. and Infield, D.G. (2008). Renewable energy powered desalination in Baja California Sur, Mexico. *Desalination* 220: 431–440.

Bigano, A., Bosello, F., Roson, R., Tol, R.S.J. (2008). Economy-wide impacts of climate change: a joint analysis for sea level rise and tourism. *Mitigation and Adaptation Strategies for Global Change* 13: 765–791.

BMU (Bundesministerium für Umwelt, Naturschutz und Reaktorsicherheit) (2008). *Repräsentativumfrage zu Umweltbewusstsein und Umweltverhalten im Jahr 2008.* Berlin: BMU.

BMV (Bundesverkehrsministerium) (1996). Verkehr in Zahlen. Berlin: Deutsches Institut fur Wirtschaftsforschung.

Bode, S., Isensee, J., Krause, K. and Michaelowa, A. (2002). Climate policy: analysis of ecological technical and economic implications for international maritime transport. *International Journal of Maritime Economics* 4: 164–184.

Boeing (2008). *Summary Outlook 2008–2027.* Available at: www.boeing.com/commercial/cmo/pdf/boeing_cmo_summary_2008.pdf. Accessed 1 August 2008.

Bohdanowicz, P. (2009). Theory and Practice of Environmental Management and Monitoring in Hotel Chains. In: Gössling, S., Hall, C.M. and Weaver, D. (eds) *Sustainable Tourism Futures: perspectives on systems, restructuring and innovations.* London: Routledge, pp. 102–130.

Bohdanowicz, P. and Martinac, I. (2007). Determinants and benchmarking of resource consumption in hotels – case study of Hilton International and Scandic in Europe. *Energy and Buildings* 39: 82–95.

Böhler, S., Grischkat, S., Haustein, S. and Hunecke, M. (2006). Encouraging environmentally sustainable holiday travel. *Transportation Research Part A*: 652–670.

Böhm, S. and Dabhi, S. (2009). Upsetting the offset: the political economy of carbon markets. Available from: http://mayflybooks.org/wp-content/uploads/2009/12/9781906948078UpsettingtheOffset.pdf. Accessed 5 March 2010.

Bony, S., Colman, R., Kattsov, V.M., Allan, R.P., Bretherton, C.S., Dufresne, J.-L., Hall, A., Hallegatte, S., Holland, M.M., Ingram, W., Randall, D.A., Soden, B.J., Tselioudis, G. and Webb, M.J. (2006). How well do we understand and evaluate climate change feedback processes? *Journal of Climate* 19: 3445–3482.

Boon, B., Schroten, A. and Kampman, B.E. (2007). Compensation Schemes for Air Transport. In: Peeters, P. M. (ed.) *Tourism and Climate Change Mitigation. Methods, greenhouse gas reductions and policies.* Breda: NHTV, pp. 77–90.

Bows, A., Anderson, K. and Footitt, A. (2009a). Aviation in a Low-carbon EU. In: Gössling, S. and Upham, P. (eds) *Climate Change and Aviation: issues, challenges and solutions.* London: Earthscan, pp. 89–109.

Bows, A., Anderson, B. and Peeters, P.M. (2009b). Air transport, climate change and tourism. *Tourism and Hospitality: Planning & Development* 6(1): 7–20.

Boykoff, M.T. (2007). Lost in translation? United States television news coverage of anthropogenic climate change, 1995–2004. *Climatic Change*, DOI 10.1007/s10584-007-9299-3.

Boykoff, M.T. and Boykoff, J.M. (2004). Balance as bias: global warming and the US prestige press. *Global Environmental Change* 14: 125–136.

Boykoff, M.T. and Boykoff, J.M. (2007). Climate change and journalistic norms: a case-study of US mass-media coverage. *Geoforum* 38(6): 1190–1204.

Brewer, P.G. (2009). A changing ocean seen with clarity. *Proceedings of the National Academy of Sciences* 106: 12213–12214.

British Standards Institute (2008). *PAS 2050:2008. Specification for the assessment of the life cycle greenhouse gas emissions of goods and services*. Carbon Trust, DEFRA and British Standards Institution: London.

Broderick, J. (2009). Voluntary Carbon Offsets: a contribution to sustainable tourism? In: Gössling, S., Hall, C.M. and Weaver, D.B. (eds) *Sustainable Tourism Futures: perspectives on systems, restructuring and innovations*. London: Routledge, pp. 169–199.

Brouwer, R., Brander, L. and Van Beukering, P. (2008). 'A convenient truth': air travel passengers' willingess to pay to offset their CO_2 emissions. *Climatic Change* 90: 299–313.

Buhaug, O. (2009). *Second IMO GHG Study 2009*. London: International Marine Organization.

Burke, J. (2010). Rickshaw pullers win right to work Delhi streets. Available from: http://www.guardian.co.uk/world/2010/feb/11/rickshaw-ruling-delhi. Accessed 8 March 2010.

Burke, M.B., Miguel, E., Satayanath, S., Dykema, J.A. and Lobell, D.B. (2009). Warming increases the risk of civil war in Africa. *PNAS* 106(49): 20670–20674. Available at: www.pnas.org/cgi/doi/10.1073/pnas.0907998106. Accessed 6 August 2010.

Butler, D. (2008). Architects of a low-energy future. *Nature* 452(7187): 520–523.

Byrnes, T.A. and Warnken, J. (2006). Greenhouse gas emissions from marine tours: a case study of Australian tourboat operators. *Journal of Sustainable Tourism* 14(3): 255–270.

Cabrini, L. (2009). Tourism, Climate Change and the Millennium Development Goals. In: D'Mello, C., Minninger, S. and McKeown, J. (eds) *Disaster Prevention in Tourism: climate justice and tourism*. Chiang Mai: Ecumenical Coalition On Tourism and German Church Development Service (EED), pp. 162–170.

Capoor, K. and Ambrosi, P. (2009). *State and Trends of the Carbon Market 2009*. Washington DC: World Bank. Available from: http://siteresources.worldbank.org/EXTCARBONFINANCE/Resources/State_and_Trends_of_the_Carbon_Market_2009-FINALb.pdf. Accessed 26 February 2010.

Carbon Trust (2010). Hospitality. Saving energy without compromising service. Available from: http://www.carbontrust.co.uk/publications/pages/publicationdetail.aspx?id=CTV013. Accessed 18 February 2010.

Caribbean Hotel and Tourism Association (2007). Caribbean Hotel Association and Caribbean Tourism Organization (2007) *CHA-CTO Position Paper of Global Climate Change and the Caribbean Tourism Industry*. Available from: http://www.caribbeanhotels.org/ClimateChangePosition0307.pdf. Accessed 20 February 2010.

CE Delft (2009). Technical support for European action to reducing greenhouse gas emissions from international maritime transport. Available from: http://ec.europa.eu/environment/air/transport/pdf/ghg_ships_%20report.pdf. Accessed 26 February 2010.

Ceron, J.-P. and Dubois, G. (2003). Tourisme et changement climatique. Impacts potentiels du changement climatique en France au XXIème siècle. *First International Conference on Climate Change and Tourism*, 9–11 April 2003. Djerba: WTO World Tourism Organisation.

Chakravarti, S., Cikkatur, A., De Coninck, H., Pacala, S., Socolow, R. and Tavoni, M. (2009). Sharing Global CO_2 Emission Reductions among One Billion High Emitters. *PNAS* early edition, available at: www.pnas.org/cgi/doi/10.1073/pnas.0905232106. Accessed 14 July 2009.

Chan, W.W. and Lam, J.C. (2003). Energy-saving Supporting Tourism: a case study of hotel swimming pool heat pump. *Journal of Sustainable Tourism* 11(1): 74–83.

Chan, Z.C.Y. and Lai, W.F. (2009). Revisiting the Melamine Contamination Event in China: implications for ethics in food technology. *Trends in Food Science and Technology* 20(8): 366–373.

Chang, P., Zhang, R., Hazeleger, W., Wen, C., Wan, X., Ji, L., Haarsma, R.J., Breugem, W.-P. and Seidel, H. (2008). Oceanic Link Between Abrupt Change in the North Atlantic Ocean and the African Monsoon. *Nature Geoscience* 1: 444–448.

Chapman, L. (2007). Transport and Climate Change: a review. *Journal of Transport Geography* 15: 354–367.

Chartered Institution of Building Services Engineers (CIBSE) (2006). *Guide A: Environmental design. Category: Heating, Air Conditioning and Refrigeration*. CIBSE: London.

Choi, H.C. and Sirakaya, E. (2006). Sustainability indicators for managing community tourism. *Tourism Management* 27: 1274–1289.

Cialdini, R., Reno, R. and Kallgren, C. (1990). A Focus Theory of Normative Conduct: recycling the concept of norms to littering in public places. *Journal of Personality and Social Psychology* 58: 749–758.

CLIA (2009). 2009 CLIA cruise market overview: statistical cruise industry data through 2008. Cruise Lines International Association.

Cohen, M.J. (2009). Sustainable Mobility Transitions and the Challenge of Countervailing Trends: the case of personal aeromobility. *Technology Analysis & Strategic Management* 21(2): 249–265.

Coles, T., Duval, D.T. and Hall, C.M. (2005). Tourism, Mobility, and Global Communities: new approaches to theorising tourism and tourist spaces. In: Theobald, W.F. (ed.) *Global Tourism*. 3rd edition. Amsterdam: Elsevier, pp. 463–481.

Commission of the European Communities (EC) (2006). *Summary of the Impact Assessment: Inclusion of Aviation in the EU Greenhouse Gas Emissions Trading Scheme (EU ETS)*. Available from: ec.europa.eu/environment/climat/pdf/aviation/sec_2006_1685_en.pdf. Accessed 20 January 2007.

Connell, J. (2006). Medical tourism: sea, sun, sand and … surgery. *Tourism Management* 27(6): 1093–100.

Connell, J.F. and Williams, G. (2005). Passengers' perceptions of low cost airlines and full service carriers: a case study involving Ryanair, Aer Lingus, Air Asia and Malaysia Airlines. *Journal of Air Transport Management* 11(4): 259–272.

Continental Airlines (2009). Continental airlines flight demonstrates use of sustainable biofuels as energy source for jet travel. Available from: http://www.continental.com/web/en-US/apps/vendors/default.aspx?i=http%3A%2F%2Fphx%2Ecorporate%2Dir%2Enet%2Fphoenix%2Ez html%3Fc%3D85779%26p%3Dirol%2DnewsArticle%26ID%3D1241576. Accessed 2 March 2010.

Cook, K.H. and Vizy, E.K. (2006). Coupled Model Simulations of the West African Monsoon System: twentieth- and twenty-first-century simulations. *Journal of Climate* 19: 3681–3703.

Copenhagen Climate Council (2009) The Copenhagen call. Available from: http://www.copenhagenclimatecouncil.com/get-informed/news/text-of-the-copenhagen-call.html. Accessed 22 December 2009.

Copenhagen Diagnosis (2009). Updating the World on the Latest Climate Science. I. Allison, N.L. Bindoff, R.A. Bindschadler, P.M. Cox, N. de Noblet, M.H. England, *et al.* Sydney: CCRC.

Costa, M.H., Yanagi, S.N.M., Souza, P.J.O.P., Ribeiro, A. and Rocha, E.J.P. (2007). Climate change in Amazonia caused by soybean cropland expansion, as compared to caused by pastureland expansion. *Geophysical Research Letters* 34(7), L07706, doi: 10.1029/2007GL029271.

Costanza, R. (ed.) (1992). *Ecological Economics: the science and management of sustainability*. New York: Columbia University Press.

Council of the European Union (2010). Report from the Commission to the European Parliament and the Council. Monitoring the CO_2 emissions from new passenger cars in the EU: Data for the year 2008. Available at: http://register.consilium.europa.eu/pdf/en/10/st05/st05515.en10.pdf.

Cox, P.M., Betts, R.A., Collins, M., Harris, P.P., Huntingford, C. and Jones, C.D. (2004). Amazonian forest dieback under climate-carbon cycle projections for the 21st century. *Theoretical and Applied Climatology* 78: 137–156.

Cox, P.M., Harris, P.P., Huntingford, C., Betts, R.A., Collins, M., Jones, C.D., Jupp, T.E., Marengo, J.A. and Nobre, C.A. (2008). Increasing risk of Amazonian drought due to decreasing aerosol pollution. *Nature* 453: 212–216.

Daley, B. (2009). Is air transport an effective tool for sustainable development? *Sustainable Development* 17: 210–219.

Daley, B. and Preston, H. (2009). Aviation and Climate Change: assessment of policy options. In: Gössling, S. and Upham, P. (eds) *Climate Change and Aviation: issues, challenges and solutions*, London: Earthscan, pp. 347–372.

Dalton, G.J., Lockington, D.A. and Baldock, T.E. (2007). A survey of tourist operator attitudes to renewable energy supply in Queensland, Australia. *Renewable Energy* 32: 567–586.

Dalton, G.J., Lockington, D.A. and Baldock, T.E. (2008a). Feasibility analysis of stand-alone renewable energy supply options for a large hotel. *Renewable Energy* 33: 1475–1490.

Dalton, G.J., Lockington, D.A. and Baldock, T.E. (2008b). A survey of tourist attitudes to renewable energy supply in Australian hotel accommodation. *Renewable Energy* 33: 2174–2185.

Dalton, G.J., Lockington, D.A. and Baldock, T.E. (2009) Case study feasibility analysis of renewable energy supply options for small to medium-sized tourist accommodations. *Renewable Energy* 34: 1134–1144.

David Suzuki Foundation (2008). Credit Check: A comparative evaluation of tree-planting and fossil-fuel emission reduction offsets. Available from: http://www.davidsuzuki.org/files/reports/Credit_Check_080701.pdf. Accessed 5 March 2010.

David Suzuki Foundation (2009). Purchasing carbon offsets. a guide for Canadian consumers, businesses, and organizations. Available from: http://www.davidsuzuki.org/files/reports/climate_offset_guide_web.pdf. Accessed 5 March 2010.

Davis, S.J. and Caldeira, K. (2010). Consumption-based accounting of CO_2 emissions. Available at: www.pnas.org/cgi/doi/10.1073/pnas.0906974107.

Dawson, J., Stewart, E.J., Lemelin, H. and Scott, D. (2009). The carbon cost of polar bear viewing tourism in Churchill, Canada. *Journal of Sustainable Tourism* 18(3): 319–336.

De Bruijn, K., Dirven, R., Eijgelaar, E. and Peeters, P. (2008). *Reizen op grote voet 2005. De milieubelasting van vakanties van Nederlanders. Een pilot-project in samenwerking met NBTC-NIPO Research*. Breda: NHTV University for Applied Sciences.

DEFRA (2005). The validity of food miles as an indicator of sustainable development. Available from: http://www.defra.gov.uk/evidence/economics/foodfarm/reports/documents/Foodmile.pdf. Accessed 6 August 2010.

DEFRA (2008). *A Framework for Pro-Environmental Behaviour*. London: DEFRA. Available at www.defra.gov.uk.

Deng, S. and Burnett, J. (2000). A study of energy performance of hotel buildings in Hong Kong. *Energy and Buildings* 31: 7–12.

Desforges, L. (2000). Traveling the world: identity and travel biography. *Annals of Tourism Research*. 27(4): 926–945.

Deutsche Bahn (2009). Paradoxe Privilegien. Mobil, October 2009. Available from: http://www.deutschebahn.com/site/bahn/de/unternehmen/bahnwelt/kundenmagazin/aktuelle_ausgabe/aktuelle_ausgabe.html Accessed 17 February 2010.

Dicken, P. (2007). Global Shift. Mapping the Changing Contours of the World Economy. 5th ed. New York: The Guildford Press.

Dickinson, J.E. (2009). Adapting Tourism for a Lower Carbon Future: a slow travel approach. In: Landré, M. (ed.) *Transport and Tourism. Challenges, issues and conflicts*. Proceedings of the Travel and Tourism Research Association Europe 22–24 April 2009 Annual Conference – Rotterdam/ Breda, the Netherlands. Breda: TTRA, pp. 32–45.

Dickinson, J. and Dickinson J. (2006). Local transport and social representations: challenging the assumptions for sustainable tourism. *Journal of Sustainable Tourism* 14: 192–208.

Dickinson, J. and Robbins, D. (2007). Using the car in a fragile rural tourist destination: a social representations perspective. *Journal of Transport Geography* 15: 116–126.

Dickinson, J. and Robbins, D. (2008). Representations of tourist transport problems in a rural destination. *Tourism Management* 29: 1110–1121.

Dickinson, J.E., Robbins, D. and Fletcher, J. (2009). Representation of transport: a rural destination analysis. *Annals of Tourism Research* 36: 103–123.

DOE/NETL (US Department of Energy, National Energy Technology Laboratory) (2009). Affordable, low-carbon diesel fuel from domestic coal and biomass. Available from: http://www.netl.doe.gov/ energy-analyses/pubs/CBTL%20Final%20Report.pdf. Accessed 2 March 2010.

Doganis, R. (2006). *The Airline Business*. 2nd edition. London: Routledge.

Downward, P., Lumsdon, L. and Weston, R. (2009). Visitor expenditure: the case of cycle recreation and tourism. *Journal of Sport & Tourism* 14(1): 25–42.

Dubois, G. and Ceron, J.P. (2006). Tourism and climate change: proposals for a research agenda. *Journal of Sustainable Tourism* 14(4): 399–415.

Dubois, G. and Ceron, J.P. (2009). Carbon Labelling and Restructuring Travel Systems: involving travel agencies in climate change mitigation. In: Gössling, S., Hall, C.M. and Weaver, D.B. (eds) *Sustainable Tourism Futures: perspectives on systems, restructuring and innovations*. London: Routledge, pp. 222–239.

Dubois, G., Ceron, J.-P., Peeters, P. and Gössling, S. (2010). The future tourism mobility of the world population: emission growth versus climate policy. *Transportation Research Part A*, in press.

Dulal, H.B., Shah, K.U. and Ahmad, N. (2009). Social equity considerations in the implementation of Caribbean climate change adaptation policies. *Sustainability* 1: 363–383.

Dwyer, L., Forsyth, P., Spurr, R. and Hoque, S. (2010). Estimating the carbon footprint of Australian tourism. *Journal of Sustainable Tourism*, in press.

Earth Policy Institute (2010). US feeds one quarter of its grain to cars while hunger is on the rise. Available from: http://www.earth-policy.org/index.php?/press_room/C68/2010_datarelease6/. Accessed 1 February 2010.

Easterling, D.R. and Wehner, M.F. (2009). Is the climate warming or cooling? *Geophysical Research Letters* 36, L08706.

Eby, M., Zickfeld, K., Montenegro, A., Archer, D., Meissner, K.J. and Weaver, A.J. (2009). Lifetime of anthropogenic climate change: millennial time scales of potential CO_2 and surface temperature perturbations. *Journal of Climate* 22: 2501–2511.

EC (2009) Energy efficiency. Energy labelling of domestic appliances. Available from: http:// ec.europa.eu/energy/efficiency/labelling/labelling_en.htm. Accessed 30 March 2010.

EHAS (2010). BioEthanol for sustainable transport. Results and recommendations from the European BEST project. Available from: http://www.best-europe.org/. Accessed 30 March 2010.

Eijgelaar, E., Thaper, C. and Peeters, P. (2010). Antarctic cruise tourism: the paradoxes of ambassadorship, 'last chance tourism' and GHG emissions. *Journal of Sustainable Tourism* 18(3): in press.

Energy Rating Australia (2010). The energy label. Available from: http://www.energyrating.gov.au/ con3.html. Accessed 10 February 2010.

Energy Star (2010). About Energy Star. Available from: http://www.energystar.gov/. Accessed 10 February 2010.

England, M.H., Gupta, A.S. and Pitman, A.J. (2009). Constraining future greenhouse gas emissions by a cumulative target. *Proceedings of the National Academy of Sciences* 106: 16539–16540.

Environment News Service (2007). Aviation industry rejects Europe's climate emissions trading system. 2 October. Available from: www.ens-newswire.com/ens/oct2007/2007-10-02-03.asp. Accessed 1 March 2008.

EUHOFA, IH&RA, UNEP (2001). Sowing the Seeds of Change. Environmental Teaching Pack for the Hospitality Industry. Paris: EUHOFA, IH&RA, UNEP.

Euractiv (2009). EU carbon tax on new Commission's agenda early next year. Available from: http://www.euractiv.com/en/climate-change/eu-carbon-tax-new-commission-agenda-early-year/article-187029. Accessed 25 February 2010.

Europa (2008). Emissions trading: commission welcomes EP vote on including aviation in EU ETS. Available from: http://europa.eu/rapid/pressReleasesAction.do?reference=IP/08/1114. Accessed 8 July 2008.

European Parliament and Council (2009) Directive 2008/101/EC of the European Parliament and of the Council of 19 November 2008 amending Directive 2003/87/EC so as to include aviation activities in the scheme for greenhouse gas emission allowance trading within the Community. *Official Journal of the EU*, 13.1.2009.

Eurostat (2008). Europe in Figures, Eurostat Yearbook 2008.

Eyring, V., Isaksen, I.S.A., Berntsen, T., Collins, W.J., Corbett, J.J., Endresen, O., Grainger, R.G., Moldanova, J., Schlager, H. and Stevenson, D.S. (2009). Transport impacts on atmosphere and climate: Shipping. *Atmospheric Environment*, doi:10.1016/j.atmosenv.2009.04.059.

Fabian, P. (1974). Residence Time of Aircraft Exhaust Contaminants in the Stratosphere. CIAP Contract No. 05-30027, US Department of Transportation, Washington, DC, June 1974.

Fabian, P. (1978). Ozone increase from Concorde operations? *Nature* 272: 306–307.

Fabry, V.J., Seibel, B.A., Feely, R.A. and Orr, J.C. (2008). Impacts of ocean acidification on marine fauna and ecosystem processes. *ICES Journal of Marine Science* 65: 414–432.

Fahrenthold, D.A. (2009). It's natural to behave irrationally. *Washington Post*, 8 December.

Fine, A.H. (ed.) (2006). *Handbook on Animal-assisted Therapy: theoretical foundations and guidelines for practice*. 2nd edition. San Diego: Elsevier.

Flohr, S. (2001). An analysis of British postgraduate courses in tourism: what role does sustainability play within higher education? *Journal of Sustainable Tourism* 9(6): 505–513.

Flybe (2010). Make your own environment label. Available from: http://www.flybe.com/pdf/eco_labels_make_own.pdf. Accessed 28 March 2010.

Font, X. (2002). Environmental certification in tourism and hospitality: progress, process and prospects. *Tourism Management* 23(3): 197–205.

Food Carbon (2009). Food carbon footprint calculator. Available from: http://www.foodcarbon.co.uk. Accessed 1 October 2009.

Forster, P.M. de F., Shine, K. P. and Stuber, N. (2007). Corrigendum to 'It is premature to include non-CO_2 effects of aviation in emission trading schemes', *Atmospheric Environment* 40(2006): 117–1121. *Atmospheric Environment*, 41: 3941.

Frändberg, L. (2008a). Paths in transnational time-space: representing mobility biographies of young Swedes, *Geografiska Annaler B* 90(1): 17–28.

Frändberg, L. (2008b). How normal is travelling abroad? Differences in transnational mobility between groups of young Swedes. *Environment and Planning A* 40, in press.

French Environment and Energy Agency (ADEME) (2006). Bilan carbone. Calcul des facteurs d'émissions et sources bibliographiques utilisées, (version 4.0). Paris: ADEME, MIES.

Friedlingstein, P.P. *et al.* (2006). Climate-carbon feedback analysis: results from the C4MIP model intercomparison. *Journal of Climate* 19: 3337–3353.

Fuglestvedt, J., Berntsen, T., Eyring, V., Isaksen, I., Lee, D.S. and Sausen, R. (2009). Shipping emissions: from cooling to warming of climate – and reducing impacts on health. *Environmental Science & Technology* 43(24): 9057–9062; doi: 10.1021/es901944r.

G8 (2009). Declaration of the leaders of the major economies forum on energy and climate. Available from: www.g8italia2009.it/static/G8_Allegato/MEF_Declarationl.pdf. Accessed 22 December 2009.

Gabriel, Y., Fineman, S. and Sims, D. (2000). *Organizing and Organizations*. 2nd edition. London: Sage Publications Ltd.

Gallastegui, I.G. and Spain, S. (2002). The use of eco-labels: a review of the literature. *European Environment* 12(6): 316–331.

Gamah, I. and Self, R. (2010). Advanced open rotors – balancing noise costs against reduced carbon emissions for future aircraft. Available from: http://www.omega.mmu.ac.uk/Downloads/Final-Reports/36%20Final%20Report%20AOR.pdf. Accessed 2 March 2010.

Gatersleben, B. (2007). Affective and symbolic aspects of car use. In: Gärling, T. and Steg, L. (eds) *Threats to the Quality of Urban Life from Car Traffic: problems, causes, and solutions*. Amsterdam: Elsevier, pp. 219–233.

Gerbens-Leenes, W., Hoekstra, A.Y. and van der Meer, T.H. (2009). The water footprint of bioenergy. *Proceedings of the National Academy of Sciences* 106(25): 10219–10223.

Getz, D. (2009). Policy for sustainable and responsible festivals and events: institutionalization of a new paradigm. *Journal of Policy Research in Tourism, Leisure and Events* 1(1): 61–78.

Giddens, A. (2009). *The Politics of Climate Change*. Cambridge: Polity Press.

Gilbert, R. and Perl, A. (2008). *Transport Revolutions: moving people and freight without oil*. London: Earthscan.

Gilg, A., Barr, S. and Ford, N. (2005). Green consumption or sustainable lifestyles? Identifying the sustainable consumer. *Futures* 37: 481–504.

Glaesser, D. (2003). *Crisis Management in the Tourism Industry*. Oxford: Elsevier.

Global Focus (2008). 12 climate entrepreneurs. Available from: http://www.wwf.se/source.php/1237577/12%20Climate%20Entrepreneurs%202.pdf. Accessed 16 February 2010.

Global Humanitarian Forum (2009) *The Anatomy of a Silent Crisis*. London: Global Humanitarian Forum.

Goddard Institute for Space Studies (GISS) (2010). GISS surface temperature analysis. Available from: http://data.giss.nasa.gov/gistemp/. Accessed 22 January 2010.

Goetz, A.R. and Vowles, T.M. (2009). The good, the bad, and the ugly: 30 years of US airline deregulation. *Journal of Transport Geography* 17: 251–263.

Gold Standard (2006). Various documents. Available from: www.cdmgoldstandard.org. Accessed 25 September 2006.

Gössling, S. (2002). Human-environmental relations with tourism. *Annals of Tourism Research* 29(4): 539–556.

Gössling, S. (2006). Ecotourism as experience-tourism. In: Gössling, S. and Hultman, J. (eds) *Ecotourism in Scandinavia: lessons in theory and practice*. Wallingford: CABI Publishing, pp. 89–97.

Gössling, S. and Hall, C.M. (eds) (2006). *Tourism and Global Environmental Change: ecological, social, economic and political interrelationships*. London: Routledge.

Gössling, S. and Hall, C.M. (2008). Swedish tourism and climate change mitigation: an emerging conflict? *Scandinavian Journal of Hospitality and Tourism* 8(2): 141–158.

Gössling, S. and Upham, P. (2009). Introduction: aviation and climate change in context. In:

Gössling, S. and Upham, P. (eds) *Climate Change and Aviation: issues, challenges and solutions*. London: Earthscan, pp. 1–23.

Gössling, S. and Schumacher, K. (2009). Implementing carbon neutral destination policies: issues from the Seychelles. *Journal of Sustainable Tourism* 18(2), in press.

Gössling, S. and Schumacher, K. (2010). Implementing carbon neutral destination policies: issues from the Seychelles. *Journal of Sustainable Tourism* 18(2), in press.

Gössling, S. and Nilsson, J.H. (2010). Frequent flyer programmes and the reproduction of mobility. *Environment and Planning A* 42: 241–252.

Gössling, S., Borgström-Hansson, C., Hörstmeier, O. and Saggel, S. (2002). Ecological footprint analysis as a tool to assess tourism sustainability. *Ecological Economics* 43(23): 199–211.

Gössling, S., Schumacher, K., Morelle, M., Berger, R. and Heck, N. (2004). Tourism and street children in Antananarivo, Madagascar. *Hospitality & Tourism Research* 5(2): 131–149.

Gössling, S., Peeters, P.M., Ceron, J.-P., Dubois, G., Patterson, T. and Richardson, R.B. (2005). The eco-efficiency of tourism. *Ecological Economics* 54(4): 417–434.

Gössling, S., Broderick, J., Upham, P., Peeters, P., Strasdas, W., Ceron, J.-P. and Dubois, G. (2007). Voluntary carbon offsetting schemes for aviation: efficiency and credibility. *Journal of Sustainable Tourism* 15(3): 223–248.

Gössling, S., Peeters, P. and Scott, D. (2008). Consequences of climate policy for international tourist arrivals in developing countries. *Third World Quarterly* 29(5): 873–901.

Gössling, S., Ceron, J.-P., Dubois, G. and Hall, C.M. (2009a). Hypermobile Travellers. In: Gössling, S. and Upham, P. (eds) *Climate Change and Aviation: issues, challenges and solutions*. London: Earthscan, pp. 131–148.

Gössling, S., Hall, C.M. and Weaver, D.B. (2009b). Sustainable Tourism Futures: Perspectives on systems, restructuring and innovations. In: Gössling, S., Hall, C.M. and Weaver, D.B. (eds) *Sustainable Tourism Futures: Perspectives on systems, restructuring and innovations*. London: Routledge, pp. 1–15.

Gössling, S., Hultman, J., Haglund, L, Källgren, H. and Revahl, M. (2009c). Voluntary carbon offsetting by Swedish air travellers: towards the co-creation of environmental value? *Current Issues in Tourism* 12(1): 1–19.

Gössling, S., Hall, C.M., Peeters, P. and Scott, D. (2010). The future of tourism: can tourism growth and climate policy be reconciled? A climate change mitigation perspective. *Tourism Recreation Research* 35(2), in press.

Green, A.E., Hogarth, T. and Shackleton, R.E. (1999). Longer distance commuting as a substitute for migration in Britain. *International Journal of Population Geography* 5: 49–68.

Green, J.E. (2009). The potential for reducing the impact of aviation on climate. *Technology Analysis & Strategic Management* 21(1): 39–59.

Greenpeace (2010). Koch Industries. Secretly funding the climate denial machine. Available from: http://www.greenpeace.org/raw/content/usa/press-center/reports4/koch-industries-secretly-fund.pdf. Accessed 31 March 2010.

Gregory, S. (2009). Twittering over JetBlue's all-you-can-jet pass. Available from: http://www.time.com/time/business/article/0,8599,1917579,00.html. Accessed 22 February 2010.

Guiver, J., Lumsdon, L., Weston, R. and Ferguson, M. (2007). Do buses help meet tourism objectives? The contribution and potential of scheduled buses in rural destination areas. *Transport Policy* 14: 275–282.

Haites, E. (2009). Linking emissions trading schemes for international aviation and shipping emissions. *Climate Policy* 9: 415–430.

Hall, C.M. (2005). *Tourism: rethinking the social science of mobility*, London: Pearson Education Limited.

Hall, C.M. (2008). Tourism and climate change: knowledge gaps and issues. *Tourism Recreation Research* 33: 339–350.

Hall, C.M. (2009a). Changement climatique, authenticité et marketing des régions nordiques: conséquences sur le tourisme finlandais et la 'plus grande marque au monde' ou 'Les changements climatiques finiront-ils par tuer le père Noël?' *Téoros* 28(1): 69–79.

Hall, C.M. (2009b). Degrowing tourism: décroissance, sustainable consumption and steady-state tourism. *Anatolia* 20(1): 46–61.

Hall, C.M. and Jenkins, J. (1995). *Tourism and Public Policy*. Routledge: London.

Hall, C.M. and Müller, D. (eds) (2004). *Tourism, Mobility and Second Homes: between elite landscape and common ground*. Clevedon: Channel View Publications.

Hall, C.M. and Higham, J. (eds) (2005). *Tourism, Recreation and Climate Change*, Clevedon: Channel View Publications.

Hall, C.M. and Williams (2008). *Tourism and Innovation*. London: Routledge.

Hall, C.M. and Lew, A. (2009). *Understanding and Managing Tourism Impacts: an integrated approach*. London: Routledge.

Hall, C.M., Scott, D. and Gössling, S. (2009). Tourism, Development and Climate Change. In: D'Mello, C., Minninger, S. and McKeown, J. (eds) *Disaster Prevention in Tourism: climate justice and tourism*. Chiang Mai: Ecumenical Coalition On Tourism and German Church Development Service (EED), pp. 136–161.

Hans Böckler Stiftung (2009). Vermögen in Deutschland zunehmend ungleich verteilt. Available from: http://www.boeckler.de/320_94199.html. Accessed 30 March 2010.

Hansen, J., Sato, M., Ruedy, R., Kharecha, P., Lacis, A., Miller, R., Nazarenko, L., Lo, K., Schmidt, G.A. and Russell, G. (2006). Dangerous human-made interference with climate: a GISS modelE study. *Atmospheric Chemistry and Physics* 7: 2287–2312.

Hares, A., Dickinson, J. and Wilkes, K. (2009). Climate change and the air travel decisions of UK tourists. *Journal of Transport Geography*, in press, corrected proof.

Harper, G.C. and Makatouni, A. (2002). Consumer perception of organic food production and farm animal welfare. *British Food Journal* 104(3–5): 287–299.

Hede, A.-M. (2008). Managing special events in the new era of the triple bottom line. *Event Management* 11(1–2): 13–22.

Helm, D., Smale, R. and Phillips, J. (2007). *Too Good To Be True? The UK's climate change record*. Oxford, New College, University of Oxford. Available from: http://www.dieterhelm.co.uk/publications/Carbon_record_2007.pdf.

Hertwich, E.G. and Peters, G.P. (2009). Carbon footprint of nations: a global, trade-linked analysis. *Environmental Science and Technology* 43: 6414–6420.

Hickman, R. and Banister, D. (2007). Looking over the horizon: transport and reduced CO_2 emissions in the UK by 2030. *Transport Policy* 14: 377–387.

Hileman, J.I., Ortiz, D.S., Bartis, J.T., Min Wong, H., Donohoo, P.E. and Weiss, M.A. (2009). *Near-Term Feasibility of Alternative Jet Fuels*. Santa Monica, CA: RAND.

Hille, J., Aall, C. and Grimstad Klepp, I. (2007). Miljøbelastninger fra norsk fritidsforbruk – en kartlegging. Available from: http://www.vestforsk.no/www/download.do?id=638. Accessed 28 February 2010.

Hille, J., Sataøen, H.L., Aall, C. and Storm, H.N. (2008). Miljøbelastningen av norsk forbruk og produksjon 1987–2007. Vestlandsforsking, Sogndal. http://www.vestforsk.no/www/show.do?page=12andarticleid=2201. Accessed 21 October 2009.

Hille, J., Ekström, F., Aall, C. and Brendehaug, E. (2009). Klimamerking av mat e er det mulig? VF-rapport 8/2009 Sogndal: Vestlandsforsking.

Hoegh-Guldberg, O., Mumby, P.J., Hooten, A.J., Steneck, R.S., Greenfield, P., Gomez, E., Harvell,

C.D., Sale, P.F., Edwards, A.J., Caldeira, K., Knowlton, N., Eakin, C.M., Iglesias-Prieto, R., Muthiga, N., Bradbury, R.H., Dubi, A. and Hatziolos, M.E. (2007). Coral reefs under rapid climate change and ocean acidification. *Science* 318(5857): 1737–1742.

Hofmann, M. and Schellnhuber, H. J. (2009). Oceanic acidification affects marine carbon pump and triggers extended marine oxygen holes. *Proceedings of the National Academy of Sciences* 106: 3017–3022.

Holden, E. (2007). *Achieving Sustainable Mobility: everyday and leisure-time travel in the EU*. Ashgate: Aldershot.

Holm Olsen, K. (2007). The Clean Development Mechanism's contribution to sustainable development: a review of the literature. *Climatic Change* 84: 59–73.

Høyer, K. (2000). Sustainable tourism or sustainable mobility? The Norwegian case. *Journal of Sustainable Tourism* 8(2): 147–160.

Humane Society (2009). Pet ownership statistics. Available from: http://www.humanesociety.org/issues/pet_overpopulation/facts/pet_ownership_statistics.html. Accessed 28 February 2010.

Hunecke, M. and Haustein, S. (2007). Einstellungsbasierte Mobilitätstypen: Eine integrierte Anwendung von multivariaten und inhaltsanalytischen Methoden der empirischen Sozialforschung zur Identifkation von Zielgruppen für eine nachhaltige Mobilität. *Umweltpsychologie* 11(2): 38–68.

Hunter, C. (1997). Sustainable tourism and an adaptive paradigm. *Annals of Tourism Research* 24(4): 850–867.

IATA (2007). New IATA financial forecast predicts 2008 downturn. Available from: http://www.iata.org/pressroom/pr/2007-12-12-01. Accessed 2 August 2008.

IATA (2008a). Jet fuel price monitor. Available from: http://www.iata.org/whatwedo/economics/fuel_monitor/index.htm. Accessed 2 August 2008.

IATA (2008b). World air transport statistics. Available from: http://www.iata.org/ps/publications/wats.htm. Accessed 14 October 2008.

IATA (2008c). Aviation carbon offset programmes. IATA guidelines and toolkit. Available from: http://www.iata.org/NR/rdonlyres/1D1D6A9C-4FBF-4627-B695-06F7FB69E5B6/61823/Carbon_Offset_Guidelines_May2008.pdf. Accessed 10 February 2010.

IATA (2009a). The IATA technology roadmap report. Available from: http://www.iata.org/NR/rdonlyres/8FC59023-919D-4719-8CEE-F20FF1BAB181/0/Technology_Roadmap_May2009.pdf. Accessed 3 March 2010.

IATA (2009b). Weak demand, falling load factors. Available from: http://www.iata.org/pressroom/pr/2009-07-30-01.htm. Accessed 3 March 2010.

IATA (2010a). IATA cuts 2010 loss forecast in half – strong start to 2010. Available from: http://www.iata.org/pressroom/pr/Pages/2010-03-11-01.aspx. Accessed 30 March 2010.

IATA (2010b). Fact . Available from: http://www.iata.org/pressroom/facts_figures/fact_sheets/carbon-offsets.htm. Accessed 10 February 2010.

ICAO (2009). Group on International Aviation and Climate Change (GIACC). Report. 1 June 2009. Available from: http://www.icao.int/env/meetings/GiaccReport_Final_en.pdf. Accessed 18 January 2010.

IEA (2001). *World Energy Outlook. Assessing today's supplies to fuel tomorrow's growth*. Paris: International Energy Agency. Available from: http://www.iea.org/textbase/nppdf/free/2000/weo2001.pdf. Accessed 18 January 2010.

IEA (2009). *World Energy Outlook 2009*. Paris: International Energy Agency.

Ilbery, B. and Kneafsey, M. (2000). Producer constructions of quality in regional speciality food production: a case study from South West England. *Journal of Rural Studies* 16(2): 217–230.

IMO (2009a). Prevention of Air Pollution from Ships. Second IMO GHG Study 2009. Available from: http://www.imo.org/includes/blastDataOnly.asp/data_id%3D26047/INF-10.pdf. Accessed 17 January 2009.

IMO (2009b). Climate change: A challenge for IMO too! Available from: http://www.imo.org/includes/blastDataOnly.asp/data_id%3D26316/backgroundE.pdf. Accessed 17 January 2010.

IMO MEPC (2009). MEPC.176(58) Amendments to the Annex of the Protocol of 1997 to amend the International Convention for the Prevention of Pollution from Ships, 1973, as modified by the Protocol of 1978 relating thereto (Revised MARPOL Annex VI). Available from: http://www.imo.org/. Accessed 14 February 2010.

Indian Tour Operators Promotion Council (2009) Domestic tourism statistics. Available from: http://www.itopc.org/travel-requisite/domestic-tourism-statistics.html. Accessed 12 September 2009.

International Tourism Partnership (2008). Available from: http://www.tourismpartnership.org/downloads/Going%20Green.pdf. Accessed 16 February 2010.

IPCC (1990). *First Assessment Report 1990*. Cambridge, UK and New York: Cambridge University Press.

IPCC (1995). *Climate change 1995. The science of climate change: Summary for policymakers and technical summary of the Working Group I Report*. Cambridge: Cambridge University Press.

IPCC (2001). *Climate Change 2001: The Scientific Basis. Contribution of Working Group I to the Third Assessment Report of the Intergovernmental Panel on Climate Change (IPCC TAR)*. Cambridge, UK and New York: Cambridge University Press.

IPCC (2007a). *Climate Change 2007: Impacts, Adaptation and Vulnerability*. Contribution of Working Group II to the Fourth Assessment Report of the Intergovernmental Panel on Climate Change, edited by M.L. Parry, O.F. Canziani, J.P. Palutikof, P.J. van der Linden and C.E. Hanson. Cambridge: Cambridge University Press, 976 pp.

IPCC (2007b). *Fourth Assessment Report: Climate Change 2007*. Cambridge: Cambridge University Press.

IPCC (2007c). Glossary of terms used in the IPPC Fourth Assessment Report. Available from: http://www1.ipcc.ch/glossary/index.htm. Accessed 26 February 2010.

Jackson, T. (2005). Motivating Sustainable Consumption. A review of evidence on consumer behaviour and behavioural change. A report to the Sustainable Development Research Network. Available from: http://www.sd-research.org.uk/post.php?p=126. Accessed 30 March 2010.

Jardine, C.N. (2009). Calculating the carbon dioxide emissions of flights. Available from http://www.eci.ox.ac.uk/research/energy/downloads/jardine09-carboninflights.pdf. Accessed 10 February 2010.

Jones, C. and Munday, M. (2007). Exploring the environmental consequences of tourism: a satellite account approach. *Journal of Travel Research* 46: 164–172.

Jørgensen, M.W. and Sørenson, S.C. (1997). Estimating Emissions from Railway Traffic. Report for the Project MEET: Methodologies for Estimating Air Pollutant Emissions from Transport, Department of Energy Engineering, Technical University of Denmark, Lyngby. Available from: http://www.inrets.fr/infos/cost319/MEETDeliverable17.PDF. Accessed 14 December 2007.

Jurowski, C. (2002). BEST think tanks and the development of curriculum modules for teaching sustainability principles. *Journal of Sustainable Tourism* 10(6): 536–545.

Kaldellis, J.K., Kavadias, K. and Christinakis, E. (2001). Evaluation of the wind-hydro energy solution for remote islands. *Energy Conversion and Management* 42: 1105–1120.

Kelly, J. and Williams, P.W. (2007). Modelling tourism destination energy consumption and greenhouse gas emissions: Whistler, British Columbia, Canada. *Journal of Sustainable Tourism* 15(1): 67–90.

Kelly, J., Haider, W. and Williams, P.W. (2007a). A behavioral assessment of tourism transportation options for reducing energy consumption and greenhouse gases. *Journal of Travel Research* 45: 297–309.

Kelly, J., Haider, W., Williams, P.W. and Englund, K. (2007b). Stated preferences of tourists for eco-efficient destination planning options. *Tourism Management* 28: 377–390.

Kemp, R. (2009). Short-haul aviation – under what conditions is it more environmentally benign than the alternatives? *Technology Analysis & Strategic Management* 21(1): 115–127.

Khisty, C.J. and Zeitler, U. (2001). Is hypermobility a challenge for transport ethics and systemicity? *Systemic Practice and Action Research* 14(5): 597–613.

Klein, J. and Dawar, N. (2004). Corporate social responsibility and consumers' attributions and brand evaluations in a product-harm crisis. *International Journal of Research in Marketing* 21(3): 203–217.

Köhler, J., Whitmarsh, L., Nykvist, B., Schilperoord, M., Bergman, N. and Haxeltine, A. (2009). A transitions model for sustainable mobility. *Ecological Economics* 68: 2985–2995.

Kok, R., Benders, R.M.J. and Moll, H.C. (2001). Energie-intensiteiten van de nederlandse consumptieve bestedingen anno 1996. IVEM, Rijksuniversiteit Groningen.

Kollmuss, A., Lazarus, M., Lee, C. and Polycarp, C. (2008). *A Review of Offset Programs: trading systems, funds, protocols, standards and retailers*. Stockholm: Stockholm Environment Institute.

KPMG (2008). Climate changes your business. Available at: www.kpmg.nl/sustainability.

Kriegler, E., Hall, J.W., Held, H., Dawson, R. and Schellnhuber, H.J. (2009). Imprecise probability assessment of tipping points in the climate system. *Proceedings of the National Academy of Sciences* 106: 5041–5046.

Kuklinski, J.H., Metlay, D.S. and Kay, W.D. (1982). Citizen knowledge and choices on the complex issue of nuclear energy. *American Journal of Political Science* 26(4): 615–642.

Kuo, N.-W. and Chen, P.-H. (2009). Quantifying energy use, carbon dioxide emission, and other environmental loads from island tourism based on a lifecycle assessment approach. *Journal of Cleaner Production* 17: 1324–1330.

Ladle, R., Jepson, P. and Whittaker, R.J. (2005). Scientists and the media: the struggle for legitimacy in climate change and conservation science. *Interdisciplinary Science Reviews* 30(3): 231–240.

Lahiri, S. (2009). Bio-fuel and Commons in India. A story of dispossession and colonisation. In: D'Mello, C., McKeown, J. and Minninger, S. (eds) *Disaster Prevention in Tourism: perspectives on climate justice*. Chiang Mai, Thailand: Ecumenical Coalition on Tourism in cooperation with EED Tourism Watch, Germany, pp. 207–217.

Laing, J. and Frost, W. (2010). How green was my festival: exploring challenges and opportunities associated with staging green events. *International Journal of Hospitality Management* 29: 261–267.

Lam, P., Lavik. G., Jensen, M.M., van de Vossenberg, J., Schmid, M., Woebken, D., Gutiérrez, D., Amann, R., Jetten, M.S.M. and Kuypers, M.M.M. (2009). Revising the nitrogen cycle in the Peruvian oxygen minimum zone. *Proceedings of the National Academy of Sciences* 106: 4752–4757.

Lamers, M. and Amelung, B. (2007). The environmental impacts of tourism, to Antarctica: a global perspective. In: Peeters, P.M. (ed.) *Tourism and Climate Change Mitigation: methods, greenhouse gas reductions and policies*. Breda: NHTV, pp. 51–62.

Larsen, J., Urry, J. and Axhausen, K.W. (2007). Networks and tourism: mobile social life. *Annals of Tourism Research* 34(1): 244–262.

Lash, S. and Urry, J. (2004). *Economies of Signs and Spaces*. London: Sage.

Lassen, C. (2006). Aeromobility and work. *Environment and Planning A* 38: 301–312.

Latouche, S. (1993). *In the Wake of the Affluent Society*. London: Zed Books.

Lawrence, P. (2009). Meeting the challenge of aviation emissions: an aircraft industry perspective. *Technology Analysis and Strategic Management* 21(1): 79–92.

Le Quéré, C. *et al.* (2009). Trends in the sources and sinks of carbon dioxide. *Nature Geosciences* 2, in press.

Lean, J. L. and Rind, D.H. (2009). How will Earth's surface temperature change in future decades? *Geophysical Research Letters* 36, L15708.

Lee, D. (2009). Aviation and Climate Change: the science. In: Gössling, S. and Upham, P. (eds) *Climate Change and Aviation: issues, challenges and solutions*. London: Earthscan, pp. 27–67.

Lee, D. and Sausen, R. (2000). New directions: assessing the real impact of CO_2 emissions trading by the aviation industry. *Atmospheric Environment* 34: 5337–5338.

Lee, D.S., Fahey, D.W., Forster, P.M., Newton, P.J., Wit, R.C.N., Lim, L.L., Owen, B. and Sausen, R. (2009). Aviation and global climate change in the 21st century. *Atmospheric Environment* 43: 3520–3537.

Lenton, T.M., Held, H., Kriegler, E., Hall, J.W., Lucht, W., Rahmstorf, S. and Schellnhuber, H.J. (2008). Tipping elements in the Earth's climate system. *Proceedings of the National Academy of Sciences* 105: 1786–1793.

Lenzen, M. (1999). Total requirements of energy and greenhouse gases for Australian transport. *Transportation Research Part D* 4: 265–290.

Liang, L. and James, A.D. (2009). The low-cost carrier model in China: the adoption of a strategic innovation. *Technology Analysis and Strategic Management* 21(1): 129–148.

Lindenberg, S. (2001a). Social rationality versus rational egoism. In: J. Turner (ed.) *Handbook of Sociological Theory*. New York: Kluwer Academic/Plenum, pp. 635–668.

Lindenberg, S. (2001b). Intrinsic motivation in a new light. *Kyklos* 54: 317–342.

Lindenberg, S. (2006). Prosocial behavior, solidarity and goal-framing processes. In: D. Fetchenhauer, A. Flache, B. Buunk and S. Lindenberg (eds.) *Solidarity and Prosocial Behavior: an integration of sociological and psychological perspectives*. Amsterdam: Kluwer.

Lloyd, B. (2007). The Commons revisited: the tragedy continues. *Energy Policy* 35: 5806–5818.

Lumsdon, L.M. (2006). Factors affecting the design of tourism bus services. *Annals of Tourism Research* 33(3): 748–766.

Lumsdon, L., Downward, P. and Cope, A. (2004). Monitoring of cycle tourism on long distance trails: the North Sea Cycle Route. *Journal of Transport Geography* 12: 13–22.

Lumsdon, L., Downward, P., Rhoden, S. (2006). Transport for tourism: can public transport encourage a modal shift in the day visitor market? *Journal of Sustainable Tourism* 14(2): 139–157.

Lyle, C. (2010). Kyoto v. Chicago: ICAO debates how to apply the principle of Common But Differentiated Responsibilities to aviation. Available from: http://www.greenaironline.com/news.php?viewStory=450. Accessed 2 April 2010.

Lynes, J.K. and Dredge, D. (2006). Going green: motivations for environmental commitment in the airline industry. A case study of Scandinavian Airlines. *Journal of Sustainable Tourism* 14(2): 116–138.

Machado-Filho, H. (2009). Brazilian low-carbon transportation policies: opportunities for international support. *Climate Policy* 9(5): 495–507.

Mann, B.I. McNeil, A.J. Pitman, S. Rahmstorf, E. Rignot, H.J. Schellnhuber, S.H. Schneider, S.C. Sherwood, R.C.J. Somerville, K. Steffen, E.J. Steig, M. Visbeck, A.J. Weaver. The University of New South Wales Climate Change Research Centre (CCRC), Sydney, Australia, 60pp.

Mann, M.E., Zhang, Z., Hughes, M.K., Bradley, R.S., Miller, S.K., Rutherford, S. and Ni, F. (2008). Proxy-based reconstructions of hemispheric and global surface temperature variations over the past two millennia. *Proceedings of the National Academy of Sciences* 105: 13252–13257.

Markussen, P. and Svendsen, G.T. (2005). Industry lobbying and the political economy of GHG trade in the European Union. *Energy Policy* 33(2): 245–255.

Marsh, P.T., Brooks, E. and Karly, D.J. (2009). Preliminary investigation into the severe thunderstorm environment of Europe simulated by the Community Climate Systems Model 3. *Atmospheric Research* 93: 607–618.

Mascarelli, A.L. (2009). Gold rush for algae. *Nature* 461 (23 September): 460–461.

Matthews, H.D. and Caldeira, K. (2008). Stabilizing climate requires near zero emissions. *Geophysical Research Letters* 35, L04705.

Mayor, K. and Tol, R.S.J. (2007). The impact of the UK aviation tax on carbon dioxide emissions and visitor numbers. *Transport Policy* 14: 507–513.

Mayor, K. and Tol, R.S.J. (2008). The impact of the EU-US Open Skies agreement on international travel and carbon dioxide emissions. *Journal of Air Transport Management* 14: 1–7.

Mayor, K. and Tol, R.S.J. (2009). Aviation and the environment in the context of the EU-US Open Skies agreement. *Journal of Air Transport Management* 15: 90–95.

Mayor, K. and Tol, R.S.J. (2010a). Scenarios of carbon dioxide emissions from aviation. *Global Environmental Change* 20: 65–73.

Mayor, K. and Tol, R.S.J. (2010b). The impact of European climate change regulations on international tourist markets. *Transportation Research Part D* 15: 26–36.

Mazar, N. and Zhong, C.-B. (2010). Do green products make us better people? *Psychological Science*, in press.

McBoyle, G. and Wall, G. (1987). Impact of CO_2 induced warming on downhill skiing in the Laurentians. *Cahiers de Géographie du Québec* 31: 39–50.

McBoyle, G., Wall, G., Harrison, R., Kinnaird, V. and Quinlan, C. (1986). Recreation and climatic change: a Canadian case study. *Ontario Geographer* 28: 51–68.

McCarty, J.A. and Shrum, L.J. (1994). The recycling of solid wastes: personal values, value orientations, and attitudes about recycling as antecedents of recycling behavior. *Journal of Business Research* 31(1): 53–62.

McDonald, S., Oates, C., Thyne, M., Alevizou, P. and McMorland, L.-A. (2009). Comparing sustainable consumption patterns across product sectors. *International Journal of Consumer Studies* 33: 137–145.

McKercher, B., Prideaux, B., Cheung, C. and Law, R. (2010). Achieving voluntary reductions in the carbon footprint of tourism and climate change. *Journal of Sustainable Tourism*, in press.

McMichael, A.J., Campbell-Lendrum, D.H., Corvalán, C.F., Ebi, K.I., Githeko, A.K., Scheraga, J.D. and Woodward, A. (2003). *Climate Change and Human Health: risks and responses*. Geneva: World Health Organization.

McNeil, B.I. and Matear, R.J. (2007). Climate change feedbacks on oceanic pH. *Tellus-B* 59B: 191–198.

Meehl, G.A., Arblaster, J. and Collins, W. (2008). Effects of black carbon aerosols on the Indian monsoon. *Journal of Climate* 21: 2869–2882.

Meinshausen, M., Meinshausen, N., Hare, W., Raper, S.C.B., Frieler, K., Knutti, R., Frame, D.J. and Allen, M.R. (2009). Greenhouse-gas emission targets for limiting global warming to 2° C. *Nature* 458(7242): 1158–1162.

Michaelowa, A. and Michaelowa, K. (2007). Does climate policy promote development? *Climatic Change* 84: 1–4.

Miller, G., Rathouse, K., Scarles, C., Holmes, K. and Tribe, J. (2007). Public understanding of sustainable leisure and tourism: a report to the Department for Environment, Food and Rural Affairs. University of Surrey. London: DEFRA.

Miller, M.M., Henthorne, T.L. and George, B.P. (2008). The competitiveness of the Cuban tourism industry in the twenty-first century: a strategic re-evaluation. *Journal of Travel Research* 46 (February): 268–278.

Mintel. (2008b). Cruises International – June 2008: Mintel Oxygen.

Mitchell, A. (2001). *Right Side Up*. London: Harper Collins Business.

Morrow, W.R., Lee, H., Gallagher, K.S. and Collantes, G. (2010). Reducing the U.S. Transportation

Sector's Oil Consumption and Greenhouse Gas Emissions. Policy Brief, Belfer Center for Science and International Affairs, Havard Kennedy School, March 2010.

Morton, D.C., DeFries, R S., Shimabukuro, Y.E., Anderson, L.O., Arai, E., del Bon Espirito-Santo, F., Freitas, R. and Morisette, J. (2006). Cropland expansion changes deforestation dynamics in the southern Brazilian Amazon. *Proceedings of the National Academy of Science* 103(39): 14637–14641.

Mote, T.L. (2007). Greenland surface melt trends 1973–2007: Evidence of a large increase in 2007. *Geophysical Research Letters* 34, L22507.

Nakicenovic, N. *et al.* (2000). *IPCC Special Report on Emissions Scenarios*. Cambridge: IPCC.

National Bureau of Statistics of China (2009). China Statistical Yearbook – 2008. Available from: http://www.stats.gov.cn/tjsj/ndsj/2006/indexee.htm. Accessed on 12 September 2009.

National Round Table on the Environment and Economy (2008). *Getting to 2050: Canada's transition to a low-emission future*. Ottawa: National Round Table on the Environment and Economy.

Naturvårdsverket (Swedish Environmental Protection Agency) (2009). Allmänhetens kunskaper och attityder till klimatförändringen. Report 1, October 2009. Stockholm: Naturvårdsverket.

Neiberger, C. (2009). China: Räumliche Disparitäten, Wirtschaftswachstum und die Bedeutung des Schienengüterverkehrs, unpublished working paper, Dept. of Geography, Bonn University, Germany.

Nilsson, J.H. (2009). Low-Cost Aviation. In: Gössling, S. and Upham, P. (eds) *Climate Change and Aviation: issues, challenges and solutions*. London: Earthscan, pp. 113–129.

Norton, L., Johnson, P., Joys, A., Stuart, R., Chamberlain, D., Feber, R., Firbank, L., Manley, W., Wolfe, M., Hart, B., Mathews, F., Macdonald, D. and Fuller, R.J. (2009). Consequences of organic and non-organic farming practices for field, farm and landscape complexity. *Agriculture, Ecosystems and Environment* 129(1–3): 221–227.

Nygren, E., Aleklett, K. and Höök, M. (2009). Aviation fuel and future oil production scenarios. *Energy Policy* 37(10): 4003–4010.

Oberthür, S. (2003). Institutional interaction to address greenhouse gas emissions from international transport: ICAO, IMO and the Kyoto Protocol. *Climate Policy* 3(3): 191–205.

OECD (1996). Towards Sustainable Transportation. OECD Publications, Paris. Available from: http://www.oecd.org/dataoecd/28/54/2396815.pdf. Accessed 18 February 2010.

Orr, J.C. *et al.*, (2005) Anthropogenic ocean acidification over the twenty-first century and its impact on calcifying organisms. *Nature* 437: 681–686.

Oschlies, A., Schulz, K.G., Riebesell, U. and Schmittner, A. (2008). Simulated 21st century's increase in oceanic suboxia by CO_2-enhanced biotic carbon export. *Global Biogeochemical Cycles* 22, GB4008.

Owen, B. (2010). Fuel efficiency development and prediction. Main thematic area: climate change. Available from: http://www.omega.mmu.ac.uk/Downloads/Final-Reports/23%20Fuel%20Efficiency%20development%20and%20Prediction%20Final.pdf. Accessed 2 March 2010.

Page, S., Yeoman, I. and Greenwood, C. (2009). Transport and Tourism in Scotland: a case of scenario planning at VisitScotland. In: Gössling, S., Hall, C.M. and Weaver, D.B. (eds) Sustainable Tourism Futures: perspectives on systems, restructuring and innovations. London: Routledge, pp. 58–83.

Palmer, A. and Boissy, S. (2009). The effects of airline price presentations on buyers' choice. *Journal of Vacation Marketing* 15: 39–52.

Palmer, C. and Engel, S. (2009). Avoided Deforestation: prospects for mitigating climate change. London: Routledge.

Parry, M., Lowe, J. and Hanson, C. (2008). The consequences of delayed action on climate change.

Available from: www3.imperial.ac.uk/pls/portallive/docs/1/53345696.PDF. Accessed 21 January 2009.

Patricola, C.M. and Cook, K.H. (2008). Atmosphere/vegetation feedbacks: a mechanism for abrupt climate change over northern Africa. *Journal of Geophysical Research (Atmospheres)* 113, D18102.

Patterson, M. and McDonald, G. (2004). How clean and green is New Zealand Tourism? Lifecycle and future environmentmal impacts. *Landcare Research Science Series* 24. Lincoln, Canterbury, New Zealand. Available from: http://www.mwpress.co.nz/store/downloads/LCRSciSeries24_Tourism_4web.pdf. Accessed 30 March 2010.

Pattullo, P. (2005). *Last Resorts: the cost of tourism in the Caribbean*. London: Latin American Bureau.

Patz, J.A., Campbell-Lendrum, D., Holloway, T. and Foley, J.A. (2005). Impact of regional climate change on human health. *Nature* 438, 310–317, doi:10.1038/nature04188.

Peeters, P.M., van Egmond, T. and Visser, N. (2004). *European Tourism, Transport and Environment*. Final Version. Breda: NHTV CSTT.

Peeters, P. and Schouten, F. (2006). Reducing the ecological footprint of inbound tourism and transport to Amsterdam. *Journal of Sustainable Tourism* 14(2): 157–171.

Peeters, P.M. and Middel, J. (2007). Historical and Future Development of Air Transport Fuel Efficiency. In: Sausen, R., Blum, A., Lee, D.S. and Brüning, C. (eds) *Proceedings of an International Conference on Transport, Atmosphere and Climate (TAC)*; Oxford, United Kingdom, 26–29 June 2006, pp. 42–47. Oberpfaffenhoven: DLR Institut für Physic der Atmosphäre.

Peeters, P. and Gössling, S. (2008). Environmental Discourses in the Aviation Industry: the social reproduction of mobility. In: Burns, P. and Novelli, M. (eds) *Tourism and Mobility: local-global connections*. Amsterdam: Elsevier, pp. 187–203.

Peeters, P. and Dubois, G. (2010a). Methods for unlikely futures: exploring tourism travel under climate change mitigation constraints. *Journal of Transport Geography*, in press.

Peeters, P. and Dubois, G. (2010b). Exploring tourism travel under climate change mitigation constraints. *Journal of Transport Geography* 18: 447–457.

Peeters, P., Szimba, E. and Duijnisveld, M. (2007a). Major environmental impacts of European tourist transport. *Journal of Transport Geography* 15: 83–93.

Peeters, P., Gössling, S. and Becken, S. (2007b). Innovation towards tourism sustainability: climate change and aviation. *International Journal of Innovation and Sustainable Development* 1(3): 184–200.

Peeters, P., Gössling, S. and Lane, B. (2009a). Moving Towards Low-carbon Tourism: opportunities for destinations and tour operators. In: Gössling, S., Hall, C.M. and Weaver, D. (eds) *Sustainable Tourism Futures*. London, New York: Routledge.

Peeters, P., Williams, V. and de Haan, A. (2009b). Technical and Management Reduction Potentials. In: Gössling, S. and Upham, P. (eds) *Climate Change and Aviation: issues, challenges and solutions*. London: Earthscan, pp. 293–307.

Pentalow, L. and Scott, D. (2009). The Impact of Climate Policy and Oil Price on Tourist Arrivals to the Caribbean Region. *Proceedings of 7th International Symposium on Tourism and Sustainability, Travel and Tourism in the Age of Climate Change*. University of Brighton, Brighton, England, July 8–10.

Peters, G.P. and Hertwich, E.G. (2008). CO_2 embodied in international trade with implications for global climate policy. *Environmental Science and Technology* 42(5): 1401–1407.

Phillips, O.L. *et al.* (2009). Drought sensitivity of the Amazon rainforest. *Science* 323: 1344–1347.

Piket, P. (2009). Indirect taxes and subsidies for international tourism passenger transport and conflicts with climate policies: a European case study. In: Landré, M. (ed.) *Transport and Tourism:*

challenges, issues and conflicts. Proceedings of the Travel and Tourism Research Association Europe 2009 Annual Conference – Rotterdam/Breda, the Netherlands, 22–24 April. Breda: TTRA, pp. 217–233.

Pitman, A.J., Narisma, G.T. and McAneney, J. (2007). The impact of climate change on the risk of forest and grassland fires in Australia. *Climatic Change* 84: 383–401.

Pounds, J.A. and Puschendorf, R. (2004). Clouded Futures. *Nature* 427: 107–109.

Putnam, R.D. (1995). *Bowling Alone: the collapse and revival of American community.* New York: Simon and Schuster.

Ramanathan, V., Chung, C., Kim, D., Bettge, T., Buja, L., Kiehl, J.T., Washington, W.M., Fu, Q., Sikka, D.R. and Wild, M. (2005). Atmospheric brown clouds: impacts on South Asian climate and hydrological cycle. *Proceedings of the National Academy of Sciences* 102: 5326–5333.

Ramírez de Arellano, A.B. (2007). Patients without borders: the emergence of medical tourism. *International Journal of Health Services* 37(1): 193–198.

Randles, S. and Bows, A. (2009). Aviation, emissions and the climate change debate. *Technology Analysis and Strategic Management* 21(1):1–16.

Randles, S. and Mander, S. (2009). Aviation, consumption and the climate change debate: 'Are you going to tell me off for flying?' *Technology Analysis and Strategic Management* 21(1): 93–113.

Raupach, M.R., Marland, G., Ciais, P., Le Quéré, C., Canadell, J.G., Klepper, G. and Field, C.B. (2007). Global and regional drivers of accelerating CO_2 emissions. *Proceedings of the National Academy of Sciences* 104: 10288–10293.

RealClimate (2010). IPCC errors: facts and spin. Available from: http://www.realclimate.org/index. php/archives/2010/02/ipcc-errors-facts-and-spin/. Accessed 24 February 2010.

Richardson, K. *et al.* (2009). Climate Change: global risks, challenges and decisions. Synthesis Report of the Copenhagen Climate Congress. (University of Copenhagen).

Riebesell, U., Körtzinger, A. and Oschlies, A. (2009). Sensitivities of marine carbon fluxes to ocean change. *Proceedings of the National Academy of Sciences* 106(49): 20602–20609.

Riehl World View (2010). UK to limit air travel abroad? Available http://www.riehlworldview. com/carnivorous_conservative/2009/02/uk-to-limit-air-travel-abroad.html. Accessed 12 February 2010.

Roberts, S. and Thumim, J. (2006). A Rough Guide to Individual Carbon Trading: the ideas, the issues and the next steps. Report to DEFRA, UK. Available from: http://www.carbonequity.info/PDFs/defranov06.pdf. Accessed 30 March 2010.

Rogelj, J., Hare, B., Nabel, J., Macey, K., Schaeffer, M., Markmann, K. and Meinshausen, M. (2009). Halfway to Copenhagen, no way to 2 °C. *Nature Reports Climate Change* (0907): 81–83.

Rosa, R. and Seibel, B.A. (2008). Synergistic effects of climate-related variables suggest future physiological impairment in a top oceanic predator. *Proceedings of the National Academy of Sciences* 105: 20776–20780.

Royal Dutch Airlines (KLM) (2010). Choose more comfort. Available from: http://www.klm.com/travel/nl_en/prepare_for_travel/checkin_options/internet_checkin/ici_help/seat_choice.htm. Accessed 16 February 2010.

Ryanair (2009). Ryanair beats recession as traffic grows 13%. Available from: http://www.ryanair. com/en/news/ryanair-beats-recession-as-traffic-grows-13-percent. Accessed 20 February 2010.

Ryanair (2010). Ryanair grows 13% with 65 million passengers in 2009. Available from: http://www. ryanair.com/en/news/ryanair-grows-13-percent-with-65-million-passengers-in-2009. Accessed 20 February 2010.

Ryghaug, M. and Sørensen, K.H. (2009). How energy efficiency fails in the building industry. *Energy Policy* 37(3): 984–991.

SAS (2010). Baggage. Available from: http://www.flysas.com/en/Travel_info/Baggage/. Accessed 16 February 2010.

Saunders, C., Barber, A. and Taylor, G. (2006). Food miles – comparative energy/emissions performance of New Zealand's agriculture industry. Available from: http://www.lincoln.ac.nz/documents/2328_rr285_s13389.pdf. Accessed 3 March 2010.

Sausen, R., Isaksen, I., Grewe, V., Hauglustaine, D., Lee, D.S., Myhre, G., Köhler, M.O., Pitari, G., Schumann, U., Stordal, F. and Zerefos, C. (2005). Aviation Radiative Forcing in 2000: An Update on IPCC (1999). *Meteorologische Zeitschrift* 14: 555–561.

Scandic (2009). We care because we are part of society. http://www.scandichotels.com/About-Us/Responsible-living/Society/. Accessed 1 October 2009.

Schahn, J. (1993). Die Rolle von Entschuldigungen und Rechtfertigungen für umweltschädigendes Verhalten. In: Schahn, J. and Giesinger, T. (eds) *Psychologie für den Umweltschutz*. Weinheim: Beltz, pp. 51–61.

Schafer, A. (1998). The global demand for motorized mobility. *Transportation Research A* 32(6): 455–477.

Schafer, A. (2000). Regularities in travel demand: an international perspective. *Journal of Transportation and Statistics* 3(3): 1–31.

Schafer, A. and Victor, D.G. (2000). The future mobility of the world population. *Transportation Research A* 34: 171–205.

Schilcher, D. (2007). Growth versus equity: the continuum of pro-poor tourism and neoliberal governance. *Current Issues in Tourism* 10(2–3): 166–193.

Schwartz, S.H. (1977). Normative Influences on Altruism. In: L. Berkowitz (ed.) *Advances in Experimental Social Psychology*, Vol. 10. New York: Academic Press, pp. 221–279.

Scott, D. (2006). Climate Change and Sustainable Tourism in the 21st Century. In: Cukier, J. (ed.) *Tourism Research: policy, planning, and prospects*. Waterloo: Department of Geography, University of Waterloo, pp. 175–248.

Scott, D. and McBoyle, G. (2007). Climate change adaptation in the ski industry. *Mitigation and Adaptation Strategies for Global Change* 12: 1411–1431.

Scott, D. and Lemieux, C. (2009). *Weather and Climate Information for Tourism*. Geneva and Madrid: WMO and UNWTO.

Scott, D. and Becken, S. (2010). Editorial: adapting to climate change and climate policy: progress, problems and potentials. *Journal of Sustainable Tourism*, in press.

Scott, D., Dawson, J. and Jones, B. (2008). Climate change vulnerability of the US Northeast winter recreation – tourism sector. *Mitigation and Adaptation Strategies for Global Change* 13: 577–596.

Scott, D., Peeters, P. and Gössling, S. (2010). Can tourism 'seal the deal' of its mitigation commitments? The challenge of achieving 'aspirational' emission reduction targets. *Journal of Sustainable Tourism* 18(2), in press.

Shaw, S. and Thomas, C (2006). Social and cultural dimensions of air travel demand: hyper-mobility in the UK? *Journal of Sustainable Tourism* 14(2): 209–215.

Sherman, L. (2007). Priciest private jets. Available from: http://www.forbes.com/2007/03/06/jets-private-travel-forbeslife_07billionaires_cz_ls_0308jets.html. Accessed 15 March 2010.

Simmons, C. and Lewis, K. (2001). *Take Only Memories, Leave Nothing but Footprints. An ecological footprint analysis of two package holidays*. Oxford: Best Foot Forward.

Simpson, M.C., Gössling, S. and Scott, D. (2008). Report on the international policy and market response to global warming and the challenges and opportunities that climate change issues present for the Caribbean tourism sector. Barbados: Caribbean Tourism Organization.

SJ (Svenska Järnvägen/Swedish Railways) (2010). Carbon Calculator. Available from: http://www.sj.se/sj/jsp/polopoly.jsp?d=280andl=enandintcmp=13196. Accessed 10 January 2010.

Smith, I.J. and Rodger, C.J. (2009). Carbon emission offsets for aviation-generated emissions due to international travel to and from New Zealand. *Energy Policy* 37(9): 3438–3447.

Smith, J.B., Schneider, S.H., Oppenheimer, M., Yohe, G.W., Hare, W., Mastrandrea, M.D., Patwardhan, A., Burton, I., Corfee-Morlot, J., Magadza, C.H.D., Füssel, H.-M., Pittock, A.B., Rahman, A., Suarez, A. and van Ypersele, J.-P. (2009a). Assessing dangerous climate change through an update of the Intergovernmental Panel on Climate Change (IPCC) 'reasons for concern'. *Proceedings of the National Academy of Sciences* 106(11): 4133–4137.

Smith, P., Martino, D., Cai, Z., Gwary, D., Janzen, H., Kumar, P., McCarl, B., Ogle, S., O'Mara, F., Rice, C., Scholes, B. and Sirotenko, O. (2009b). Agriculture. In: Metz, B., Davidson, O.R., Bosch, P.R., Dave, R. and Meyer, L.A. (eds) *Climate change 2007: Mitigation*. Contribution of Working Group III to the Fourth Assessment Report of the Intergovernmental Panel on Climate Change. Cambridge and New York: Cambridge University Press.

Solomon, S., Plattner, G.-K., Knutti, R. and Friedlingstein, P. (2009). Irreversible climate change due to carbon dioxide emissions. *Proceedings of the National Academy of Sciences* 106, 1704–1709.

South West Tourism (2009). Various documents. Available from: www.swtourism.org.uk/. Accessed 15 March 2010.

SSP Sweden (2009). Vårt miljöarbete. Available from: http://www.foodtravelexperts.com/sweden/. Accessed 8 August 2009.

(SCB/SIKA) (2001). RES 2000. Den nationella reseundersökningen. Stockholm: Birger Gustafsson AB.

STCRC (2009) Australian Tourism Futures: Redefining the Future. Communiqué, 2009. Available from: http://www.tourismfutures.com.au/Publications/2009Communique.pdf. Accessed 18 February 2010.

Steg, L. and Vlek, C. (2009). Encouraging pro-environmental behaviour: an integrative review and research agenda. *Journal of Environmental Psychology* 29: 309–317.

Stern, N. (2006). *The economics of climate change: the Stern Review*. Cambridge: Cambridge University Press.

Stern, N. (2009). *The Global Deal: climate change and the creation of a new era of progress and prosperity*. New York: Public Affairs.

Stern, P.C., Dietz, T., Abel, T., Guagnano, G.A. and Kalof, L. (1999). A value-belief-norm theory of support for social movements: the case of environmentalism. *Human Ecology Review* 6: 81–97.

Sterner, T. (2007). Fuel taxes: an important instrument for climate policy. *Energy Policy* 35: 3194–3202.

Stoll-Kleemann, S., O'Riordan, T. and Jaeger, C.C. (2001). The psychology of denial concerning climate mitigation measures: evidence from Swiss focus groups. *Global Environmental Change* 11: 107–117.

Stramma, L., Johnson, G.C., Sprintall, J. and Mohrholz, V. (2008). Expanding oxygen-minimum zones in the tropical oceans. *Science* 320: 655–658.

Swarbrooke, J. and Horner, S. (2001). *Business Travel and Tourism*. Oxford: Butterworth-Heinemann.

T&E (2009a). *Bunker Fuels and the Kyoto Protocol: how ICAO and the IMO failed the climate change test*. Brussels: Transport and Environment.

T&E (2009b). Pressure grows for aviation and shipping to be given specified climate target. Available from: http://transportenvironment.org/News/2009/7/Pressure-grows-for-aviation-and-shipping-to-be-given-specified-climate-target/. Accessed 12 September 2009.

Tesco (2009). Our carbon label findings. Available from: http://www.tesco.com/assets/greenerliving/content/documents/pdfs/carbon_label_findings.pdf. Accessed 21 November 2009.

Thomas, C.D., Cameron, A., Green, R.E., Bakkenes, M., Beaumont, L.J., Collingham, Y.C., Erasmus,

B.F.N., Ferreira de Siqueira, M., Grainger, A., Hannah, L., Hughes, L., Huntley, B., van Jaarsveld, A.S., Midgley, G.F., Miles, L., Ortega-Huerta, M.A., Peterson, A.T., Philips, O.L.,and William, S.E. (2005). Extinction risk from climate change. *Nature* 427: 145–148.

Thornley, P., Upham, P. and Tomei, J. (2009). Sustainability constraints on UK bioenergy development. *Energy Policy* 37(12): 5623–5635.

Thurlow, C. and Jaworski, A. (2006). The alchemy of the upwardly mobile: symbolic capital and the stylization of elites in frequent-flyer programmes. *Discourse and Society* 17(1): 99–135.

Tol, R.S.J. (2007). The impact of a carbon tax on international tourism. *Transportation Research Part D* 12: 129–142.

Torres, R. (2002). Toward a better understanding of tourism and agriculture linkages in the Yucatan: tourist food consumption and preferences. *Tourism Geographies* 4(3): 282–306.

Trapp, R.J., Diffenbaugh, N.S., Brooks, H.E., Baldwin, M.E., Robinson, E.D. and Pal, J.S. (2007). Changes in severe thunderstorm environment frequency during the 21st century caused by anthropogenically enhanced global radiative forcing. *Proceedings of the National Academy of Sciences* 104: 19719–19723.

Trapp, R.J., Diffenbaugh, N.S. and Gluhovsky, A. (2009). Transient response of severe thunderstorm forcing to elevated greenhouse gas concentrations. *Geophysical Research Letters* 36, L01703.

Traveldaily (2010). Business class guide. Available from: http://archives.traveldaily.com.au/2010/Supplements/TD_Business_Class_Guide_2010.pdf. Accessed 15 March 2010.

Trick, C.G., Bill, B.D., Cochlan, W.P., Wells, M.L., Trainer, V.L. and Pickell, L.D. (2010). Iron enrichment stimulates toxic diatom production in high-nitrate, low-chlorophyll areas. *Proceedings of the National Academy of Sciences*, early edition, www.pnas.org/cgi/doi/10.1073/pnas.0910579107.

Trung, D.N. and Kumar, S. (2005). Resource use and waste management in Vietnam hotels. *Journal of Cleaner Production* 13: 109–116.

Tufts Climate Initiative (2006, updated 2007). Voluntary offsets for air-travel carbon emissions. Evaluations and recommendations of voluntary offset companies. (Kollmuss, A. and Bowell, B.) Available from: http://www.tufts.edu/tie/tci/pdf/TCI_Carbon_Offsets_Paper_April-2–07.pdf. Accessed 2 March 2008.

TUI Fly Nordic (2010). TUIfly Nordics miljöpåverkan. Available from: http://www.fritidsresor.se/36665/Ansvar--Klimat/Flyg/Flyg/. Accessed 30 March 2010.

Tyedmers, P. (2001). Energy consumed by North Atlantic Fisheries. Available from: http://sres.management.dal.ca/Files/Tyedmers/Energy_Tyedmers1.pdf. Accessed 21 October 2009.

UIC (2007). Energy efficiency technologies for railways – database, International Union of Railways, Paris. Available from: http://www.railway-energy.org/tfee/index.php?ID=200. Accessed 14 December 2007.

UK Department for Energy and Climate Change (2009). Various documents. Available from: http://www.decc.gov.uk/. Accessed 15 March 2010.

UKERC (2009). Global oil depletion. An assessment of the evidence for a near-term peak in global oil production. Available from: http://www.ukerc.ac.uk/support/tiki-index.php?page=Global+Oil+Depletion. Accessed 25 February 2010.

UNDP (2007). *Human Development Report 2007/2008. Fighting Climate Change: Human Solidarity in a Divided World*. Published for the United Nations Development Programme (UNDP). Basingstoke: Palgrave Macmillan.

UNEP–Oxford University-UNWTO-WMO (2008). *Climate Change Adaptation and Mitigation in the Tourism Sector: frameworks, tools and practice*. Paris: UNEP–Oxford University–UNWTO–WMO.

UNFCCC (1998). Kyoto Protocol to the United Nations Framework Convention on Climate Change.

Available from: http://unfccc.int/resource/docs/convkp/kpeng.pdf#page=20. Accessed 14 January 2010.

UNFCCC (2009). Copenhagen Accord. Available from: http://unfccc.int/files/meetings/cop_15/application/pdf/cop15_cph_auv.pdf. Accessed 15 January 2010.

UNFCCC (2010a). GHG data. Times series – Annex I. Available from: http://unfccc.int/ghg_data/ghg_data_unfccc/time_series_annex_i/items/3814.php. Accessed 1 March 2010.

UNFCCC (2010b). Article 2: Objective. Available from: http://unfccc.int/essential_background/convention/background/items/1353.php. Accessed 12 January 2010.

UNFCCC (2010c). The United Nations Framework Convention on Climate Change. Available from: http://unfccc.int/essential_background/convention/items/2627.php. Accessed 12 January 2010.

UNFCCC (2010d). UNFCCC receives governments' climate pledges. Available from: http://unfccc.int/files/press/news_room/press_releases_and_advisories/application/pdf/pr_accord_100201.pdf. Accessed 8 February 2010.

UNFCCC (2010e). Quantified, economy wide targets for 2020. Available from: http://unfccc.int/home/items/5264.php. Accessed 8 February 2010.

UNFCCC (2010f). GHG data from UNFCCC. Available from: http://unfccc.int/ghg_data/ghg_data_unfccc/items/4146.php. Accessed 2 April 2010.

UNSD (2009) Environment Data. Available at: http://unstats.un.org/unsd/environment/air_co2_emissions.htm. Accessed 8 September 2009.

UNWTO (2001). *Tourism 2020 Vision: global forecasts and profiles of market segments*. Madrid: UNWTO.

UNWTO (2003). Djerba Declaration. Available from: http://www.world-tourism.org/sustainable/climate/decdjerba-eng.pdf. Accessed 2 April 2010.

UNWTO (2007). Davos Declaration. Available from: http://www.unwto.org/pdf/pr071046.pdf. Accessed 2 April 2010.

UNWTO (2008). Emerging tourism markets – the coming economic boom, Press Release, UNWTO Madrid, 24 June 2008.

UNWTO (2009a). Discussion Paper on Climate Change Mitigation Measures for Intenational Air Transport. Discussion Paper. August.

UNWTO (2009b). Roadmap for recovery. Available from: http://www.unwto.org/conferences/ga/en/pdf/18_08.pdf. Accessed 15 March 2010.

UNWTO (2009c). World Tourism Barometer, volume 7, no. 2, June 2009. Available from: http://www.unwto.org/facts/eng/pdf/barometer/UNWTO_Barom09_2_en_excerpt.pdf. Accessed 15 July 2009.

UNWTO (2009d). From Davos to Copenhagen and beyond: advancing tourism's response to climate change. Available from: http://www.unwto.org/conferences/ga/en/pdf/18_08.pdf. Accessed 15 March 2010.

UNWTO (2010a). Historical perspective of world tourism. Available from: http://www.unwto.org/facts/eng/historical.htm. Accessed 24 February 2010.

UNWTO (2010b). UNWTO World Tourism Barometer, volume 8, no. 1, January 2010. Available from: http://www.unwto.org/facts/eng/pdf/barometer/UNWTO_Barom10_1_en_excerpt.pdf.

UNWTO-UNEP-WMO (2007). Davos Declaration. Climate change and tourism: responding to global challenges. *Second International Conference on Climate Change and Tourism*, Davos, Switzerland.

UNWTO-UNEP-WMO (2008). *Climate Change and Tourism: responding to global challenges*. Madrid: UNWTO.

Upham, P., Tomei, J. and Boucher, P. (2009a). Biofuels, aviation and sustainability. In: Gössling,

S. and Upham, P. (eds) *Climate Change and Aviation: issues, challenges and solutions*. London: Earthscan, pp. 309–328.

Upham, P., Thornley, P., Tomei, J. and Boucher, P. (2009b). Substitutable biodiesel feedstocks for the UK: a review of sustainability issues with reference to the UK RTFO. *Journal of Cleaner Production* 17: 537–545.

USA TODAY (2007). 'Saudi Prince Alwaleed buys his own A380 jumbo jet', *USA Today*. 13 November. Available from: http://www.usatoday.com/money/industries/travel/2007–11–12-prince-alwaleed-a380_N.htm. Accessed 9 July 2008.

Van der Werf, G.R., Morton, D.C., DeFries, R.S., Olivier, J.G.J., Kasibhatla, P.S., Jackson, R.B., Collatz, G.J. and Randerson, J.T. (2009). CO_2 emissions from forest loss. *Nature Geoscience* 2: 737–738.

Vasedua, R. (2008). Trend analysis of greenhouse gas emissions from the Indian aviation sector: a study of the implications of future civil aviation demand. M.Sc. Thesis, International Master's Programme in Environmental Sciences and Sustainability Studies, Lund University, Sweden.

Veggiedag 2010. DonderdagVeggiedag. Available from: http://www.donderdagveggiedag.be/. Accessed 13 February 2010.

Vera-Morales, M. and Schäfer, A. (2009). Final report: fuel-cycle assessment of alternative aviation fuels. University of Cambridge, Institute for Aviation and the Environment. Available from: http://www.omega.mmu.ac.uk/Downloads/Final-Reports/10%20Final%20Report%20Sustainable%20Fuels%20for%20Aviation.pdf. Accessed 16 February 2010.

Virgin-Atlantic (2008). Biofuel demonstration. Available from: http://www.virgin-atlantic.com:80/en/gb/allaboutus/environment/biofuel.jsp. Accessed 2 March 2010.

Vos, E. (2000). EU food safety regulation in the aftermath of the BSE crisis. *Journal of Consumer Policy* 23(3): 227–255.

Wall, G. (1998). Climate change, tourism and the IPCC. *Tourism Recreation Research* 23(2): 65–68.

Wall, G., Harrison, R., Kinnaird, V., McBoyle, G. and Quinlan, C. (1986). The implications of climatic change for camping in Ontario. *Recreation Research Review* 13(1): 50–60.

Walz, A., Calonder, G.-P., Hagedorn, F., Lardelli, C., Lundström, C. and Stöckli, V. (2008). Regional CO_2 budget, countermeasures and reduction aims for the Alpine tourist region of Davos, Switzerland. *Energy Policy* 36: 811–820.

Washington Post (2009). Fewer Americans believe in global warming, polls show. Available from: http://www.washingtonpost.com/wp-dyn/content/article/2009/11/24/AR2009112402989.html. Accessed 16 February 2010.

WBGU (2009). *Solving the Climate Dilemma: the budget approach*. Berlin: WBGU.

Weaver, D. (2004). Tourism and the Elusive Paradigm of Sustainable Development. In: Lew, A., Hall, C.M. and Williams, A. (eds) *Companion to Tourism*. Oxford: Blackwell, pp. 510–521.

Weaver, D. (2007). Toward sustainable mass tourism: paradigm shift or paradigm nudge? *Tourism Recreation Research* 32(3): 65–69.

Weber, C.L. and Matthews, H.S. (2008). Food-miles and the relative climate impacts of food choices in the United States. *Environment, Science, and Technology* 42: 3508–3513.

Westerling, A.L., Hidalgo, H.G., Cayan, D.R. and Swetnam, T.W. (2006). Warming and earlier spring increase. Western U.S. forest wildfire activity. *Science* 313: 940–943.

Wilkinson, P.F. (2003). Tourism Policy and Planning in St. Lucia. In: Gössling, S. (ed.) *Tourism and Development in Tropical Islands: political ecology perspectives*. Cheltenham: Edward Elgar Publishing, pp. 88–120.

Williams, A.M. and Montanari, A. (1995). Tourism regions and spaces in a changing social framework. *Tijdschrift Voor Economische en Sociale Geografie* 86(1): 3–12.

Winebrake, J.J., Corbett, J.J., Green, E.H., Lauer, A., and Eyring, V. (2009). Mitigating the health impacts of pollution from international shipping: an assessment of low-sulfur fuel mandates. *Environmental Science and Technology* 49(13): 4776–4782.

WEF (2009). Climate policies: from Kyoto to Copenhagen. Available from: http://www.weforum. org/en/knowledge/Themes/Enviroment/ClimateChange/KN_SESS_SUMM_28001?url=/en/ knowledge/Themes/Enviroment/ClimateChange/KN_SESS_SUMM_28001. Accessed 22 December 2009.

Worldwatch Institute (2010). *State of the World. Transforming cultures. From consumerism to sustainability*. New York, London: W.W. Norton.

WRI (2004). Good stuff? Available from: http://www.worldwatch.org/system/files/GS0000.pdf. Accessed 15 March 2010.

WTO (1997). *Tourism market trends 1997. World overview*. Madrid: World Tourism Organisation.

WTO (2000). *Tourism 2020 vision. Volume 7. Global forecasts and profiles of market segments*. Madrid: World Tourism Organisation.

WTRG Economics (2010). Oil price history and analysis. Available from: http://www.wtrg.com/ prices.htm. Accessed 30 March 2010.

WTTC (2009). *Leading the Challenge on Climate Change*. London: World Travel and Tourism Council.

WWF-UK (2002). Holiday footprinting: a practical tool for responsible tourism. Available from: http://www.wwf.org.uk/filelibrary/pdf/holidayfootprintingfull.pdf. Accessed 20 October 2009.

Xuereb, M. (2005). Food miles: environmental implications of food imports to Waterloo region. Available from: http://www.region.waterloo.on.ca/web/health.nsf/4f4813c75e78d71385256e5a0057f5e1/ 54ED787F44ACA44C852571410056AEB0/$file/FOOD_MILES_REPORT.pdf?openelement. Accessed 3 March 2010.

Yeoman, I. and McMahon-Beattie, U. (2006). Understanding the impact of climate change on Scottish tourism. *Journal of Vacation Marketing* 12(4): 371–379.

Yeoman, I., John Lennon, J., Blake, A., Galt, M., Greenwood, C. and McMahon-Beattie, U. (2007). Oil depletion: what does this mean for Scottish tourism? *Tourism Management* 28(5): 1354–1365.

Zahavi, Y. (1981). The UMOT-Urban Interactions. DOT-RSPA-DPB 10/7. Washington, DC: US Department of Transportation.

Zmeureanu, R.G., Hanna, Z.A. and Fazio, P. (1994). Energy performance of hotels in Ottawa. *ASHRAE Transactions* 100(1): 314–322.

Index